KT-577-987

TRADE AND ENVIRONMENTAL LAW
IN THE EUROPEAN COMMUNITY

Trade and Environmental Law in the European Community

ANDREAS R. ZIEGLER

CLARENDON PRESS · OXFORD
1996

Oxford University Press, Great Clarendon Street, Oxford OX2 6DP

Oxford New York

Athens Auckland Bangkok Bogota Bombay
Buenos Aires Calcutta Cape Town Dar es Salaam
Delhi Florence Hong Kong Istanbul Karachi
Kuala Lumpur Madras Madrid Melbourne
Mexico City Nairobi Paris Singapore
Taipei Tokyo Toronto

and associated companies in
Berlin Ibadan

Oxford is a trade mark of Oxford University Press

Published in the United States
by Oxford University Press Inc., New York

© Andreas R. Ziegler 1996

All rights reserved. No part of this publication may be reproduced,
stored in a retrieval system, or transmitted, in any form or by any means,
without the prior permission in writing of Oxford University Press.
Within the UK, exceptions are allowed in respect of any fair dealing for the
purpose of research or private study, or criticism or review, as permitted
under the Copyright, Designs and Patents Act, 1988, or in the case of
reprographic reproduction in accordance with the terms of the licences
issued by the Copyright Licensing Agency. Enquiries concerning
reproduction outside these terms and in other countries should be
sent to the Rights Department, Oxford University Press,
at the address above

British Library Cataloguing in Publication Data
Data available

Library of Congress Cataloging in Publication Data
Zeigler, Andreas R.
Trade and environmental law in the European community / Andreas,
R. Zeigler.
p. cm.
Originally presented as the author's thesis (doctoral—University
of St. Gallen, Switzerland, 1995).
Includes bibliographical references.
1. Environmental law—European Union countries. 2. Trade
regulation—European Union countries. 3. Environmental policy—
Economic aspects—European Union countries. I. Title.
KJE6242.Z54   1996   341.7'62'094—dc20   96–26277
ISBN 0–19–826246–9

1 3 5 7 9 10 8 6 4 2

Typeset by Hope Services (Abingdon) Ltd.
Printed in Great Britain
on acid-free paper by
Bookcraft Ltd., Midsomer Norton, Somerset

Foreword

The state-based international system in Europe has been changed by the continual enforcement of the competences, activities, and law of the European Community. Even if the main object of European integration was at first economy, the political dimension existed from the beginning; and the far-reaching consequences of that integration have now become evident, as the Community has been included in the broader framework of the European Union which deals with foreign policy, as well as justice and home affairs. The Member States are no longer sovereign in the traditional sense; sovereignty is divided between the Community and the Member States.

Andreas R. Ziegler illustrates this sharing of sovereignty in his remarkable book by analyzing the competences and activities of the Community and the Member States in the domain of protection of the environment. He explains the steps taken by the Community to fulfil its responsibility to contribute to the preservation of the natural bases of life. Protection of the environment is expressly mentioned in the EC Treaty as one of the aims of the Community, and responsibility in this field is shared, as the author demonstrates, between the Community and the Member States. The tensions existing between this aim and the other aims of the Community, in particular the realization of the Common and Internal Market, is the main subject considered by the author; but he also emphasizes the many conflicts which exist or may arise because of the very real responsibilities which still fall on Member States.

The author makes a thorough analysis of the various rules, instruments, and procedures available under Community law to overcome, or at least to diminish, such tensions and conflicts, arising from opposite standpoints. Special attention is given to the relevant decisions of the Court of Justice. The author's arguments are closely-reasoned, and take into account not only legal and technical requirements but also the economic and social contexts. His ideas are a contribution to the continuing discussion between all concerned parties in the Community, which is necessary in an open society.

The message which emerges from this study seems to be clear. The problems and difficulties experienced by the Community as a result of tasks and competences being divided between different decision-makers cannot be solved by confrontation and a struggle for power, but only by co-operation and mutual loyalty. It is necessary for everyone involved in the decision-making process, at the Community or national level, to pay attention to the common aims, and to aid in the search for the right balance between those aims, and between the Community and its Member States. In practice, the reality is often very different.

The author of this book is Swiss, and therefore not a citizen of the European Union. This is not in itself exceptional, as many outside observers contribute remarkably to our understanding of Community law. However, it must be remembered that Switzerland chose not to join the Community. While the people's free decision must be respected, it is possible that reading this book may inspire the sceptics among the author's compatriots to reflect further on whether, in the modern world, a country is able to solve its problems on its own, and on whether it is wise still to go its way alone, within an otherwise unified Europe.

ULRICH EVERLING

Professor at the University of Bonn
Former Judge of the Court of Justice of the European Communities

Foreword

Not so long ago the European integration efforts under the different treaties on the European Communities, the European Treaty on Coal and Steel, and the Euratom Treaty, were referred to, in the English language, as the 'Common Market'. At that time, British pragmatism, for whatever reason, refused to see in the different efforts of institutionalizing Western European integration anything more than measures to establish and ensure the functioning of a common market among Western European States. This may be history or not: it is a fact that even today, in early 1996, the common market—the internal market—for products and services, capital and labour, is the core of the European Union. And all efforts to set up a European Union, a common currency, joint economical or financial policies, or other measures are implicitly built and constructed around this internal market concept, which was in the EEC Treaty right from its beginnings.

An internal market, where State frontiers are no longer seen or perceived as national frontiers, will inevitably have impacts on the shaping and implementation of environmental policies. Only in 1987, thirty years after the conclusion of the EEC Treaty, were environmental policy considerations inserted into that Treaty. However, a considerable time before 1987, environmental issues started to impinge on the concept of an 'ideal' internal market, where uniform rules for products and services exist. Indeed, the protection, preservation, and the improvement of the quality of the environment are very largely influenced by diverse geographical, climatic, geological, and other conditions. Thus a policy aiming at the protection of the environment normally and actually tries to optimize local or regional environmental protection—without taking into consideration the concerns of the market. Such a policy must inevitably enter into conflict with a policy that aims at establishing a level playing field for economic operators on this internal market, at preventing distortions of competition, and at setting uniform standards.

The inherent tensions between environmental protection rules and provisions for marketing of goods and services are well known within all Member States. At EC level, however, these different policy objectives are further increased by the more general question of who is to act in environmental matters, the Member States or the EC. While it is clear, under internal market provisions of primary law—Articles 30 and 36 in particular—and secondary EC law—the numerous EC regulations and directives—that it is essentially for the EC to fix common standards for products and services, this question is much less obvious in environment matters. Indeed, the environment—comparable in that to other general-interest matters such as human rights or health and safety of persons—must not remain unprotected: where the EC has not fixed EC-wide standards for environmental protection, it cannot, in principle, prevent Member States from adopting such measures, if Member States deem it necessary to protect the local, regional, or national environment.

Dr Ziegler's book tries to establish principles for striking the balance, under EC law, between legitimate environmental protection considerations at Member-State level, and the EC need to establish common rules for setting up and seeing functioning a common market for products and services; between the need to create uniform product standards and the need to apply other, in particular more stringent, environmental rules at national level; between the need to create a level playing field for economic operators within the internal market and the legitimate concerns of public authorities to optimize the protection of the environment.

Under the EC Treaty, such striking of the balance between different, sometimes diverging, interests of common market standards on the one hand and of ensuring optimal environmental protection on the other hand, will never be accomplished once and for all, since market conditions change as well as environmental needs—or are perceived differently by citizens or public authorities. Western European integration is a process; so are the efforts to protect the environment and so are the efforts to find an appropriate equilibrium between the market and the environment.

Therefore, as long as efforts continue in order to create an effective European Union, the inherent tensions between internal market standards and environmental protection requirements will continue to exist. It will be useful, then, to refer to Dr Ziegler's analysis, which very carefully researches the underlying principles that influence these policies and that determine their consequences.

DR. LUDWIG KRÄMER

Former Head of Legal Matters and Application
of Community Law in DG XI of the
European Commission

Acknowledgements

This book is a revised edition of my doctoral thesis accepted by the thesis committee of the University of St Gallen (Switzerland) on 27 June 1995. The original stimulus for my thesis was given by Professors Ernst–Ulrich Petersmann and Heinz Hauser during my graduate studies at the University of St. Gall. I would like to thank Professor Ernst–Ulrich Petersmann for the freedom he granted me when writing my thesis and for his support for the completion of this challenging study, in particular, during the time when I was working as his research assistant at the Institute of European, Economic and Comparative Law at the University of St Gall.

I am particularly grateful to Professor Heinz Hauser for giving me the opportunity to use my knowledge and findings from this study for a related research project on international trade policy funded by the Swiss National Fund for Research at the Swiss Institute for Research into International Economic Relations, Economic Structures and Regional Science at the University of St Gall. It is to his merit that the relationship between economic theory and legal rules has become one of my favourite research interests. I also would like to thank him for his continuing support with regard to this revised edition and my ongoing research.

An important part of this thesis was written during the academic year 1992–3 when I attended the Master Programme in European, Comparative and International Law at the European University Institute in Florence (Italy). I benefited enormously from the stimulating environment and the truly European and international spirit at the Institute. I would like to thank the Swiss Federal Ministry of Education and Science (*Bundesamt für Bildung und Wissenschaft*) for providing the financial resources for this study and research period. For their supervision and readiness for constructive criticism and discussion of my work I would like to thank my supervisors at the Institute, Professors Francis Snyder (EUI, Florence/College of Europe, Bruges/University College, London) and Christian Joerges (EUI, Florence/University of Bremen).

I am also very grateful to Professor David Cameron who allowed me to spend a most interesting research period at the Foundation of International Environmental Law and Development (University of London) and the Bodleian Library (University of Oxford). I am indebted to Professor Rainer J. Schweizer (University of St Gall) for the interest he took in my work and my enthusiasm for European and international law without ever letting me completely forget questions of domestic public and administrative law, as well as of legal theory in general.

The final corrections to my manuscript have benefited from the more than stimulating environment of the Georgetown University Law Centre (GULC) and the International Law Institute (ILI), both in Washington, DC. I would like to thank Professors Edith Brown Weiss and Don Wallace (both Georgetown University), as well as Stewart Kerr (International Law Institute) for their hospitality. I also benefited enormously from the computer systems and the working environment which I found during an extended visiting period at the Chicago–Kent College of Law and I would like to express my gratitude to Frederick Abbott.

For comments and suggestions regarding my work I would like to thank Rafael Stieger (Dr oec. HSG) and Christoph Henrichs (Dr iur., LL.M. (EUI), Assessor), for their linguistic support and careful assistance. Thanks go to Ronald William Ewart (MA, Lecturer at the University of St Gall), Rebecca Haynes (LL.M. (Lond.), Barrister), and Melanie Thomas (LL.B., BCL (Oxon.)). I am indebted to many friends and colleagues among whom for their understanding and moral support I want to mention, in particular, Anna, Anne, Bente, Fernando, Gallus, and Thomas.

For this edition the case law of the European Court of Justice and legal literature until December 1995 have been taken into account. I have tried to include most of the comments and corrections that have been made with regard to earlier versions. In particular, I would like to thank Dr. Ludwig Krämer (former Head of the Legal Service, Directorate General XI, Environment, Nuclear Safety, and Civil Protection, European Commission) and Professor Ulrich Everling for their assistance in improving the original manuscript and their willingness to write a foreword for this edition. For the very pleasant co-operation and their understanding of my editorial inexperience I would like to express my warmest gratitude to Richard Hart (Chief Editor Law, Oxford University Press) and my copy editor Kate Elliott. Obviously, all mistakes, shortcomings, and opinions expressed in this book are my own. All comments and corrections with regard to this book should be sent to the author's address and will be most appreciated.

St Gallen and Washington, D.C., Winter 1995/6

Andreas R. Ziegler
Swiss Institute for Research into International Economic Relations (SIASR), University of St Gallen, Dufourstrasse 48, CH–9000 St Gallen (Switzerland)

Contents

Abbreviations

AgrarR	*Agrarrecht*
AJIL	*American Journal of International Law*
AJP	*Aktuelle Juristische Praxis*
BB	*Der Betriebsberater*
BGE	Entscheide des Schweizerischen Bundesgerichts (Official reports of judgments of the Swiss Federal Supreme Court)
BGBl.	Bundesgesetzblatt (Germany)
BISD	Basic Instruments and Selected Documents (GATT)
BVerfGE	Entscheidungen des Bundesverfassungsgerichts (Official reports of judgments of the German Constitutional Court)
BVerwG	Bundesverwaltungsgericht (Germany)
BYIL	*British Yearbook for International Law*
CDE	Cahiers du Droit Européen
CMLR	Common Market Law Reports
CMLRev.	*Common Market Law Review*
DB	Der Betrieb
DV	Die Verwaltung
DVBl.	Deutsches Verwaltungsblatt
EA	*Europa-Archiv*
EC	European Community [Treaty]
ECR	Reports of the European Court of Justice
EEA	European Economic Area
EEC	European Economic Community (now European Community)
EFTA	European Free Trade Association
ELRev.	*European Law Review*
EP	European Parliament
EuGRZ	*Europäische Grundrechte–Zeitschrift*
EuR	*Europarecht*
EuZW	*Europäische Zeitschrift für Wirtschaftsrecht*
EUI	European University Institute
EWG	Europäische Wirtschaftsgemeinschaft (=EEC)
EWS	*Europäisches Wirtschafts- und Steuerrecht*
EWR	Europäischer Wirtschaftsraum (=EEA)
GATT	General Agreement on Tariffs and Trade
GYIL	*German Yearbook for International Law*
ICLQ	*The International and Comparative Law Quarterly*
ILM	International Legal Materials

ILO	International Labour Organization
IUCN	The Word Conservation Union
JA	*Juristische Ausbildung*
JCMS	*Journal of Common Market Studies*
J Env. L	*Journal of Environmental Law*
JuS	*Juristische Schulung*
JWT	*Journal of World Trade*
JZ	*Juristenzeitung*
KSE	*Kölner Schriften zum Europarecht*
LIEI	*Legal Issues on European Integration*
MEA	Multilateral Environmental Agreement
MLR	*Modern Law Review*
NAFTA	North American Free Trade Agreement
NILR	*Netherlands International Law Review*
NJB	*Nederlands Juristenblad*
NJW	*Neue Juristische Wochenschrift*
NuR	*Natur und Recht*
NVwZ	*Neue Zeitschrift für Verwaltungsrecht*
OECD	Organization for Economic Co-operation and Development
OJ	Official Journal of the European Community
ÖZW	*Österreichische Zeitschrift für Wirtschaftsrecht*
RabelsZ	*Rabels Zeitschrift*
RIW	*Recht der Internationalen Wirtschaft*
RMC	*Revue du Marché Commun*
RMCUE	*Revue du Marché Commun et de l'Union Européenne*
RTDE	*Revue Trimestrielle du Droit Européen*
SEA	Single European Act
SEW	*Sociaal–Economische Wetgeving*
SPS	Sanitary and Phitosanitary [Measures]
SZW	*Schweizerische Zeitung für Wirtschaftsrecht/Revue suisse de droit des affaires*
TBT	Technical Barriers to Trade
TREMs	Trade-related Environmental Measures
TRIPs	Trade-related Intellectual Property Rights
UNCED	United Nations Conference on Environment and Development
UNEP	United Nations Environment Programme
UPR/DEP	Umwelt- und Planungsrecht
UTR	Schriftenreihe des Instituts für Umwelt- und Technikrecht der Universität Trier
WTO	World Trade Organization
WuW	*Wirtschaft und Wettbewerb*
WWF	World-wide Fund for Nature

YEnv. L	*Yearbook of Environmental Law*
YEL	*Yearbook of European Law*
ZfU	*Zeitschrift für Umweltpolitik und Umweltrecht*
ZHR	*Zeitschrift für das gesamte Handelsrecht und Wirtschaftsrecht*
ZVgl. R Wiss.	*Zeitschrift für verlgeichende Rechtstwissenschaft*

Table of Cases

Judgments of the European Court of Justice
(The judgments by the European Court of Justice delivered in late 1992 and 1993 have not yet been published in the official reports (ECR), they are marked with an asterisk (*) and indicated with their date of delivery. Wherever available, the (CMLR) reference has been given.)

GATT Panel Decisions

Australia
High Court

Germany
Federal Constitutional Court (Bundesverfassungsgericht)

Federal Administrative Court (Bundesverwaltungsgericht)

Finanzgericht Bremen

Oberlandesgericht Köln (OLG Köln)

Switzerland
Swiss Federal Court (Bundegericht)

United Kingdom
English High Court

1

Integration of Trade and Environment

Liberalized Trade and Protection of the Environment

The co-ordination of trade liberalization and environmental protection is one of the biggest challenges facing all existing trade agreements[1] today. Since World War II the liberalization of trade has been one of the main objectives of international relations and politics. The protection of the environment, on the other hand, has become a priority only in the last twenty years, since the 1972 UN Environmental Conference in Stockholm. In recent years there has been increasing discussion about the compatibility of liberalized trade and environmental protection and the limitation of either in the interests of the other. The integration of sustainable development and economic growth was also a main issue of the 1992 Rio Earth Summit, i.e. the United Nations Conference for the Environment and Development (UNCED).[2]

In order to promote the liberalization of trade at a global level, a legal system—GATT—was created in 1947. This system works as a rule-oriented forum which aims at eliminating quantitative trade restrictions and technical barriers to trade, as well as at reducing customs duties. Within this framework many regional trade agreements have established free trade areas.[3] In these regional agreements customs duties have been abolished and the application of non-tariff barriers to trade has been prohibited. In many aspects they follow the development of the creation of internal markets in federal states or divided power systems in general.[4] The foundation of the World Trade Organization

---

[1] See e.g. OECD (Council at ministerial level), *Trade and Environment* (OECD, Paris, 1991); Congress of the United States, *Trade and Environment, Background Paper* (US Congress, Washington, D.C., 1992); P. Low (ed.), *International Trade and the Environment, World Bank Discussion Paper* (World Bank, Washington, D.C., 1992); GATT Secretariat, *Trade and the Environment* (GATT, Geneva, 1992); E.U. Petersmann, 'International Trade Law and International Environmental Law' [1993] *JWT* 43 to 81; T. Anderson (ed.), *NAFTA and the Environment* (Pacific Research Institute for Public Policy, San Francisco, 1993).

[2] See, in particular, UNCED, *Agenda 21* (ch. 38) and UNCED, *The Rio Declaration on Environment and Trade* (Rio Declaration), Principle 12, as reprinted e.g. in [1992] 31 ILM 874.

[3] Such as provided for by Art. XXIV GATT.

[4] See e.g. for the United States: D. Kommers and M. Waelbroeck, 'Legal Integration and the Free Movement of Goods: The American and European Experience' in M. Cappelletti, M. Seccombe, and J. Weiler (eds.), *Integration through Law* (W. de Gruyter, New York, 1985), Vol. I, Book 3, 165 to 230; T. Sandalow and E. Stein, 'The Two Systems: An Overview' in T. Sandalow and E. Stein (eds.), *Courts and Free Markets* (Oxford University Press, Oxford, 1982); for Australia: C. Staker, 'Free Movement of Goods in the EEC and Australia: A Comparative Study' [1990] *YEL*

(WTO) on 1 January, 1995 is considered to provide an even stronger framework for the prevention of protectionism and the establishment of worldwide liberalized trade.

The establishment of a common market for goods and the protection of the environment do not necessarily contradict each other *per se*. In economic analysis trade is an instrument for the optimal allocation of production resources.[5] The protection of the environment, particularly in terms of the concept of sustainable development, aims at the maintenance of our natural habitats and the existing ecological equilibrium in the interest of a balanced long-term coexistence of natural variety, production, and consumption. It thereby aims also at the preservation of natural production factors for future generations and the ecological equilibrium allowing for economic development. By giving environmental resources their just price and value, the principle of sustainability seeks to preserve their production capacity.[6] In this regard there is no contradiction between the principles of liberalized trade and environmental protection.

Obstacles to Trade through National Regulation

Nevertheless, the protection of the environment often requires State intervention to avoid the negative effects of certain economic activities. 'Environmental problems have traditionally been viewed as unwanted side effects of economic activities which should be controlled by a range of regulatory measures. A less widely held view is that environmental problems stem from failures within economies—and, therefore, market-based measures are needed to resolve them. Though the former approach has dominated EC and Member State environmental policies so far, the balance of view is changing.'[7]

As the environment can be considered to be a 'public good'[8] which has neither a price nor a particular owner, the intervention by the authorities in the public interest is in many cases the only way of safeguarding our natural habi-

209 to 242; for Switzerland see e.g. J.-P. Müller, *Die Grundrechte der Schweizerischen Bundesverfassung* (Schulthess, Zürich, 1991), 355; K. Vallender, *Wirtschaftsfreiheit und begrenzte Staatsverantwortung* (2nd edn., Stämpfli, Bern, 1991), 49.

[5] See e.g. M. W. Corden, 'The Normative Theory of International Trade' in R. W. Jones and P. B. Kenen (eds.), *Handbook of International Economics* (North-Holland, Amsterdam, 1984), 63 at 69 or R. E. Caves, J. A. Frankel and R. W. Jones, *World Trade and Payments* (6th edn., Harper Collins College Publishers, New York, 1993), 30.

[6] See e.g. UNCED, n. 2 above, 874; World Commission on Environment and Development, *Brundlandt Report, Our Common Future* (United Nations, New York, 1987); IUCN, UNEP, and WWF, *Caring for the Earth* (WWF, Gland, 1991), 8 to 13; H. Siebert, *Economics of the Environment* (3rd edn., Springer, Berlin, 1992), 245.

[7] Taken from N. Lee, 'Environmental Policy' in M. Artis and N. Lee, *The Economics of the European Union* (Oxford University Press, Oxford, 1994), 238.

[8] See for economic considerations on public goods in general e.g. H. R. Varian, *Intermediate Microeconomics* (3rd edn., W. W. Norton, New York, 1993), 579; for the differentiation between the environment as a common-property resource and environmental quality as a public good see Siebert, n. 6 above, 18 and 63 to 94.

tat.[9] Such intervention by regulations, prohibitions, and economic instruments, such as taxes and state aids, can lead to different regulatory systems in different countries. Such regulatory differences, however, hinder trade by creating different conditions for market access.[10]

Trade agreements, in general, aim at promoting trade through the reduction of obstacles to the free movement of goods. Free trade agreements have the objective of eliminating all barriers to trade including tariffs among the parties involved. Apart from the elimination of customs duties, quantitative restrictions, and tax discrimination, this objective often involves the reduction of trade barriers created by different product standards and administrative rules and procedures.[11] A third aspect is the elimination of trade-distorting financial incentives[12] or competition-distorting private agreements.[13] When such rules, standards or economic instruments are intended to safeguard the environment, conflicts between trade liberalization and national environmental policy may arise.

The Common Market and the Environment

The European Community (EC) has as one of its original and most important objectives the creation of a common market.[14] Apart from its far-reaching political integration objectives,[15] the Community aims at establishing one common market without internal borders or trade barriers in the form of custom duties,[16] quantitative restrictions on trade, or any measures having equivalent effect.[17] A

---

[9] See Siebert, n. 6 above, 59. See, however, also the outstanding considerations on the possible development of private negotiations on environmental quality in R. H. Coase, 'The Problem of Social Cost' [1960] *Journal of Law and Economics* 1 to 44; on the scarcity of such spontaneous private agreements see E.-U. Petersmann, 'Freier Warenverkehr und nationaler Umweltschutz in EWG und EWR' [1993] *Aussenwirtschaft* 95 at 96. These interventions are described by C. Joerges as 'social regulation', see C. Joerges, 'European Economic Law, the Nation State and the Maastricht Treaty' in R. Dehousse (ed.), *The European Union Treaty* (C. H. Beck, München, 1994), 1 at 23.

[10] See e.g. H. Gröner, 'Umweltschutzbedingte Produktnormen als nichttarifäres Handelshemmnis' in H. Gutzler (ed.), *Umweltpolitik und Wettbewerb* (NOMOS, Baden-Baden 1981), 143 to 162.

[11] See e.g. in the framework of the WTO, the Agreements on Technical Barriers to Trade (TBT Agreement) and the Sanitary and Phytosanitary Measures (SPS Agreement), e.g. in GATT Secretariat (ed.), *The Results of the Uruguay Round of Multilateral Trade Negotiations—The Legal Texts* (GATT, Geneva, 1994), 138; see for comments e.g. E.-U. Petersmann, 'Trade Policy, Environmental Policy and the GATT' [1991] *Aussenwirtschaft* 197 at 219; see also Arts. 11 and 12 of the Agreement on the European Economic Area (EEA).

[12] See e.g. in the framework of the World Trade Organization (WTO) the Agreement on Subsidies and Countervailing Measures, in its new version after the Uruguay Round in GATT Secretariat (ed.), n. 11 above.

[13] See e.g. E.-U. Petersmann, 'International Competition Rules for the GATT–MTO World Trade and Legal System' [1993] *JWT* 35 to 86 or the relevant sections in the US–Canada Free Trade Agreement and NAFTA. [14] Art. 2 EC.

[15] In particular, since the coming into force of the Treaty on the European Union on 1 November 1993 (EU Treaty or Maastricht Treaty).

[16] Arts. 9, 12 EC.

[17] Arts. 30 and 34 EC (prohibitions of quantitative restrictions on trade and measures having equivalent effect).

further element to ensure the establishment of the common market is the creation of a system ensuring undistorted competition within the Community.[18] Finally, the Community has undertaken the approximation of national laws to the extent required for the establishment of the common market[19] and in certain areas has established common policies.[20] In all these areas the possibilities for Member States to take autonomous action in pursuit of domestic objectives are strictly limited by the Community legal order.

When the Community was founded in 1957 the protection of the environment was not an explicit objective of the Treaty; nevertheless, the elimination of technical barriers to trade soon raised questions concerning European and national environmental policy. Divergent national product standards constitute obstacles to trade[21] and thereby lead to market fragmentation, while production and process measures as well as differences in taxation or the allocation of state aids influence the competitive situation within the common market.[22] Thus, regulatory differences between the Member States hinder the establishment of the common market.[23] This is also true if such measures are taken in the interest of environmental protection. On the other hand, there is a genuine interest in maintaining certain measures necessary for the efficient safeguarding of the environment. With the entry into force of the Single European Act (SEA) the Community itself has been entrusted with the protection of the environment at a high level.[24]

The Community in Search of Reconciliation

The pursuit of both a common market and adequate protection of the environment, demands, however, certain mechanisms which co-ordinate the two aims. Legal theory has to elaborate adequate solutions to balance the interests concerned. As Community law stands, the (*prima facie*) dilemma between national environmental measures and the elimination of trade-hindering regulatory differences has been tackled mainly in two ways.

One approach is to establish certain basic principles concerning the application of national (environmental) measures: the Treaty provides an important

---

[18] Art. 3 EC.   [19] Art. 3 EC.   [20] Such as under Arts. 43, 75, 84 (2), 113 etc. EC.

[21] See e.g. Case 302/86 *Commission* v. *Denmark* (*Danish Bottles*) [1988] *ECR* 4607.

[22] See, however, e.g. J. A. Tobey, 'The Effects of Domestic Environmental Policies on Patterns of World Trade: An Empirical Test' [1990] *Kyklos* 191 to 209.

[23] See e.g. Case 91/79 *Commission* v. *Italy* (*Detergents*) [1980] *ECR* 1099 at 1106 or Case 92/79 *Commission* v. *Italy* (*Maximum Sulphur Content of Liquid Fuels*) [1980] *ECR* 1115 at 1122; see also M. Seidel, 'Umweltrecht in der Europäischen Gemeinschaft—Träger oder Hemmnis des Fortschritts' [1989] *DVBl.* 441 at 444.

[24] Art. 130r EC. The Treaty does not contain a clear definition of the terms 'environment' or 'environmental policy'. This book uses a rather broad concept which allows one also to include such issues as the well-being of animals or specific aspects of human health. For a detailed treatment of the problem see L. Krämer, *EC Treaty and Environmental Law* (2nd edn., Sweet & Maxwell, London, 1995), 41 to 44.

number of rules for the application of national environmental standards, regulations, and prohibitions as well as for the use of economic instruments and voluntary agreements. While this amounts in many cases to the application of a mere non-discrimination principle,[25] there are areas where Member States are prohibited from applying certain instruments because of their general trade-hindering or competition-distorting effect.[26] However, there are exceptions for specific interests, such as the protection of the environment, which allow Member States to deviate from the general rules in cases where this is necessary to achieve these specific objectives. The Commission and, in particular, the Court of Justice,[27] have developed certain guidelines which allow for the application of domestic measures and instruments for optimal protection of the environment at the national and local level without, however, allowing Member States to jeopardize the establishment of the common market.[28] To find the balance is often a very delicate and difficult task.[29]

Another way of eliminating the remaining obstacles to trade is the harmonization of environmental standards.[30] Under the Treaty of Rome the Member States have given the European Community a broad power to harmonize national laws, rules, and administrative measures which hinder the establishment of the common market. This power has also been used to harmonize national environmental standards.[31] In certain areas the Community has the power to establish common policies such as a common agricultural policy, a common transport policy, or a common commercial policy. These policies also have important environmental aspects. Under the Single European Act the existing set of competences was complemented by an explicit power to introduce a comprehensive environmental policy at Community level.[32]

Recently, however, the harmonization of national rules has come under

---

[25] E.g. Arts. 7, 34, 95 etc. EC.

[26] Such as Arts. 85, 92 and, through the Court's case law, 30 EC applying the *Dassonville* formula first developed in Case 8/74 *Procureur du Roi* v. *B. and G. Dassonville* (*Dassonville*) [1974] *ECR* 837.

[27] On the important role of the Court in the development of Community law see e.g. H. Rasmussen, *On Law and Policy in the European Court of Justice* (Martinus Nijhoff, Dordrecht, 1986); M. Cappelletti, 'Is the European Court of Justice "running wild"?' (1987) 12 *ELRev.* 3; J.-P. Colin, *Le gouvernement des juges dans les Communautés Européennes* (Librairie générale de droit et de jurisprudence, Paris, 1966); P. Pescatore, 'La carrence du législateur communautaire et le devoir du juge' in G. Lüke, G. Rees, and M. R. Will (eds.), *Rechtsvergleichung, Europarecht und Staatsintegration, Gedächtnisschrift für Leontin-Jean Constantinesco* (Heymann, Köln, 1983), 559 to 580.

[28] See Art. 5 EC; on the constitutional function of international trade rules in general and the freedoms of the Treaty see E.-U. Petersmann, *Constitutional Functions and Constitutional Problems of International Economic Law* (Fribourg University Press, Fribourg, 1991), 453.

[29] See also C. Joerges, n. 9 above, 8 to 10 on the replacement of national regulatory traditions by a common European framework through the Court of Justice.

[30] See also the recent developments in NAFTA and GATT: E.-U. Petersmann, n. 9 above, 127 or D. Esty, 'Making Trade and Environmental Policies work together: Lessons from NAFTA' [1994] *Aussenwirtschaft* 59 to 80.

[31] Arts. 100, 43, 75, 99, and 113 EC.

[32] Art. 130s EC, but see also the accelerated harmonization of rules under Art. 100a.

repeated criticism. The principles of subsidiarity[33] and competition of regulatory systems[34] express a strong desire to limit the harmonization measures taken by the Community to those absolutely necessary. Some of the Member States might wish to apply national environmental measures more stringent than those at Community level,[35] but the Community has the task of ensuring both objectives: the establishment of the common market and the protection of the environment at a high level. The established principle of subsidiarity, however, requires the application of mechanisms which allow a certain degree of choice as to the local level of protection.

OBJECTIVES AND FOCUS OF THIS BOOK

The Questions to be Answered

This book seeks to answer the following question: how far does the existing Community legal framework co-ordinate the shared responsibility for the protection of the environment and the establishment of the common market between Community and Member States? It thus asks for a two-fold co-ordination problem under Community law: first, how does the Community legal order co-ordinate the establishment of the common market and the protection of the environment, both explicit Community tasks and objectives? Secondly, how does the Community integrate the Member States into these tasks, e.g. in cases in which the optimal protection of the environment requires the intervention of Member States and thus sets a limit to harmonization at Community level? The second question involves the aspects of subsidiarity and competition of regulatory systems under Community law.

In my view, two sets of mechanisms exist in the Treaty to co-ordinate Community law and national environmental law: (a) the Treaty provisions concerning the four freedoms and the system ensuring undistorted competition within the common market, including implicit and explicit exceptions for domestic environmental policy, and (b) harmonized Community rules which create mechanisms for the application of diverging national rules. How do these com-

---

[33] See e.g. A. G. Toth, 'The Principle of Subsidiarity in the Maastricht Treaty' (1992) 29 *CMLRev.* 1079 to 1106 or D. Z. Cass, 'The Word that Saves Maastricht? The Principle of Subsidiarity and the Division of Powers Within the European Community' (1992) 29 *CMLRev.* 1107.

[34] See e.g. P. Nicolaides, 'Competition Among Rules' [1992] *World Competition* 113 to 121 or H. Hauser, 'Harmonisierung oder Wettbewerb nationaler Regulierungssysteme in einem integrierten Wirtschaftsraum' [1993] *Aussenwirtschaft* 459 to 476.

[35] For a long time there has been an environmentalist fear that the Community was going to harmonize environmental standards at the 'lowest possible denominator', in particular, under Art. 100 EC, see e.g. E. Steindorff, 'Umweltschutz in Gemeinschaftshand?' [1984] *RIW* 767 at 771 and 772; Seidel, n. 23 above, 443; see also 'Keine EG-Harmonisierung des Umweltschutzes nach unten', *Neue Zürcher Zeitung* (13 Feb. 1990, no. 36) 21.

plementary mechanisms work and which principles govern the relation between Community law and domestic environmental policy?

Existing Literature and Research

This book does not intend to discuss the subject of existing Community competences to adopt environmental measures and the appropriate legal basis. There are a large number of publications which deal in detail with the Community's competence to regulate environmental policy.[36] It is, however, necessary to show how the chosen legal basis affects the applicable mechanisms.

A second range of publications has been dedicated to the interpretation of Article 100a and its relationship to Article 130s.[37] These have analyzed the provisions in detail, but their interpretation remains controversial. I intend rather to place Article 100a(4) and also Article 130t within the framework of the existing mechanisms without entering into the argument about the range of their possible interpretations.[38]

A third category of existing literature focuses on the justification of national environmental measures under the general principles of the common market, mainly under the free movement of goods principle. However, focusing as they do only on the admissibility of product measures under Article 36 and the rule of reason,[39] these neglect the possible consequences from production and process measures, taxes, and state aids, as well as the existing harmonization of

---

[36] See I. Pernice, 'Kompetenzordnung und Handlungsbefugnisse der Europäischen Gemeinschaft auf dem Gebiete des Umwelt- und Technikrechts' [1989] *DV* 1 to 54; A. Vorwerk, *Die umweltpolitischen Kompetenzen der Europäischen Gemeinschaft und ihrer Mitgliedstaaten nach Inkrafttreten der EEA* (VVF, München 1990); F. Hochleitner, *Die Kompetenzen der Europäischen Wirtschaftsgemeinschaft auf dem Gebiet des Umweltschutzes* (VWGO, Wien, 1990); T. Schröer, *Die Kompetenzverteilung zwischen der Europäischen Wirtschaftsgemeinschaft und ihren Mitgliedstaaten auf dem Gebiet des Umweltschutzes* (Duncker & Humblot, Berlin, 1992) with many references to the abundant German literature.

[37] See C. E. Palme, *Nationale Umweltpolitik in der EG—Zur Rolle des Art. 100a IV im Rahmen einer Europäischen Umweltgemeinschaft* (Duncker & Humblot, Berlin, 1991); see partly also A. Furrer, *Die Sperrwirkung des sekundärrechtlichen Gemeinschaftsrechts auf die nationalen Rechtsordnungen* (Nomos, Baden-Baden, 1994) or in English D. Geradin, 'Trade and Environmental Protection: Community Harmonization and National Standards' [1993] *YEL* 151 to 199.

[38] Furthermore, a case concerning Art. 100a(4) was recently decided by the Court of Justice: the application of Art. 100a(4) was, however, not clarified as the relevant decision by the Commission was annulled on procedural grounds: Case C–41/93 *France* v. *Commission* (*PCP Decision*) [1994] *ECR* I–1829; see [1992] *OJ* C334/8 and [1993] *OJ* C70/11; see also Ch. 8.

[39] See L. Krämer, 'Environmental Protection and Art. 30 EEC Treaty' (1993) 30 *CMLRev.* 111 to 143; U. Becker, *Der Gestaltungsspielraum der EG-Mitgliedstaaten im Spannungsfeld zwischen Umweltschutz und freiem Warenverkehr* (Nomos, Baden-Baden, 1991); A. Epiney and T. M. J. Möllers, *Freier Warenverkehr und nationaler Umweltschutz* (Heymann, Köln, 1992); from a broader perspective but focusing on the free movement of goods Petersmann, n. 9 above; A. Middeke, *Nationaler Umweltschutz im Binnenmarkt* (Heymann, Köln, 1994); D. Demiray, 'The Movement of Goods in a Green Market' [1994] *LIEI* 73 to 110 or recently J. Scherer, 'Regional Perspectives on Trade and the Environment: The European Union' in W. Lang (ed.), *Sustainable Development and International Law* (Graham & Trotman, London, 1994), 253 to 271.

laws.[40] Economic theory shows how closely all these measures are connected, as they are easily interchangeable to attain the same effect by other means.[41] The general tendency to use more diversified instruments for the protection of the environment[42] makes it necessary to analyse the field using a more systematic approach.

The Approach used in this Book

All of the publications mentioned above have been strongly influenced by German legal literature and particularly by the concept of the *Nationaler Alleingang*.[43] My objective, however, is to show how the Community order and, in particular, the Court of Justice, have established a system where both the Community and the Member States have environmental responsibilities. The effective and adequate protection of the environment has become a shared responsibility of the Community and the Member States.[44] For the combination of regulation by several actors certain coordinating principles are needed.[45]

It will become clear that the Community uses different instruments in different contexts, depending on the degree of homogeneity needed for the establishment of the common market. Until comprehensive harmonization takes place, the Member States remain free to act, bound only by the basic principles of the Treaty. These principles contain certain specific exceptions clauses for national interests and the Court has developed a broad case law which takes into account the need of locally adequate environmental protection. It will also be shown that the interpretation of certain Treaty provisions has been influenced by a growing ecological awareness. This applies also to the practice of the Commission.

In its harmonization projects, by using safeguard clauses and minimum requirements, the Community provides for the application of more stringent

[40] See, however, the recently published study by O. Brunetti, *EG-Rechtsverträglichkeit als Kriterium der nationalen Umweltpolitik* (Schulthess und Stämpfli, Zürich and Bern, 1993). This very interesting work focuses on the different instruments of national environmental policy. It does not, however, elaborate on the system of environmental tasks and responsibilities of the Community but mainly discusses the existing Community law concerning the domestic application of technical rules, state aids, taxes, and voluntary agreements.

[41] See e.g. Siebert, n. 6 above, 127 to 148.

[42] See e.g. W. E. Oates, 'Market Incentives for Environmental Protection: a Survey of Some Recent Developments' in M. H. Peston and R. E. Quandt (eds.), *Prices, Competition and Equilibrium* (P. Allan, Oxford, 1986), 251 to 267; K.-H. Hansmeyer, 'Marktwirtschaftliche Elemente in der Umweltpolitik—Eine Zusammenfassung der Argumente' [1988] *ZfU* 231 to 241.

[43] May be best translated as 'divergent national measures'; see K. Hailbronner, 'Der nationale Alleingang im Gemeinschaftsrecht am Beispiel der Abgasstandards für PKW' [1989] *EuGRZ* 101 to 122. Krämer uses the term 'unilateral action', see L. Krämer, *Focus on European Environmental Law* (Sweet & Maxwell, London, 1993), 179 to 208.

[44] The use of the term 'shared responsibility' as well as the idea of a systematic approach to the Community system regulating environment and trade have been heavily influenced by publications by *Ludwig Krämer*, see Krämer, n. 39 above, 143 and L. Krämer, 'Community Environmental Law— Towards a Systematic Approach' [1992] *YEL* 151 to 184.

[45] Joerges, n. 9 above, 32.

national environmental measures. The introduction of systematic options for diverging national measures under Article 100a(4) and Article 130t EC has provided a complementary instrument. The mutual information and the compulsory notification of planned national measures constitute an essential element in this system for balancing the interests in question.

Member States and local authorities have important regulatory competences and tasks. Only in cases where such measures are abused for non-ecological aims or interfere with the common market in a disproportionate way will the Community intervene. In these cases it is, however, sometimes difficult to find a satisfactory solution for the reconciliation of trade and environment.[46] In certain cases the harmonization of laws, including mechanisms for the application of higher national standards, can be a means of achieving both objectives to a certain extent. While the use of such mechanisms tries to take into account regional differences and the principle of subsidiarity, cases may again emerge where the unity of the common market and regional preferences or needs for environmental protection do not converge. These situations still demand an element of choice. The Community and its Member States have to 'weigh Community interests against national policy choices and then arrive at workable compromises between market integration objectives and national autonomy'.[47]

In spite of the possible incidence of such situations, the Community has established a very comprehensive system for the balancing of ecological and trade interests. The variety of mechanisms developed and the establishment of the protection of the environment as an autonomous objective of the Community will help to combine economic prosperity and development with the protection of the natural habitats and species within the Community. In this sense, this book is also intended to be a contribution to today's global search for a legal solution to the possible conflicts arising from the integration of trade rules and the need for environmental regulation.[48]

STRUCTURE AND ORGANIZATION

After this introduction, Part I will deal with the general freedoms and principles of the common market and their implications for domestic environmental measures. Chapter 2 will discuss the consequences of different regulatory models and their implications for domestic policy and national sovereignty when adopting environmental measures. Chapter 3 provides a survey of the current Community concept of the free movement of goods while Chapter 4 will survey the specific

---

[46] See e.g. Case 302/86 *Danish Bottles*, n. 21 above.   [47] Joerges, n. 9 above, 32.

[48] See for the current discussion in the GATT/WTO system, e.g. J. H. Jackson, 'World Trade Rules and Environmental Policies: Congruence or Conflict?' (1992) 49 *Washington & Lee Law Review* 1227 to 1275, or in NAFTA, e.g. B. Zagaris, 'The Transformation of Environmental Enforcement Cooperation Between Mexico and the USA in the Wake of NAFTA' (1993) 18 *North Carolina Journal of International Law and Commercial Regulation* 59 to 133.

rules and case law applicable to domestic measures in the interest of the environment. Chapter 5 is dedicated to a detailed analysis of the conditions governing the admissibility of domestic environmental measures under Article 36 and the rule of reason. Chapter 6 contains an analysis of the Treaty's rules governing undistorted competition and their compatibility with national economic instruments and incentives for undertakings to protect the environment.

Part II elaborates upon the Community system for the combination of Community environmental action and domestic environmental policy. Chapter 7 will focus on the general development of the Community's environmental policy and the changing awareness of the need for such action in the last thirty years. Chapter 8 will explain the mechanisms for harmonized standards under the general harmonization of laws, while Chapter 9 will present the various special areas of harmonization and common policies which have an impact on national environmental measures. Chapter 10 is dedicated to the use of economic instruments for the protection of the environment. In Chapter 11 the external relations of the Community concerning the environment are analysed. Finally, in Chapter 12 a systematic overview of the mechanisms used and the principles underlying the Community legal order is given.

For a better understanding of the mechanisms discussed, I have tried to include a large number of examples from existing Community law and, in particular, the case law of the European Court of Justice.[49] Apart from the Court's case law, many examples are taken from the Commission's reports and, in the case of unpublished proceedings, from the publications by *Ludwig Krämer* (Head of Legal Matters and Application of Community Law in Directorate General XI of the European Commission).

Apart from explicitly mentioned exceptions, the term EC Treaty refers throughout the integral text to the Treaty establishing the European Community in its current form after the coming into force of the Treaty on European Union (EU). Whenever possible, the case law of the European Court of Justice and the general development of Community environmental law have been taken into account until January 1996.

---

[49] The examples are given in small print.

PART I

Undistorted Trade and Competition and Domestic Environmental Measures

2

The Common Market and National Regulation

INTRODUCTION

The common market is one of the main means available to the Community for the promotion of its objectives. The protection of the environment at a high level has to be taken into consideration in the establishment of the common market. The common market relies on different elements: the four economic freedoms, a system ensuring undistorted competition, and the approximation of laws to the extent required for the functioning of the common market. In the field of competition the Community has established a system which tries to avoid the reconstruction of abolished state trade barriers by private undertakings. The underlying concepts of the Treaty provisions concerning the establishment of the common market have important effects on domestic environmental policy.

It is often an essential feature of international trade agreements that the relevant Treaty requires the equal application of national administrative rules and financial burdens to both imported and domestic goods. In the European Community the 'national treatment' test is applied in a way which also covers national measures affecting domestic and foreign goods disparately although applied *prima facie* equally to both categories. Nevertheless, such an interpretation of the non-discrimination principle does not preclude differentiation for justified interests by the Member States. The Community sets certain rules, however, to avoid the abuse of such measures for protectionist goals.

Apart from the mere 'non-discrimination' requirement of national policy measures, the scope of the general freedoms of the Treaty and the rules applying to private undertakings can also include eliminating measures which hinder or interfere with trade between the Member States. Measures adopted by the Member States or private undertakings can have such an effect despite their equal application to domestic and foreign products. In a system where, besides the mere prohibition of protectionism, 'federalist values' such as the promotion of a unified market and an integrated economy are aspired to, such measures must be eliminated. The Court applies different concepts under different provisions of the Treaty. In distinct cases the trade hindering effect of a private or State action is considered to be sufficient to make it unlawful under the system of the Treaty despite its non-discriminatory application.

THE COMMON MARKET AND DOMESTIC ACTIONS

The Concept of a Common Market

Article 2 EC mentions as the Community's first instrument for the promotion of its objectives the establishment of a common market.[1] The Community uses two principal means to establish this market. The first is a set of economic freedoms and principles aimed at the elimination of any trade- or competition-distorting behaviour by Member States and undertakings operating in the market. The second means is the complementary approximation of laws of the Member States to the extent required for the proper functioning of the common market.[2] In addition, the implementation of common policies, which constitutes another means of promotion of the Community objectives, is also very much related to the concept of the common market.[3]

The first set of instruments used for the establishment of the common market are the four freedoms of the Treaty and the establishment of a system ensuring that competition within the common market is not distorted. The four freedoms include the free movement of goods, the free movement of services, the free movement of persons, and the free movement of capital.[4] The two main elements of the Community system ensuring undistorted competition are the prohibition of trade-distorting behaviour of, and agreements between, undertakings[5] on the one hand and the general prohibition of state aids distorting, or threatening to distort, competition[6] on the other. While the wording of the four freedoms suggests that they are aimed mainly at the regulation of Member-State action, whereas the prohibition of competition-distorting behaviour seems to focus on private behaviour, these have to be conceptualized as a set of rules regulating the behaviour of both for the establishment of the common market.[7]

While the first set of prohibitions or principles governing the common mar-

---

[1] In terms of the Treaty of Rome this task was accompanied by the progressive approximation of the economic policies of the Member States, which now, under the Treaty on European Union (EU Treaty), has been developed into the 'establishment of an economic and monetary union' (Art. 2 EU).

[2] Art. 3 EC.

[3] See e.g. P. J. G. Kapteyn and P. VerLoren van Themaat, *The Law of the European Communities* (2nd edn., Kluwer, Deventer, 1989), 75; see also Ch. 9.

[4] Art. 3(c) EC. Sometimes the freedom of payments is included as a fifth freedom; see e.g. R. Barents, 'The Community and the Unity of the Common Market' [1990] *GYIL* 308 at 312.

[5] Arts. 85 ff. EC.   [6] Arts. 92 ff. EC.

[7] See e.g. for the consequences of Art. 85 on the Member States' behaviour: Case 311/85 *A.S.B.L. Vereniging van Vlaamse Reisebureaus* v. *A.S.B.L. Sociale Dienst van de Plaatselijke en Gewestelijke Overheidsdiensten* [1987] *ECR* 3801 at 3817; or recently: Case C–185/91 *Bundesanstalt für den Güterfernverkehr* v. *Gebrüder Reiff*, Judgment of 17 Nov. 1993, reprinted in [1995] 5 *CMLR* 145 or [1993] *EuZW* 769; for details see Ch. 6; for the role of private undertakings when relying on commercial property legislation or unfair competition legislation to prevent certain imports: e.g. Case 15/74 *Centrafarm BV* v. *Sterling Drug* [1974] *ECR* 1147 or Case 187/80 *Merck* v. *Stephar BV* [1981] ECR 2063; see also Kapteyn and VerLoren van Themaat, n. 3 above, 83 and 380.

ket is often referred to as negative harmonization,[8] the second set (the approximation of laws of Member States) is called positive harmonization. Both have important effects on the Member States' powers to use regulatory instruments in the pursuit of national policy objectives.

In the field of the environment, the use of national regulatory instruments such as prohibitions on the use of certain substances or product standards, as well as economic instruments, such as state aids, charges, or levies etc., is severely restricted by the rules of the Treaty, as well as by the existing Community secondary law in various areas. Still, the protection of the environment is an autonomous objective of the Community.[9] The principal rules governing the common market can therefore not be interpreted as having the aim of eliminating every domestic environmental policy which interferes with Community trade and competition. This is supported by Articles 2 and 130r(2) EC. The protection of the environment is a common task which requires common action by both the Community and its Member States.[10]

On the other hand, the rules of the Treaty are aimed at the elimination of national measures which jeopardize the establishment of the common market by distorting trade and competition. In this sense domestic environmental measures may not be abused for objectives which do not relate to the interests of the environment. Such domestic policy contradicts the spirit of the Treaty and is incompatible with the Member States' commitments, in particular with their duty of loyalty towards the Community (Article 5).

In this sense the freedoms of the Treaty and the established system for the elimination of competition-distorting behaviour by undertakings are general guarantees[11] by the Treaty for the establishment of the common market. At the same time they have to be applied in a way which respects the environment.[12] From this it follows that all actions by Member States must be analysed in two respects: (a) their effect on the common market, i.e. their distorting effect on trade or competition within the common market, and (b) their positive effect on the quality of the environment throughout the Community. In both areas, the development and concretization of the Treaty principles and the development of the ecological principles of the Treaty, the Court of Justice has played an important role. Not only has it conceptualized the scope of certain Treaty pro-

---

[8] See e.g. P. Behrens, 'Die Konvergenz der wirtschaftlichen Freiheiten' [1992] *EuR* 145 at 150, which is, however, in my view only appropriate in cases where differences among the regulatory systems of the Member States are actually harmonized through the jurisdiction of the Court (such as under Art. 30 EC) and not for provisions which apply a mere non-discrimination principle: see below in this chapter the section on the concept of the free movement of goods. For similar considerations in the field of the free movement of workers see E. Johnson and. D. O'Keeffe, 'From Discrimination to Obstacles to Free Movement: Recent Developments Concerning the Free Movement of Workers' (1994) 31 CMLRev. 1313 at 1329.

[9] Arts. 2 and 3(k) EC. See on the development of the Communiy environmental policy Ch. 7.

[10] Art. 130r(4); see also L. Krämer, 'Environmental Protection and Article 30 EEC Treaty' (1993) 30 *CMLRev.* 111 at 113.

[11] See e.g. Behrens, n. 8 above, 145 at 147 or Barents, n. 4 above, 308.

[12] Art. 2 EC.

visions and their constitutional character,[13] but it has also developed methods for the co-ordination of economic integration and protection of the environment.[14] The achievement of an equilibrium between these two aspects is the main problem which the following chapters will describe.[15]

Different Categories of Economic Freedoms

As derived from the case law of the Court and the proceedings brought by the Commission against Member States, the main principles of the Treaty which conflict with national environmental policy measures are, on the one hand, the freedom of goods principle[16] and, on the other, the rules of the Treaty concerning competition-distorting behaviour by the Member States when favouring agreements with or between undertakings,[17] or applying state aids[18] or charges for the pursuit of their domestic environmental goals.[19]

When applying the freedoms and principles of the Treaty to domestic laws, it is important to note that the concepts underlying those Community guarantees differ according to the specific provisions.[20] One can probably distinguish three categories of Community rules concerning the application of domestic regulations in areas where action by a Member State is still compatible with the Treaty.[21] As the free movement of goods is the most controversial principle of the Treaty as far as domestic environmental measures are concerned, I shall concentrate in this Chapter on the concepts and objectives underlying trade in goods. There exist, however, similar problems and conceptual differences in the application of the other freedoms of the Treaty.[22] The underlying principles of

[13] See e.g. E.-U. Petersmann, 'Constitutionalism, Constitutional Law and European Integration' [1991] *Aussenwirtschaft* 247 at 256; see also Ch. 3.

[14] See e.g. I. Koppen, *The Role of the European Court of Justice in the Development of the European Community's Environmental Policy*, EUI Working Paper (European University Institute, San Domenico di Fiesole, 1993), 14 ff.; see also Chs. 4 and 5.

[15] Apart from the Community example here described, such problems arise in all divided power systems which have to reconcile environmental measures (by their sub-entities) and the establishment of a common market or commercial freedoms: see e.g. for the United States, D. Geradin, 'Free Trade and Environmental Protection in an Integrated Market: A Survey of the Case Law of the United States Supreme Court and the European Court of Justice' [1993] 2 *Journal of Transnational Law and Policy* 141 at 142, or for Australia C. Staker, 'Free Movement of Goods in the EEC and Australia: A Comparative Study' [1990] *YEL* 209 at 219.

[16] Arts. 30 ff. EC, in conjunction with Art. 95; see Chs. 3 to 5.

[17] Arts. 85 ff. in conjunction with Art. 5; see Ch. 6.   [18] Arts. 92 ff.; see Ch. 6.

[19] The freedom-of-services principle may also interfere with domestic prohibitions of certain dangerous activities or export restrictions concerning recyclable waste, see e.g. U. Everling, 'Die Wiederaufbereitung abgebrannter Brennelemente in anderen Mitgliedstaaten der Europäischen Gemeinschaft' [1993] *RIW* (suppl. 2) 14 to 19 or H.-W. Rengeling, 'Schadlose Verwertung radioaktiver Reststoffe durch Wiederaufbearbeitung in anderen EG-Mitgliedstaaten' [1991] *DVBl.* 914 at 919. In view of its limited relevance to the framework of this book, however, it will not be dealt with here.   [20] See for details Behrens, n. 8 above, 147.

[21] The following concept is heavily influenced by the analysis of Kapteyn and VerLoren van Themaat, n. 3 above, 92 ff. and 355 ff.

[22] See Behrens, n. 8 above, 145.

certain Treaty provisions explain to a large extent the difficulties which arise between the various levels of regulation in a divided power system such as the Community.[23]

The Prohibition of Protectionist Measures

First, the Treaty contains prohibitions on domestic actions which are directly aimed at hindering trade between the Member States. The classical examples are quantitative trade restrictions and customs duties. Normally, these are easily recognizable and take the form of trade restrictions or financial charges and levies which concern only imported goods and do not apply to domestic goods at all. In these cases the Treaty's objective is the abolition of any protectionist national measures which discriminate openly against imported goods, i.e. which differentiate between imported goods and domestic goods only because of the fact that the former cross an inter-state border. As the Community is based on the creation of a common market and the abolition of all trade barriers between Member States, such domestic action is always incompatible with the Treaty, except in specific cases provided for by the Treaty.[24]

As in classical trade agreements[25] the most appropriate examples in the EC Treaty of the proscriptions of purely protectionist measures are Articles 9 and 12 which prohibit the use of any customs duties, while Articles 30 and 34 prohibit quantitative restrictions on imports and exports.[26] The main aim of both trade restrictions and customs duties is the reduction of trade and the favouring of domestic production. It is an inherent characteristic of these measures that they do not apply to domestic goods and therefore do not only openly discriminate against imported goods, but have as their only justification the hindrance

---

[23] M. Cappelletti, M. Seccombe, and J. H. H. Weiler, 'Introduction' in M. Cappelletti, M. Seccombe, and J. H. H. Weiler (eds.), *Integration through Law* (W. de Gruyter, New York, 1986), i, book 1, 3 at 11 to 15; see also E. Stein, 'Towards a European Foreign Policy?' in Cappelletti, Seccombe, and Weiler (eds.), n. 23 above, 3 at 5.

[24] This is already the case in less far-reaching agreements which aim only at the establishment of a free trade area, see e.g. W. Molle, *The Economics of European Integration* (Brookfield, Aldershot, 1990), 15 and 83 to 112. It should be noted that I always speak of imported goods as opposed to domestic goods in the following sections. I would like to stress, however, that protectionist measures can also be adopted against domestic production which is meant to be exported. Here again specific measures are sometimes taken to hinder trade and these also constitute obstacles to trade in the form of export restrictions. The reasons for their adoption can be many. To keep my argument simple I will refer only to imported goods throughout this Chapter. The conclusions are, however, *mutatis mutandis*, also applicable to measures concerning exported goods.

[25] See e.g. the prohibition on quantitative restrictions on trade in GATT (Art. XI), which does not, however, prohibit the use of customs duties but aims at a constant reduction of the latter (Art. II). For real free trade agreements and their provisions see e.g the EFTA Agreement: Arts. 3 and 8 (Tariffs) and Arts. 10 and 11 (Quantitative Restrictions on Trade); for the Switzerland–EC Free Trade Agreement Arts. 3 to 7 (Tariffs) and Art. 13 (Import Restrictions) or for NAFTA: Art. 300 section B (Tariff Elimination) and section C (Import and Export Restrictions).

[26] See, however, the prohibition of measures/charges having equivalent effect which underlies a far more complex control by the Court; see Ch. 3.

of trade and the protection of domestic industry. Such action by the Member States is clearly in opposition to the main objectives of the establishment of the common market.[27]

The Non-discrimination Principle

Secondly, the Treaty contains certain rules concerning the application of domestic instruments which are not only aimed at the reduction of trade between Member States but which apply to both imported and domestic goods. In dealing with these national measures, most traditional international trade agreements require their parties to abstain from any discrimination between domestic goods and imported goods (national treatment). This applies mainly to the administrative treatment of goods, or the imposition of specific taxes and levies upon goods.[28] In most cases the discrimination will lead to the protection of domestic production, and the prohibition of the discriminatory application of domestic rules is thus a special means to avoid protectionism. The 'obviously' protectionist effect is not always an essential element of the prohibition of the discriminatory application of domestic rules.[29] Normally the hindrance of trade by applying different rules or standards to domestic and imported goods is presumed to be protectionist.[30] Most treaties and federal constitutions, however, provide for escape clauses enumerating justified objectives for the differential treatment of domestic and imported goods, such as health protection, national security etc.[31]

The general non-discrimination principle is also a basic element of the Community's principles concerning domestic action by the Member States. The equal application of domestic rules and charges to imported and domestic goods must guarantee that the abolition of customs duties and quantitative trade restriction is not jeopardized by the unfavourable application of administrative rules and charges. The non-discrimination principle prevents the circumvention

[27] e.g. Arts. 2 and 3 EC.

[28] See e.g. GATT, Art. III (National Treatment); EFTA, Art. 6 (Non-Discriminatory Taxation) or, NAFTA, Art. 300, section A (National Treatment) referring explicitly to Art. III GATT.

[29] See e.g. the definition of the scope of s. 92 of the Australian Constitution as 'the prohibition of measures which burden interstate trade and commerce and which also have the effect of conferring protection on interstate trade and commerce of the same kind', Decision by the High Court of Australia, in *Cole* v. *Whitfield* (1988) 165 *Commonwealth Law Reports* 360 at 394; see Staker, n. 15 above, 224 and 225.

[30] Such a protectionist effect is, however, presumed whenever domestic and imported goods are treated in a different manner (without a justification for differentiation apart from their origin) and thereby the import of non-domestic products is hindered; see e.g. the case law by the Court of Justice of the European Community (see Ch. 3) or the case law of the US Supreme Court e.g. in *Philadelphia* v. *New Jersey*, 437 US at 618, 626; see Geradin, n. 15 above, 157, or the Australian High Court in *Cole* v. *Whitfield*, n. 29 above, 394; see Staker, n. 15 above, 224 and 225.

[31] See Art. 36 EC, also Art. XX GATT and Art. 20–EC Switzerland Free-Trade Agreement etc.; see, for the conditions governing the applicability of such escape clauses and their relationship to the protection of the environment, Ch. 4.

of the free trade rules.[32] In principle discrimination can take place in two different ways. One is the open application of different rules and charges for imported goods in comparison to like domestic goods. The second possibility is that similar products are treated in different ways without any objective justification for the differential treatment.[33]

Article 95 EC, for example, prohibits any discrimination in the field of taxes and the Court generally applies a broad discrimination requirement which may incidentally include measures which are *prima facie* applied equally to imported and domestic goods.[34] This principle is also applied in the field of charges having equivalent effects to customs duties under Articles 9 and 12.[35]

Similarly, under Article 34 EC, domestic laws which affect exports are forbidden if they have as their objective the establishment of a difference in treatment between imported goods and domestic goods.[36] Article 30 EC contains a prohibition on measures having equivalent effect to import restrictions; this clearly includes a prohibition on discriminatory measures, but the Court's case law has extended this prohibition to encompass non-discriminatory measures, provided they fulfil certain other conditions.[37]

The Inter-state Trade Approach

If the objective of a commercial agreement is only the abolition of protectionist measures between its parties, then the prohibition of customs duties and quantitative restrictions on trade, in conjunction with a non-discrimination principle for all other State measures, is a sufficient means for the pursuit of this objective.[38] If a divided power system seeks, however, to foster trade between Member States in general and tries to create a single market where goods (as well as other production factors) can move without any hindrance, this may imply the abolition of certain regulatory differences between the Member States even in the absence of discrimination.[39]

[32] See the similar provisions under Arts. 40(3), 48(2), 65 etc. EC.

[33] Often referred to as disguised discrimination, see e.g. C. W. A. Timmermanns, 'Verboden Discriminatie of (Geboden) Differentiatie' [1982] *SEW* 426 at 430.

[34] See e.g. Case 148/77 *H. Hansen Jun. et al.* v. *Hauptzollamt Flensburg* [1978] *ECR* 1787 at 1806; see also Kapteyn and VerLoren van Themaat, n. 3 above, 357; for details see Ch. 3.6.

[35] e.g. Case 77/72 *Carmine Capolongo* v. *Azienda Agricola Maya* [1973] *ECR* 611, which distinctively showed the difference between this and the mere 'equal application' concept; see also Kapteyn and VerLoren van Themaat, n. 3 above, 357.

[36] e.g. Case 15/79 *P. B. Groenveld BV* v. *Produktschap voor Vee en Vlees* (*Horse Meat*) [1979] *ECR* 3409 at 3415; see for details Ch. 3.

[37] See below the section on 'Discrimination despite Equal Application', and Ch. 3.

[38] See e.g. the GATT system (Arts. I, III, XI etc.) which however, allows the maintenance of certain tariffs.

[39] See e.g. D. Kommers and M. Waelbroeck, 'Legal Integration and the Free Movement of Goods' in Cappelletti, Seccombe, and Weiler (eds.), n. 23 above 165 ff. or T. Sandalow and E. Stein, 'On the Two Systems' in T. Sandalow and E. Stein (eds.), *Courts and Free Markets* (Oxford University Press, Oxford, 1982), 1 to 46; Geradin, n. 15 above, 152, or for Australia's s. 92 of the Constitution: Staker, n. 15 above, 228.

The approximation of laws[40] and the mutual recognition of equivalent standards[41] are means to facilitate trade in those areas where regulatory differences among the Member States of the Community hinder trade.[42] In these areas, the trade-hindering effect of existing differences necessitates, under the rubric of desirable integration, a harmonization of trade and competition-related rules. The Court follows this approach in the field of the free movement of goods, especially in relation to domestic rules which hinder imports.[43]

Certain domestic measures, applied to domestic commerce and international trade equally, may be prohibited by the Treaty just because of their hindering effect on trade between Member States. Examples are the scope of Article 85 (prohibition of trade-distorting agreements between undertakings) and, particularly important for environmental measures, Article 30 EC (measures having equivalent effect to import restrictions). The far-reaching scope of both measures is mainly due to the influence of the Court.[44] In this last category the Court, in its case law,[45] has established rules previously known only in the relationship between federal states and their sub-national entities.[46] The pure application of the non-discrimination principle would accept the existing regulatory differences between the members of a free trade area. If the Court, however, does not accept certain non-discriminatory domestic measures because of their trade effects, this leads to the negative harmonization of regulatory systems within the Community.[47]

Domestic Regulation and Community Principles

The economic system applied by the Community in relation to action by its Member States thus combines classical elements of international trade agree-

---

[40] See, in particular, Arts. 100 to 102 EC; to a certain extent also the common policies e.g. under Arts. 43, 75, 113 etc.; see also Kapteyn and VerLoren van Themaat, n. 3 above, 76, who speak of the 'indivisible unity of common market and common policies'.

[41] See Case 120/78 *Rewe Zentralverwaltung AG* v. *Bundesmonopolverwaltung für Branntwein* (*Cassis de Dijon*) [1979] *ECR* 649 and the introduction of Art. 100b under the Single European Act.

[42] See the 'extensive use' of the commerce clause by the US federal government to legislate in the field of the environment; see e.g. Geradin, n. 15 above, 144, with many references.

[43] In its famous case law concerning 'measures having equivalent effect', mainly elaborated in the decisions following its judgment in Case 8/74 *Procureur du Roi* v. *B. and G. Dassonville* (*Dassonville*) [1974] *ECR* 837.

[44] For Art. 30: Case 8/74 *Dassonville*, n. 43 above and Case 120/78 *Cassis de Dijon*, n. 41 above; for Art. 85 see e.g. Case 5/69 *Völk* v. *Etablissement J. Vervaecke* [1969] *ECR* 295 at 302. See for the similarities Kapteyn and VerLoren van Themaat, n. 3 above, 379.

[45] See e.g. Behrens, n. 8 above, 149.

[46] See e.g. for the development in Switzerland J.-P. Müller, *Die Grundrechte der schweizerischen Bundesverfassung* (Schulthess, Zürich, 1991), 355, or K. Vallender, *Wirtschaftsfreiheit und begrente Staatsverantwortung* (2nd edn., Stämpfli, Bern 1991), 49; for Australia: Staker, n. 15 above, 209 to 242; in the United States this approach is sometimes disputed: certain authors adhere to the non-discrimination principle, for comments see Kommers and Waelbroeck, n. 39 above, 165 ff. or Sandalow and Stein, n. 39 above, 24 ff.

[47] See e.g. Behrens, n. 8 above, 150, and Barents, n. 4 above, 314.

ments[48] with integrative instruments of federal states or, more generally, divided power systems aiming at the elimination of technical barriers to trade. The classical instruments are the prohibition of purely trade-oriented (protectionist) instruments, such as customs duties and quantitative restrictions, combined with a general non-discrimination principle for administrative measures and taxes. So far, it is only in the area of domestic measures having equivalent effect to import restrictions (Article 30) that the Court has applied a more developed interstate trade approach which leads to negative harmonization of regulatory systems.[49]

In the general context of the rules governing the common market and, taking into account the existing shared responsibility for the environment, it is important to know which concepts concerning actions by Member States underlie which provisions in the Treaty and their interpretation by the Court. As long as there are several actors taking Community-wide and local action for the optimal protection of the environment, we have to observe the implications of the possible concepts of market or economic freedoms for action at domestic level.

THE NON-DISCRIMINATION PRINCIPLE: TWO FACES

Article 6 and Specific Non-discrimination Provisions

Article 6 EC[50] explicitly contains the general non-discrimination principle governing the Community legal order. It is accompanied by various specific anti-discrimination provisions throughout the Treaty.[51] While Article 6 prohibits any discrimination on grounds of nationality,[52] other provisions concern the discrimination between imported and domestic goods. In the field of the free movement of goods Articles 30 and 34, in conjunction with Article 36, prohibit 'arbitrary discrimination' among domestic and imported goods while Article 95

---

[48] See, however, the recent developments in world trade law under the WTO and its new Agreements on Technical Barriers to Trade (TBT) and on Sanitary and Phytosanitary Measures (SPS), e.g. reprinted in GATT Secretariat (ed.), *The Results of the Uruguay Round of Multilateral Trade Negotiations–The Legal Texts* (Geneva, 1994), 138. In my view, these agreements introduce a new generation of integration measures into the world trading system by restricting domestic measures to proportionate and necessary measures despite their equal application to domestic and traded goods. See for comments e.g. J. Cameron and H. Ward, *The Uruguay Round's Technical Barriers to Trade Agreement* (WWF, Gland, 1993).

[49] See on the political and institutional consequences J. H. H. Weiler, 'Journey to an Unknown Destination: A Retrospective and Prospective of the European Court of Justice in the Arena of Political Integration' [1993] *JCMS* 417 at 426 and 429.

[50] Art. 7 before the coming into force of the Treaty on European Union and the resulting modification of the Treaty of Rome.

[51] See Kapteyn and VerLoren van Themaat, n. 3 above, 92; examples are Arts. 36, 95, 40(3), 48 etc. EC.

[52] See e.g. for a case of the direct application of Art. 6 (before Art. 7 of the Treaty); Joined cases C–92/92 *Phil Collins* v. *Imtrat Handelsgesellschaft mbH* and C–326/92 *Patricia Im- und Export Verwaltungsgesellschaft mbH et al.* v. *EMI Electrola*, [1993] 3 *CMLR* 773.

prohibits any tax discrimination between products of other Member States and similar domestic goods.

As has been mentioned before, there are, in principle, two concepts of discrimination between imported goods and domestic goods.[53] A first approach is the requirement that charges, administrative measures, and any domestic action are equally applied to all like goods and do not 'openly' discriminate against imported goods. Even under this stringent principle, the term 'like products or goods' includes, not only equal goods, but also similar goods.[54] Otherwise, the meaning of this principle would be completely undermined. A second, more elaborate, concept is to ask what consequences certain measures have and whether, despite their equal application to imported goods and domestic goods they may have the final objective, or effect, of discriminating against imported goods. While the first approach looks mainly at the surface of the domestic rules, the second concept looks at their effect and therefore involves a much more complex and delicate test.

Prima Facie Equal Application

Certain domestic measures discriminate openly or 'facially' against imported goods. This is what we call open or *prima facie* discrimination. Against such measures the application of a test which in a very static way looks at existing differences in treatment of imported goods and domestically produced and/or consumed goods is efficient. Nevertheless, such a non-discrimination test which is based only on the *prima facie* equal application of domestic rules to domestic goods and imported goods is relatively ineffective if the protectionist instruments used are more sophisticated. In the absence of the production of a certain product within a country, certain rules affect imported goods only and are still not openly discriminatory.[55] The same is true if very similar or equivalent products are treated unequally.[56] Most products are not absolutely equal and therefore such an approach opens a wide gap for abusive domestic measures against imported products.

Most trade agreements and national rules therefore apply a discrimination test

---

[53] See for a much more detailed analysis: P. VerLoren van Themaat, *Rechtsgrondlagen van een Nieuwe Internationale Economische Orde, Studies over Internationaal Economisch Recht* (Asser Institute, s'Gravenhage, 1979, ii); W. Kewenig, *Der Grundsatz der Nichtdiskriminierung im Völkerrecht der Internationalen Handelsbeziehungen*, vol. 1: *Der Begriff der Diskriminierung* (Athenäum, Frankfurt a. M., 1972); W. A. McKean, 'The Meaning of Discrimination in International and Municipal Law' [1970] *BYIL* 177 ff.

[54] For details of the definition of similar products in the EC see e.g. Case 21/79 *Commission v. Italy* [1980] *ECR* 1; Case 170/78 *Commission v. United Kingdom* [1980] *ECR* 417; see also R. Barents, 'The Prohibition of Fiscal Discrimination in Art. 95 of the EEC Treaty' (1981) 18 *CMLRev.* 521 ff.; see also the abundant case law within the framework of GATT: e.g. T. Schoenbaum, Free International Trade and Protection of the Environment [1992] *AJIL* 700 at 722 or E.-U. Petersmann, 'International Trade Law and International Environmental Law' [1993] *JWT* 43 at 63.

[55] e.g. Case 249/84 *Ministère Public et Ministère des Finances v. PROFANT* [1985] *ECR* 3237.

[56] Case 21/79, n. 54 above, 1; Case 170/78, n. 54 above, 417.

which also looks at the effects of a measure. The Community has through the interpretation of the Court developed a system which always considers the effect of domestic measures and thus applies more stringent controls than under the *prima facie* test.[57] The mere *prima facie* test is applied only to clear cases such as the prohibition on import and export duties or quantitative restrictions on trade, as they fall exclusively on imports and exports.[58]

Discrimination despite Equal Application

Despite their equal application to like products, certain domestic measures can have a disparate effect and thereby indirectly discriminate against imported goods.[59] In cases where the measure or financial burden applies mainly to imported goods, while similar or equivalent domestic products are treated differently, there is a danger of hidden or disguised discrimination.[60] Three elements seem to be necessary to render a measure discriminatory in the view of the Court:[61] (a) it must have a negative effect on the goods concerned, (b) the situations or objects must be comparable, and (c) the differentiation must be unjustified or arbitrary.

The main question which rises under these considerations is whether the administrative or fiscal differentiation is justified or amounts to discrimination against similar or equivalent products.[62] This question, however, is often very difficult to deal with.[63] For the Community 'the criteria for judging the objective justification of different treatment, just like the concept of discrimination itself, have to be assessed in the light of the objectives of the particular provisions of Community or national law'.[64] As in national systems, however, the question when a differentiation amounts to unjustified discrimination is mainly developed through case law[65] and difficult to reduce into an easy formula.[66]

---

[57] See Kapteyn and VerLoren van Themaat, n. 3 above, 382 ff.

[58] See, however, the extension to charges having equivalent effect which applies a more sophisticated non-discrimination test; see e.g. Case 77/72, n. 35 above, 611.

[59] See, for an overview on direct and indirect discrimination in the field of the free movement of workers, Johnson and O'Keeffe, n. 8 above, 1327.

[60] Such measures are sometimes referred to as 'disguised discrimination' e.g. by Timmermanns, n. 33 above, 426, or also as 'facially neutral' measures, e.g. by Geradin, n. 15 above, 155, while the French doctrine speaks of 'discrimination indirecte', i.e. P. Garrone, 'La discrimination indirecte en droit communautaire: vers une théorie générale' [1994] *RTDE* 425 at 426.

[61] See for details Timmermanns, n. 33 above, 431.

[62] See Case 25/67 *Firma Milch, Fett- und Eierkontor GmbH* v. *Hauptzollamt Saarbrücken* [1968] *ECR* 305; and Garrone, n. 60 above, 427, who proposes a framework for the distinction between indirect distinction and indirect discrimination.

[63] See e.g. Timmermanns, n. 33 above.

[64] Kapteyn and VerLoren van Themaat, n. 2 above, 95.

[65] See for an interesting overview Timmermanns, n. 33 above, 426 to 460.

[66] See, however the Court's attempt in its reasoning in Case 106/83 *Sermide SpA* v. *Cassa Conguaglio Zucchero et al.* [1984] *ECR* 4209 at 4231 where it held, with reference to the special non-discrimination principle incorporated under Art. 40(3) EC: 'comparable situations must not be treated differently and different situations must not be treated in the same way unless such treatment is objectively

Distortion through Different Regulatory Systems

The Community is much more than a mere trade agreement, but it still does not provide a coherent non-discrimination principle which eliminates differences between the regulatory systems of the Member States. The Treaty applies only if the unequal treatment can be imputed to one legal subject, e.g if one Member State treats similar products in an unequal way without being able to justify this differentiation.[67] This means also that the application of national legislation cannot be held contrary to the principle of non-discrimination merely because other Member States allegedly apply less strict rules.[68] Differences in treatment which result from the limited territorial scope of domestic regulations do not constitute a discrimination on grounds of nationality.[69] The Treaty contains, however, special provisions for the approximation of laws of the Member States to eliminate such inequality of treatment.[70]

No Favourable Treatment for Domestic Goods

One might even ask whether the non-discrimination principle as it is laid down in the Treaty is in fact only a principle which requires merely that foreign products be treated no worse than national goods. The principle is intended to protect imported goods against any differential treatment which is detrimental to trade. The concept behind this principle is thereby to eliminate protectionist measures which would hinder trade by favouring domestic products. It is, however, questionable whether such a concept requires absolute equal treatment of foreign and imported goods. If not, such a principle cannot be invoked by nationals who feel they suffer more stringent measures or less favourable treatment than non-nationals.[71] Even if the Community's legal order does not pro-

---

justified'. This formula is reminiscent of the formulas used by other courts previously, e.g. Swiss Federal Court, in BGE 110 Ia 7 at 13: 'Like issues must be treated alike according to their likeness and different issues must be treated differently according to their different character', see e.g. U. Häfelin and G. Müller, *Grundriss des Allgemeinen Verwaltungsrechts* (Schulthess, Zürich, 1990), 86 ff.; or the German Federal Constitutional Court's . . . 'the principle of equal treatment prohibits only that substantially like issues be treated differently, but not that substantially different issues be treated differently according to their different character' (BVerfGE 1, 52).

[67] See Kapteyn and VerLoren van Themaat, n. 3 above, 95.

[68] See e.g. the recent decision in Case C–379/92 *Criminal Proceedings against Matteo Peralta* [1994] *ECR* I–3453.

[69] J. Jan, 'Transfrontier Environmental Policy' [1988] *LIEI* 21 at 27 with reference to the Answer of the Commission to Written Question 664/86 [1987] *OJ* C91/6.

[70] See for details A. Epiney and T. M. J. Möllers, *Freier Warenverkehr und nationaler Umweltschutz* (Heymann, Köln, 1992), 32 to 48; on the Treaty's system for the elimination of such distortion see e.g. Case 173/83 *Commission* v. *Italy (Family Allowances)* [1974] *ECR* 709.

[71] See for details on discrimination against nationals Epiney and Möllers, n. 70 above, 32 ff.; for the limited protective effect of Art. 7 on nationals against measures by their own Member State see, however, Case 14/68 *Wilhelm Rau et al.* v. *Bundeskartellamt* [1969] *ECR* 1 or Case 115/78 *J. Knoors* v. *Secretary of State for Economic Affairs* [1979] *ECR* 399.

vide for an absolute guarantee for the citizens of a Member State to be treated by its own authorities in the same way as citizens of other Member States, this does not preclude the application of existing national fundamental rights which guarantee such treatment.[72]

The same applies to goods. Here again, the principle underlying ordinary international trade agreements dictates that it is not necessary to grant domestic products equally favourable treatment to imported goods. The main objective of the non-discrimination principle in trade agreements is the elimination of protectionist abuse of national measures. This also seems to be the concept underlying the non-discrimination principle as applied by the Court to the free movement of goods.[73] Thus the Court[74] considers it sufficient that the imported goods are not treated less favourably, while a 'discrimination of purely domestic goods' seems acceptable.[75] In these areas the non-discrimination principle in its trade-related form is not yet equivalent to an individual right, as in national or federal states.[76]

THE CONCEPT OF THE FREE MOVEMENT OF GOODS

Two Basic Concepts

Since the end of the transitional period on 31 December 1969 the free movement of goods—as well as the other basic freedoms of the Treaty—is guaranteed by the Treaty as directly binding upon all Member States. It is directly effective and can be relied upon by private parties in their national courts.[77] There are, however, different basic conceptions of the character of the principle of free movement of goods. While some see it as a general individual freedom from trade-hindering State action, which can be enforced against the authorities like any other human right,[78] others consider it rather to be a mere non-dis-

---

[72] See Case C–132/93 *Volker Steen* v. *Deutsche Bundespost* [1994] *ECR* I–2715 concerning the access to the civil service.

[73] See e.g. E.-U. Petersmann, 'Freier Warenverkehr und nationaler Umweltschutz in EWG und EWR' [1993] *Aussenwirtschaft* 95 at 117 and 118.

[74] See e.g. Joined cases 80 and 159/85 *Nederlandse Bakkerij et al.* v. *Edah BV* [1986] *ECR* 3359; Case 355/85 *Driancourt* v. *Michel Cognet* [1986] *ECR* 3231; Case 407/85 *Drei Glocken et al.* v. *USL Centro Sud* [1988] *ECR* 4233.

[75] See Case 155/80 *Administrative Proceedings against Sergius Oebel* [1981] *ECR* 1993.

[76] See e.g. also Behrens, n. 8 above, 161. See for criticism of the Court's case law A. Bleckmann, 'Die umgekehrte Diskriminierung' [1985] *RIW* 917 at 918 or P. Nicolaysen, 'Inländerdiskriminierung im Warenverkehr' [1995] *EuR* 95 at 103; R. Streinz, 'Das Problem der umgekehrten Diskriminierung im Bereich des Lebensmittelrechts' [1990] *Zeitschrift für das gesamte Lebensmittelrecht* 487 to 515; for similar cases concerning the free movement of persons see e.g. Case 35/82 *Morson* v. *The Netherlands* [1982] *ECR* 3723.

[77] Kapteyn and VerLoren van Themaat, n. 3 above, 355.

[78] See e.g. H. Hauser and K. Vallender, *Zur Bindung des Wirtschaftsgesetzgebers durch Grundrechte* (Stämpfli, Bern, 1989), 12 ff. or E.-U. Petersmann, *Constitutional Functions and Constitutional Problems of International Economic Law* (Fribourg University Press, Fribourg, 1991), 452 ff.; see also Case 124/81

crimination principle applicable to State measures with a protectionist effect or objective.[79]

The Comprehensive Non-discrimination Approach

The less-restrictive view of the principle of the free movement of goods interprets this freedom as a prohibition on national measures affecting exclusively imports or exports from or to another Member State.[80] Measures reflecting this view discriminate against imported goods. Purely domestic regulations which concern trade in domestic and imported goods equally and not disparately, are not covered in this view. The individual is guaranteed only the absence of national measures affecting trade in goods only which cross or are intended to cross the national borders.[81] In terms of this view the freedom of movement of goods can be understood as a guarantee of the absence of national measures which discriminate against goods by reason of their country of origin or destination.[82]

It will be argued below that this test is the one underlying the Court's interpretation of Article 34 concerning national restrictions on exports and measures having equivalent effect.[83] The Court has never extended the interpretation of Article 34 to a prohibition on domestic measures hindering inter-state trade in general. The same is true for the Court's interpretation of the prohibition on fiscal discrimination. Articles 95 to 97 concerning domestic taxes forbid only fiscal discrimination, although heavy taxation can limit the trade in certain goods.[84] However, the Court applies more than a mere *prima facie* non-discrimination test.[85]

Certain authors suggest that the prohibition of discriminatory taxation under Article 95 has been extended in the case law to include even 'non-discriminatory' cases. This is the situation where national taxation hinders imports or disadvantages them.[86] With reference to the Court's case law,[87] Everling calls this an infringement of the competitive neutrality of taxation by distorting competition.[88]

Commission v. *United Kingdom* [1983] *ECR* 203 or Case 57/65 *Firma Alfons Lütticke GmbH* v. *Hauptzollamt Saarlouis* (*Lütticke*) [1966] *ECR* 293.

[79] See e.g. N. Marenco, 'Pour une interprétation traditionelle de la notion de mesure équivalent à une restriction quantitative' [1984] *CDE* 291 to 364 at 312; F. Burrows, *Free Movement in European Community Law* (Oxford University Press, Oxford, 1987), 54; or M. Waelbroeck, 'Le rôle de la Cour de Justice dans la mise en œuvre de l'Acte Unique Européen' [1989] *CDE* 41 at 49.

[80] See Ch. 2 above, section on different categories of economic freedoms.

[81] Kapteyn and VerLoren van Themaat, n. 3 above, 357.

[82] See Kapteyn and VerLoren van Themaat, n. 3 above, 356.   [83] See Ch. 3.

[84] See Kapteyn and VerLoren van Themaat, n. 3 above, 357.

[85] Case 57/65 *Lütticke*, n. 78 above, 293.

[86] R. Barents, 'Artikel 95 en de gemeenschappelijke Markt' [1983] *SEW* 438 at 461 and 477.

[87] Case 15/81 *Gaston Schul* v. Inspecteur der Invoerrechten en Accijnzen droits d'importation [1982] ECR 1409.

[88] U. Everling, 'Zur neueren EuGH-Rechtsprechung zum Wettbewerbsrecht' [1982] *EuR* 301 at 307, as referred to by Kapteyn and VerLoren van Themaat, n. 3 above, 369.

The Market-unity Approach

A more restrictive view of the principle of free movement of goods would require Member States to be generally deprived of the right to adopt any measure which 'even incidentally touches on inter-state trade and hinders or tampers with inter-state trade'.[89] In terms of this view the law-making power of Member States is greatly restricted and the free movement of goods can be considered to be a substantial individual freedom protecting the individual against any interference by the State with trade.[90] This restrictive interpretation prohibits national measures whether they affect inter-state trade alone or both domestic and inter-state trade. This view includes, in principle, the prohibition of commercial restrictions on already imported goods and even domestic goods. Restrictions on trade imposed by national regulations are only lawful on grounds of certain public interests, defined by the superior level of the divided power system.[91]

The more restrictive view is often typical in domestic law, particularly where federal authorities or regions retain law making power to restrict the free movement of goods.[92] In the application of this principle 'other "federalist" values such as promoting a unified market and a more integrated economy' are involved which are not covered by an 'anti-protectionist' or 'non-discrimination approach'.[93] It will be argued that this more restrictive view is the one underlying the Court's interpretation of Article 30 on restrictions on imports and measures having equivalent effect,[94] while it has not been extended to similar measures concerning imports. On the other hand, the Commission and many legal writers had originally interpreted Article 30 as a mere non-discrimination principle, relying on the Treaty provisions for the approximation of laws to achieve the unity of the Single Market. The Court's case law, however, complemented the positive harmonization of laws with its own negative harmonization.[95]

Nevertheless, even under this broad approach there has so far been no comprehensive elimination of regulatory differences between Member States. First,

[89] See Kapteyn and VerLoren van Themaat, n. 3 above, 356.

[90] This is the concept generally referred to in US constitutional law as the Commerce Clause, see e.g. L. H. Tribe, *American Constitutional Law* (2nd edn., Foundation Press, Mineola NY, 1988), 305 ff. or Sandalow and Stein, n. 39 above.

[91] Kapteyn and VerLoren van Themaat, n. 3 above, 356.

[92] See e.g. the most recent proposals by the Swiss Government to introduce domestic regulations to ensure non-discrimination between market participants within Switzerland. The law-making power of the cantons has so far led to the discriminatory application of sub-national laws, mainly in the field of free movement of persons and services; see the new proposal for an Internal Market Law (*Binnenmarktgesetz*); for comments and the proposal see e.g. R.J. Schweizer, 'Betrachtungen zum Vorentwurf eines Bundesgesetzes über den Binnenmarkt' [1994] *AJP* 739 to 748.

[93] Sandalow and Stein, n. 39 above, 26.

[94] See Ch. 3.

[95] See e.g. Behrens, n. 8 above, 150.

the Court requires that trade be (potentially) affected by the domestic measures.[96] Purely domestic measures which have no effect on trade between Member States are not covered by Article 30.[97] Another consequence is that individuals cannot rely on the guarantee of Article 30 against their own Member State by claiming the less favourable treatment of domestic goods in comparison to non-domestic goods, as Article 30 applies only to import-hindering measures.[98] Secondly, domestic measures can be justified despite their trade-hindering effect if they are adopted for the safeguard of certain public interests. Under Article 36 and for the compliance with mandatory requirements of the Treaty, as developed by the Court, domestic measures remain applicable if they are proportionate.[99] In these cases it is, however, the Court who decides on the acceptability of domestic measures and thereby limits recourse to situations falling within these exceptions.[100]

The Double-headed Concept of the Court

From the general considerations above it seems that the free movement of goods, as it is understood in the Treaty and interpreted by the Court, combines two elements: in general it provides a guarantee against protectionist measures by Member States which hinder trade within the common market through any form of custom duties, quantitative trade restrictions, and open or disguised discrimination (protectionism). In the area of domestic measures equivalent to quantitative import restrictions (Article 30), however, the Court interprets the concept underlying the Treaty as prohibiting any national measures which hinder trade between Member States and are not justified for specific public interests, as recognized by the Court[101] (elimination of technical barriers to trade).

Both sets of provisions, Article 30 to 36 concerning quantitative trade restrictions and Articles 95 to 97, correspond in their original wording or draft to the equivalent provisions of the General Agreement on Tariffs and Trade (GATT). They concern administrative and fiscal treatment, as well as the application of all domestic rules, to imported and domestic goods. While the Community's case law on Articles 34 and 95 is relatively similar to the existing Treaty practice and

---

[96] See e.g. Case 75/81 *Blesgen* v. *Belgium* [1982] *ECR* 1211 at 1229 or Case 148/85 *Direction générale des impôts et Procureur de la République* v. *Marie-Louise Forest, née Sangoy, et SA Minoterie Forest* [1986] *ECR* 3449 at 3475; for details see O. Dörr, 'Die Warenverkehrsfreiheit nach Art. 30 EWG-Vertrag—doch bloss ein Diskriminierungsverbot?' [1990] *RabelsZ* 677 at 681.

[97] For details on the development of the Court's notion of trade-hindering effects and the most recent case law see Ch. 3.

[98] This applies, however, only in relation to national measures while Art. 30 EC implies for the Community itself a true non-discrimination duty; see Barents, n.4 above, 325.

[99] See Chs. 3, 4, and 5.

[100] See, for details on Art. 36, the rule of reason and, in particular, the relevant environmental justifications, Ch. 4.

[101] See, however, for the recent development of the conception of trade-hindering measures, Ch. 3.

the existing panel reports under GATT,[102] there are important differences as far as measures having equivalent effect to import restrictions under Article 30 are concerned. Here the Court has gone much further in providing the Community with a guaranteed freedom from any interference by Member States which hinders or tampers with trade.[103] A concept similar to this has so far only been known in federal states.[104]

Environmental Measures and Free Movement of Goods

The distinction between these theoretical concepts about the free movement of goods has important implications for the potential of Member States to take national measures, especially on grounds of public interests such as the protection of the environment. An approach which aims at the negative harmonization of regulatory differences between Member States requires the Member States to justify their objectives and the chosen measures on grounds recognized by the Community as a whole.[105]

If a Member State wants to protect its environment it may want to take measures concerning the production of certain goods. In these cases imported goods are usually not involved and trade is only hindered in so far as domestic producers have also to apply more stringent environmental standards for the products they intend to export. Here the Court's jurisdiction on Article 34 does not pose major problems if a Member State regulates domestic environmental issues. Article 34 covers only protectionist attempts or measures which aim specifically at exports.[106]

On the other hand, the strict application of the Court's case law on the principle underlying Article 30 on domestic measures affecting imports results in important restraints upon domestic authorities. If they want to apply domestic environmental measures regulating the sale, marketing, use, and general product standards for certain goods, they are bound by a significant limitation of their regulatory power by virtue of the Court's case law with regard to Article 30.[107] As the Community recognizes the protection of the environment to be an

---

[102] See e.g. Petersmann, n. 73 above, 112.

[103] See, however, the recent developments in the WTO's Agreements on Technical Barriers to Trade (TBT) and Sanitary and Phytosanitary Measures (SPS), as reprinted in GATT Secretariat (ed.), *The Results of the Uruguay Round of Multilateral Trade Negotiations—The Legal Texts* (GATT, Geneva, 1994), 138: for comments see e.g. Cameron and Ward, n. 48 above.

[104] See e.g. the commerce clause of the United States; see in general on the topic Sandalow and Stein, n. 39 above, 25.

[105] See for the recognized grounds Ch. 4 and for the conditions for lawful measures Ch. 5.

[106] See for details Ch. 3.

[107] See e.g. the environmentalists' fears that the Court's case law following the decisions in Cases 8/74 *Dassonville*, n. 43 above, 873 and Case 120/78 *Cassis de Dijon*, n. 41 above, might lead to harmonization at the lowest common denominator, see e.g. M. Seidel, 'Umweltrecht der Europäischen Gemeinschaft' [1989] *DVBl.* 441 at 443; E. Steindorff, 'Umweltschutz in Gemeinschaftshand?' [1984] *RIW* 767 at 771 and 772.

important element of all its policies, it has also to guarantee this protection under its concept of free movement of goods. I will demonstrate in Chapter 3 how the Community, mainly through the case law of the Court and later through the introduction of new provisions under the Single European Act, has tried to find an equilibrium between the harmonizing and trade-fostering effect of its concept of the free movement of goods on one side and the protection of the environment at a high level on the other.

THE COMPETITION CONCEPT OF THE COMMUNITY

While the prohibition on trade-distorting measures and the establishment of a non-discrimination principle by the Member States or parties to a trade agreement are relatively common, the direct effect of competition rules and trade rules on undertakings is a very distinct element of the Community legal order.[108] Nevertheless, as far as state aids and distorting subsidies are concerned, they are often regulated within international trade agreements, as they concern directly the distorting behaviour of governments bound by the Treaty.[109]

Regulations on the behaviour of private parties or soft agreements between governments and private parties are less common areas of international regulation. The rules concerning agreements between undertakings and their competition-distorting behaviour correspond to national competition rules and have never before been addressed by international agreements.[110] The Community's principles governing such behaviour and, in particular, agreements between undertakings were very much influenced by the German model after World War II.[111]

The Court has always emphasized the importance of Article 85 concerning the trade- and competition-distorting behaviour of private undertakings in the framework of the common market. With reference to the preamble to the Treaty the Court considers 'the elimination of barriers' and the establishment of 'fair

---

[108] See for details and the implications on the environment Ch. 6.

[109] See e.g. the new Agreement on Subsidies and Countervailing Measures (generally referred to as *Subsidy Code*) as included in GATT Secretariat (ed.), n. 103 above, or for EFTA, Art. 13 (State Aids) of the Free Trade Agreement between Switzerland and the EC, Art. 23 (Competition Rules).

[110] See, however, the new developments and suggestions in GATT, described in e.g. E.-U. Petersmann, 'International Competition Rules for the GATT–MTO World Trade and Legal System' [1993] *JWT* 35 to 86; D. P. Fidler, 'Competition Law and International Relations' [1992] *ICLQ* 563 ff.; or E. Vermulst, 'A European Practitioner's View of the GATT–System: Should Competition Law Violations Distorting International Trade Be Subject to GATT Panels?' [1993] *JWT* 55 to 75; see also the relevant sections in the US–Canada Free Trade Agreement and NAFTA.

[111] The so-called 'Freiburger Schule', sometimes referred to as ordoliberalism, including the economists Walter Eucken, Franz Böhm, and Wilhelm Röpke, had an important influence on the development of German competition law (*Gesetz gegen Wettbewerbsbeschränkungen*, effective as at 1 Jan. 1958) and the German delegation (Ludwig Erhard and Alfred Müller-Armack) to the negotiations of the Treaty of Rome took their ideas to the negotiation table, see for details T. Oppermann, *Europarecht* (C. H. Beck, München, 1991), 345.

competition' as basic elements of the common market.[112] Thus the provisions in Articles 85 and 92 EC are important complements to the free movement of goods as well as the other elements of the Single Market as established in the Treaty. The Court has held that the abolition of trade barriers by the Member States must not be jeopardized through the erection of new obstacles to trade by private undertakings.[113]

As the framework of this study is mainly oriented on the shared competences and responsibilities of the Member States and the Community, the main question here is the role of Member States in the Community's system ensuring competition within the common market. The chief areas of conflict between national (environmental) policy instruments and Community law are the granting of state aids and, to a lesser but increasing degree, actions which favour, facilitate, or allow distorting behaviour by private agreements. The concept underlying Article 85 is also interesting as it evidences many similarities to the concept applied by the Court under Article 30. Both are very far-reaching prohibitions of measures hindering inter-state trade, even in the absence of any discrimination between domestic products or undertakings and those of another Member State.[114]

Article 85 produces similar questions as arise under Articles 30–7 (free movement of goods). Agreements between undertakings 'which may affect trade between Member States and which have as their object or effect the prevention, restriction or distortion of competition within the common market' are prohibited in Article 85. As in the case of Article 30, discrimination against non-domestic goods is not a condition for the application of this Article.[115] Article 85 'affects also agreements on prices and other competition-restricting agreements applying indiscriminately to imports and home products'.[116]

Under the general competition principle of the Treaty, both voluntary agreements and state aids are prohibited whenever they distort competition and may thereby lead to a distortion of trade. The Treaty, however, establishes a large number of exceptions for specific areas, where certain interests may legitimize the use of these 'generally banned' instruments. Chapter 6 will demonstrate, in detail, how far Member States may rely on financial incentives and voluntary agreements or covenants with undertakings to promote their own environmental aims.

---

[112] See Kapteyn and VerLoren van Themaat, n. 3 above, 501.

[113] Joined cases 56 and 58/64 *Consten and Grundig* v. *Commission* [1966] *ECR* 429: 'Finally, an agreement between producer and distributor which might tend to restore the national divisions in trade between Member States might be such as to frustrate the most fundamental objectives of the Community. The Treaty, whose preamble and content aim at abolishing the barriers between States, and which in several provision gives the evidence of a stern attitude with regard to their reappearance, could not allow undertakings to reconstruct such barriers.'

[114] See for details Kapteyn and VerLoren van Themaat, n. 3 above, 377.

[115] See Kapteyn and VerLoren van Themaat, n. 3 above, 356 and 507.

[116] Kapteyn and VerLoren van Themaat, n. 3 above, 377.

3

The Free Movement of Goods

The free movement of goods, one of the four freedoms of the Treaty, covers the trade in goods between the Member States. Apart from a few explicitly exempted goods or products, the general principles of Articles 9 to 37 protect the import, export, and transit of all goods even if they are ecologically dangerous. In principle waste products are considered to be 'goods' in the sense of the Treaty, but their special characteristics may allow additional restrictions under Articles 30 to 36.

The prohibition of customs duties and charges having equivalent effect prohibits any levy which is charged solely because goods cross a border between Member States. Charges levied for border controls or administrative measures may be justified, *inter alia*, for environmental reasons if they are not higher than the charges applied to domestic goods and do take into account existing controls in the country of origin. Charges which are levied on domestic goods and imported goods equally may not be refunded in a way which benefits only or mainly domestic products or producers. The same system applies to fiscal measures which have to be applied equally to domestic and foreign products; they may not have a disparate effect (Article 95).

Apart from the prohibition on customs duties and quantitative restrictions on trade, the principle of the free movement of goods includes, in particular, a prohibition on measures having equivalent effect to restrictions on imports or exports. With respect to import restrictions this concept has traditionally been interpreted by the Court in a very broad way, covering most national product and even certain marketing requirements. For export restrictions the Court usually applies a mere non-discrimination test.

As environmental measures and rules are often taken in the form of product requirements, they usually fall under the prohibition in Article 30 EC if they hinder imports. The Court has, however, developed, in its 'Cassis de Dijon' doctrine (rule of reason), a set of mandatory requirements which, if adhered to, do exempt national measures from the prohibition in Article 30, provided they are applied in a non-discriminatory way. The protection of the environment is one of these requirements. Furthermore, specific exceptions exist under Article 36 to allow certain national measures in spite of their infringement of Article 30 to 34.

THE DEFINITION OF GOODS

General Observations

Environmental measures are often linked to certain types of products, because of their physical characteristics, their effects on the environment, or their production mode. It is therefore particularly important to know what kinds of products enjoy the guarantees of the Treaty, i.e. which goods are covered by the Treaty provisions on free movement of goods.[1] The guarantees of Articles 30–7 EC cover only the trade in 'goods'.[2] In other words, the prohibition on certain measures by Member States applies only to those products or goods which fall within the terms of Articles 9, 12 to 17, and 30 to 37. In the field of the protection of the environment the most controversial discussion has been whether waste and other environmentally harmful or dangerous goods fall within this category.[3]

Certain goods are explicitly exempted from the application of the general rules. Goods which are covered by Article 232 EC fall under the more specific provisions of the Treaty on the European Coal and Steel Community (ECSC) or the Euratom Treaty. With regard to agricultural products, Article 38 provides that the general rules concerning the free movement of goods apply only if no special provisions exist under Articles 39 to 46 EC.[4]

For all other items Article 9(2) EC defines the term 'goods' as referred to in Articles 12 to 17 and 30 to 37 EC, as 'products originating in Member States and . . . products coming from third countries which are in free circulation in Member States.'[5] This definition, however, gives no clear indication of any particular requirements concerning the application of the relevant provisions, as it merely replaces the term 'goods' with the term 'products'.

The Court of Justice has never given a comprehensive definition of the term 'goods' but it seems possible to derive from its case law certain characteristics which trigger the relevant Treaty provisions. In an early decision in 1968 the Court defined goods in the sense of Article 9(2) EC as products which have an economic value and may thus be the object of commercial transaction.[6] The term 'products', however, does not require that they must have undergone a

---

[1] See also the recent survey by A. Middeke, *Nationaler Umweltschutz und Binnenmarkt* (Heymann, Köln, 1994), 116 to 123.

[2] See A. Skordas, *Umweltschutz und freier Warenverkehr in EWG-Vertrag und GATT* (Apelt, Steinbach, 1986), 45, and J. Henke, *EuGH und Umweltschutz* (VVF, München, 1992), 157, referring to K. v. Kempis, 'Überlegungen zu der Vereinbarkeit des Grundsatzes der Abfallbeseitigung im Inland mit dem EWG-Vertrag' [1985] *UPR* 354.

[3] In economics this category is sometimes even referred to as 'bads', implying a negative value, see H. R. Varian, *Intermediate Economics* (3rd. edn., W. W. Norton, New York, 1993), 41.

[4] Joined cases 80 and 81/77 *Société Les Commissionaires Réunis* v. *Receveur des Douanes (Charge on Italian Wine)* [1978] *ECR* 927 at 946.

[5] On the second category see Arts. 10 and 115 EC.

[6] Case 7/68 *Commission* v. *Italy (Taxes on Italian Art Treasures)* [1968] *ECR* 617 at 642.

production process.[7] This follows from the fact that substances or raw materials have to be included in this definition.[8] Furthermore, the definition covers not only goods imported for the purposes of trade, but also goods which are taken from one Member State to another for purely private use.[9] In its most recent case law[10] the Court no longer requires that goods under Article 9 must have a positive value which is paid by the buyer to the seller.[11] The economic value of goods can also be 'negative' in the economic sense.

This definition, however, does not preclude the possibility that trade in certain products which can be valued in money and form the subject of commercial transactions may fall within the category of services[12] or possibly means of payment[13] and thus would be governed by the application of the more specific Treaty provisions.[14] In order to distinguish between the applicability of the free movement of goods principle and the other freedoms, 'goods' in the sense of Article 30 EC have to be 'tangible objects'.[15]

On the other hand many aspects of the freedom to provide services may have important impacts on the free movement of goods as is easily seen in the Court's case law, e.g. in the field of technical assessment tests or certification procedures through authorized undertakings.[16] Furthermore, it is important to observe that Articles 30–7 EC do not apply to situations in which the rules of a Member State govern the general conditions which must be observed when services are being provided. This is particularly important in cases where transport is concerned. Here, the possible restrictions imposed on the transport of goods brought about by such rules may, however, constitute an infringement of the provisions governing the freedom of services.[17]

---

[7] See the reasoning in Case 7/68 *Taxes on Italian Art Treasures*, n. 6 above, 642; see also Skordas, n. 1 above, 45. See, however, the different conception of the word 'to produce' by an English court in: judgment of the English High Court (Queen's Bench Division) of 22 May 1992, *Commissioners of Customs and Excise* v. *Alibaba Tex Ltd.* [1992] 3 *CMLR* 725.

[8] Case 139/84 *Van Dijk's Boekhuis BV* v. *Staatssecretaris van Financiën* [1984] *ECR* 1405; for raw material and mixtures see also Henke, n. 1 above, 157, and Skordas, n. 1 above, 45.

[9] Case 215/87 *Heinz Schuhmacher* v. *Hauptzollamt Frankfurt a.M.-Ost* [1989] *ECR* 617; see also P. Oliver, *Free Movement of Goods in the EEC* (2nd edn., European Law Centre, London, 1988), 21.

[10] See Ch. 3. on waste.

[11] Case C–2/90 *Commission* v. *Belgium (Walloon Waste Case)* [1992] *ECR* I–4431.

[12] Such as television programmes in Case 155/73 Criminal Proceedings against Giuseppe Sacchi *(Sacchi)* [1974] *ECR* 409 at 428, but not videocassettes, such as in Joined cases 60 and 61/84 *Cinéthèque SA* v. *Fédération nationale des cinémas français (Cinéthèque)* [1985] *ECR* 2605 at 2623.

[13] Case 7/78 *Regina* v. *Thompson* [1978] *ECR* 2247 at 2275.

[14] Freedom of services (Arts. 59 to 66) and freedom of payments (Arts. 67 to 73), respectively.

[15] See Joined cases 60 and 61/84 *Cinéthèque*, n. 12 above, 2623; Case 155/73 *Sacchi*, n. 12 above, 428; see also L. Krämer, 'Environmental Protection and Article 30 EEC Treaty' (1993) 30 *CMLRev.* 111 at 116 or U. Becker, *Der Gestaltungsspielraum der EG-Mitgliedstaaten im Spannungsfeld zwischen Umweltschutz und freiem Warenverkehr* (Nomos, Baden-Baden, 1991), 46.

[16] See e.g. Case C–55/93 *Criminal Proceedings against Johannis Gerrit Cornelis van Schaik* [1994] *ECR* I–4837.

[17] See for such considerations Case C–379/92 *Criminal Proceedings against Matteo Peralta* [1994] *ECR* I–3453.

In Case C–379/92 *Criminal Proceedings against Matteo Peralta*[18] the Court had to decide on the lawfulness of certain criminal proceedings brought by the Italian authorities against Matteo Peralta, the master of a tanker especially equipped for the transport of chemicals. It had been established that during 1990 Mr Peralta had repeatedly ordered the discharge into the sea of water which had been used to flush tanks which previously contained caustic soda, an activity penalized by Italian Law 979 of 31 December 1982 for the protection of the Sea. The Court did not address the alleged infringement of Article 30 as it considered that Community law did not preclude Member States from prohibiting vessels from discharging harmful chemical substances into its internal or international waters.

Waste

The reduction of waste and the regulation of its transport and disposal have become very important factors in the formulation of national and Community environmental policy in recent years.[19] If, however, wastes are considered to be goods in terms of Article 9(2) EC[20] they then enjoy all the guarantees under the provisions of the free movement of goods.[21] While the Court has heard several cases on waste in the last two decades[22] without giving a clear statement about the classification of waste as goods, the situation has recently been clarified in a decision concerning regional import restrictions for waste.[23] The Court has recognized, in principle, that wastes are goods in the sense of the Treaty.[24] Thus all types of waste, whether recyclable[25] or 'only' disposable, fall under the

---

[18] Case C–379/92, n. 17 above.

[19] See for details e.g. P. v. Wilmowsky, *Abfallwirtschaft im Binnenmarkt* (Werner Verlag, Düsseldorf, 1990), 87; A. Schmidt, 'Transboundary Movement of Waste under EC Law: The Emerging Regulatory Framework' [1992] *Journal of Environmental Policy* 57 at 71 with further references; see also M. Hoffmann, *Grundfragen der grenzüberschreitenden Verbringung von Abfall nach nationalem Recht und nach EG-Recht* (Duncker & Humblot, Berlin, 1994).

[20] See Krämer, n. 15 above, 117, for the Community's secondary legislation and its definition of waste.

[21] The question concerning the processing of waste can also fall under the provisions governing the freedom of services, see I. Pernice, 'Gestaltung und Vollzug des Umweltrechts im europäischen Binnenmarkt' [1990] *NVwZ* 414 at 416 or U. Everling, 'Die Wiederaufbereitung abgebrannter Brennelemente in anderen Mitgliedstaaten der Europäischen Gemeinschaft' [1993] *RIW* (Suppl. 2).

[22] Most cases concerned the Community's regulations on waste oils: e.g. Case 172/82 *Syndicat national des fabricants raffineurs d'huile de graissage et al.* v. *Groupement d'intérêt économique 'Inter-Huiles' et al.* (*Inter-Huiles*) [1983] *ECR* 555; Case 295/82 *Groupement d'intérêt économique 'Rhône Alpes Huiles' et al.* v. *Syndicat national des fabricants raffineurs d'huile de graissage* (*Rhône Alpes Huiles*) [1984] *ECR* 575; Case 173/83 *Commission* v. *France* (*Waste Oil*) [1985] *ECR* 491; Case 240/83 *Procureur de la République* v. *Association de défense des brûleurs d'huiles usagées* (*ADBHU*) [1985] *ECR* 531. Another case was concerned with the character of poultry offal: Case 118/86 *Openbaar Ministerie* v. *Nertsvoederfabriek Nederland BV* (*Poultry Offal*) [1987] *ECR* 3883 at 3909, where the Court also applied the provisions on the free movement of goods. See for details Becker, n. 15 above, 51.

[23] For the considerations of the Commission on this question before the judgment in C–2/90 *Walloon Waste Case*, n. 11 above,; see e.g. Becker, n. 15 above, 48 ff.

[24] See also Krämer, n. 15 above, 116.

[25] See for considerations on reactor rods Everling, n. 21 above, 4 to 6.

provisions of the Treaty governing the free movement of goods.[26] This clarification by the Court confirms in many respects the Commission's approach[27] which is traditionally to include waste in its definition of goods.[28] At the same time the Court has held that specific principles may apply to waste because of its particular characteristics.[29] The Court takes into account that the trade in certain harmful products and waste, in particular, can lead to problems in regions where an important afflux of such products takes place.

The clarification by the Court is particularly important and welcomed at a time when recycling of waste, as well as the management of technology and knowledge concerning its treatment become more and more important industrial activities. A very dynamic industry for its treatment has emerged in recent years.[30] The Community's fast-growing secondary law in this field shows the importance of the issue at stake.[31]

Packaging

While waste and the movement of waste have always caused controversy in the field of the protection of the environment, the limitation placed on packaging for environmental reasons is a relatively new, but fast-growing, area.[32] As a big part of today's domestic waste is caused by packaging materials from consumer goods, the elimination and reduction of these particular 'goods' have become

[26] Case C–2/90 *Walloon Waste Case*, n. 11 above, 4478 reads 'Waste, which can be recycled or not, should be considered as a product; the free movement of which . . . should not be hindered' (para. 28) and recently repeated in Case C–155/91 *Commission* v. *Council* (*Waste Directive*) [1993] *ECR* I–939; see for the case law of the Court before these decisions e.g. Henke, n. 1 above, 157 to 161; Becker, n. 15 above, 45 to 53; Skordas, n. 1 above, 42 to 55, although their arguments in favour of the classification of 'waste' as lying outside the scope of Article 30 EC are no longer applicable under the Court's recent case law.

[27] See for the various elements of the definition of ordinary waste in the relevant Community legislation, e.g. Art. 1 of Council Dir. 75/442/EEC on waste [1975] *OJ* L194/47; Art. 1 of Council Dir. 78/319/EEC on toxic and dangerous waste [1978] *OJ* L84/43 and the relevant amendments. For comments see Becker, n. 15 above, 49.

[28] See Becker, n. 15 above, 49 to 51, referring to Dir. 75/442/EEC, n. 27 above, while his considerations on the economic value of waste are no longer valid after the Court's decision in C–2/90 *Walloon Waste Case*, n. 11 above, 4431; see also Joined cases 206 and 207/88 *Ministero Pubblico* v. *Vessosso and Zanetti* [1990] *ECR* I–1461 concerning the Commission's interpretation of waste in Community secondary law. See also M. Wheeler, 'The Restrictions on Waste Movements under Community Law' [1993] *Journal of Environmental Law* 133 to 148.

[29] The Court uses the term 'particular nature', referring to the principles of self-sufficiency and autarky as mentioned in the Basel Convention on Transboundary Movement of Hazardous Waste, reprinted e.g. in (1995) 28 *ILM* 657 and the principle of correction at source (Art. 130r(2)) EC.

[30] See (1989) 9 *EC Bulletin* 8 or 'Umweltbranche: Der Müll, die Multis und der Wettbewerb' [1995] *EU Magazin* 6.

[31] See e.g. for an overview A. Schmidt, 'Trade in Waste under Community Law' in J. Cameron, G. Demaret, and D. Geradin (eds.), *Trade and the Environment: The Search for Balance* (Cameron May, London, 1994), 184 to 202.

[32] See for the Community e.g. Dir. 85/339/EEC on Containers of Liquids for Human Consumption [1985] *OJ* L176/18 and more recently Council Dir. 94/62/EC on Packaging and Packaging Waste [1994] *OJ* L365/10; for comments see I. Persaud, 'The Packaging and Packaging Waste Directive' [1995] *Environmental Law Review* 318 to 323.

very important elements of every environmental policy. National governments and the Community itself have adopted measures to replace or prohibit certain substances,[33] to favour recyclable packaging materials,[34] and to reduce the amount of packaging material in general.[35]

From the definition above, it follows that packaging materials must undoubtedly be considered to be goods under Article 9 EC, whether they are traded alone or as packaging of other products, i.e. before and during their use as mere containers for other goods. While some authors suggest that certain Court decisions indicate a differentiation between packaging materials and 'ordinary goods',[36] this differentiation does not imply the exclusion of packaging materials from the provisions of Article 30 EC.[37] Particularly after the Court's decision on waste in the *Walloon Waste Case*, a special treatment for packaging does not seem appropriate. However, this does not preclude any national regulation or limitation concerning packaging materials, as long as it conforms to the Treaty requirements of Articles 30 and 36 or the rule of reason.[38]

THE ABOLITION OF CUSTOMS DUTIES (ARTICLES 9 AND 12)

Definition

Articles 9 and 12 EC provide for 'the prohibition between Member States of customs duties on imports and exports and of all charges having equivalent effect'. The abolition of customs duties between Member States is a basic pillar of the establishment of a common market. The provision has direct effect.[39] While the elimination of 'official' customs duties posed no problem for the Community, charges having equivalent effect have led to several cases before the Court of Justice. They have been defined by the Court as 'any pecuniary charge, however small and whatever its designation and mode of application,

---

[33] Case 302/86 *Commission* v. *Denmark (Danish Bottles)* [1988] *ECR* 4607; Case 380/87 *Enichem Base S.p.A. et al.* v. *Commune die Cinsello Balsamo (Italian Plastic Bags)* [1989] *ECR* 2491 for the prohibition of non-biodegradable plastic bags.

[34] Case 302/86 *Danish Bottles*, n. 33 above, for the duty to recycle certain drink containers.

[35] Some Member States have already taken very ambitious measures which may influence the outcome of future Community regulations, e.g. Germany by introducing its new 'Packaging Ordinance' of 12 June 1991 [1991] I BGBl. 1234, effective on 1 Jan. 1993, reprinted in [1992] 31 *ILM* 1135 ff.; see also S. Schwarzer, 'Nationale und internationale Verpackungsreglementierung als Unternehmensdatum' [1993] *ÖZW* 16 to 23.

[36] See Becker, n. 15 above, 47, with reference to Case 261/81 *Walter Rau* v. *P.V.B.A. De Smedt (Margarine Packaging)* [1982] *ECR* 3961 and Case 16/83 *Criminal Proceedings against K. Prantl (Bocksbeutel)* [1984] *ECR* 1299 at 1327.

[37] Becker, n. 15 above, 48.   [38] See Ch. 5.

[39] Case 26/62 *NV Algemene Transport- en Expeditie Onderneming Van Gend en Loos* v. *Nederlandse Administratie der Belastingen (Van Gend en Loos)* [1963] *ECR* 3 at 25.

which is imposed unilaterally on domestic and foreign goods by reason of the fact that they cross a frontier'.[40]

Charges for Services Rendered

The only charges allowed are payments for services actually rendered to the importer. Nevertheless, this exception is very strictly interpreted so as not to cover any compulsory frontier formalities such as statistical fees. The authorization and administrative procedure for the crossing of the frontier itself cannot be considered as the type of service rendered which would justify a special charge.[41]

In the field of health protection, border levies for special compulsory controls and inspections[42] are considered to be unlawful if they are applied using criteria other than those which are applied to domestic goods.[43] Where such controls are applied to domestic and imported goods in a non-discriminatory way, the charges must still be compatible with the provisions of Article 95 EC[44] and the existing secondary law in the field.[45] Such control and inspection procedures must, however, take into account controls already in place in the country of origin. An additional control which simply repeats a procedure, whose results are known or can be easily obtained by the importing country, cannot be regarded as a service rendered.[46] The same is true for environmentally justified controls.[47]

Parafiscal Charges

Certain charges may be applied without distinction to national and foreign products and then refunded wholly or partly to national producers in the form of

---

[40] Case 24/68 *Commission* v. *Italy (Statistical Levy)* [1969] *ECR* 193 at 201; see for more references P. J. G. Kapteyn van Themaat, *The Law of the European Communities* (2nd edn., Kluwer, Deventer, 1989), 362, n. 33. See also for a recent decision Case C–130/93 *Lamaire NV* v. *Nationale Dienst voor Afzet van Land- en Tuinbouwprodukten (NDALPT)* [1994] *ECR* I–3215.

[41] See A. Falkenstein, *Freier Warenverkehr in der EG* (Nomos, Baden-Baden, 1989), 83.

[42] So-called sanitary and phyto-sanitary measures or controls.

[43] Case 35/76 *Simmenthal S.p.A.* v. *Ministero delle Finanze (Simmenthal I)* [1976] *ECR* 1871 at 1881; Case 18/87 *Commission* v. *Germany (Animal Inspection Fees)* [1988] *ECR* 5427; Case C–69/88 *Krantz* v. *Ontvanger der Directe Belastingen (Seizure of Goods by Tax Authorities)* [1990] *ECR* I–583.

[44] For the difference see Case 132/78 *SARL Denkavit Loire* v. *Administration des Douanes (Denkavit)* [1979] *ECR* 1923 at 1934.

[45] See e.g. Case C–426/92 *Germany* v. *Deutsches Milch-Kontor GmbH* [1994] *ECR* I–2757, where the relevant Community Dir., 1725/79/EEC, provided only for controls based on spot checks and not a systematic control as executed by the German authorities; such an over-rigorous practice and the excessive costs it entailed were considered by the Court to be a custom duty under Arts. 9 and 12 EC.

[46] See e.g. Joined cases C–277, C–318, and C–319/91 *Ligur Carni srl et al.*, judgment of 15 Dec. 1993 (1993) 36 *Proceedings of the Court* 1.

[47] See Becker, n. 15 above, 70; see also the new developments in the WTO under its Agreement on the Application of Sanitary and Phytosanitary Measures, such as reprinted in GATT Secretariat (ed.), *The Results of the Uruguay Round of the Multilateral Trade Negotiations—The Legal Texts* (Geneva, 1994), 69.

subsidies e.g. for particular ecological production methods or research activities. These refunded charges are considered to be parafiscal charges. If this refunding system is designed exclusively to favour activities which specifically benefit domestic products or producers, it must, however, be regarded as a system implementing a charge having equivalent effect to an import duty under Article 12 EC.[48]

An environmental fund for the support of domestic producers only, but financed by a levy on both imported and domestic goods, would thus fall under the prohibition in Article 12. Such policy instruments for the support of certain ecological behaviour have to be applied in a non-discriminatory manner and therefore must be equally beneficial to all goods fulfilling the relevant requirements.[49] Furthermore, such refunds may raise problems under the specific Treaty provisions on subsidies.[50]

Case: In its decision in Joined cases C–78 to C–83/90 *Compagnie Commerciale de l'Ouest*[51] the Court of Justice was confronted with a French charge on products derived from crude oil. The charge was levied in a non-discriminatory way on domestic and imported petrol, diesel, and fuel oil. The charge had been introduced in 1978 after the price for these products had dropped because of the lower exchange rate for the US dollar leading to a lower price for crude oil. It constituted a complementary element of the price fixation by the French authorities for crude-oil products. The main purpose of the charge was to avoid a rise in consumption of crude-oil products after the price had fallen for monetary reasons; the charge was used for the funding of the *Agence pour les Economies d'Energie* (Energy Saving Agency), a national public institution for the promotion of energy saving and 'the efficient use of non adequately used energy resources'. Several importers of manufactured crude-oil products argued that the charge was incompatible with the provisions of the Treaty, as it favoured national producers. The Court confirmed its former case law indicating that a charge which was used to favour certain domestic (production) activities was incompatible with Articles 12 or 95 EC despite the fact that it was levied equally on domestic and imported goods. It was, however, for the domestic court to decide whether in this case the French system favoured domestic producers.

---

[48] See Case 77/72 *Carmine Capolongo* v. *Azienda Agricola Maya* [1973] *ECR* 611; Case 78/76 *Steinike and Weinlig* v. *Germany (Absatzfonds der deutschen Agrarwirtschaft)* [1977] *ECR* 595 at 614; Case 105/76 *Interzuccheri* v. *Società Rezzano e Cavassa* [1977] *ECR* 1029 at 1042. If the system refunds domestic producers only part of their costs under the charge, it falls instead under Art. 95 (tax discrimination) of the Treaty. Joined cases 78 to 83/90 *Compagnie Commerciale de l'Ouest et al.* v. *Receveur principal des douanes de la Pallice Port* [1992] *ECR* I–1847; Case C–261/91 *CELBI* v. *Fazenda Pública* [1993] *ECR* I–4337; Case C–72/92 *H. Scharatke GmbH* v. *Federal Republic of Germany*, judgment of 27 Oct. 1993, (1993) 30 *Proceedings of the Court* 17. For export charges see e.g. Case 130/93 *NDALPT*, n. 40 above.

[49] See the most recent case law on a fund for agricultural forestry and food: Case C–72/92, n. 48 above.

[50] Case 47/69 *France* v. *Commission (Union of Textile Industries)* [1970] *ECR* 487 at 495.

[51] Joined cases C–78 to C–83/90, n. 48 above, 1847; for notes see [1992] *EWS* 309 to 312.

THE ABOLITION OF QUANTITATIVE RESTRICTIONS (ARTICLES 30, 34)

Quantitative Restrictions on Imports

Apart from customs duties, trade between Member States could also be restricted by a quota system or other quantitative restrictions. Article 30, in conjunction with Article 36, prohibits the use of quotas and restrictions as well as the application of 'measures having equivalent effect'. The prohibition covers all measures which restrict wholly or in part the import of goods, including the transit of goods.[52] Any comprehensive prohibition or restriction of imports for certain goods,[53] parts of goods, as well as ingredients,[54] constitutes in principle an infringement of the prohibition on quantitative restrictions on imports. It may, however, be justified under the exceptions provided for by the Treaty, i.e. to avoid the spreading or the transmission of pests or animal diseases.[55] Quota systems never posed a serious problem for the Community[56] and the imposition of quantitative restrictions was always easily recognizable. Also ecological reasons can lead to the imposition of an import ban or quantitative restrictions on imports.[57]

Quantitative Restrictions on Exports

Article 34 operates as a complement to Article 30. It creates a prohibition on quantitative restrictions on exports and measures having equivalent effect. While Article 30 covers directly protectionist attempts by a Member State to prevent the import of goods from other Member States, Article 34 applies to national measures which hinder the export of goods. There are various reasons for doing this, including the protection of the supply of the domestic manufacturing industry.[58] When raw materials or an important element of a product cannot be exported to another country where it is scarce, domestic production may obtain an important comparative advantage.[59] Similarly, national authorities can be

---

[52] See Case 2/73 *Riseria Luigi Geddo* v. *Ente Nazionale Risi* [1973] *ECR* 865 at 879; see Henke, n. 1 above, 162.

[53] See e.g. Case 54/85 *Ministère Public* v. *Xavier Mirepoix (Mirepoix)* [1986] *ECR* 1067 at 1078.

[54] Case 274/87 *Commission* v. *Germany (Sausages)* [1988] *ECR* 229 at para. 4.

[55] Art. 36 and rule of reason, e.g. Case C–2/90 *Walloon Waste Case*, n. 11 above; see Ch. 4.

[56] See Kapteyn and VerLoren van Themaat, n. 40 above, 375.

[57] See e.g. the quantitative limitation of imports of soft drinks bottled in non-recyclable bottles in Case 302/86 *Danish Bottles*, n. 33 above, 4629; for an import ban see Case C–2/90 *Walloon Waste Case*, n. 11 above, or Case 169/89 *Criminal Proceedings against Gourmetterie Van den Burg (Scottish Red Grouse)* [1990] *ECR* I–2143 at 2154. All these cases are described in detail in Ch. 5.

[58] See Case 172/82 *Inter-Huiles*, n. 22 above, 566, para. 12.

[59] See for similar cases in GATT: e.g. Canada—Measures Affecting Exports of Unprocessed Salmon and Herring, [1989] *GATT BISD*, 35th suppl., 98 to 115. For a detailed comparison to EC law see E.-U. Petersmann, *International and European Trade and Environmental Law after the Uruguay Round* (Kluwer, Deventer, 1995), 62 ff.

tempted to ensure the profitability of local recycling plants or regenerating industries by using export restrictions for recyclable wastes or offal.[60]

In these cases Article 34 which has direct effect and allows individuals to rely on it before domestic courts[61] is an essential element of the system of free movement of goods under the Treaty. The environmental reasons mostly invoked by Member States to justify export restrictions are the protection of domestic natural resources (wood, fish, etc.)[62] and the protection of the environment of the importing country.[63] Often a limitation of exports is justified by the domestic authorities with the need to avoid any opportunity for market participants to circumvent domestic recycling and process regulations or to endanger the functioning of a domestic recycling system (so called 'level-playing-field' argument).[64]

MEASURES HAVING EQUIVALENT EFFECT

General Observations

In contrast to the abolition of quantitative restrictions, it is much more difficult to evaluate and recognize measures having equivalent effect. Hitherto there have been two interpretations of Article 30 EC suggested as bases for the classification of a national measure as a measure having equivalent effect to a trade restriction. The traditional concept, as applied in most (classical) trade agreements, is the non-discrimination principle as a 'national treatment' requirement.[65] All domestic measures are lawful, provided they are applied without distinction and thereby do not directly or indirectly discriminate between domestic and imported goods to the detriment of imports.[66]

Only cases of obvious misuse of equally applicable measures are prohibited. This is usually the case if equally applicable measures have very disparate effects on domestic and imported goods. This concept was the one suggested by the Commission for the free movement of goods in its first communication relating to this topic at the end of the transitional period.[67]

---

[60] See Ch. 5 for the case law in this area.

[61] Case 83/78 *Pigs Marketing Board* v. *R. Redmond* [1978] *ECR* 2347 at 2374.

[62] See e.g. the equivalent cases in GATT: e.g. Canada—Measures Affecting Exports of Unprocessed Salmon and Herring, n. 59 above, 98 to 119.

[63] See the arguments in Case 118/86 *Poultry Offal*, n. 22 above, 3883.

[64] See Ch. 5 on the disputed justification of this argument in the European Community.

[65] See, for considerations on the equivalent interpretation of Art. III:4 and 5 GATT, where the national treatment principle is explicitly mentioned for internal measures, as opposed to Arts. 30 and 34 EC where the wording is not explicit and first and foremost refers to measures directed against imported goods, Petersmann, n. 59 above, 62 ff. or E.-U. Petersmann, 'Freier Warenverkehr und nationaler Umweltschutz in EWG und EWR' [1993] *Aussenwirtschaft* 95 at 111 and 114 to 115.

[66] See for details Ch. 2.

[67] Dir. 70/50/EEC [1970] *OJ* L13/29; see also J. Steiner, 'Drawing the Line: Uses and Abuses of Article 30 EEC Treaty' (1992) 29 *CMLRev.* 749 at 753; Kapteyn and VerLoren van Themaat, n. 40 above, 378.

Another more integrative and federalist approach, however, will also cover indistinctly applicable domestic measures if they hinder trade or marketing opportunities for imported goods. Such a concept would entail that all domestic measures which hinder trade in goods in general, and thereby also have an influence on imported goods, are subject to judicial control by the Court under Article 36. In the interest of inter-state trade and with respect to the domestic sovereignty of the Member States, this principle implies that measures adopted by national authorities are only covered by the prohibition of Article 30 only if they (also) affect imported goods. Purely domestic measures which never affect imported goods do not fall within this concept. The distinction between purely domestic measures and those also affecting imported goods might, however, be very difficult and somewhat unpredictable.[68]

Examination of the Court's View

Which view of the principle of the free movement of goods the Court of Justice should apply was for a long time disputed and still causes much controversy.[69] For a long time it seemed that the Court had chosen different interpretations of the principle for the evaluation of the prohibited effect of measures restricting imports and those restricting exports. For measures having an equivalent effect to export restrictions the Court has in principle developed a classical non-discrimination principle.[70] For import restrictions, however, the Court uses a more comprehensive, integrative principle which covers also indistinctly applicable measures if they disproportionately affect trade.

For a long time, the possible trade-hindering effects of a measure affecting imports were interpreted in a very broad way (*Dassonville* formula[71]). The far-reaching effects of this interpretation were, however, moderated by allowing Member States to adopt measures which were necessary to satisfy certain public interests (*Cassis de Dijon* doctrine[72]). While for a long time this system seemed

[68] See the case law on national marketing restrictions and shopping hours e.g. Joined cases C–267 and 268/91 *Criminal Proceedings against Bernard Keck and Daniel Mithouard*, judgment of 24 Nov. 1993 (1993) 33 *Proceedings of the Court* 1.

[69] See for details Steiner, n. 67 above, 750; for interesting overviews see also E. L. White, 'In Search of Limits to Article 30 EEC Treaty' (1989) 26 *CMLRev.* 235 to 280 or K. Mortelsmann, 'Article 30 of the EEC Treaty and Legislation Relating to Market Circumstances: Time to Consider a New Definition' (1991) 28 *CMLRev.* 115 to 136.

[70] e.g. Case 15/79 *P. B. Groenveld BV* v. *Produktschap voor Vee en Vlees* (*Horse Meat*) [1979] *ECR* 3409 at 3415; see the next section below.

[71] Case 8/74 *Procureur du Roi* v. *B. and G. Dassonville* (*Dassonville*) [1974] *ECR* 837.

[72] Case 120/78 *Rewe Zentralverwaltung AG* v. *Bundesmonopolverwaltung für Branntwein* (*Cassis de Dijon*) [1979] *ECR* 649 at 662; see Ch. 4.

[73] See for detailed descriptions M. Dauses, 'L'interdiction des mesures d'effet équivalent à des restrictions quantitatives à la lumière de la jurisprudence de la CJCE' [1992] *RTDE* 607 to 629; O. Dörr, 'Die Warenverkehrsfreiheit nach Artikel 30EWG-Vertrag—doch bloss ein Diskriminierungsverbot?' [1990] *RabelsZ* 677; L. Gormley, 'Recent Case Law on the Free Movement of Goods: Some Hot Potatoes' (1990) 27 *CMLRev.* 825 to 857.

relatively well established,[73] there are now new indications by the Court that it may in the future narrow its interpretation, limiting the concept of trade hindrance to cases where the effect of a domestic measure is disparate on domestic and imported products.[74] The question whether this is the return to a pure non-discrimination principle is still open.

Import Measures: The *Dassonville* Formula

Under Article 30 both categories—restrictions on imports and measures having equivalent effect—are prohibited. Because of the insignificant incidence of the first group and the sometimes difficult differentiation between the two groups, the Court itself often refers to a mere infringement of Article 30 without distinction.[75]

In its decision in Case 8/74 *Dassonville*[76] in 1974 the Court introduced a very broad concept of 'measures having equivalent effect' to restrictions on imports when concerned with the lawfulness of a Belgian requirement to prove the genuineness of Scottish Whisky. The Court held: 'all trading rules enacted by Member States which are capable of hindering, actually or potentially, directly or indirectly, intra-Community trade are to be considered as measures having equivalent effect to quantitative restrictions.'[77]

In the Court's view this very broad definition renders irrelevant the question whether a measure is applied on a non-discriminatory basis or not.[78] In the legal regime of the European Community, as developed by the Court, discrimination is a sufficient but not a necessary element for deciding whether a national measure is capable of hindering trade between Member States and therefore falling under the prohibition of Article 30 EC. As an ultimate consequence this concept of free movement of goods guarantees that, in principle, the free trade of goods within the common market is not hindered by any national measures or restrictions.[79] Furthermore, the Court does not require proof that a national measure has actually led to trade distortion. The mere potential effect is

---

[74] e.g. Joined cases C–267 and C–268/91, n. 68 above, or Joined cases C–401/92 and C–402/92 *Criminal Proceedings against Tankstation 't Heuske vof and J. B. E. Boermans* [1994] *ECR* I–2199 concerning the opening hours of petrol stations.

[75] See Henke, n. 1 above, 162, referring to Joined cases 51 to 54/71 *International Fruit Company NV v. Produktschap voor Groenten en Fruit (Import Licences)* [1971] *ECR* 1107 at 1116; Case 173/83, n. 22 above, 507.

[76] Case 8/74 *Dassonville*, n. 71 above.

[77] Case 8/74 *Dassonville*, n. 71 above, 852.

[78] See Kapteyn and VerLoren van Themaat, n. 40 above, 379 to 381.

[79] The term 'trading rules' has to be interpreted in a broad sense to include restrictive measures which are not aimed particularly at trade: e.g. Case 4/75 *Rewe Zentralfinanz GmbH* v. *Landwirtschaftskammer (Phyto-sanitary Measures)* [1975] *ECR* 843 at 858 or even restrictions on domestic production: Case 190/73 *Officier van Justitie* v. *J. W. J. Van Haaster* [1974] *ECR* 1123; see Kapteyn and VerLoren van Themaat, n. 40 above, 379.

considered unlawful.[80] Thus, the Court has often refused to limit the applicability of Article 30 to perceptible[81] or even severe restrictions.[82]

This very wide concept used by the Court has been extremely controversial ever since.[83] As demonstrated before, it is much closer to the principle of a national market established, for example, by the commerce clause in the United States or the 'freedom of commerce and business' under Article 31 of the Swiss Constitution,[84] than to the ordinary non-discrimination principle of a classical free trade agreement[85] or the 'national treatment requirement' in GATT.[86] The prohibition covers, however, only national rules and practices which affect trade between Member States. Article 30 is not applicable if such measures are applied only to domestic products.[87] It is thus only an 'almost constitutional right'[88] to trade and not to business activities in general.[89]

The Court's concept may include product requirements, certain commercialization, or marketing restrictions etc. This broad concept leads to a number of problems in the field of environmental measures.[90] While under GATT and other trade agreements Member States remain, in principle, free to take national measures for the protection of the environment, provided they are applied on a non-discriminatory basis,[91] the Member States of the Community have to

---

[80] See also Case 12/74 *Commission* v. *Germany (Indirect Appellation of Origin)* [1975] *ECR* 181 at 185 or Case 2/69 *Sociaal Fonds voor de Diamantarbeiders* v. *Brachfeld & Sons SA* [1969] *ECR* 211 at 221.

[81] e.g. Case 4/75 *Phytosanitary Measures*, n. 79 above, 864, or Case 16/83 *Bocksbeutel*, n. 36 above, 1326.

[82] See the case law referred to in Henke, n. 1 above, 163; particularly Case 16/83 *Bocksbeutel*, n. 36 above, 1326.

[83] See the survey by J. Pipkorn, 'Das Verbot von Massnahmen gleicher Wirkung wie mengenmässige Beschränkungen' in E.-W. Fuss (ed.), *Der Beitrag des Gerichtshofes der Europäischen Gemeinschaften zur Verwirklichung des Gemeinsamen Marktes* (Nomos, Baden-Baden, 1981), 9 at 13.

[84] 'Handels- und Gewerbefreiheit' as laid down in Art. 31 of the Swiss Constitution of 1874, see e.g. H. Marti, *Die Wirtschaftsfreiheit der schweizerischen Bundesverfassung* (Helbing & Lichtenhahn, Basel, 1976) or K. Vallender, *Wirtschaftsfreiheit und begrenzte Staatsverantwortung* (2nd edn., Stämpfli, Bern, 1989), 28 to 50.

[85] See e.g. for the free trade agreement between Switzerland and the European Community and its corresponding articles, J. Borer, *Massnahmen gleicher Wirkung im Freihandelsabkommen Schweiz-EWG* (Stämpfli, Bern, 1988) or M. Baldi, 'Direct Applicability of the Free Trade Agreements between the EEC and the EFTA Countries from a Swiss Perspective' [1985] *Swiss Review of International Competition Law* 31 to 38.   [86] See Ch. 2.

[87] Often referred to as 'discrimination against nationals', see e.g. A. Skordas, n. 1 above, 14 to 165; A. Epiney and T. M. J. Möllers, *Freier Warenverkehr und nationaler Umweltschutz* (Heymann, Köln, 1992), 32 ff.; Case 237/82 *Jongeneel Kaas BV et al.* v. *The Netherlands (Nisin)* [1984] *ECR* 483 at 504, with regard to Art. 34.

[88] See, for the constitutional function of international trade rules in general, E.-U. Petersmann, 'Trade Policy as a Constitutional Problem—On Domestic Policy Functions of International Trade Rules' [1986] *Aussenwirtschaft* 405 to 439.

[89] See e.g. H.-W. Rengeling, *Grundrechtsschutz in Europäischen Gemeinschaft* (C. H. Beck, München, 1993), 18 to 20.

[90] For details, procedures, and cases, see the proportionality principle in Ch. 5.

[91] See e.g. E.-U. Petersmann, 'International Trade Law and International Environmental Law—Prevention and Settlement of International Disputes in GATT' [1993] *JWT* 43 at 53. See, however, the new provisions in the Agreement on Technical Barriers to Trade (TBT–Agreement) after the Uruguay Round, i.e. the 'necessity test' as laid down by Art. 2.2., in GATT Secretariat (ed.) n. 42 above.

observe the principles of Articles 30–7 EC and their interpretation by the Court of Justice.

Particularly in cases where the Member States would like to introduce requirements regarding the product characteristics of certain products they are usually limited by the *Dassonville* formula. National restrictions on the use of cars,[92] prohibitions of certain dangerous or harmful substances,[93] packaging requirements,[94] limitations or prohibition of use of certain materials for certain purposes,[95] domestic measures prescribing noise levels,[96] labelling requirements[97] etc., have effects on the market situation for imported goods. Most environmental measures related to product characteristics fall under the concept referred to by the *Dassonville* formula.[98]

Limiting the Scope of the *Dassonville* Formula?

Nevertheless, the Court's definition of 'measures having equivalent effect to import restrictions' remains somewhat difficult to apply. This is attested to by the enormous case law that has been produced by the Court of Justice during the last twenty years.[99] While the *Dassonville* formula was welcomed by many as a substitute for the slow and difficult harmonization of national laws by the Council[100] this development was also criticized by many, as the Court was confronted with the effect that its approach was 'capable of embracing a variety of measures introduced for wholly desirable and necessary purposes beyond those for which derogation was specifically provided under Article 36'.[101]

As a consequence the Court was confronted with the task of moderating and restricting the use of its jurisprudence to those cases which were justified under the objectives of the Treaty. For the time being, the Court has used two main

[92] See e.g. the regulations introduced by several German *Länder* on the use of cars without catalytic converter during smog-alarm periods; see e.g. C. Moench, 'Die Fahrverbotsregelungen der Smogverordnungen auf dem Prüfstand des EG-Rechts' [1989] *NVwZ* 335 to 339 and K. Heinz, 'Nochmals: Die Fahrverbotsregelungen der Smogverordnungen auf dem Prüfstand des EG-Rechts' [1989] *NVwZ* 1035 to 1038.

[93] See e.g. Case C–125/88 *Criminal Proceedings against Nijman* [1989] *ECR* 3533 at 3557.

[94] Case 302/86 *Danish Bottles*, n. 33 above, concerning a return system for bottles.

[95] See e.g. Case 380/87 *Italian Plastic Bags*, n. 33 above.

[96] See e.g. *R.* v. *London Boroughs Transport Committee, ex parte Freight Transport Association Ltd.*, CA, 31 July 1990 [1990] 3 *CMLR* 495 and HL, 24 July 1991, [1992] 1 *CMLR* 5 concerning noise levels for lorries in residential areas; see also a Danish regulation on noise levels for windmills as described by Krämer, n. 15 above, 134; see also Ch. 5.

[97] See e.g. Case C–369/89 PIAGEME v. Peeters PVBA (*Labelling in Regional Language*) [1991] *ECR* I–2971.

[98] See M. Dauses, 'Dogmatik des freien Warenverkehrs in der europäischen Gemeinschaft' [1984] *RIW* 197 at 201.

[99] See A. Falkenstein, *Freier Warenverkehr in der EG* (Nomos, Baden-Baden, 1989).

[100] The term 'negative harmonization', as opposed to 'positive harmonization' under the specific Treaty provisions, reflects this development, see e.g. P. Behrens, 'Die Konvergenz der wirtschaftlichen Freiheiten im europäischen Gemeinschaftsrecht' [1992] *EuR* 308 at 314; see also Ch. 2.

[101] Steiner, n. 67 above, 752.

instruments for this purpose: first, the introduction of areas of justified domestic regulation affecting trade which preclude the application of Article 30 (rule of reason) and, secondly, a limitation of the concept applied to trade hindrance which limits the scope of the *Dassonville* formula (*Keck* case law).

First, the Court has moderated the effect of its wide concept by introducing a set of reasons which precludes the application of Article 30. If Member States try to satisfy certain recognized public interests, referred to by the Court as 'mandatory requirements', national measures do not fall within the prohibition in Article 30 if they are necessary and proportionate (*Cassis de Dijon* doctrine). As the Court has never given a complete list of the recognized objectives of national policy under this doctrine and applies a proportionality test which used not to be familiar to many national courts,[102] the development of this case law has proved to be a relatively difficult way of limiting the effects of the *Dassonville* formula. In the case of the protection of the environment, the rule of reason has, however, allowed the Court to integrate the environment clearly into its case law even before the introduction of the Single European Act.[103]

Secondly, as far as the possible hindrance to trade is concerned, the Court has even after the *Dassonville* judgment, delivered a few judgments where the reasoning seemed to contradict the developed concept to some extent.[104] In these cases, concerning national marketing and distribution rules, the Court considered the (potential) effect on trade as 'too problematic and remote'[105] or not impeding trade at all. Simultaneously, the Court decided similar cases by applying the *Dassonville* formula and allowing certain restrictions by reference to the *Cassis-de-Dijon* doctrine.[106] In both groups of cases the Court was concerned with equally applicable national measures which were justified by the national governments with certain public interests. Several authors have tried to develop a general theory to explain why the Court apples the *Dassonville* formula in certain cases and in others not.[107]

---

[102] See e.g. Steiner, n. 67 above, 750, with reference to *Hoffmann* J in a case before an English court: *Council of the City of Stoke-on-Trent* v. *B & Q* [1990] 3 *CMLR* 31, leading later to a preliminary ruling before the Court of Justice, Case C–169/91 *Council of the City of Stoke-on-Trent* v. *B & Q* [1992] *ECR* I–6635.

[103] Because of its particular importance for domestic environmental measures the rule of reason under Art. 30 EC will be outlined in the next sect. and explained in detail in the following two chs. together with Art. 36.

[104] See Case 75/81 *Blesgen* v. *Belgium* (*Marketing Restriction on Alcohol*) [1982] *ECR* 1211 at 1229; Case 155/80 *Administrative Proceedings against Sergius Oebel* (*Nightwork in Bakeries*) [1981] *ECR* 1993 at 1210, para. 7; Case 148/85 *Direction Générale des Impôts and Procureur de la République* v. *Forest* (*Milling Quotas*) [1986] *ECR* 3449; Case C–69/88 *Seizure of Goods by Tax Authorities*, n. 43 above, 583; C–23/89 *Quietlynn Ltd.* v. *Southend-on-Sea BC* (*Limitation of Sales of Sex Articles*) [1990] *ECR* I–3059.

[105] Case C–69/88 *Seizure of Goods by Tax Authorities*, n. 43 above.

[106] Case 286/81 *Criminal Proceedings against Osthoek's Uitgeversmaatschappij BV* (*Gifts for Promotional Purposes*) [1982] *ECR* 1013; Case 238/82 *Duphar BV et al.* v. *The Netherlands* (*Restriction of Refundable Pharmaceuticals*) [1984] *ECR* 523 at 541; Joined cases 60 and 61/84 *Cinéthèque*, n. 12 above; Case 382/87 *Buet* v. *Ministère Public* (*Door-to-Door Selling*) [1989] *ECR* 1235; Case C–362/88 *GB INNO-BM* v. *Confédération du Commerce Luxembergeois* (*Restrictions on Sales Promotions*) [1990] *ECR* I–667.

[107] See for references Steiner, n. 67 above, 762; L. Gormley, ' "Actually or Potentially, Directly

No Trade Effects from General Marketing Regulations

Only recently, however, the Court has openly admitted that it tends towards a reformulation of the *Dassonville* formula. Confronted with an increasing number of cases related to equally applicable national rules with relatively small trade effects, the Court considered a re-examination and clarification of its own case law.[108] After an impressive series of judgments concerning national marketing restrictions, where the Court applied the *Dassonville* formula, the Court has indicated its intention to limit the scope of Article 30. While the Court usually held that domestic marketing restrictions were capable of affecting trade in spite of their equal application to both domestic and imported goods,[109] there is now a new series of decisions where such indistinctly applied restrictions are regarded as lying outside the scope of Article 30.[110]

The marketing of goods with explicit reference to environmental qualities and advantages of certain products becomes increasingly important for the consumer goods industry. The use of, in particular, specific 'green' or environmental labels awarded by private or semi-statal organizations is very popular for the distinction of environmentally friendly products.[111] On the other hand, producers and retail sellers are tempted to use environmental selling arguments for the information of customers in order to gain a comparative advantage in relation to ordinary, i.e. not environmentally friendly, products. While the use of marketing instruments in the form of general information and product declarations is generally helpful for transparency within the market and the information and awareness of customers it can also be abused for illegitimate purposes. In general, Member States have established certain rules and restriction against the abuse of marketing instruments in order to protect consumers and (also)

---

or Indirectly?" Obstacles to the Free Movement of Goods' [1989] *GYIL* 197 at 198; Dörr, n. 73 above, 677 to 691.

[108] Joined cases 267 and 268/91, n. 68 above, para. 14.

[109] See the abundant case law on the so-called 'Sunday Trading Cases': comments e.g. by M. van der Woude, 'The Limits of Free Circulation: The Torfaen Borough Case' [1990] *LJIL* 57 to 63 or W. Alt and J. Sack, 'Nationale Werbebeschränkungen und freier Warenverkehr' [1990] *EuZW* 311 to 314.

[110] Joined cases 267 and 268/91, n. 68 above; also Case C–292/92 *Hünermund* v. *Landesapothekenkammer Baden-Württemberg*, judgment of 15 Dec. 1993 (1993) 36 Proceedings of the Court 1; Joined cases C–401/92 and C–402/92, n. 74 above, 2199; Joined cases C–69/93 and C–258/93 *Punto Casa SpA* v. *Sindaco del Comune di Capena et al.* [1994] *ECR* I–2355; for comments see M. Petschke, 'Die Warenverkehrsfreiheit in der neuesten Rechtsprechung des EuGH' [1994] *EuZW* 107 to 111 and J. Sedemund and F. Montag, 'Die Entwicklung des Europäischen Gemeinschaftsrechts' [1994] *NJW* 625 at 627; M. Waldhäusl, 'EuGH zum freien Warenverkehr: Das Keck-Urteil' [1994] *Ecolex* 367 to 371; A. Dubach, 'Der freie Warenverkehr in der neusten Rechtsprechung des Europäischen Gerichtshofs' [1994] *SZW* 219 ff.; or F. Emmert, *Lange Stange im Nebel oder neue Strategie? Basler Schriften zur europäischen Integration Nr. 7* (Europainstitut der Universität Basel, Basel, 1994).

[111] See e.g. A. Wiebe, 'EG-rechtliche Grenzen des deutschen Wettbewerbsrechts am Beispiel der Umweltwerbung' [1994] *EuZW* 41.

competitors against misleading (environmental) information.[112] While such restrictions are often related to market circumstances and thereby apply equally to all suppliers they may also have important effects on the product labelling and packaging and thereby on the characteristics and presentation of products.

In my view, marketing restrictions for the use of environmental labels and product declaration still fall under the *Dassonville* formula, as they concern the products and their packaging and therefore would partition the common market into separate segments by requiring different packagings for different countries.[113] In these cases the *Dassonville* formula is still applicable.[114] The case is different if marketing restrictions relate only to the mode of selling or other market circumstances surrounding the sale of products.[115] Here the Court has established the principle that such measures do not fall within the scope of Article 30.[116] In my view this limitation in scope applies also if the domestic marketing restrictions require an adaptation of marketing strategies and concepts used in other markets without asking for different product or packaging characteristics.[117] Admittedly, such domestic measures will lead to a certain segmentation of markets and therefore the line between measures relating to the product characteristics themselves and the marketing strategies used will have to be defined more explicitly by the Court.[118]

Cassis de Dijon Doctrine or the Rule of Reason

As submitted in the case of environmental labels and product declarations, most authors argue that the restriction of the scope of the *Dassonville* formula applies

[112] e.g. the German *Gesetz gegen den unlauteren Wettbewerb* (UWG); for details see Wiebe, n. 111 above, 41; see also Case C–470/93 *Verein gegen Unwesen im Handel und Gewerbe* v. *Mars GmbH*, judgment of 6 July 1995, comments by T. Lüder, 'Mars: Zwischen Keck und Cassis'[1995] *EuZW* 609 to 610.

[113] See e.g Case 27/80 *Criminal Proceedings against A. A. Fietje (Fietje)* [1980] *ECR* 3839 at 3853.

[114] See e.g. the Court's decision in Case C–317/92 *Commission* v. *Germany (Expiry Dates)* [1994] *ECR* I–2039 where the Court noted that the German measure which required the compulsory indication of only two possible expiry dates per year on the packaging of medicinal products was likely to affect intra-Community trade in so far as it might reduce the selling period of imported products and therefore constituted a measure prohibited by Art. 30 despite its non-discriminatory character. The alleged simplification of the handling of such products by traders and the corresponding economic advantages were not recognized as a ground of justification.

[115] Mortelsmann, n. 69 above, 115, defines the latter as 'market circumstances' such as the prohibition on opening shops on Sundays or on selling products by going from door to door or general legislation related to publicity and commercials, e.g. Case C–412/93 *Société d'Importation Edouard Leclerc-Siplec* v. *TF1 Publicité SA* [1995] *ECR* I–179. See e.g. M. Dauses, 'Die Rechtsprechung des EuGH zum Verbraucherschutz und zur Werbefreiheit im Binnenmarkt' [1995] *EuZW* 425 to 443.

[116] See Joined cases 60 and 61/84 *Cinéthèque*, n. 12 above, 2605; Joined cases C–267 and C–268/91 n. 68 above; Case C–292/92, n. 110 above.

[117] In the existing case law measures which required a change of marketing strategies or prohibited the use of a selling method whereby a trade usually realizes most of its sales fell under the *Dassonville* formula and were only justifiable if they were covered by Art. 36 or one of the grounds of the rule of reason, see e.g. Case 382/87 *Door-to-Door-Selling*, n. 106 above; Case C–362/88 *Restrictions on Sales Promotion*, n. 106 above.

[118] See also Petschke, n. 110 above, 111.

only to marketing regulations and leaves the prohibition on product requirements or measures relating to characteristics of products intact.[119] Thus, in the
field of national measures related to product characteristics which hinder the
import of goods from other Member States the Court regularly applies the strict
view developed in the *Dassonville* formula. In principle, the ultimate consequence
of such a broad interpretation of Article 30 would be that Member States no
longer have the power to apply domestic measures for the protection of their
territory or their population. An elimination of all national measures falling
under the *Dassonville* formula would lead to the erosion of national regulations
for the protection of national interests and public order.

In the absence of comprehensive and adequate Community legislation and in
the light of existing differences between the Member States, such a result would
be very unsatisfactory.[120] Although the Treaty itself provides a general exception in Article 36 from the application of Articles 30 and 34 EC, the Court has
always preferred a very narrow interpretation of Article 36 as it has for the
Treaty's exception clauses in general.[121] In this situation the Court itself has
introduced the concept of 'mandatory requirements' to allow the application of
national measures for the protection of certain public interests even if they hinder the free movement of goods between Member States.[122] The landmark
judgement was delivered in Case 120/78 *Cassis de Dijon*[123] in 1979 and the concept applied in the case law that followed is often referred to as the *Cassis de Dijon*
doctrine or rule of reason.[124] In this decision the Court found that in spite of
the applicability of the *Dassonville* formula certain national measures did not fall
within the prohibition of Article 30 as

Obstacles to movement within the Community resulting from disparities between the
national laws relating to the marketing of the products in question must be accepted in
so far as those provisions may be recognized as being necessary in order to satisfy mandatory requirements relating in particular to the effectiveness of fiscal supervision, the protection of public health, the fairness of commercial transactions and the defence of the
consumer.[125]

---

[119] See e.g. White, n. 69 above, 235; Mortelmans, n. 69 above, 115.

[120] See e.g. L. Gormley, *Prohibiting Restrictions on Trade within the E.E.C.* (North Holland, Amsterdam, 1985), 52 to 53.

[121] See e.g. Steiner, n. 67 above, 752; there are more details in Ch. 4.

[122] The view expressed by Skordas, n. 1 above, 31, that the application of the rule of reason relies on a previous infringement of Art. 30 is not compatible with the Court's case law.

[123] Case 120/78 *Cassis de Dijon*, n. 72 above, 662.

[124] For classical surveys on the rule of reason see P. VerLoren van Themaat, 'La libre circulation des marchandises après l'arrêt "Cassis de Dijon" ' [1982] *CDE* 123 to 135 or A. Mattera,
'L'arrêt "Cassis de Dijon": Une nouvelle approche pour la réalisation et le bon fonctionnement du
marché intérieur' [1990] *RMC* 505 to 513; J.-C. Masclet, 'Les articles 30, 36 et 100 du Traité CEE
à la lumière de l'arrêt "Cassis de Dijon" ' [1980] *RTDE* 611 to 634; J.-C. Masclet, 'La libre circulation des marchandises dans les Communautés européennes' [1986] *RTDE* 243 to 267.

[125] Case 120/78 *Cassis de Dijon*, n. 72 above, 662.

From a substantive point of view this doctrine enlarges the catalogue of justi-fied national measures under Article 36, but in terms of a more systematic or formal aspect the Court seems to treat the doctrine as a limitation of the scope of Articles 30 and 34. The Court therefore treats the relevant measures not as restrictive measures in the sense of Article 30 but considers them to lie beyond the scope of this provision and therefore to be lawful under the general princi-ples of the Treaty. The application of any exceptional clause, such as Article 36, is not necessary.[126] The *Cassis de Dijon* doctrine is therefore a further develop-ment of the Court's authoritative interpretation of Article 30, moderating to an important extent the effect of the *Dassonville* formula. The list of mandatory requirements has subsequently been enlarged by the Court and is, in principle, open.[127] The protection of the environment has also been included within the mandatory requirements of the Treaty.[128]

Rule of Reason and Mutual Recognition

Nevertheless, the scope for national product requirements and measures related to the characteristics of products under Article 30 remains limited. This is par-ticularly so, since the Court stated in the same decision that a Member State has no justification for prohibiting the marketing of goods which have been lawfully produced or placed on the market in another Member State.[129] This declara-tion should, however, be interpreted in the context of the Court's case law. It merely creates a rebuttable presumption[130] and each case must still be judged on its merits. As long as there is insufficient harmonization of standards within the Community the Member States will have to retain their own protective regimes.[131] The measures have, however, to be suitable, necessary, and propor-tionate. They are not considered to be necessary or proportionate if the level of protection achieved by measures and regulations in the exporting Member State is equivalent to the desired level in the importing Member State.[132]

It is, thus, important to distinguish two principles implicit in the *Cassis de Dijon* doctrine. First, the doctrine restricts the prohibition in Article 30 in so far as Member States are authorized to adopt national safeguards in the interest of cer-tain 'mandatory requirements' if they are suitable, necessary, and proportion-

---

[126] See Kapteyn and VerLoren van Themaat, n. 40 above, 389.

[127] See for a comprehensive collection of case law: G. Meier, *Die Cassis- Rechtsprechung des Gerichtshofs des Europäischen Gemeinschaften* (Behr, Hamburg, 1988).

[128] See Case 302/86 *Danish Bottles*, n. 33 above; to a lesser extent already indicated in Case 240/83 *ADBHU*, n. 22 above; see also Ch. 4.

[129] See Case 120/78 *Cassis de Dijon*, n. 72 above, 664.

[130] See also the communication by the Commission concerning the *Cassis de Dijon* decision [1980] *OJ* C256/2.

[131] See Kapteyn and VerLoren van Themaat, n. 40 above, 286.

[132] See e.g. Case C–373/92 *Commission* v. *Belgium* (*Sterilized Instruments*) [1993] *ECR* I–3107 which concerned a compulsory examination of sterilized instruments which had already undergone similar tests in the country of origin.

ate.[133] Such measures do not constitute measures having equivalent effect to import restrictions. Secondly, this authorization is limited by the compulsory recognition of equivalent measures and regulations applied in other Member States. National measures to implement 'mandatory requirements' are only justified if they are necessary to guarantee the higher national standard in the absence of an equivalent level of protection in other Member States.[134]

Restrictions on Exports

Using the same wording as Article 30 EC, Article 34 creates the prohibition on 'quantitative restrictions on exports and all measures having equivalent effect'. Although this principle is the equivalent of Article 30, the Court has developed different principles governing the treatment of restrictions on exports. When looking at measures applicable only to exports, the Court applies the basic principles of the *Dassonville* formula.[135] The same is true for indistinctly applicable measures in the agricultural sector covered by common market organizations at Community level.[136] Whenever a national measure outside the excepted agricultural sectors is involved, however, the Court allows measures affecting trade as long as they are imposed irrespective of the destination of the goods. In contrast to the *Dassonville* formula the Court applies here a classic non-discrimination principle when referring to Article 34 EC.[137] In several cases the Court held:

Article 34 concerns national measures which have as their specific object or effect the restriction of patterns of exports and thereby the establishment of a difference in treatment between the domestic trade of a Member State and its export trade, in such a way to provide a particular advantage for national production or for the domestic market of the State in question.[138]

The first group of cases in which this concept was used concerned very sensitive areas of the production and distribution of goods, such as the use of horsemeat[139] and the prohibition of night work.[140] It was therefore reasonable to imagine that the *Dassonville* formula remained in principle applicable also to Article 34, but that the Court wished to moderate its effect.[141] Nevertheless, in subsequent cases the Court has made it clear that the non-discrimination

---

[133] Case 120/78 *Cassis de Dijon*, n. 72 above, 662.　　　　[134] Ibid., 664.

[135] e.g. Case 53/76 *Procureur de la République de Besançon* v. *Bouhelier et al.* [1977] *ECR* 197.

[136] e.g. Case 94/79 *Criminal Proceedings against Pieter Vriend* v. *Public Ministry of The Netherlands* [1980] *ECR* 327.

[137] See Kapteyn and VerLoren van Themaat, n. 40 above, 382.

[138] e.g. Case 15/79 *Horse Meat*, n. 70 above, 3415; Case 155/80 *Night Work in Bakeries*, n. 104 above, 2009; Case 174/84 *Bulk Oil AG* v. *Sun Limited and Sun Oil Trading Company* (*Sun Oil*) [1986] *ECR* 559 at 589.

[139] Case 15/79 *Horse Meat*, n. 70 above, 3415.

[140] Case 155/80 *Night Work in Bakeries*, n. 104 above, 2009.

[141] For a similar approach, by applying the rule of reason, see Case 75/81 *Marketing Restrictions on Alcohol*, n. 104 above, 1229; see Kapteyn and VerLoren van Themaat, n. 40 above, 382.

criterion is the general test for national measures having equivalent effect as restrictions to exports.[142]

In the field of the environment, measures having equivalent effect to export restrictions often concern the treatment or the transport of such sensitive goods as hazardous waste or specific categories of dangerous products.[143] These restrictions would fall within the wide concept of the *Dassonville* formula but are not within the scope of Article 34 EC as long as they are applied irrespective of the destination of the product. Therefore domestic measures affecting exports remain lawful provided they are accompanied by equivalent domestic restrictions or prohibitions.[144]

'Local grab measures', however, are covered by the prohibition in Article 34 EC.[145] This applies, for example, to the requirement that waste or certain chemical substances have to be recycled or deposited within the national territory.[146] From an ecological point of view the non-discrimination requirement is sufficient for an effective environmental policy, as it allows national or domestic authorities to require certain precautions for the treatment and transport of waste or hazardous substances within the country without opening a gap for protectionist measures or inefficient measures.[147] It remains to be clarified what effect the 'principles of autarky' or 'self-sufficiency'[148] and the principle of correction at source, as laid down by Article 130r(2),[149] will have on export restrictions.[150]

Thus, from a systematic point of view, national measures concerning exports are subject to less stringent restrictions than measures concerning imports.[151] This may be explained by the Court's respect for national sovereignty and the Member States' right to regulate 'purely internal matters' concerning the pro-

---

[142] See Kapteyn and VerLoren van Themaat, n. 40 above, 382; in Case 155/80 *Nightwork in Bakeries*, n. 104 above, 1993 and in Case 15/79 *Horse Meat*, n. 70 above, Caportorti AG still suggested the application of the *Dassonville* formula.

[143] After the decision in Case C–2/90 *Walloon Waste Case*, n. 11 above, it is clear that waste falls under the provisions of Art. 34; the considerations by e.g. Becker, n. 15 above, 63, and others are therefore no longer applicable.

[144] Same opinion Henke, n. 2 above, 164, referring to Skordas, n. 2 above, 33.

[145] See Kapteyn and VerLoren van Themaat, n. 40 above, 383.

[146] Case 172/82 *Inter-Huiles*, n. 22 above, 555, and Case 173/83, n. 22 above, 507, and Case 240/83 *ADBHU*, n. 22 above, 531; Case C–37/92 *Criminal Proceedings against J. Vanacker et al.*, judgment of 12 Oct. 1993 (1993) 28 *Proceedings of the Court* 2; Case C–366/89 *Commission v. Italy (Recycling of Chemical Waste)*, judgment of 2 Aug. 1993 (1993) 24 *Proceedings of the Court* 1.

[147] For the problem of possible discrimination against nationals by applying very strict requirements internally see Henke, n. 2 above, 165 at 169; E. Steindorff, 'Probleme des Art. 30' [1984] *ZHR* 338 at 353; U. F. Kleier, 'Freier Warenverkehr (Art. 30 EWG-Vertrag) und die Diskriminierung inländischer Erzeugnisse' [1988] *RIW* 623 at 628.

[148] Basel Convention on Transboundary Movements of Hazardous Waste, reprinted e.g. in (1989) 28 *ILM* 657.

[149] As applied by the Court in its decision in Case C–2/90 *Walloon Waste Case*, n. 11 above.

[150] For more details and the existing case law see Ch. 5 or Middeke, n. 1 above, 146 to 161.

[151] For problems arising from the fact that other Member States have lower environmental standards for the recycling of waste or production of certain goods which may lead to a critical environmental situation abroad or to the circumvention of national regulations see Ch. 5.

duction or the treatment of goods. In these cases the measures apply only to domestic products and therefore cannot discriminate against products from other Member States.[152] In spite of their trade-inhibiting effect they do not distort competition among products, nor among undertakings recycling or disposing of waste, as long as the requirements concern the products themselves.[153]

DISCRIMINATORY TAXATION (ARTICLE 95)

General Observations

In spite of its location in the chapter on general fiscal provisions[154] Article 95 is an important element ensuring the free movement of goods in the European Community.[155] While Articles 9 and 12 prohibit any financial charge levied for the mere fact that goods cross the border within the Community,[156] Article 95 constitutes the necessary complement for a general prohibition on the discriminatory imposition of financial burdens.[157] In conjunction with Articles 30–7 these provisions allow for undistorted trade within the Community.[158]

While Article 95 aims at the elimination of fiscal discrimination leading to a distortion of trade it does not preclude differential taxation of different goods if it is objectively justified.[159] This applies also in the case of environmental charges or taxes. The Community recognizes the importance of these instruments, in particular, under the polluter pays principle.[160] A differentiation on environmental grounds is justified if the taxes are levied equally on imported and domestic goods and do not constitute a disguised restriction on trade.[161]

The Scope of Article 95

Article 95, first sentence, provides that no Member State 'shall impose, directly

---

[152] See Henke, n. 2 above, 168.

[153] See Ch. 5 for possible infringements of Art. 34 by national export restrictions concerning the treatment and ecological situation in the country of destination; see also Everling, n. 21 above, 9; D. H. Scheuing, *Grenzüberschreitende atomare Wiederaufbereitung im Lichte des europäischen Gemeinschaftsrechts* (Nomos, Baden-Baden, 1991), 36; H.-W. Rengeling, 'Schadlose Verwertung radioaktiver Reststoffe durch Wiederaufbereitung in anderen EG-Mitgliedstaaten' [1991] *DVBl.* 914 at 919.

[154] Ch. 2: Tax Provisions (Arts. 95 to 99).

[155] Case 57/65 *Firma Alfons Lütticke GmbH* v. *Hauptzollamt Saarlouis (Lütticke)* [1968] ECR 293.

[156] See Ch. 3.

[157] See the corresponding provision in GATT: Art. III GATT.

[158] Case 142/77 *Statens Kontrol* v. *Preben Larsen* [1978] ECR 1543 or Case 168/78 *Commission* v. *France (Tax Arrangement Applicable to Spirits I)* [1980] ECR 347.

[159] e.g. Case 200/85 *Commission* v. *Italy (Diesel Engines)* [1986] ECR 3953 at 3971, para. 8.

[160] Art. 130r(2) EC.

[161] See E. Steindorff, 'Umweltschutz in Gemeinschaftshand?' [1984] *RIW* 767 at 770 or H. R. Glatz, 'Die Verträglichkeit nationaler umweltpolitischer Initiativen mit dem EWG-Vertrag: Das Beispiel der PKW-Schadstoffbegrenzung' in J. Schwarze and R. Bieber, *Das europäische Wirtschaftsrecht vor der Herausforderung der Zukunft* (Nomos, Baden-Baden, 1985), 161, as referred to by Becker, n. 15 above, 69.

or indirectly, on the products of other Member States any internal taxation of any kind in excess of that imposed directly or indirectly on similar domestic products'. The distinction of such internal taxation from custom duties and in particular charges having equivalent effect (Articles 9, 12 EC) is not always easy.¹⁶² The distinction is important as Article 12 prohibits any imposition of such duties or charges whereas Article 95 permits the imposition of taxes on imported goods provided there is an equivalent taxation of internal products.¹⁶³ The Court has recognized that Articles 12 and 95 cannot be applied at the same time for the same situation.¹⁶⁴ The terminology is, however, somewhat puzzling.¹⁶⁵

Article 95 includes, in principle, all indirect internal charges and taxes¹⁶⁶ whether they are product-related charges, parafiscal charges,¹⁶⁷ or fees for services rendered.¹⁶⁸ If the charges, however, are only applied to imported goods on occasion or because of their border crossing, they have to be considered as charges and custom duties prohibited under Articles 9 and 12 EC.¹⁶⁹ The question of how the charge or tax has been levied has no importance for the distinction between custom duties and taxes.

The use of the contribution, however, may have an impact on its classification. The case law of the Court has extended the application of Article 95 to 'non-discriminatory internal taxation which hinders imports or disadvantages them'.¹⁷⁰ Certain charges are reimbursed in whole or in part, directly or indirectly, to national producers (so-called parafiscal charges). The case law of the European Court of Justice has clarified¹⁷¹ the terminology used for such financial burdens under the Treaty: if they are completely refunded to domestic producers or used for a public service which benefits only domestic producers,¹⁷² they have to be considered charges equivalent to customs duties under Articles 9 and 12 EC. If these parafiscal charges, however, are refunded only partly to domestic producers, they fall under Article 95 as discriminatory taxes.¹⁷³

---

¹⁶² See Ch. 3.   ¹⁶³ See Kapteyn and VerLoren van Themaat, n. 40 above, 368.
¹⁶⁴ Case 57/65 *Lütticke*, n. 155 above, 211.
¹⁶⁵ See R. Breuer, 'Umweltrechtliche und wirtschaftslenkende Abgaben im europäischen Binnenmarkt' [1992] *DVBl.* 485 to 496.
¹⁶⁶ T. Oppermann, *Europarecht* (C. H. Beck, München, 1991) 395.
¹⁶⁷ See Case 94/74 *Industria Gomma Articoli Vari IGAV* v. *Ente Nazionale per la Cellulosa e per la Carta* [1975] *ECR* 699; Case 74/76 *Ianelli and Volpi S.p.A.* v. *Meroni* [1977] *ECR* 557; Case 78/76 *Steinike und Weinlig*, n. 48 above.
¹⁶⁸ Case 35/76 *Simmenthal I*, n. 43 above, 1871; Case 46/76 *Bauhuis* v. *The Netherlands* [1977] *ECR* 5.
¹⁶⁹ See A. Furrer, 'Nationale Umweltschutzkompetenzen in der EG und im EWR' [1992] *AJP* 1517 at 1522; E. Grabitz, 'Handlungsspielräume der EG-Mitgliedstaaten zur Verbesserung des Umweltschutzes: Am Beispiel der Umweltabgaben und -subventionen' [1989] *RIW* 623 at 635.
¹⁷⁰ See Kapteyn and VerLoren van Themaat, n. 40 above, 369, with reference to R. Barents, 'Article 95 en de Gemeenschappelijke Markt' [1983] *SEW* 438 at 461. See also Case 15/81 *Gaston Schul* v. *Inspecteur des droits d'importation* [1982] *ECR* 1409.
¹⁷¹ Joined cases C–78 to 83/90, n. 48 above, 1884.
¹⁷² See above in this chapter the section on parafiscal charges and in particular the case law referred to in n. 48 above.
¹⁷³ The question whether such reimbursed charges constitute distorting state aids under Art. 92 does not depend on their classification under Art. 12 or 95; see Ch. 6.

Charges, fees, special levies, and taxes are, generally speaking, financial burdens which are imposed on certain goods. Such charges are generally able to hinder trade and might therefore constitute measures having equivalent effect as trade restrictions under Article 30. The Court has, however, on several occasions stated that they normally fall under the more specific provisions of Articles 12 or 95 EC.[174] In view of the Court's broad conception of disguised discrimination most unjustified cases will fall under the prohibition of Article 95. Still, it seems that the Court wants to avoid a gap in the Treaty allowing Member States to introduce heavy taxes for products not produced at all within a Member State. The Court seems to indicate that it might perhaps apply the provisions of Articles 30–7 in cases where national taxation jeopardizes the free movement of goods without falling under the prohibition of Article 95.[175] Normally, however, all kind of eco-taxes fall under Article 95 EC.

The Non-discrimination Requirement

Article 95(1) requires a non-discriminatory application of national taxes.[176] This can be the case for generally higher taxation of foreign products[177] or a tax reduction which applies only to domestic producers.[178] This principle constitutes an absolute guarantee and applies even to cases with very small tax differences.[179] The prohibition of Article 95 applies also to the imposition of a higher tax on exported goods,[180] while it does not cover the imposition of a lower tax on imported goods in relation to domestically produced goods.[181] Article 95(2) is intended to eliminate protectionist attempts in the form of *prima facie* indistinctly applicable tax barriers.[182]

Additionally, Article 96 provides that any reimbursement of internal taxation should not exceed the internal taxation imposed on the goods concerned

---

[174] Case 74/76, n. 166 above, 557; Joined cases C–78 to 83/90, n. 48 above, 1884.

[175] See Case 31/67 *August Stier* v. *Hauptzollamt Hamburg* [1968] *ECR* 351 at 359 and more recently Case C–47/88 *Commission* v. *Denmark (Registrstion Duty)* [1990] *ECR* I–4509 at 4530 ff.

[176] It is very similar to Art. III:2 GATT, first sentence. See e.g. P. Demaret and R. Stewardson, 'Border Tax Adjustment under GATT and EC Law and General Implications for Environmental Taxes' [1994] *JWT* 5 at 41.

[177] Case C–105/91 *Commission* v. *Greece (Automobile Taxes)* [1992] *ECR* I–5871 or Case C–327/90 *Commission* v. *Greece (Different Taxable Amounts)* [1992] *ECR* I–3033.

[178] Case 148/77 *H. Hansen Jun. et al.* v. *Hauptzollamt Flensburg* [1978] *ECR* 1787 at 1806.

[179] Case C–105/91 *Automobile Taxes*, n. 177 above, 5871.

[180] Case 142/77, n. 158 above, 1557.

[181] A case of discrimination against nationals; see e.g. Case 86/78 *SA des Grandes Distilleries Peureux* v. *Directeur des Services Fiscaux* [1979] *ECR* 897, as referred to by O. Brunetti, *EG-Rechtsverträglichkeit als Kriterium der nationalen Umweltpolitik* (Schulthess und Stämpfli, Zürich und Bern, 1993) 114; see also Ch. 2 for general considerations on the non-discrimination principle.

[182] This corresponds to GATT Art. III:2 second sentence. See e.g Demaret and Stewardson, n. 176 above, 41 or E.-U. Petersmann, 'Settlement of International Environmental Disputes in GATT and the EC—Comparative Legal Aspects' in N. Blokker and S. Muller, *Towards More Effective Supervision by International Organizations—Essays in Honour of Henry G. Schermers* (Martinus Nijhoff, Dordrecht, 1994) 165 at 167 ff.

whether directly or indirectly.[183] Article 96 applies only to indirect taxes and does not cover taxes which are not imposed on products but 'upon the producing undertaking in the very varied aspects of its general commercial and financial activity'; the latter cannot be reimbursed under Article 96.[184] In relation to specific prior-stage taxes[185] the Court refuses to allow Member States to levy an adjusting charge on imports in respect of a domestic specific prior charge. In the *Denkavit* case[186] the Court held that a 'charge to which an imported product is subject must impose the same duty on national products and identical imported products *at the same marketing stage* . . . and the *chargeable event* giving rise to the duty must also be identical in the case of both products'.[187] This may have important consequences for the applicability of border tax adjustments related to a general energy tax or carbon tax, if the Court treats them in the same way.[188]

General differences in taxation of different categories of products are not covered by Article 95.[189] Nevertheless, this provision applies to 'similar products'.[190] It is interpreted by the Court in a way which shall prevent any unjustified differentiation between categories of equivalent goods. The Court considers products to be similar if they 'have similar characteristics and meet the same needs from the point of view of consumers'.[191] Article 95 does not apply only to identical products. The Court also considers a product's competitive character on the market[192] and the possible substitution of one product by another.[193] Thus,

[183] The term 'directly' does not imply that direct taxes can also be reimbursed but merely relates to taxes levied on final products while 'indirectly' relates to raw-materials and semi-finished goods used in the manufacture of exported goods; see Case 45/64 *Commission* v. *Italy* (*Tax Refund*) [1965] *ECR* 1057; see also D. Wyatt and A. Dashwood, *European Community Law* (3rd edn., Sweet & Maxwell, London, 1993), 203 to 204.

[184] Case 45/64, n. 183 above, 1066. See for details Demaret and Stewardson, n. 176 above, 42.

[185] This does not apply to the VAT (Value Added Tax) which is governed by a specific Community regime, see Ch. 10.

[186] Case 132/78 *Denkavit*, n. 44 above.   [187] *Ibid.*, 1934 to 1935.

[188] See for more detailed considerations on this point and the possible solutions: Demaret and Stewardson, n. 176 above, 46 and 47.

[189] The issue of 'border tax adjustments' according to differences in the tax systems of several Member States is treated in Ch. 10.

[190] See the abundant discussion on 'like products' in the GATT under Arts. I and III, e.g. Petersmann, n. 91 above, 63.

[191] See Case 45/75 *Rewe Zentrale des Lebensmittel-Großhandels GmbH* v. *Hauptzollmat Landau Pfalz* [1976] *ECR* 181 at 194 and Case 169/78 *Commission* v. *Italy* (*Tax Arrangements Applicable to Spirits II*)[1980] *ECR* 385 at 400.

[192] A Member State has, however, also to take into account the possible evolution of the market situation, such as stated by the Court in a case concerning the British tax differentiation for beer and wine: Case 170/78 *Commission* v. *United Kingdom* (*Tax Arrangements Applying to Wine*) [1980] *ECR* 417 at 433 or Case 184/85 *Commission* v. *Italy* (*Consumer Tax on Bananas*) [1987] *ECR* 2013 at 2026.

[193] See, however, the earlier decisions where the Court tried to find a set of criteria normally applied in the field of tax law, customs law, or in statistics for the differentiation of certain classes of goods, such as in Case 27/67 *Fink-Frucht GmbH* v. *Hauptzollamt München-Landsbergerstrasse* [1968] *ECR* 327 at 347, as referred to by Brunetti, n. 181 above, 116. This more static principle is also applied in certain GATT panel decisions on like products, see e.g. Australia—Subsidy on Ammonium Sulphate [1952] 2 *GATT BISD* 188, para. 8 or Germany—Treatment of Imports of Sardines [1953] *GATT BISD*, 1st suppl., 53 to 59; see also J. H. Jackson and W. Davey, *Legal Problems of International Economic Relations* (West Publ. Co., St. Paul, 1986), 443 ff.

Article 95's second sentence has to be read in a manner which also prohibits indirect protection to domestic goods which can be used for the same purpose.[194] This is also important in cases where a specific product is not produced internally and therefore a strict prohibition of discrimination against equal goods would not apply.[195]

Case: Recently, there has a risen a dispute on the compatibility of a planned Belgian charge on non-reusable food containers and products.[196] The Belgian Government planned the introduction of such a charge where manufacturers and distributors of mineral water, beer, and soft drinks did not introduce reusable containers on a voluntary basis. It was planned that the charge should cover non-reusable bottles made of PVC but not those made of glass, PET, or aluminium, as the latter could more easily be recycled or destroyed with less environmental harm. While Belgian producers mostly used PET for their plastic bottles, imports from France consisted mainly of PVC bottles. The French producers and the Belgian importers concerned, backed by the Commission, considered the planned measure to be discriminatory as it mainly hit imports from France. In the meantime the introduction of the tax was postponed several times and limited in scope by special exemptions for materials other than PVC.[197]

Environmental Charges and Taxes

While certain differentiations are considered to be unjustified cases of discrimination which affect trade,[198] others may be justified for legitimate reasons.[199] Under the current case law objective criteria can include grounds of differences in the products themselves or of differences in production process, raw material, or origin.[200] This applies also to any differentiation on environmental grounds.[201] Community law recognizes the importance of environmental taxes

---

[194] See Kapteyn and VerLoren van Themaat, n. 40 above, 370.

[195] See for a detailed overview of the existing case law Demaret and Stewardson, n. 176 above, 49 ff.

[196] See e.g. notes in [1993] *EuZW* 108; see also *Neue Zürcher Zeitung* (23 Dec. 1993) 25; the project has, however, for the time being been postponed, see *Neue Zürcher Zeitung* (31 Mar. 1994) 33.

[197] It is interesting to observe that the Commission's proposal for a new dir. on packaging introduced a limitation to domestic environmental charges on goods (Art. 15) which hindered Belgian taxation of PVC bottles and was highly controversial in the Council. It was rejected by Germany, The Netherlands, Denmark, and Belgium in a first attempt in June 1994, see *Neue Zürcher Zeitung* (10 June 1994) 22; In a second round, however, the dir. was adopted after Belgium decided to support the Commision's proposal.

[198] See the abundant case law of the Court of Justice: e.g. Case 148/77, n. 178 above, 1787, for an unjustified discrimination between liquors; Case 168/78, n. 158 above, 347, for an unjustified differentiation between Whisky and Cognac.

[199] see e.g. Case 184/85, n. 192 above, 2013, for a justified differentiation between bananas and Italian fruit; Case 21/79 *Commission v. Italy (Recycled Oil)* [1980] *ECR* 1: justified differentiation between fresh oil and recycled oil; Case 200/85 *Diesel Engines*, n. 159 above, 3971, for a justified differentiation between diesel engines and others.

[200] See Case 243/84 *Criminal Proceedings against John Walker & Sons* [1986] *ECR* 877 at 884; for details see Demaret and Stewardson, n. 176, above, 54.

[201] Grabitz, n. 169 above, 635; Becker, n. 15 above, 69.

as an essential element of national environmental policy.[202] In the case of green taxes, the tax itself and its amount must be justified for environmental reasons.[203] The importance of environmental or 'green' taxes will increase as they constitute important and efficient instruments for the implementation of the 'polluter pays' principle.[204]

Environmental charges are normally used to internalize environmental costs which arise from certain products without being expressed in their market price.[205] By imposing an additional charge and thereby raising the price of a product, the authorities try to correct market failures and to internalize the additional environmental costs of the products concerned. The cost can arise from the consumption of certain goods, from their production or their difficult recycling or disposal. By using the collected charges for the reparation or prevention of certain damage the authorities try to correct market failure. In certain cases, however, such a correction or adjustment of the consumer price is not possible and the charges are used to guide consumers away from certain goods and to make other similar goods with better environmental characteristics more attractive.[206] This is, for example, the case for carbon dioxide-taxes or the preferential treatment of certain types of fuel.[207]

Case: An example is a recently introduced tax on non-biodegradable plastic bags in Italy. Every non-biodegradable plastic bag which is produced or marketed carries an environmental tax of 100 Lire to be paid by the consumer. As a non-discriminatory measure which does not constitute a disguised restriction on trade this measure seems perfectly acceptable under Article 30 as well as under Article 95 EEC Treaty.[208]

Several German municipalities, among them, for example, Frankfurt am Main and Kassel, have imposed local taxes on certain non-reusable packaging products such as disposable containers and cutlery, mostly used in fast-food restaurants. In an answer to several questions in the European Parliament the Commission underlined that such taxes, in general, did not contravene Article 95 or the existing secondary law in the field.[209] 'However, as the individual measures and obligations introduced . . . do not form a uniform set of rules, the Commission is also examining the measures, to see whether the

---

[202] Art. 130r(2) EC; Case 200/85 *Diesel Engines*, n. 159 above, 3971.

[203] See Case 433/85 *Jacques Feldain* v. *Directeur des Services Fiscaux du Haut Rhin* [1987] *ECR* 3521.

[204] See on this instrument e.g. J. Stenger, *Das Steuerrecht als Instrument des Umweltschutzes— Möglichkeiten und Grenzen des Steuerrechts zur Erfüllung umweltpolitischer Ziele* (Peter Lang, Frankfurt a.M., 1995), or M. Rodi, *Umweltsteuern: das Steuerrecht als Instrument der Umweltpolitik* (Nomos, Baden-Baden, 1993).

[205] See e.g. W. J. Baumol and W. E. Oates, *The Theory of Environmental Policy* (2nd edn., Cambridge University Press, Cambridge, 1988), 23 to 25.

[206] See e.g. a recent German decision on the *Länder's* competence to introduce a special tax on fast-food containers for the prevention of waste, questions of Community law were not at stake: Bundesverwaltungsgericht (Germany), 19 Aug. 1994, Aktennotiz 8 N 1.93, reported in *Süddeutsche Zeitung* (20/21 Aug. 1994) 1; see, however, the questions in the European Parliament (E–327/95 and P–387/95) and the answer by the Commission, [1995] *OJ* C175/33.

[207] See for details Brunetti, n. 181, above, 112.

[208] Example cited by Krämer, n. 15 above, 142.

[209] Art. 3(2) of Dir. 92/12/EEC on indirect taxation [1992] *OJ* L76/1.

local rules adopted constitute infringements of the provisions of the Treaty concerning the free movement of goods (Articles 30 to 36 EC)'.[210]

Environmental Differentiation or Discrimination

Although Article 95 aims at eliminating any discriminatory taxation concerning similar products it is sometimes very difficult to draw the line between environmentally justified taxes and those taken for protectionist means. Normally, environmental taxes should be applied to all like goods in the same way, whether they are of domestic or foreign origin, as their environmental impact remains the same. Therefore national measures taken on environmental grounds must apply to domestic and imported goods in a way which does not favour national production. The argument of the difficult decision of whether foreign products fulfil certain domestic requirements is normally not acceptable.[211]

In a very recent decision in Case C–157/91 *Commission* v. *Greece*[212] the Court was confronted with a Greek special consumption tax on cars not being provided with a special anti-pollution equipment. This tax was not levied on those cars which had been built according to new technology, irrespective of their internal or foreign origin. Cars which were still built according to the old technology were exempted from the tax under certain conditions. Greek cars were automatically exempted if they had been built before a certain date, while imported cars had to undergo complex administrative procedures to benefit from the same reduction. The Court considered such discriminatory treatment as contrary to Article 95 despite the Greek objections concerning the examination of the production method of imported cars.

Still, even if national taxes apply to domestic and imported goods in the same way the concrete market situation may lead to cases where the tax indirectly discriminates against foreign producers.[213] In these cases it is particularly important to consider the environmental justification of such measures. The justified differentiation on environmental grounds may take into account e.g. the content of pollutants, the mode of production[214] or the effects of a product after its use, such as the possibilities for its recycling.[215]

---

[210] Questions in the European Parliament, n. 206 above.

[211] Case 21/79 *Recycled Oil*, n. 199 above, 8; Case C–105/91 *Automobile Taxes*, n. 177 above, 5895.

[212] Case C–105/91 *Automobile Taxes*, n. 177 above, 5897.

[213] See Ch. 2 and, in particular, P. Garrone, 'La discrimination indirecte en droit communautaire: vers une théorie générale' [1994] *RTDE* 425 to 449.

[214] Nevertheless, this may raise very important issues with regard to the territoriality principle and the sovereignty of Member States to decide their own level of environmental protection. The Court did not approach this problem in Case 21/79 *Recycled Oil*, n. 199 above, 12. See for a similar problem arising in GATT: United States—Restrictions on Imports of Tuna, unadopted Panel Report of 16 Aug. 1991, reprinted in (1992) 32 *ILM* 1594 ff. or the Belgian Family Allowances Case [1953] *GATT BISD*, 1st supplement, 59 to 62.

[215] See also M. Danusso and R. Denton, 'Does the European Court of Justice look for a Protectionist Motive under Article 95?' [1990] *LIEI* 67 at 89.

In Case 21/79 *Commission* v. *Italy*[216] the Court was confronted with an Italian measure favouring oil produced from recycled waste oil. This type of oil was granted a tax reduction which did not apply to normal oil. Nevertheless, physically regenerated oil and fresh oil could not be distinguished. The Italian government justified its tax differentiation, among other reasons, by environmental considerations. The Court did at least not object to these arguments. The Court held that Italy was permitted to distinguish between 'physically' identical products on the grounds of production process and raw materials used. As the tax reduction, however, applied only to the domestic production (imports were not eligible for the tax reduction) it was considered a discriminatory measure prohibited under Article 95.

The Court will always analyse whether the distinction is made on the basis of an objective criterion. Even in those cases where the objective seems reasonable the Court will look behind such measures to analyse whether they constitute disguised protectionist measures.[217] Such a situation can arise even if the differentiation seems to be reasonable from a *prima facie* assessment[218] but only or mostly[219] affects imported goods and thus should be replaced by a non-protectionist measure. There are a few cases concerning car taxes where the Commission has appealed to the Court after a Member State had introduced national tax incentives or disincentives, or charges in its national legal system in order to differentiate between different types of motor vehicles.[220] They illustrate how difficult it is for the Court of Justice to distinguish between differential taxes for genuine environmental reasons[221] and those used in an ambiguous way to hinder imports and favour national producers.[222]

[216] Case 21/79 *Recycled Oil*, n. 199 above, 12.

[217] See for details on the Court's non-discrimination test and protectionist domestic measures Danusso and Denton, n. 215 above, 67 ff., and Brunetti, n. 181 above, 115 to 141.

[218] See e.g. Case C–132/88 *Commission* v. *Greece (Taxation of Motor Cars)* [1990] *ECR* I–1567 at 1593, para. 17 with reference to the consistent case law. See for a detailed analysis of the test applied by the Court under Art. 95 in Danusso and Denton, n. 215 above, 67.

[219] See e.g. also Case C–343/90 *M. J. Lourenço Dias* v. *Director da Alfândaga do Porto* [1992] *ECR* I–4673.

[220] These cases make only implied reference to environmental protection. The tax differentiation is mostly justified by the different engines and cubic capacities. Powerful engines and high cubic capacities are typical for expensive luxury cars; see the considerations in Case 200/85 *Diesel Engines*, n. 159 above, 3971. They are, however, also important factors for the ecological classification of a car. It seems therefore very important to analyse these cases in this context.

[221] e.g. in Case C–132/88, n. 218 above, 1567, the Court considered the Greek tax system to be reasonable although its highest tax class hit only foreign cars. Competition among foreign cars and national cars was still guaranteed in other tax classes.

[222] In Case 112/84 *Michel Humblot* v. *Directeur des Services Fiscaux* [1985] *ECR* 1367 at 1375 and Case 433/85, n. 203 above, 521, the Court considered the effects of the tax to be protectionist. See, for a tax difference concerning newly imported used cars and domestic used cars, Case C–345/93 *Fazenda Pública and Ministério Público* v. *Américo João Nunes Tadeu* [1995] *ECR* I–479.

4

Environmental Justification for National Restrictions

INTRODUCTION

As has been shown, the Community principle of free movement of goods, in particular through the Court's broad interpretation of Article 30 under the *Dassonville* formula, sets very important restraints on national measures for the protection of the environment. A great number of domestic measures risk being incompatible with Community law even if they are applied in a non-discriminatory way. The Treaty itself, however, contains an exception from the prohibitions in Articles 30 and 34. Under Article 36 national measures for the protection of the life and health of humans, animals, and plants, as well as for other selected reasons, are justified in spite of their infringement of the free movement of goods principle.

The environment is not explicitly mentioned in Article 36 and the Court favours a narrow interpretation of this provision. Nevertheless, domestic measures for the protection of the environment can be included in Article 36 if they have a direct effect on the life and health of humans, animals, and plants. Because of the narrow interpretation of Article 36 and the awareness of the need for local and national responses to specific environmental preferences and problems in the absence of comprehensive Community solutions, the Court has developed a second set of bases which enable Member States to adopt domestic safeguards. Under the *Cassis de Dijon* doctrine, or the rule of reason, the Court has established that domestic measures for the safeguard of certain 'mandatory requirements' of the Treaty, such as the protection of the environment, are not covered by the prohibition in Article 30 EC. Domestic measures are, however, only covered by this doctrine if they are applied to domestic and imported goods equally. The Court also applies the conditions, laid down in Article 36 second sentence, to measures under the *Cassis de Dijon* doctrine.

The protection of health and life of humans, animals, and plants under Article 36 is most often very closely linked to environmental protection in general. Thus, the two sets of reasons—Article 36 and the rule of reason—become very similar in their effect and it is difficult to evaluate the differences in their application. Nevertheless, they differ in concept. Article 34 does not usually require the application of the rule of reason, as non-discriminatory domestic measures are not covered by its prohibition.

GENERAL CONCEPT

In spite of the existence of abundant case law on the free movement of goods
and, in particular, on national measures having equivalent effect to restrictions
on trade, there are few cases which have been dealt with on environmental
grounds by the Court. This is particularly interesting if one takes into account
the fact that environmental standards and regulations are typical examples of
domestic measures which hinder trade.[1]

On the other hand, the protection of the environment was for a long time
only very weakly established in the Treaty[2] and it was thus difficult for the Court
to refer to ecological reasons when interpreting Community law.[3] Nevertheless,
it will be shown that the Court in its case law relatively early took into account
the protection of the environment, although it did so sometimes when referring
to other (economic) objectives of the Treaty.[4] In the absence of any environmental provisions in the Treaty, the most important case law on environmental
questions has for a long time been the application of Article 36 for the protection of health and life of humans, animals, and plants.

JUSTIFICATION OF NATIONAL RESTRICTIONS UNDER ARTICLE 36

Exception Clause

Article 36 EC represents a classic exception clause, as found in most international agreements on trade and particularly those regulating free trade.[5] Many
bilateral co-operation treaties, commercial treaties, and naval treaties include
such safeguard measures which permit the exceptional non-application of certain treaty provisions for reasons of public health and disease or pest control.[6]

---

[1] See e.g. B. Beutler, R. Bieber, J. Pipkorn, and J. Streil, *Die Europäische Gemeinschaft—Rechtsordnung
und Politik* (3rd. edn., Nomos, Baden-Baden, 1987), 282.

[2] See Ch. 7.

[3] As laid down in Art. 164 EC: '[t]he Court of Justice shall ensure that in the interpretation and
application of this Treaty the law is observed.' The Court gives rulings concerning the interpretation of the Treaty by means of a preliminary ruling under Art. 177 EC .

[4] Besides referring to Article 36 EC the Court repeatedly invoked 'the economic development of
the Community'; see Joined cases 3, 4, and 6/76 *Criminal Proceedings against Cornelis Kramer et al.
(Biological Resources of the Sea)* [1977] *ECR* 1279 or Case 91/79 *Commission* v. *Italy (Detergents)* [1980]
ECR 1099 at 1106.

[5] See e.g. Art. XX GATT or Art. 20 of the Free Trade Agreement between Switzerland and the
EC; on safeguard clauses in general see I. B. Kravis, *Domestic Interests and International Obligations:
Safeguards in International Trade Obligations* (University of Pennsylvania Press, Philadelphia, 1963).

[6] For a detailed analysis of the agreements concluded by the United States, see S. Charnovitz,
'Exploring the Environmental Exceptions in the GATT Art. XX' [1991] *JWT* 37 to 55; see also the
explanations on the drafting of Art. 36 and its connections to Art. XX GATT by E.-U. Petersmann,
'Freier Warenverkehr und nationaler Umweltschutz in EWG und EWR' [1993] *Aussenwirtschaft* 95
at 107.

The general system of the Treaty must allow Member States to take certain measures on grounds of public order or national interest. As long as the Community does not itself take all the necessary measures to prevent specific negative or dangerous consequences from the free movement of goods, the Member States must bear the responsibility for these areas.[7]

The development of the approximation of laws within the Community shows, however, that the Community works towards a continuous limitation of the application of Article 36 by the Member States.[8] The position of the Court has also been to insist that Article 36 be strictly interpreted and not extended to justifications not referred to therein.[9] The exceptional admissibility of diverging national measures does not change their trade-hindering character. In view of the establishment of the common market and of the necessary protection at Community level, national measures under Article 36 are only legitimate as long as the Community itself has not taken comprehensive measures to avoid the inherent dangers.[10] After harmonization of standards or approximation of national laws in the areas mentioned by Article 36 or developed under the rule of reason, application of Article 36 or invocation of the rule of reason by national governments is no longer possible in principle.[11] Article 36 does not operate as a general exemption for domestic action in the areas referred to therein but can only be invoked where no comprehensive harmonization at Community level exists.[12]

Recent developments in this area, however, might indicate that in most cases the Community no longer attempts the complete or comprehensive harmonization of standards throughout the Community. Certain Member States require the ability to retain or introduce higher environmental standards than the rest of the Community. In response to this, the Community often acts only to establish minimum levels or explicitly to provide the Member States with the opportunity of enacting higher domestic standards. A result of this strategy is Article

[7] See e.g. Case 120/78 *Rewe Zentral AG* v. *Bundesmonopolverwaltung für Branntwein* (*Cassis de Dijon*) [1979] *ECR* 649 at 662; Case 788/79 *Criminal Procedure against Gilli and Andres* [1980] *ECR* 2071 at 2078; see also J. Henke, *EuGH und Umweltschutz* (VVF, München, 1992), 170.

[8] See Ch. 7.

[9] See Case 113/80 *Commission* v. *Ireland* (*Buy Irish Case*) [1981] *ECR* 1625 at 1638; Case 229/83 *Association des Centres Distributeurs Edouard Leclerc* v. *Sàrl 'Au Blé Vert' et al.* [1985] *ECR* 1 at 35. The Court provides, however, a certain reconciliation and dynamic element by the application of the rule of reason or *Cassis de Dijon* doctrine; see above in this chapter on the rule of reason..

[10] See Chs. 8 to 11.

[11] See Part II, Ch. 8, and the consistent case law of the Court, such as Case 5/77 *Carlo Tedeschi* v. *Denkavit* (*Tedeschi/Denkavit*) [1977] *ECR* 1555 at 1576; Case 251/78 *Denkavit Futtermittel* v. *Minister of Food, Agriculture and Forests* (*Denkavit*) [1979] *ECR* 3369 at 3388; for the environment, in particular, Case 172/82 *Syndicat National des Fabricants Raffineurs d'Huile de Graissage et al.* v. *Groupement d'Intérêt Economique Inter-Huiles* (*Inter-Huiles*) [1983] *ECR* 555 or Case C-169/89 *Criminal Proceedings against Gourmetterie Van den Burg* (*Scottish Red Grouse*) [1990] *ECR* I-2143, see most recently C-2/90 *Commission* v. *Belgium* (*Walloon Waste Case*) [1992] *ECR* I-4431.

[12] See M. Dauses, 'L'interdiction des mesures d'éffet équivalent à des restrictions quantitatives à la lumière de la jurisprudence de la CJCE' [1992] *RTDE* 607 at 622.

100a(4), which establishes this model for the general harmonization of laws in the interest of the establishment of the Internal Market. Article 100a(4), as well as specific provisions in recent Community legislation on environmental standards, therefore refers to the general principles of Article 36 and the rule of reason despite an existing harmonization.[13]

The Environment and Article 36

Article 36 explicitly mentions four areas where the provisions of Articles 30 and 34 shall not apply given certain conditions are fulfilled. The first is public morality, public policy, or public security. This, however, does not include general economic objectives.[14] Secondly, it refers to the protection of health and life of humans, animals, or plants; thirdly, the protection of national treasures possessing artistic, historic, or archaeological value; and, finally, the protection of industrial and commercial property. On the whole, Article 36 has provoked an abundance of case law, though not equally concerning all the different areas.[15] In the area of national environmental measures it is first and foremost the second area which provides Member States with the opportunity to take domestic safeguard measures.[16]

Public policy and security seem, in principle, possible grounds for environmental action. The case law on these two terms is, however, somewhat nebulous.[17] It seems that it covers only fundamental national interests which are not covered by one of the other more specific grounds.[18] For environmental measures, the reliance on grounds of protection of health and life of humans, animals, and plants has proved to be much more important.

---

[13] See for details Part II of this study.

[14] Case 95/81 *Commission* v. *Italy* (*Advance Payments*) [1982] *ECR* 2187 at 2204.

[15] See e.g. P. Oliver, *Free Movement of Goods in the E.E.C.* (2nd edn., European Law Centre, London, 1988), 187.

[16] See also U. Becker, *Der Gestaltungsspielraum der EG-Mitgliedstaaten im Spannungsfeld zwischen Umweltschutz und freiem Warenverkehr* (Nomos, Baden-Baden, 1991), 73 and the interesting arguments of A. Skordas, *Umweltschutz und freier Warenverkehr in EWG-Vertrag und GATT* (Apelt, Steinbach, 1986), 103 to 120 on resource management and the guarantee of sufficient energy supply.

[17] See P. J. G. Kapteyn and P. VerLoren van Themaat, *Introduction to the Law of the European Communities* (2nd edn, Kluwer, Deventer, 1989), 393 with reference to the relevant case law and commentaries.

[18] An example from British domestic case law is *R.* v. *Her Majesty's Treasury and the Bank of England, ex parte CENTRO-COM srl*, QBD, 6 Sept. 1993 [1994] 1 *CMLR* 109, where the British authorities invoked public policy reasons under Art. 36 EC for the justification of certain measures related to trade sanctions against Serbia and Montenegro pursuant to UN Security Council Resolution 757; in general, see also Becker, n. 16 above, 72 and 73. The use of the concepts of 'public policy' or 'public security' for environmental measures is rather hard to imagine, see also B. Jadot, 'Mesures nationales de police de l'environnement, libre circulation des marchandises et proportionnalité' [1990] *CDE* 408 at 412 or D. Geradin, 'Free Trade and Environmental Protection in an Integrated Market: A Survey of the Case Law in the United States Supreme Court and the European Court of Justice' (1993) 2 *Journal of Transnational Law and Policy* 141 at 179.

Health and Life of Humans, Animals, and Plants

Including the protection of health and life of humans, animals, and plants as an integrative part of the protection of the environment, Article 36 also provides a basis for national measures for the protection of the environment.[19] The state of the environment clearly has an influence on the health and eventually the life of human beings. On the other hand, the Court has always underlined that it wishes to interpret Article 36 narrowly.[20] Thus it has always linked the application of Article 36 to the protection of health and life of humans, animals, and plants even if it sometimes added the protection of the environment as a further element without indicating, however, whether it was generally included in the mentioned grounds of Article 36.

Finally, the Court has clearly recognised the protection of environment as a mandatory requirement of the Treaty, instead of including it in a general way in Article 36. The Court's distinction, however, is not always clear and seems to be of little importance in view of the existing similarities between Article 36 and the rule of reason.[21]

The most remarkable case law under Article 36 concerns the influence of pesticides on health and the environment.[22] In several cases the Court had to decide on the lawfulness of trade prohibitions and restrictions on pesticides or pesticide-treated products.[23] While in certain cases the Court mentioned only the grounds of protection explicitly referred to in Article 36[24] (health of humans, animals, and plants), it sometimes added the protection of the environment.[25] The level of protection necessary for safeguarding public health is in principle to be set by the Member States.[26]

---

[19] Case 104/75 *Criminal Proceedings against Adriaan De Peijper (De Peijper)* [1976] *ECR* 613 at 635.

[20] See e.g. Case 46/76 *Bauhuis* v. *The Netherlands* [1977] *ECR* 5; Case 113/80 *Buy Irish Case*, n. 9 above; Case 95/81, n. 14 above.

[21] Some authors suggest a criterion of 'direct effect', e.g. L. Krämer, 'Environmental Protection and Art. 30 EEC Treaty' (1993) 30 *CMLRev.* 111 at 118; see also below in this chapter on convergence.

[22] See T. Van Rijn, 'A Review of the Case Law of the Court of Justice on Arts. 30–6 in 1986 and 1987' (1988) 25 *CMLRev.* 593 at 598.

[23] Case 125/88 *Criminal Proceedings against Nijman (Pesticide Residues on Apples)* [1989] *ECR* 3533; a similar case eight years earlier was still treated only under the aspect of health protection, see Case 272/80 *Criminal Proceedings against FNMBP (Plant Protection Products)* [1981] *ECR* 3277 at 3291; see also Case 94/83 *Criminal Proceedings against Heijn (Pesticides)* [1984] *ECR* 3263; Case 54/85 *Ministère Public* v. *Xavier Mirepoix (Pesticides on Fruit)* [1985] *ECR* 1067.

[24] See Case 272/80, n. 23 above, in spite of the fact that The Netherlands and Denmark had referred to environmental reasons; see for their submissions to the Court, 3284 and 3291; see also Henke, n. 7 above, 171.

[25] e.g. Case 125/88, n. 23 above; more oriented towards the health argument because of the pesticides being applied on imported fruit: Case 94/83, n. 23 above, 3280; Case 54/85, n. 23 above, 1077. The climatic conditions mentioned might, however, include an environmental aspect.

[26] Case 104/75 *De Peijper*, n. 19 above, 635. See also the most recent decision in Case 131/93 *Commission* v. *Germany (Freshwater Crayfish)* [1994] *ECR* I–3303. Ludwig Krämer emphasizes, however, that in his view these two judgments are somewhat contradictory and even, to a certain extent,

In its decision in Case 125/88 *Criminal Proceedings against Nijman*[27] the Court had to evaluate the lawfulness of a Dutch measure prohibiting the use and sale of certain kinds of pesticides. The Dutch authorities had begun criminal proceedings against Mr Nijman because he had been found in possession of a prohibited substance. The Netherlands justified their national rules prohibiting this substance by the dangerous effects it could have on the health of the users and the environment. The Commission agreed, adding that there was no comprehensive harmonization of the field by Community law itself and that therefore the Member States were responsible for taking the necessary action. The Court accepted the Dutch measures indicating the dangerous effects of pesticides for the health of humans and animals as well as the environment. Given that the other conditions were also fulfilled, the Court concluded that the measure was lawful under Article 36 EC.

Livestock and Plantations

Apart from the above-mentioned cases concerning the protection of health and life of humans, animals, and plants in general, Article 36 has often been invoked for national measures concerning the protection of livestock and plantations against dangerous pests or diseases.[28] A classical example is the prevention of rabies in rabies-free Member States[29] or more recently 'mad-cow disease'.

Besides the protection of plantations or livestock against pests[30] such an interpretation also includes the objective of guaranteeing the well-being of domestic animals and livestock, for example with respect to the treatment of cows in their stalls or hens in battery-cages.[31] The Community itself has taken many environmental measures to regulate animal experimentation, the transport conditions of animals, the pre-slaughter stunning or the marketing of livestock.[32]

Wild Flora and Fauna

Another important sector in this field is the protection of endangered species of plants and animals. Although there are some indications that Article 36 was primarily aimed at the protection of livestock and agricultural crops, it is today also

incompatible. In his view, Member States are allowed to establish a reasonable degree of protection, but not necessarily the highest degree possible, see L. Krämer, *European Environmental Law, Case Book* (Sweet & Maxwell, London, 1993), 94 to 108. See also Ch. 5 for more details .

[27] Case 125/88, n. 23 above.

[28] See Case 40/82 *Commission* v. *United Kingdom* (*Newcastle Disease*) [1984] *ECR* 283 at 300; see also A. Epiney and T. M. J. Möllers, *Freier Warenverkehr und nationaler Umweltschutz* (Heymann, Köln, 1992), 101.

[29] D. Lasok and J. W. Bridge, *The Law and Institutions of the European Communities* (5th edn., Butterworths, London, 1991), 75.

[30] See Matthies, Art. 36, para. 15, in E. Grabitz and M. Hilf (eds.), *Kommentar zur EU* (2nd edn., C. H. Beck, München, 1990 ff.).

[31] Joined cases 141 to 143/81 *Criminal Proceedings against G. Holdijk et al.* (*Protection of Animals for Fattening*) [1982] *ECR* 1299 at 1314.

[32] See L. Krämer, 'Community Environmental Policy—Towards a Systematic Approach' [1992] *YEL* 151 at 153.

applicable to the protection of wild species.[33] As they belong to the natural heritage of a country[34] it is important that Member States be allowed to take the necessary measures to protect their own natural treasures and resources.[35] As in the field of livestock or plantations, the Court initially exhibited a tendency to consider the protection of natural treasures such as fishery resources to be a mandatory 'economic' requirement of the Treaty which allowed the Member States to protect the existence and the future prosperity of certain economic sectors. In its decision in Joined cases 3, 4, and 6/76 *Biological Resources of the Sea*[36] the Court considered the measures taken by The Netherlands to protect the existing fishery resources to be a mandatory requirement to ensure 'a steady optimum yield from fishing' and thereby the optimal and continuing prosperity of the fishing sector,[37] in spite of the Advocate General's proposal that the measures should be considered as justified for environmental reasons.[38]

Case: In Joined cases 3, 4, and 6 /76 *Biological Resources of the Sea*[39] in 1976 the Court was concerned with Dutch participation in an international fishery resources protection agreement and the national implementing measures. Apart from the very interesting questions concerning the external competence of the Member States and the Community in the field of fishery resources[40] the Court had to adjudicate on the trade-hindering character of the established quotas under the Dutch regulation. The Court held that such a measure was capable of affecting the production and trade in fish but that it was decisive 'that in the long term these measures are necessary to ensure a steady, optimum yield from fishing'.[41]

In a later judgment concerning a Dutch measure for the protection of a specific species of birds,[42] in my opinion, the Court implicitly approved national measures for the protection of certain wild species under Article 36,[43] as is also

[33] Implicitly also submitted by Krämer, n. 21 above, 118.

[34] See, however, the important Community legislation in this area and e.g. the reference to species of wild birds as a common heritage of the Community. See Case C–169/89 *Scottish Red Grouse*, n. 11 above.

[35] See the relevant case law under Art. XX GATT, e.g. Canada—Measures Affecting Exports of Unprocessed Salmon and Herring [1989] *GATT BISD*, 35th suppl., 98 to 115.

[36] Joined cases 3, 4, and 6/76 *Biological Resources of the Sea*, n. 4 above, 1315; for comments see D. Wyatt, 'European Court of July 14, 1976, cases 3, 4, and 6/76' [1977] *ELR* 47.

[37] Later, however, the Community itself introduced measures for the protection of fishery resources; see e.g. Council Reg. 3094/86/EEC laying down certain technical measures for the conservation of fishery resources [1986] *OJ* L288/1.

[38] See the Opinion of Advocate General Trabucchi in Joined cases 3, 4, and 6/76 *Biological Resources of the Sea*, n. 4 above, 1327; see also Henke, n. 7 above, 171.

[39] *Ibid.*, n. 4 above.   [40] See Ch. 11.

[41] The Court held further: 'therefore, the fact that such measures have the effect, for a short time, of reducing the quantities that the States concerned are able to exchange between themselves, cannot lead to these measures being classified among those prohibited by the Treaty': Joined cases 3, 4, and 6/76 *Biological Resources of the Sea*, n. 4 above, 1313.

[42] Case C–169/89 *Scottish Red Grouse*, above, n. 11.

[43] By referring to the existing Community law, the non-existing danger for the species concerned and the extraterritorial scope of the Dutch measure: Case C–169/89 *Scottish Red Grouse*, n. 11 above, 2161 to 2165. For the same opinion see Geradin, n. 18 above, 179.

provided for by the existing Community secondary legislation.[44] Nevertheless, there remain many open questions concerning the geographical scope of such measures and the actual existing danger for the relevant species.[45]

Case: In its decision in Case C–169/89 *Criminal Proceedings against Gourmetterie Van den Burg (Scottish Red Grouse)*[46] the Court was concerned with a Dutch law for the protection of birds and its compatibility with the Treaty obligations. The owner of a grocery shop had been found in possession of certain species of birds which were protected by Dutch legislation while the corresponding Community secondary law did not include them among the protected species. The Court dealt with the case under the aspect of existing Community law and came to the result that the Dutch legislation was incompatible with the exhaustive character of the existing Community rules. Advocate General Van Gerven, however, referred also to Article 36 which, in his view, also indirectly concerned the protection of the environment.[47] The Advocate General held that Article 36 included the protection of birds or other endangered species, possibly even of wild species in general.[48] The case was, however, complicated by the fact that the Dutch measure aimed at the protection of a species which did not occur in The Netherlands.[49]

RULE OF REASON (*CASSIS DE DIJON* DOCTRINE)

General Observations

As has been demonstrated in Chapter 3, the Court has given a very broad interpretation to 'measures having equivalent effect to quantitative restrictions on imports' under Article 30 EC (*Dassonville formula*).[50] At the same time its interpretation of the lawful exceptions granted under Article 36 of the Treaty is rather narrow. Both developments together make it literally impossible for a Member State to take measures to safeguard certain public interests which are not covered explicitly or implicitly by Article 36.

Mandatory Requirement

The Court has developed, in its *Cassis de Dijon* doctrine, a concept which allows for non-discriminatory national measures which are justified by public interests, although they would otherwise constitute measures having equivalent effect to quantitative restrictions on trade in the sense of the *Dassonville* formula. The orig-

---

[44] Reg. 3626/82/EEC [1982] *OJ* L384/1: Art. 15 refers to Art. 36 EC.
[45] See Ch. 5.
[46] Case C–169/89 *Scottish Red Grouse*, n. 11 above.
[47] Van Gerven AG concentrated on the application of Art. 36 as only imported birds were concerned, Case 169/89 *Scottish Red Grouse*, n. 11 above, 2154.
[48] See the AG's view in Case C–169/89 *Scottish Red Grouse*, n. 11 above, 2154.
[49] See, on the extraterritorial scope of national environmental measures, Ch. 5.
[50] Mainly through its *Dassonville* formula, developed first in Case 8/74 *Procureur du Roi* v. *B. and G. Dassonville (Dassonville)* [1974] *ECR* 837; see Ch. 3.

inal list of mandatory requirements as given by the Court, however, was only indicative and not a complete enumeration of accepted grounds of justification.[51] Since then the Court has indicated that national measures are also justified in the interests of the improvement of working conditions, the reduction of costs in public health, the promotion of culture in general etc.[52]

Obviously, the protection of the environment is not referred to as an autonomous field in Article 36. Although certain measures can be considered as being covered by the 'protection of health and life of humans, animals or plants' this is a rather unsatisfactory way of guaranteeing the protection of the environment.[53] It seemed therefore very convenient and necessary to extend the open list of 'mandatory requirements' under the rule of reason[54] to the protection of the environment.[55] The Court had previously called the protection of the environment a mandatory requirement of the Treaty,[56] but in relation to national measures, it was first and foremost in its decision in the Case 302/86 *Danish Bottles* in 1988 that the Court integrated the environment into the existing list of areas covered by the *Cassis de Dijon* doctrine.[57]

Case: In its famous decision in Case 302/86 *Commission* v. *Denmark (Danish Bottles)* the Court was confronted with a Danish measure concerning the use of containers for beer and soft drinks. The measure obliged domestic producers and importers to use only re-usable bottles and to establish a deposit-and-return system for empty containers. The Court held that in principle such national measures were in the interests of the protection of the environment and therefore had to be accepted under the rule of reason as long as they fulfilled the Court's set of conditions. The installed return-system for bottles was considered lawful, while certain accompanying rules which limited the number of authorized bottle types were held disproportionate.[58]

---

[51] See Case 120/78 *Cassis de Dijon*, n. 7 above, 662, by using the term 'in particular'.

[52] See for an overview on the precedents Kapteyn and VerLoren van Themaat, n. 17 above, 389 to 390.

[53] See also C. Joerges, J. Falke, H.-W. Micklitz, and G. Brüggemeier, *Die Sicherheit von Konsumgütern und die Entwicklung der Europäischen Gemeinschaft* (Nomos, Baden-Baden, 1988), 311.

[54] Kapteyn and VerLoren van Themaat, n. 17 above, 387.

[55] For the first time explicitly in Case 240/83 *Procureur de la République* v. *Association de Défense des Brûleurs d'Huiles Usagées (ADBHU)* [1985] *ECR* 531, commented on e.g. by R. Kreutzberger, 'Der Umweltschutz als Aufgabe der Europäischen Gemeinschaften' [1986] *ZfU* 169 to 180; but see also Joined cases 3, 4, and 6/76 *Biological Resources of the Sea*, n. 4 above; see Jadot, n. 18 above, 411.

[56] Case 240/83 *ADBHU*, n. 55 above, 549, para. 13.

[57] Case 302/86 *Commission* v. *Denmark (Danish Bottles)* [1988] *ECR* 4607. For comments see e.g. P. Kromarek, 'Environmental Protection and Free Movement of Goods: The Danish Bottle Case' [1990] *J Env. L* 87 to 107 or T. Sexton, 'Enacting National Environmental Laws More Stringent than Other States' Laws under the European Community' (1991) 100 *Cornell International Law Journal* (1991) 563 to 593; J. Jan, 'European Environmental Law and Free Trade' [1989] *Journal of the Law Society of Scotland* 211 to 214; Jadot, n. 18 above, or K. H. Kohlepp, 'Beschränkungen des freien Warenverkehrs in der EG durch nationale Umweltschutzbestimmungen' [1989] *DB* 1455 to 1457; H.-W. Rengeling and K. Heinz, 'Die dänische Pfandflaschenregelung' [1990] *JuS* 613 to 617 or W. Schutt and J. Steffens, 'EuGH-Entscheidung' [1989] *RIW* 447 to 449.

[58] Case 302/86 *Danish Bottles*, n. 57 above, 4608; see for details Ch. 5.

From the Court's declaration in this case and in later cases[59] it seems that the protection of the environment has now found its place among the grounds of justification under the rule of reason. The development of Community law, and particularly the changes in the Treaty with the coming into force of the Single European Act,[60] have given the protection of the environment its character as an essential aspect of the Treaty which has to be taken into account when establishing the common market and in all other areas of Community policy.[61]

Nevertheless, there are still only a few cases where the Court has used its principles as developed under the rule of reason for the protection of the environment. Since the *Danish Bottles Case* there has been only one case where the Court itself explicitly referred to the protection of the environment as a mandatory requirement recognized by Community law for the justification of a national measure challenged under Article 30.[62]

Case: In Case C–2/90 *Commission v. Belgium (Walloon Waste Case)*[63] the Commission challenged the lawfulness of a decree by the Walloon Regional Executive which banned waste imports from other regions. As far as transfrontier movements of dangerous waste were concerned the Court considered the existing Community legislation in the field to be exhaustive;[64] for transboundary movements of general waste, however, the Court found that the Walloon Region could maintain its regional legislation. In this field Community law did not contain an exhaustive regulation.[65] On the applicability of Article 36 or the rule of reason the Court ruled that the accumulations of waste 'even before they reach levels that will present dangers to health, constitute a danger for the environment, especially when considering the limited capacity of each region or locality to receive them'. The Court thus accepted the invocation of the rule of reason, considering that the Walloon measure was not discriminating.[66]

In its decision in Case 380/87 *Enichem et al.* v. *Comune di Cinisello Balsamo (Italian Plastic Bags)*[67] the Court was concerned with a local measure which prohibited the local shopkeepers to provide their customers with non-biodegradable plastic bags or similar containers. The local authorities justified the measure with the difficult environmental

---

[59] Case C–2/90 *Walloon Waste Case*, n. 11 above.
[60] See e.g. Arts. 100a(4) and (5), 130r ff., and 118a EC.   [61] Art. 130r(2) EC.
[62] See Case C–2/90 *Walloon Waste Case*, n. 11, above; see, .however, also Case C–195/90 *Commission v. Germany (Tax on Heavy Goods Vehicles)* [1992] *ECR* I–3141 at 3184 where the Court referred to its case law but did not apply Art. 30.
[63] Case C–2/90 *Walloon Waste Case*, n. 11 above; for comments see e.g. P. v. Wilmowsky, 'Waste Disposal in the Internal Market: The State of Play after the ECJ's Ruling on the Walloon Import Ban' (1993) 30 *CMLRev.* 541 to 570 (in German: P. v. Wilmowsky, 'Abfall und freier Warenverkehr: Bestandesaufnahme nach dem EuGH-Urteil zum wallonischen Einfuhrverbot' [1992] *EuR* 414 to 433); W. T. Douma, 'Walloon Waste Import Ban' [1993] *European Business Law Review* (Feb.) 34; A. Epiney, 'Einbeziehung gemeinschaftlicher Umweltschutzprinzipien in die Bestimmung mitgliedstaatlichen Handlungsspielraums' [1993] *DVBl.* 93 to 100; S. Tostmann, 'EuGH-Verbot des Ablagerns von Abfall aus einem anderen Mitgliedstaat' [1992] *EuZW* 577 to 580.
[64] Dir. 84/631/EEC on the supervision and control within the European Community and the trans-frontier shipment of hazardous waste [1984] *OJ* L326/31.
[65] Dir. 75/442/EEC on waste [1975] *OJ* L194/47 was not considered to be exhaustive.
[66] See Ch. 5 on the questions related to non-discrimination.
[67] Case 380/87 *Enichem Base et al.* v. *Commune die Cinisello Balsamo (Italian Plastic Bags)* [1990] *ECR* I–2491.

problems arising from non-biodegradable plastic waste in the area.[68] As the referring national court, however, did not refer the question concerning the compatibility of such a measure with Article 30, the Court of Justice had only to consider whether the local measure was compatible with the existing Community secondary legislation.[69] The Advocate General *Francis G. Jacobs*, however, referred explicitly to Article 30 and the similarities to the Court's decision in the *Danish Bottles Case*.[70]

THE CONVERGENCE OF ARTICLE 36 AND THE RULE OF REASON

Conceptual Differences

The distinction between the application of Article 36 and the rule of reason is sometimes rather difficult, particularly as the Court itself has indicated the protection of health as being a mandatory requirement under the rule of reason in spite of its explicit mention in Article 36[71] and does not always clearly distinguish between the application of Article 36 and the rule of reason. Nevertheless, it would be well to remember that the underlying concepts are philosophically distinct. The rule of reason neither falls within the general terms of public policy reasons of Article 36's first sentence nor is it simply an expansion of the grounds set out in Article 36 EC.[72] While the *Cassis de Dijon* doctrine leads to a restriction of the scope of Article 30, Article 36 justifies national measures for exceptional reasons although they represent infringements of Article 30.

Connected Objectives

Through their close interconnection many aspects of environmental protection may be covered by Article 36 although they could also fall under the rule of reason.[73] While the Court considers the prohibition of certain pesticides in

---

[68] See for a similar case decided by the German Adminstrative Tribunal: BVerwG, judgment of 7 Sept. 1992, Prohibition on one-way containers by local authorities/NB 2/92 (München) [1993] *NJW* 411 to 412, where the local authorities were not entitled to adopt such measures under German Federal law.

[69] Case 380/87 *Italian Plastic Bags*, n. 67 above, 2515 and 2516.

[70] Case 380/87 *Italian Plastic Bags*, n. 67 above, 2505.

[71] See for a detailed analysis: M. Dauses, 'Dogmatik des freien Warenverkehrs in der Europäischen Gemeinschaft' [1984] *RIW* 197 at 202 or C. Moench, 'Die Fahrverbotsregelungen der Smog-Verordnungen auf dem Prüfstand des EG-Rechts' [1989] *NVwZ* 335 at 337 considering this to be an unintended mistake of the Court, while K. Heinz, 'Nochmals: Die Fahrverbotsregelungen der Smog-Verordnungen auf dem Prüfstand des EG-Rechts' [1989] *NVwZ* 1035 at 1038 refers to later judgments where this has been restated: Case 788/79, n. 7 (above), 2078 and Case 130/80 *Criminal Proceedings against Kelderman* [1981] *ECR* 527 at 535. See for an overview without a systematic conclusion, however, Henke, n. 7 above, 174.

[72] Kapteyn and VerLoren van Themaat, n. 17 above, 389.

[73] See also Krämer, n. 21 above, 118, who takes as his criterion for distinction the 'direct effect' of a measure on health, fauna, and flora.

non-harmonized areas to be covered by Article 36,[74] other areas, such as national measures concerning the reduction of waste or its sound treatment, have been dealt with under the rule of reason.[75] The distinction is not completely clarified.[76]

However, it seems reasonable to use a criterion of direct effect on human health or the health of animals and plants.[77] Measures which aim directly at the protection of health and life of humans, animals, and plants would fall under Article 36, while the general protection of the environment, despite its indirect effects on humans, animals, and plants, would fall under the rule of reason. It seems, however, from the Court's case law that 'a differentiation between measures to protect health and life and other environmental measures [is] almost superfluous'.[78]

Equal Conditions

The Court conceives Article 36 as an exception to the general prohibitions of Articles 30 and 34 and has always insisted that it must be interpreted narrowly.[79] In its case law the Court has developed a set of conditions that must be fulfilled for the application of Article 36. The Court has extended the conditions derived from Article 36's second sentence to the application of the rule of reason in spite of their different concepts.[80] The interconnection of the objectives concerned and the similarity of the conditions applied make the proposed conceptional difference between Article 36 and the rule of reason almost disappear.

This becomes particularly evident when we consider that the only coherent difference in their application, the absolute non-discrimination requirement for the rule of reason, seems to vanish or at least be moderated in its absolute nature.[81] The non-discrimination principle, when applied to measures under the rule of reason, has to take into account objectively justified differentiations. Under environmental considerations this can sometimes also justify a differentiation between goods from different regions or imported goods and domestic goods. In the case of waste the Court considers the proximity principle and the principle of correction at source as objectively justified reasons for the unequal treatment of local and imported waste.[82]

---

[74] Case 272/80, n. 23 above, 3291; Case 94/83, n. 23 above, 3279; Case 54/85, n. 23 above, 1078; Case 125/88, n. 23 above.
[75] To a limited extent already in Case 240/83 *ADBHU*, n. 55 above, 549; definitely in Case 302/86 *Danish Bottles*, n. 57 above, 4630; and recently in Case C–2/90 *Walloon Waste Case*, n. 11 above.
[76] See Becker, n. 16 above, 74; Moench, n. 71 above, 337; Henke, n. 7 above, 174 to 176.
[77] As suggested e.g. by Krämer, n. 21 above, 118.   [78] Krämer, n. 21 above, 118.
[79] Kapteyn and VerLoren van Themaat, n. 17 above, 392.
[80] See Kapteyn and VerLoren van Themaat, n. 17 above, 402, with reference to Case 8/74 *Dassonville*, n. 50 above, 852.
[81] A. Middeke, *Nationaler Umweltschutz im Binnenmarkt* (Heymann, Köln, 1993), 182 to 184 refers explicitly to the problems in the classification of the Court's decision in Case C–2/90 *Walloon Waste Case*, n. 11 above.
[82] See Case C–2/90 *Walloon Waste Case*, n. 11 above, 4480, para. 34.

5

The Conditions for Domestic Environmental Measures

INTRODUCTION

Despite the different legal concepts underlying Article 36 and the rule of reason, the Court of Justice uses a very similar test when applying them to domestic measures. In the view of the Court, the conditions, as laid down in Article 36's second sentence, are also applicable to the rule of reason. In its abundant case law the Court has basically developed four conditions.

First, the national measure has to regulate an area where no exhaustive Community secondary law exists or where the latter leaves the Member States with the opportunity to adopt additional rules. Article 36 and the application of the rule of reason can only be invoked for objectives which are not already comprehensively covered and sufficiently guaranteed by Community law. Community law may, however, provide exceptions where diverging national measures are employed in spite of an existing harmonization at Community level.

Secondly, the measures must be taken in the genuine interest of one of the recognized objectives of Article 36 or the mandatory requirements of the Treaty as developed by the Court under the rule of reason. In the field of the environment, the nature and scope of these objectives can involve difficult questions concerning the level of protection, the level of proof, and geographic scope. Apart from a purely national interest the European interest has to be observed, too.

Thirdly, the measures may not constitute a means of arbitrary discrimination or disguised protectionism. There may, however, be legitimate grounds for a differentiation according to objective reasons, although the rule of reason covers only measures which are applicable to domestic and foreign goods in the same way.

Fourthly, the Court applies a specific test concerning the relationship between the measures chosen and the objectives attempted. The test applied by the Court includes a threefold analysis: (a) whether the measure is capable of attaining the indicated objective, (b) whether the measure chosen is the least trade-restrictive measure leading to the desired level of protection, and (c) whether the restrictive character of the measure is proportionate, that is, not excessive in relation to the improvement in environmental quality.

EXCEPTIONAL CHARACTER OF NECESSARY MEASURES

Both Article 36 and the rule of reason provide, to a certain extent, for derogations from the general system of free movement of goods within the Community. This mechanism creates or maintains, in principle, obstacles to trade which the Community seeks to eliminate.[1] To accomplish the aim of minimizing obstacles to trade, the Community and, in particular, the Court seek therefore to limit the application of derogations to the absolutely necessary extent. The Court has regularly stated that it considers the application of Article 36 exceptional and that it therefore interprets its legitimate grounds for derogation in a very narrow way.[2] Nevertheless, the effect of this interpretation has been moderated by the application of the rule of reason under Article 30.

At the same time the Community has to ensure the protection of legitimate interests, as referred to in Article 36 and recognized under the rule of reason. The protection of the environment is an important aspect of the objectives the Community is entrusted to promote. At the same time environmental measures should not be abused, hindering trade unnecessarily or unduly protecting domestic industry. A set of conditions should help the Court to strike the balance between the establishment of the common market for goods and the maintenance of the necessary[3] protection of legitimate interests.[4]

Apart from the narrow interpretation of the grounds of derogation under Article 36 and use of a limited (but constantly amended) list of mandatory requirements under the rule of reason, the Court seeks to limit the application of these principles by submitting them to several conditions.[5] Into its necessity test the Court has integrated a proportionality principle which is used to strike out measures which are considered excessive in relation to the improvement they

---

[1] See P. J. G. Kapteyn and P. VerLoren van Themaat, *Introduction to the Law of the European Communites* (2nd edn., Kluwer, Deventer, 1989), 396 to 397.

[2] e.g. Case 7/68 *Commission* v. *Italy* (*Taxes on Italian Art Treasures*) [1968] *ECR* 423 at 431; Case 229/83 *Association des Centres Distributeurs Edouard Leclerc* v. *SA Thouars Distribution et al.* [1985] *ECR* 1 at 35.

[3] In my view, there is a certain insecurity about the terminology of the Court. The term necessity is sometimes used to refer to the set of conditions as a whole, while sometimes it is applied only to the aspect of the use of the least restrictive measure available. The fact that different languages and judicial traditions use different concepts may have added some confusion. See e.g. J. Steiner, 'Drawing the Line: Uses and Abuses of Art. 30 EEC' (1992) 29 *CMLRev.* 749 at 760.

[4] See e.g. Case 302/86 *Commission* v. *Denmark* (*Danish Bottles*) [1988] *ECR* 4607 at 4630 (paras. 8 to 12). See for this balancing act in relation to the free movement of goods D. Geradin, 'Balancing Free Trade and Environmental Protection—The Interplay between the ECJ and the Community Legislator' in J. Cameron, P. Demaret, and D. Geradin (eds.), *Trade and the environment: The Search for the Balance* (Cameron May, London, 1994), 204 to 240.

[5] For a survey of the conditions applied see e.g. G. Dannecker and I. Appel, 'Auswirkungen der Vollendung des Europäischen Binnenmarktes auf den Schutz der Gesundheit und Umwelt' [1990] *ZVglRWiss* 127 at 150, J. Scherer, 'Umweltrecht: Handelshemmnis im EG-Binnenmarkt?' [1992] *URP/DEP* 76 at 79.

achieve.[6] Nevertheless, justified environmental objectives have to be taken into account when deciding on the necessity of a national measure.[7]

As an overview, domestic measures are generally compatible with Community law if they (a) do not jeopardize or contradict existing Community secondary law in a specific field, (b) are in the genuine interest of the protection of the environment as interpreted by the Court, (c) are not arbitrarily discriminatory or protectionist, and (d) are suitable, necessary, and proportionate. The last condition is fulfilled only if a domestic measure is (i) reasonable for the achievement of the environmental objective in view, if the measure used is (ii) the least restrictive that leads to the achievement of this objective, and (iii) the incidental burden on trade is not excessive in relation to the benefits.

Before analysing the different elements of the Court's test to balance domestic environmental measures against the Community's interest in the free movement of goods, it might be interesting to note the obvious similarities this test has with the one applied by the United States Supreme Court when trying to balance the legitimate interests of states with the federal objective of inter-state trade as protected by the commerce clause. Apart from the pre-emptive effect of US federal law, the language of the Supreme Court is reminiscent in many cases of the terminology used by the Court of Justice of the European Community.[8] In *Pike* v. *Bruce Church*[9] the Supreme Court restated its balancing test as follows:

> where the statute regulates *evenhandedly* to effectuate a *legitimate local public interest*, and its *effects on interstate commerce are only incidental*, it will be upheld unless the burden imposed on such commerce is *clearly excessive* in relation to the putative local benefits. . . . If a legitimate local interest is found, then the question becomes one of degree. And the extent of the burden that will be tolerated will of course depend on the nature of local interests involved, and on *whether it could be promoted as well with lesser impact on interstate activities*.[10]

THE REMAINING RESPONSIBILITY OF THE MEMBER STATES

Whenever applying Article 36 or the rule of reason the Court considers first the question whether the current state of Community law makes it necessary for the

---

[6] See for the dogmatic allocation of the proportionality test Kapteyn and VerLoren van Themaat, n. 1 above, 402.

[7] This derives from Arts. 2 and 130r(2) EC as well as from the Court's case law: Case 240/83 *Procureur de la République* v. *Association de Défense des Brûleurs d'Huiles Usagées (ADBHU)* [1985] *ECR* 531; Case 302/86 *Danish Bottles*, n. 4 above, 4639; and Case C–2/90 *Commission* v. *Belgium (Walloon Waste Case)* [1992] *ECR* I–4431 at 4479.

[8] See for a very interesting comparison D. Geradin, 'Free Trade and Environmental Protection in an Integrated Market: A Survey of the Case Law of the United States Supreme Court and the European Court of Justice' (1993) 2 *Journal of Transnational Law and Policy* 141 at 152 and his interesting views on the interplay of the judiciary and the legislator in Geradin, n. 4 above, 232 to 235.

[9] 397 US 137 (1970) as referred to by Geradin, n. 8 above, 152.

[10] *Pike* v. *Bruce Church*, n. 9 above, at 142. The emphasis has been added by the author.

Member States to apply specific measures for the safeguard of certain justified objectives. The Community system does not permit a reliance on Article 36 or the rule of reason for measures which have been harmonized at Community level[11] or where a common policy exists.[12] It is, however, necessary for Community legislation to cover the area exhaustively and leave no space for further regulation by the Member States.[13]

The Court also regularly applies this rule to the protection of the environment. National or local environmental measures are not justified if the Court considers that there is no room for additional national regulations or that they infringe the existing Community secondary legislation.[14] The absence of a Community system covering the area entirely is a prerequisite of the application of Article 36 or the rule of reason.[15] In the absence of such complete Community harmonization the Member States may take measures as long as these are compatible with their other obligations under the Treaty and do not jeopardize the existing Community system.[16]

Case: Examples are the Danish introduction of noise levels for windmills, the German intention to prohibit the use of lead caps for alcoholic beverages, or the Danish regulation limiting the lead content of ammunition for hunting purposes. In all these cases there is as yet no relevant Community legislation.[17] In the absence of relevant secondary legislation, these national measures have only to be compatible with the Treaty obligations, in particular with Article 30. The case law shows that all these measures may constitute trade-hindering obstacles but are lawful as long as they are justified for the protection of the environment or the health of humans, animals, and plants, and are non-discriminatory and proportionate.

In spite of existing Community law in the area, national bans of certain substances are considered to be lawful, if the existing Community secondary law is not exhaustive, that is, it does not exclude the prohibition or regulation of national bans of certain additional substances. This is, for example, the case for mercury, prohibited in Denmark, cadmium, prohibited in The Netherlands or atrazina which is banned in Germany. Their toxicity and risk for the environment and thus for man are generally recognized and accepted.[18]

---

[11] See Ch. 8. and, for an extensive comparison with the doctrine of pre-emption, see Ch. 7 and Geradin, n. 8 above, 172.

[12] See Ch. 9.

[13] Case 5/77 *Carlo Tedeschi* v. *Dansk Denkavit (Tedeschi/Denkavit)* [1977] *ECR* 1555.

[14] e.g. Case C–169/89 Criminal Proceeding against Gourmetterie Van den Burg (*Scottish Red Grouse*) [1990] *ECR* I–2143 or Case C–2/90 *Walloon Waste Case*, n. 7 above, 4477. See, for the principle of pre-emption and the precluding character of a Community measure, Ch. 2.

[15] Case 8/74 *Procureur du Roi* v. *B. and G. Dassonville (Dassonville)* [1974] *ECR* 837 at 852; Joined cases 3, 4, and 6/76 *Criminal Proceedings against Cornelis Kramer et al. (Biological Resources of the Sea)* [1976] *ECR* 1279; Case 148/78 *Pubblico Ministero* v. *Ratti* [1979] *ECR* 1629 at 1644; Case 247/84 *Criminal Proceedings against Leon Motte* [1985] *ECR* 3887 at 3903 to 3905.

[16] See Case 154/77 *Procureur du Roi* v. *Dechmann* [1978] *ECR* 1573.

[17] Cases reported by L. Krämer, 'Environmental Protection and Art. 30 EEC Treaty' (1993) 30 *CMLRev.* 111 at 134, who indicates, however, the possible introduction of a Community regulation on a complete ban of lead caps on alcoholic beverages.

[18] Examples reported by Krämer, n. 17 above, 133.

A total harmonization of the regulations concerning the use of these substances, for example under Article 43 EEC, would, however, change the situation.[19]

In spite of existing harmonization, Article 36 or the rule of reason may still be invoked if this is explicitly provided for by safeguard clauses in secondary law (express savings[20]) or under the systematic provisions of the Treaty, such as in Articles 100a(4) or 130t.[21] The scope of these provisions is limited by the principles of the Treaty or, in the case of express savings, by explicit authorization.[22]

Case: Although the Community has introduced an exhaustive regulation concerning certain chemical substances, including PCP, Germany was allowed to maintain a total ban on PCP. This domestic provision fell within the scope of Article 100a(4).[23] It thus had to be compatible with the other conditions for the application of Article 36 or the rule of reason. The complete ban on an admittedly dangerous substance by one Member State can be lawful under Article 36 and the rule of reason if it is not discriminatory, not protectionist, and proportionate.

It is important to distinguish two different situations. In some cases we find Community legislation adopted precisely in order to harmonize a specific sector of the common market, precluding any additional national requirements.[24] In other cases, existing Community harmonization has a more general character and allows for local or domestic measures to take into account any particular needs or preferences.[25] Many Community measures adopted ensure free trade in goods and do not preclude local authorities from adopting measures which apply to all goods alike and do not preclude the use of certain goods in general,[26] but only restrict it in emergency situations[27] or during certain periods for justified reasons. Such measures do not jeopardize the establishment of the

[19] Dir. 91/414/EEC concerning the authorization of pesticides [1991] *OJ* L230/1 provides in Annex A for a list enumerating all forbidden pesticides within the Community. See Part II.

[20] See also E. D. Cross, 'Pre-emption of Member States, Law in the European Economic Community: A Framework for Analysis' (1992) 29 *CMLRev.* 447 at 456 or Geradin, n. 8 above, 173.

[21] See for details Part II.

[22] See e.g. Art. 14 of Dir. 79/409/EEC on the conservation of wild birds [1979] *OJ* L103/1; its scope is limited to more restrictive measures for the conservation of migratory birds and seriously endangered birds and not birds in general; see however L. Krämer, n. 17 above. See also Case C–169/89 *Criminal Proceedings against Gourmetterie Van den Burg (Scottish Red Grouse)* [1990] *ECR* I–2143 at 2164.

[23] See Ch. 4.

[24] See Case 60/86 *Commission v. United Kingdom (Dim-Dip Car Lights)* [1988] *ECR* 3921.

[25] See Case *R. v. London Boroughs Transport Committee, ex parte Freight Transport Association Ltd.*, CA, 31 July 1990 [1990] 3 *CMLR* 495 and HL, 24 July 1991 [1992] 1 *CMLR* 5 to 21. The same approach is used by the US Supreme Court in cases where it finds no overlap of a federal statute and local measures, see *Huron Portland Cement v. Detroit*, 362 US 440 (1960) at 445 as referred to by Geradin, n. 8 above, 149.

[26] See, however, Case 60/86 *Dim-Dip Car Lights*, n. 24 above.

[27] See the smog regulations introduced by the German *Länder*; see e.g. C. Moench, 'Die Fahrverbotsregelungen der Smog-Verordnungen auf dem Prüfstand des EG-Rechts' [1989] *NVwZ* 335; K. Heinz, 'Nochmals: Die Fahrverbotsregelungen der Smog-Verordnungen auf dem Prüfstand des EG-Rechts' [1989] *NVwZ* 1035; see also Krämer, n. 17 above, 132.

common market and the scope of existing Community law if they are compatible with the other conditions applied by the Court.[28]

Case: Local authorities in the London area imposed a night ban on lorry traffic in order to reduce noise pollution, only allowing exceptions for heavy goods vehicles which had been individually licensed. If the lorries were fitted with a device to silence air brakes they were eligible for such a licence. While the English Court of Appeal held that Community law[29] was exhaustive in this area and therefore precluded the imposition of any special devices,[30] the House of Lords came to a different conclusion. In the second appeal, the House of Lords did not consider the relevant Community legislation to be applicable and thus held that '[i]t is permissible for planning and zoning authorities to restrict the movement of compliant but large or noisy vehicles during the night or in residential areas in the interest of environmental protection.'[31] In the view of the House of Lords the existing Community law had been created to abolish trade hindering technical requirements in general and did not exclude the local protection of residents. The objective of the local measure was the noise reduction in a specific borough at night. All trucks were concerned and the measure seemed proportionate for the attainment of its objective.[32]

The German _Länder_ in 1988 introduced legislation prohibiting use of certain types of cars during periods of smog-alert.[33] While cars with a diesel-engine or a traditional motor system are banned during these periods, those equipped with a catalytic converter can be used. Although there is Community legislation concerning the exhaust standards of cars in general,[34] it is only intended to facilitate trade in cars in general. Its nature does not preclude certain emergency measures during a smog-alert, although a car purchaser may be aware of the potential restrictions in use. The scope of the existing Community standards is not to ensure the complete freedom of traffic throughout the Community without reference to local emergency situations but to establish a common market for goods.[35]

THE GENUINE PROTECTION OF THE ENVIRONMENT

General Observations

When a Member State wants to rely on the exceptions referred to in Article 36 or invoke the applicability of the rule of reason it will have to invoke one of the objectives set out in Article 36 or accepted (or supposed to be included) by the

---

[28] See e.g. Krämer, n. 17 above, 132, referring to the view of the Commission. The same approach is used by the US Supreme Court, see e.g. Geradin, n. 8 above, 151.

[29] Dir. 70/157/EEC (_Sound Level Directive_) on the approximation of exhaust systems [1970] _OJ_ L42/16 and Dir. 71/320/EEC (_Brake Directive_) [1971] _OJ_ L202/37.

[30] See e.g. Case 60/86 _Dim-Dip Car Lights_, n. 24 above.

[31] Case n. 25 above.

[32] See also S. Ball and S. Bell, _Environmental Law_ (Blackstone, London, 1991), 53 and Krämer, n. 17 above, 131.

[33] See for references Moench, n. 27 above, 336.

[34] Dir. 770/220/EEC [1970] _OJ_ L76/1, amended several times; see Heinz, n. 27 above, 337.

[35] See for the same conclusion Krämer, n. 17 above, 132; Moench, n. 27 above, 337; Heinz, n. 27 above, 1036.

Court under the rule of reason.[36] These objectives are recognized as legitimate state ends in the view of the Community and the Court of Justice.[37] As has been demonstrated in Chapter 4, the protection of the environment in general is recognized as a mandatory requirement of the Treaty[38] and certain aspects thereof are also covered by Article 36.

However, a comprehensive explication of the term 'protection of the environment' has never been given by the Community institutions. Neither in the Environmental Action Programmes nor in the Single European Act[39] are there clear indications. The Court has decided each case on its merits. This may raise several questions related to the scope of and nature of domestic policy objectives in relation to the protection of the environment, as understood by the Court when applying Article 36 and the rule of reason.

First, when assessing the need for any domestic measures related to a specific environmental objective, the Court regularly asks whether there is any danger or risk at all which justifies specific domestic action. Member States must be able to demonstrate that they are attempting to achieve an environmental objective which is justified in the presence of certain real or potential environmental dangers. If there is no such danger or potentially risky situation which justifies the intervention of trade-hindering measures, the Member State cannot claim that its measures are justified on the basis of environmental concerns. It is therefore important to know how much discretion a Member State has in evaluating the possible dangers of a situation and what level of proof is required by the Court.

Secondly, a Member State can aim at the achievement of different levels of environmental protection and this may have implications for the choice of the relevant instruments. A very high level of protection may lead to the introduction of very stringent measures and a comprehensive set of rules, as the level of protection in the other Member States might generally be lower. It is therefore important to know whether there is a limit to the Member States' discretion when defining their own level of protection. In its current state, the Community is still very heterogeneous, in particular as far as environmental awareness and preferences are concerned. This may lead to very marked differences between domestic regulatory systems within the Community.

Thirdly, the geographical scope of a national environmental objective is not yet definitively clarified. While it is clear under the existing case law that a Member State may invoke Article 36 or the rule of reason for the protection of life, health, and the environment within its own territory, it is not so clear

---

[36] This derives from the narrow interpretation of the grounds of derogation in Art. 36 and the Court's restricted acceptance of mandatory requirements under the rule of reason.

[37] See for the similar situation in the United States Geradin, n. 8 above, 153.

[38] Case 240/83 *ADBHU*, n. 7 above, 537; Case 302/86 *Danish Bottles*, n. 4 above, 4637; Case C–2/90 *Walloon Waste Case*, n. 7 above; see also Case C–195/90 *Commission* v. *Germany (Tax on Heavy Goods Vehicles)* [1992] *ECR* I–3141.

[39] See A. Epiney and T. M. J. Möllers, *Freier Warenverkehr und nationaler Umweltschutz* (Heymann, Köln, 1992), 70.

whether it may do this for the protection of the non-domestic environment. National import measures for the protection of certain species or ecological systems abroad as well as export measures concerning ecologically sensitive goods, such as waste, definitely hinder trade. They are often justified by the environmental dangers trade in those goods causes in another country. It is questionable whether such measures are lawful if they are taken in relation to trade with another Member State.

Evaluation of Environmental Dangers

In the presence of scientific uncertainty, the question whether a dangerous situation exists at all is sometimes disputed and the Court has to find a way in which to determine the conditions under which Member States are entitled to adopt environmental measures. This question does not relate to the measure itself, but rather to the objective and its general justification.[40]

The Court's case law in the field of health protection has shown that a lot of measures are taken for the elimination of dangers such as infectious diseases or the introduction of dangerous micro-organisms from other countries, including other Member States, or for the reduction of dangerous substances within their own territory.[41] In some cases, however, it has been disputed whether the dangerous situation existed at all or it was argued that the scientific knowledge of the potential dangers did not justify taking any measures which restricted trade.[42] If one considers that an environmental measure to combat certain dangers (which is a legitimate objective) is only justified if sufficient scientific proof or certainty of the existence and risks from this danger exist, the national measure would also have to fulfil certain requirements in this respect.

In terms of the case law of the Court, a national objective such as the combat of specific environmental, sanitary, or phytosanitary dangers is only justified if there is clear evidence or scientific uncertainty about the existence of such a

---

[40] In my view only the necessity of a measure for the achievement of a specific objective, as understood by the Court when asking for the application of the 'least trade restrictive measure', is a question of proportionality, see Ch. 5 on arbitrary discrimination, below; This approach is also used by Epiney and Möllers, n. 39 above, 74. I deal with the objective and its justification under the more general question whether the objective is covered by Art. 36 or the rule of reason, while other authors seem to consider the question whether a potentially dangerous situation is required in the necessity element of the proportionality test, see e.g. J. Henke, *EuGH und Umweltschutz* (VVF, München, 1993), 182; U. Becker, *Der Gestaltungsspielraum der EG-Mitgliedstaaten im Spannungsfeld zwischen Umweltschutz und freiem Warenverkehr* (Nomos, Baden-Baden, 1991), 88; B. Jadot, 'Mesures nationales de police de l'environnement, libre circulation des marchandises et proportionnalité' [1990] *CDE* 401 at 416. For a survey see also A. Middeke, *Nationaler Umweltschutz und Binnenmarkt* (Heymann, Köln, 1994), 189 and 190.

[41] See e.g Case 272/80 *Criminal Proceedings against FNMBP* [1981] *ECR* 3277 or recently Case C–131/93 *Commission* v. *Germany (Freshwater Crayfish)* [1994] *ECR* I–3303.

[42] See the dispute between the United Kingdom and Germany on the transmission of 'mad cow disease' through meat imports from the UK to Germany or Case 97/83 *Criminal Proceedings against CMC Melkunie BV* [1984] *ECR* 2367.

danger.[43] Otherwise the protection of the environment could be invoked in a completely discretionary way by Member States which would open the door to an abuse of Article 36 and the rule of reason. It is the task of Member States to prove the existence of a dangerous situation or at least to give reasonable indications for its existence.[44]

Case: In its decision in Case C-2/90 *Commission* v. *Belgium*[45] the Court had to consider whether the afflux of waste from other Member States created a real danger in the Walloon region, which justified the adoption of domestic measures. The Belgian argument that the afflux was very heavy and the existing disposal facilities very limited was accepted by the Court. It considered such a situation to be potentially dangerous. 'S'agissant de l'environnement, il convient de relever que les déchets sont des objets de nature particulière. Leur accumulation . . . constitue un danger pour l'environnement. . . .[L]e gouvernement belge a fait valoir . . . qu'un afflux massif et anormal de déchets provenant d'autres régions s'est produit . . . constitutant ainsi un danger réel pour l'environnement eu égard aux capacités limitées de cette region. Il s'ensuit que l'argument selon lequel des exigences impératives tenant à la protection de l'environnemnt justifient les mesures considére comme fondé'.

As other authors have argued before,[46] the justification of an environmental measure as necessary in the interests of combatting certain existing dangers for human health or the environment is sometimes difficult. From the Court's case law in the field of health protection[47] so far the conclusion can be drawn that the existence of a dangerous situation justifies State action to eliminate possible risks. Such a danger, however, has to be probable and the mere possibility of a danger under extreme circumstances will not be recognized by the Court.[48] Scientific proof of the absence of a specific danger renders its combat unjustified as it is unnecessary or useless.[49] It is the duty of the Member State[50]

[43] e.g. Case 174/82 *Criminal Proceedings against Sandoz BV (Vitamins)* [1983] *ECR* 2445 at 2463.

[44] Case 104/75 *Criminal Proceedings against Adriaan De Pijper* [1976] *ECR* 613; Case 227/82 *Criminal Proceedings against Van Bennekom* [1983] *ECR* 3883; Case 247/81 *Commission* v. *Germany (Marketing of Pharmaceutical Products)* [1984] *ECR* 1111 at 1120; Case 304/84 *Ministère Public* v. *Claude Muller* [1986] *ECR* 1511 at 1529; Case 90/86 *Criminal Proceedings against Zoni* [1988] *ECR* 4285 or recently Case C-17/93 *Criminal Proceedings against J. J. J. Van der Veldt* [1994] *ECR* I-3537. In the field of environmental protection, however, the introduction of Art. 130t might lead to a different situation. Here the burden of proof could lie with the Commission who has to prove that the chosen measure is excessive or can be replaced by another measure with fewer trade effects. This would lead to a stronger emphasis on the precautionary principle to the detriment of the coherence of the common market.

[45] Case C-2/90 *Walloon Waste Case*, n. 7 above, 4479.

[46] See Becker, n. 40 above, 88 and 89; Henke, n. 40 above, 182 and 183; Epiney and Möllers, n. 39 above, 74 to 80.

[47] See, in particular, Epiney and Möllers, n. 39 above, 74 to 80.

[48] See e.g. Case 178/84 *Commission* v. *Germany (German Purity Law)* [1987] *ECR* 1227 at 1276, concerning the potential danger from an accumulation of chemical residues resulting from an excessive consumption of beer.

[49] It is, however, often difficult to prove the complete absence of any danger; the Court may rely on the indications of international organizations such as the recommendations in the CITES Agreement in Case C-169/89 *Scottish Red Grouse*, n. 14 above, 2163.

[50] e.g. Case 227/82, n. 44 above, 3905 or Case 304/84, n. 44 above, 1529; for more references see Henke, n. 40 above, 189.

claiming the existence of a danger to give at least some indications of the possible danger of certain substances or mixtures.[51]

However, as long as there remains scientific uncertainty, it seems reasonable to allow Member States to set high environmental objectives which tend to protect the environment rather than to risk uncertain dangers.[52] The Member States, however, have a duty to take into account the newest scientific research[53] and to abandon measures which are no longer justified.[54] In most cases, however, the Member States retain a relatively high level of discretion for the realization of their own level of environmental protection against such dangers.[55] In the framework of the environmental policy of the Community this seems particularly important in view of the precautionary principle as laid down in Article 130r(2).

The Level of Protection

The reasonableness, or even the necessity, of an environmental measure may be very greatly influenced by the level of protection of the objective chosen. Very ambitious environmental objectives may require specific and restrictive measures which are only reasonable by reference to the high level of the objective in question.[56] It seems that the Court, when applying its test of whether a measure is the least restrictive among several alternatives, always relates it to the

---

[51] Case 178/84 *German Purity Law*, n. 48 above, 1274; Case 51/83 *Commission* v. *Italy* (*Gelatine*) [1984] *ECR* 2793 at 2806; or recently Joined cases C–13/91 and C–113/91 *Criminal proceedings against Michel Debus* [1992] *ECR* I–3617 (paras. 18 ff.) where the national government could not give any reasonable indications; see also M. Dauses, 'L'interdiction de mesures d'éffet équivalent à des restrictions quantitatives à la lumière de la jurisprudence de la CJCE' [1992] *RTDE* 607 at 625 and 626; Henke, n. 40 above, 189 or A. Skordas, 'Das griechische Bierreinheitsgebot und die erforderliche Reform des Lebensmittelrechts' [1992] *RIW* 977 at 979. He indicates the problems of certain Member States, i.e. Greece, in providing scientific data. See also Middeke, n. 40 above, 192.

[52] Case 40/82 *Commission* v. *United Kingdom* (*Newcastle Disease*) [1984] *ECR* 283 at 299 (para. 16); Case 174/82 *Vitamins*, n. 43 above, 2463 (para. 19); Case C–375/90 *Commission* v. *Greece* (*Scientific Uncertainty*) [1993] *ECR* I–2055.

[53] Case 247/84, n. 15 above, 3904; Case C–228/91 *Commission* v. *Italy* (*New Scientific Evidence*) [1993] *ECR* I–2701.

[54] See Case 54/85 *Ministère Public* v. *Xavier Mirepoix* (*Pesticides on Fruit*) [1986] *ECR* 1067 at 1079. See Becker, n. 40 above, 89; Epiney and Möllers, n. 39 above, 76 and 77. The fact that a measure does not seem necessary because the exporting country has taken equivalent measures is an element of the necessity test within the proportionality test, see Ch. 5 on arbitrary discrimination below; other authors deal with it, however, under the rubric of risk evaluation see e.g. also Middeke, n. 40 above, 192; see for the most recent developments in international trade law the provisions of Art. 5 of the Agreement on Sanitary and Phytosanitary Measures (SPS Agreement), included in GATT Secretariat (ed.), *The Results of the Uruguay Round of Multilateral Trade Negotiations—The Legal Texts* (GATT, Geneva, 1994), 69.

[55] The opinion expressed by Becker, n. 40 above, 89; Epiney and Möllers, n. 39 above, 79.

[56] While it is possible to evaluate the acceptable level of a national environmental objective under the aspect of the necessity of a measure, in my view, it is preferable to consider it under the more general question whether a certain measure serves a legitimate environmental objective. See, the different approaches by U. Becker, n. 40 above, 84 or Henke, n. 40 above, 182 to 186.

pre-given objective.[57] There seems to be no control over the chosen level of protection.[58]

Case: In its decision in Case 302/86 *Danish Bottles*[59] the Court did not analyse the objective of the Danish measure. The Court held that a system which required the comprehensive re-use of bottles covering 100 per cent of the containers was in the interests of the reduction of waste and thus legitimate for the protection of the environment. The Advocate General Sir Gordon Slynn had proposed that the level of protection had to be reasonable.[60] The Court did not enter into this discourse even if it considered the restrictive character of certain parts of the Danish regulation disproportionate although they were capable of ensuring 'a maximum rate of re-use of bottles and therefore a very considerable degree of protection of the environment'.[61]

While certain authors argue that this implies that the Court restricts itself to a mere examination of the relationship between the measure used and the given objective without analysing the level of the latter,[62] other authors deduce from the limited scope of the judgment that the question remains still to be answered.[63] Most authors agree, however, that even if the Court were in the future to analyse the level of a national environmental objective, it would still leave the Member States with a significant discretion as to the extent to which the chosen level is necessary.[64] This also corresponds to the existing case law in the field of health protection and protection of the health of animals and plants concerning sanitary and phytosanitary measures.[65]

In relation to other grounds of derogation under Article 36 the Court has emphasized that in the absence of harmonized rules, Member States should choose their desired level of protection: '[i]n principle, it is for each Member

---

[57] See e.g. Case 302/86 *Danish Bottles*, n. 4 above, 4630; same opinion: Epiney and Möllers, n. 39 above, 73; It is not clear whether Henke, n. 40 above, 181 shares this view.

[58] Epiney and Möllers, n. 39 above, 73; W. Schutt and J. Steffens, 'EuGH-Entscheidung zu Verpackungsvorschriften in Dänemark' [1989] *RIW* 448 ff. or Middeke, n. 40 above, 187, with reference to other German authors hold a different opinion. In their view, the question of the excessiveness of a measure is closely linked to the level of protection and thus leads to an evaluation of the domestic level of protection. Furthermore Middeke considers the question whether a national measure is reasonable as an element of the evaluation of the domestic environmental aim. In my view these aspects have to be treated under different headings. The domestic environmental aim has to be covered by the Community notion of environmental protection but the admissible level has not yet been clearly established by the Court.

[59] Case 302/86 *Danish Bottles*, n. 4 above.   [60] *Ibid.*, 4626.   [61] *Ibid.*, 4632.

[62] As Epiney and Möllers, n. 39 above, 72, consider.

[63] Schutt and Steffens, n. 58 above, 447, derive from the missing indications in the judgment that the decision on the desirable level should remain within the complete discretion of the Member States.

[64] See e.g. Schutt and Steffens, n. 58 above, 448 or F. Montag, 'Umweltschutz, freier Warenverkehr und Einheitliche europäische Akte' [1987] *RIW* 935 at 938.

[65] Case 40/82 *Newcastle Disease*, n. 52 above, 283 and 295; Case 74/82 *Commission* v. *Ireland* (*Poultry and Eggs*) [1984] *ECR* 317 and 340; Case 94/83 *Officier van Justitie* v. *Heijn* (*Pesticides on Apples*) [1984] *ECR* 3263 and 3280, as referred to by A. Vorwerk, *Die umweltpolitischen Kompetenzen der Europäischen Gemeinschaft und ihrer Mitgliedstaaten* (VVF, München, 1990), 140 ff.

State to determine in accordance with its own scale of values and in the form selected by it the requirements of public morality in its territory'.[66]

Similarly, in the case of health protection the Court of Justice has declined to set a standard for the legitimate level of protection applicable in each Member State. With reference to the existing insecurity the Court has declared that Member States should be capable of deciding which level they consider to be appropriate. Nevertheless, the Court has added that Member States should take into consideration the requirements of the free movement of goods.[67] The Court has also referred to the margin of discretion which Member States should have when deciding on local needs. 'In so far as the relevant Community rules do not cover certain pesticides, Member States may require the presence of residues of those pesticides in a way which may vary from one country to another according to the climatic conditions, the normal diet of the population and their state of health.'[68]

It seems reasonable to apply these principles also to the protection of the environment where a Member State should be allowed to attempt a very high level of protection. This also seems to comply with the Community's own principles of environmental policy, namely the precautionary principle and the principle that environmental policy should take into account the diversity of situations in the various regions of the Community.[69] Nevertheless, the measures used for the achievement of this level must be necessary[70] and reasonable.[71]

The Geographical Scope

As has been demonstrated in Chapter 4, most cases of legitimate trade restrictions under Article 36 or the rule of reason have been instituted to protect the domestic environment and the health and lives of humans, animals, and plants in that environment. If a country has justified reasons to ban or restrict the use of certain goods in the interests of the protection of the environment in its own territory, it is allowed to do so. The same is true for the protection of a national species of plants or animals. In the case of waste, the Court has legitimized the ban of imports of waste from other regions if the disposal of this imported waste causes serious problems for the environment of a particular region.[72]

Another question is whether the exceptions of Article 36 and the rule of reason also legitimize the restriction on the free movement of goods to protect

---

[66] Case 34/79 *R.* v. *Henn & Darby (Henn & Darby)* [1979] *ECR* 3795.
[67] See e.g. Case 272/80, n. 41 above, 3290; Case 174/82 *Vitamins*, n. 43 above, 2663; Case 97/83, n. 42 above, 2386. See for more references Henke, n. 40 above, 182.
[68] Case 94/83 *Pesticides on Apples*, n. 65 above, 3280 (para. 16).
[69] Art. 130r(2) EC.   [70] See Ch. 5 below concerning the proportionality requirement.
[71] See Ch. 5 below on arbitrary discrimination and the abundant case law in the area of health protection e.g. Case 247/84, n. 15 above, 3905 or Case 304/84, n. 40 above, 1528.
[72] See Case C-2/90 *Walloon Waste Case*, n. 7 above, and Case C-155/91 *Commission* v. *Council (Waste Directive)* [1993] *ECR* I-939.

the non-domestic environment or the health of humans, animals, and plants in another country.[73] A Member State might adopt import restrictions or measures having equivalent effect because of the environmental danger the trade in a certain species of animals or plants causes to the population of a certain species or the environment in general in another Member State.[74]

Case: In Case 118/86 *Openbaar Ministerie* v. *Nertsvoederfabriek Nederland BV (Poultry Offal)*[75] the Court of Justice was confronted with a Dutch measure implementing a licensing system for the treatment of poultry offal. The producers of poultry offal were obliged to deliver their offal to the local undertaking holding a state licence for its treatment. The implicit export restriction resulting from such an obligation was challenged before the Court. The Netherlands invoked Article 36 in support of their measure arguing that the measure was necessary and proportionate for the protection of the health and life of humans and animals against dangers arising from the transport of poultry offal. As far as the implicit export restrictions were concerned the Court held that they had to fulfil the requirements of Article 36. '[I]t does not appear necessary to prohibit the exportation of poultry offal, provided that the conditions relating to health . . . are satisfied with respect to removal and transport on national territory.'[76] Does this imply that measures may not be taken to ensure such aims in another Member State, as the importing Member State must be allowed to apply its own rules concerning the transport of poultry offal?

Mutual Recognition and Loyalty

Most legal authors consider that the geographical scope of Article 36 or the rule of reason justifies only national measures for the protection of domestic territory, as a Member State's responsibility under the principle of territorial sovereignty does not go beyond national borders.[77] They consider that sovereignty to decide the desired level of protection has to be used in the national interest only and does not allow a State to consider the 'supposed interests' of another Member State.[78]

---

[73] Until recently only a few authors have discussed this question: e.g. Krämer, n. 17 above, 118; D. H. Scheuing, *Grenzüberschreitende atomare Wiederaufarbeitung im Lichte des europäischen Gemeinschaftsrechts* (Nomos, Baden-Baden, 1991); H.-W. Rengeling, 'Schadlose Verwertung radioaktiver Reststoffe durch Wiederaufarbeitung in anderen EG-Mitgliedstaaten' [1991] *DVBl.* 914 at 919; U. Everling, 'Die Wiederaufbereitung abgebrannter Brennelemente in anderen Mitgliedstaaten der Europäischen Gemeinschaft' [1993] *RIW*, suppl. 2.

[74] See, for Community measures related to the protection of the environment outside the Community and existing secondary law for the protection of non-domestic species in other Member States, P. Demaret, 'Trade-Related Environmental Measures (TREMs) in the External Relations of the European Community' in Cameron, Demaret, and Geradin (eds.), n. 4 above, 315 ff.; see also in detail Ch. 6.

[75] Case 118/86 *Openbaar Ministerie* v. *Nertsvoederfabriek Nederland BV (Poultry Offal)* [1987] *ECR* 3883.

[76] *Ibid.*; 3909 (para. 16).

[77] See J. Jan, 'Art. 7 EEC and a Non-Discriminatory Transfrontier Environmental Policy' [1988] *LIEI* 21 at 28; Everling, n. 73 above, 10; referring to P. Müller-Graff, Art. 36, para. 31 in H. v. d. Groeben, J. Thiesing, and C.-D, Ehlermann (eds.), *Kommentar zum EWG-Vertrag* (Nomos, Baden-Baden, 1983 ff.) or K.-H. Matthies, Art. 36, paragraph 15 in E. Grabitz and M. Hilf (eds.), *Kommentar zur EU* (2nd edn., C. H. Beck, München, 1990 ff.); see also P. v. Wilmowsky, *Abfallwirtschaft im Binnenmarkt* (Werner Verlag, Düsseldorf, 1990) 328. Rengeling, n. 73 above, 919 does not reveal whether he shares this view.   [78] Everling, n. 73 above, 10.

The principle of Community law that the Member States and the Community have a duty to co-operate in comity[79] is interpreted as forbidding any interference with the sovereign decisions of another Member State within its discretion attributed by Community law.[80] National choices concerning the definition of public interest have to be accepted provided they do not openly interfere with existing Community law.[81] In cases where Community secondary law exists, Member States have to accept the different national solutions.[82]

Case: In its decision in Case 172/82 *Inter-Huiles*[83] the Court was confronted with a French measure for the implementation of Community Directive 75/439/EEC for the recycling of waste oils.[84] To fulfil the requirements of the regulation cited, the French government had introduced a system of licensed undertakings for the recycling of waste oil. The recycling of such waste oil was organized in a way which allowed only one undertaking per district to operate and the producers of waste oil were required to use its services. The export of waste oil was thereby implicitly prohibited.[85] The Court declared such a prohibition contrary to the principle of Article 34. Economic considerations such as the use of the existing capacities of the domestic undertakings were rejected. In the same way the Court rejected the French argument that the measure was in the interests of the protection of the environment as not being justified. The Court held that the other Member States were also bound by the existing Community legislation in the field and thus the protection of the environment was adequately ensured.[86]

Common Heritage and Responsibility

There are, however, voices defending the extra-domestic application of Article 36 and the rule of reason. This has also been suggested by the Commission in several cases.[87] Krämer maintains in his works 'that a Member State may protect the fauna and flora in another Member State where there is a threat to life of plants and animals'.[88] It seems, however, that he derives this conclusion mainly from the existing secondary law such as the implementing directive of the CITES Convention[89]. He concludes from the fact that Member States are

---

[79] As declared by the Court in Case 230/81 *Luxembourg* v. *Parliament* [1983] *ECR* 255 (para. 37) referring to Art. 5 EC.

[80] See Everling, n. 73 above, 10.

[81] See for a very similar problem D. Barrington, 'The Emergence of a Constitutional Court' in J. O'Reilly (ed.), *Human Rights and Constitutional Law* (Round Hall Press, Dublin, 1992), 251 at 260 on the dispute arising about the Irish prohibition of abortion and related services in other Member States under the principle of free movement of services; see Case 159/90 *SPUC* v. *Grogan et al.* [1991] *ECR* I-4685.

[82] See e.g. Van Gerven AG in Case C-169/89 *Scottish Red Grouse*, n. 14 above, 2155.

[83] Case 172/82 *Syndicat National des Fabricants Raffineurs d'Huiles de Graissage et al.* v. *Groupement d'Intérêt Economique Inter-Huiles (Inter-Huiles)* [1983] *ECR* 555.

[84] Council Dir. 75/439/EEC on the disposal of waste oils [1975] *OJ* L194/23.

[85] Case 172/82 *Inter-Huiles*, n. 83 above, 564 (para. 5).

[86] Case 172/82 *Inter-Huiles*, n. 83 above, 566.

[87] Submissions of the Commission in Case C-169/89 *Scottish Red Grouse*, n. 14 above, referred to by Van Gerven AG at 2155.

[88] Krämer, n. 17 above, 119; see also the survey on the German doctrine in Middeke, n. 40 above, 165 to 168.

[89] Reg. 3626/82/EEC [1982] *OJ* L384/1.

explicitly allowed to protect global commons such as the ozone layer or the global climate that this must also include permission to protect the environment in another Member State.[90]

Case: The Commission's position is illustrated by the following example: Germany prohibited the marketing of products made from *corallum rubrum*, a species of coral occurring in the Mediterranean Sea which is not protected under Community rules or Italian law, although its existence is threatened.[91] The coral is used in Italy to produce jewellery. The Commission accepted the German import restriction in order to protect the Italian or Mediterranean environment. The German government relied for its measure on a Community regulation[92] implementing the CITES Convention on trade in endangered species in the Community. This regulation provides the Member States *inter alia* with the capacity to take environmental measures for 'the conservation of a species or a population of a species in the country of origin'.[93] The relevant provision requires, however, that the domestic measures 'comply with the Treaty, and in particular Article 36 thereof'.[94] In this case the Commission seemed to consider the German measure as compatible with Article 36 EC.[95]

In my opinion this view does not fully take into account the particular mechanisms of the Treaty. The fact that the system of the free movement of goods and the connected harmonization of (environmental) standards for the protection of the Community environment apply only to the Member States of the Community must allow for a differentiation. The Member States have accepted a limitation on their sovereignty in the interests of the common market and the common legislation under the Community's system for the approximation of laws. The environmental interests of the Community as a whole or any environmental problem with trans-border effects should be tackled at Community level.[96]

In my view this conclusion should follow from the principle of subsidiarity. The adoption of unilateral measures with such important effects on another Member State's sovereignty is not compatible with the Treaty system and particularly its Article 5. As the Treaty itself provides for the introduction of

---

[90] See, in particular, L. Krämer, *EC Treaty and Environmental Law* (2nd edn., Sweet & Maxwell, London, 1995), 113.

[91] See Krämer, n. 17 above, 118; there is, however, no international convention which acknowledges its threatened status.

[92] Reg. 3626/82/EEC on trade with endangered species, n. 89 above.

[93] Reg. 3626/82/EEC, n. 89 above, Art. 15(1)c.

[94] Reg. 3626/82/EEC, n. 89 above, Art. 15(1) first sentence.

[95] Unpublished proceedings, reported by L. Krämer, 'Community Environmental Law— Towards a Systematic Approach' [1992] *YEL* 151 at 166 to 167.

[96] See e.g. the protection of natural habitats and fauna and flora within the Community under Dir. 92/43/EEC [1992] *OJ* L206/7 and the comments by N. De Sadeleer, 'La directive 92/43/ECEE concernant la conservation des habitats naturels ainsi que de la faune et de la flore sauvages: vers la reconnaissance d'un patrimoine naturel de la Communauté Européenne' [1993] *RMC* 25 and 26 or W. P. J. Wils, 'La protection des habitats naturels en droit communautaire' [1994] *CDE* 398 to 430.

measures where the Community environment is better protected at Community level,[97] there seems to be no room for unilateral measures by Member States.[98]

Nevertheless, when specific areas, habitats, or species of animals or plants have been recognized by the Community as a whole as being of European interest, every Member State will have the capacity and responsibility to take common or unilateral action to protect the common heritage of the Community.[99] In my view, Member States have to use the Community harmonization and co-operation procedures for the adoption of common environmental principles and objectives without falling back upon unilateral measures.[100]

Nevertheless, I understand the desirability of such measures under a more ecologically aware point of view. Similar problems with environmental measures with an extraterritorial effect have arisen under the General Agreement on Tariffs and Trade (GATT) and will continue to be discussed in the framework of the new World Trade Organization (WTO). While most trade lawyers fear the risk of a new wave of 'green protectionism' or 'ecological imperialism', many 'environmentalists' ask for unilateral measures to ensure the protection of the 'global' environment in countries where low standards prevail.[101] Here again, as in other areas, the balance has to be found between the two issues at stake. In the Community framework, however, in my view, the co-operative spirit should prevail.

Open Questions

Even Krämer admits that he doubts whether the Court will follow his reasoning.[102] The existing case law is, however, somewhat unclear. The only case in

---

[97] See e.g. the existing secondary legislation and case law concerning the disposal of waste oil which precludes additional measures by Member States, e.g. recently Case C–37/92 *Criminal Proceedings against J. Vanacker et al.*, judgment of 12 Oct. 1993 (1993) 28 *Proceedings of the Court* 2; in the case of nuclear waste see also e.g. Council Dir. 92/3/Euratom on the supervision and control of shipments of radioactive waste between Member States and into and out of the Community [1992] *OJ* L35/24.

[98] See for the implications by Community law for national regulations on waste in general H.-W. Rengeling, 'Gemeinschaftsrechtliche Aspekte der Abfallentsorgung' in J. F. Baur, P.-C. Müller-Graff, and M. Zuleeg (eds.), *Europarecht, Energierecht, Wirtschaftsrecht—Festschrift für B. Börner* (Heymann, Köln, 1992), 359 to 376; or W. Möschel, 'Altautoverwertung und europäische Gemeinschaft' in Baur, Müller, and Zuleeg (eds.), above, 289 to 301; K. H. Friauf, 'Abfallrechtliche Rücknahmepflichten' in Baur, Müller, and Zuleeg (eds.), above, 701 to 716.

[99] See also Art. 14 of Dir. 79/409/EEC on the conservation of wild birds, n. 22 above, or the suggestions by S. Walker, *Environmental Protection versus Trade Liberalization: Finding the Balance* (Publications des Facultés Universitaires Saint-Louis, Brussels, 1993), 102 taking up a proposal by P. Sands, 'European Community Environmental Law: Legislation, the European Court of Justice and Common-Interest Groups' [1990] 53 *MLR* 685 at 698.

[100] See e.g. the amending Annex II to Dir. 79/409/EEC on the conservation of wild birds, n. 22 above. Here the Member States are required to ensure that the practice of hunting complies with the principle of intelligent and ecologically balanced control of the species of birds concerned [1994] OJ L164/1.

[101] See for many others T. Schoenbaum, 'Free International Trade and Protection of the Environment' [1992] *AJIL* 700 to 727 or E.-U. Petersmann, *International and European Trade and Environmental Law after the Uruguay Round* (Kluwer, London, 1995).

[102] Krämer, n. 17 above 119.

which a measure has involved the legitimacy of a national import measure for the protection of the non-domestic environment has not produced a clear answer.[103]

Case: In its decision in Case C–169/89 *Criminal proceedings against Gourmetterie Van den Burg BV (Scottish Red Grouse)*[104] the Court did not really consider the geographical scope of the rule of reason or of Article 36. The case concerned a Dutch import restriction on a wild species of birds (the Scottish red grouse) which did not occur in The Netherlands and was not endangered in Scotland, the only Member State where it occurred. In its statement the Commission described the geographical scope of Article 36 as including the health and life of humans, animals, and plants in other Member States and was partly followed by the Advocate General who, however, considered the measure in any case to be disproportionate.[105] The Court, however, did not consider the scope of Article 36 as it found the relevant area exhaustively covered by secondary Community legislation which did not in the case concerned allow for additional national measures, as certain conditions set out in the relevant directive were not fulfilled.

In a decision in 1977, the Court declared that it was lawful under Articles 30 and 36 for two contiguous Member States to decide to carry out a sanitary control in the interests of the importing State within the territory of the exporting State.[106] This case, however, concerned a mutual agreement to facilitate trade and is therefore not relevant for the question under discussion here.[107] As far as export restrictions on dangerous materials or waste are concerned, the Court has usually rejected the argument that this was necessary for the protection of the environment. 'Clearly, the environment is protected just as effectively when the oils are sold to an authorized disposal or regenerating undertaking of another Member State as when they are disposed of in the Member State of origin.'[108]

The dangers arising in another Member State from the import and transport of such waste in its territory thus most probably lie within the sovereignty and responsibility of the importing Member State.[109] Nevertheless, it seems reasonable to base this conclusion on the principle that the exported waste or

---

[103] Case C–169/89 *Scottish Red Grouse*, n. 14 above, 2163.

[104] *Ibid.* The hunting of birds has subsequently been regulated at a European level; see e.g. the amending Annex II to Dir. 79/409/EEC on the conservation of wild birds. Here the Member States are required to ensure that the practice of hunting complies with the principle of intelligent and ecologically balanced control of the species of birds concerned [1994] *OJ* L164/1. See also L. Krämer, *European Environmental Law—Case Book* (Sweet & Maxwell, London, 1993), 152 to 161, who holds that Dir. 79/409/EEC protects all species of birds as stated in Art. 1 of the Dir.

[105] Opinion of Van Gerven AG of 20 Mar. 1990 in Case C–169/89 *Scottish Red Grouse*, n. 14 above, 2157.

[106] Case 46/76 *Bauhuis* v. *The Netherlands* [1977] *ECR* 5 (para. 45).

[107] Same opinion Everling, n. 73 above, 11, and Van Gerven AG in his opinion in Case C–169/89 *Scottish Red Grouse*, n. 14 above, 2155, criticizing the Commission's proposal.

[108] Case 172/82 *Inter Huiles*, n. 83 above, 555 (para. 14). This case, however, concerned a situation where the Community had adopted a dir. which was to be implemented by the Member States.

[109] See, for specific considerations on the German waste legislation and, in particular, the provision concerning waste exports subject to a proof of equality of foreign treatment with domestic provisions, Rengeling, n. 98 above, 371.

dangerous substance is lawfully treated in the other Member State.[110] If it becomes clear that the exported goods will be handled contrary to the security provisions of the importing Member State, the exporting Member State has a certain responsibility towards the importing Member State and population concerned. This also follows from the principle of mutual loyalty and co-operation in the Community. Everling derives this principle of co-operation and mutual recognition of existing legal differences from the general Treaty system and particularly Article 5.[111]

Today the result of the above-mentioned waste cases might be influenced by the aspects of self-sufficiency in the recycling of waste, as stated in Article 130r(2) EC or in the Court's decision concerning import restrictions for waste in the *Walloon Waste Case*.[112] From this principle one might conclude that it is also a legitimate principle of national environmental policy to limit the export of waste to other regions or countries. If this principle justifies import restrictions for environmental reasons it should also be applicable to export restrictions. The specific character of waste would here justify an exception from the general prohibition of Article 34.

ARBITRARY DISCRIMINATION OR DISGUISED RESTRICTION ON TRADE

General Observations

Article 36's second sentence submits national measures to the condition that they 'shall not constitute a means of arbitrary discrimination or a disguised restriction on trade between Member States'. This prohibition is designed to prevent misuse of any of the permitted justifications referred to in Article 36, first sentence.[113] The Court has repeatedly stated that Article 36, second sentence, applies also to measures in respect of which the rule of reason is invoked.[114]

Discrimination and Unequal Application

In principle, Article 36 also allows national measures which apply to domestic and imported goods in different ways. Nevertheless, such a differentiation must be objectively and genuinely justified,[115] otherwise it would have to be regarded

---

[110] See Everling, n. 73 above.   [111] Everling, n. 73 above, 11.

[112] Case C–2/90 *Walloon Waste Case*, n. 7 above, para. 34.

[113] Such as clearly declared by the Court in Case 144/81 *Keurkoop BV* v. *Nancy Kean Gifts BV* [1982] *ECR* 2853 at 2872 to 2873; see also Case 34/79 *Henn & Darby*, n. 66 above, 3815; Case 40/82 *Newcastle Disease*, n. 52, 2825, as referred to by Kapteyn and VerLoren van Themaat, n. 1 above, 402.

[114] e.g. Case 8/74 *Dassonville*, n. 15 above, 852; see Kapteyn and VerLoren van Themaat, n. 1 above, 402.

[115] e.g. Case 4/75 *Rewe-Zentralfinanz GmbH* v. *Landwirtschaftskammer (Phyto-Sanitary Examinations)* [1975] *ECR* 843 at 860.

as an arbitrary discrimination. In the case of health protection the Court has stated 'that any suspicion that products are dangerous or that health rules have not been complied with must be a genuine suspicion based on reasonable grounds and may not be simply an excuse for interfering systematically or in an arbitrary manner with interstate trade'.[116]

The usual test for the discriminatory application of measures is a comparison with the treatment of domestic goods.[117] In some cases the Court will treat the unequal treatment of imported products in comparison to domestic products as a prohibited discrimination *per se*.[118]

As has been demonstrated earlier, the Court has held that the rule of reason may only be invoked if the national measures apply equally to domestic and imported goods.[119] In principle the prohibition of arbitrary discrimination and disguised protectionism is already included in the more general test for the applicability of the rule of reason. The effect and purpose are at least very similar to the test applied under Article 36, although the requirement of equal application of the measures may differ from the prohibition spelled out in Article 36. Also, from an environmental point of view the discriminatory treatment of domestic and foreign products only leads to distortions of trade and the inefficient allocation of resources.[120]

Disguised Restriction of Trade

The Court will look behind domestic measures under Article 36 to eliminate purely or mainly protectionist measures taken in favour of domestic industry.[121] Similarly, when applying the rule of reason the Court uses a broad discrimination approach[122] which may also embrace equally applicable measures if they have disparate effects on imported and domestic goods or aim at the protection of domestic production.[123] The Court has repeatedly stated that a national

---

[116] Kapteyn and VerLoren van Themaat, n. 1 above, 403, with reference to Case 42/82 *Commission* v. *France (Wine War)* [1983] *ECR* 1013 at 1043.

[117] D. Wyatt and A. Dashwood, *European Community Law* (3rd edn., Sweet & Maxwell, London, 1993), 226.

[118] See Kapteyn and VerLoren van Themaat, n. 1 above, 402, with reference to Case 152/78 *Commission* v. *France (Recommendation for Alcoholic Beverages)* [1980] *ECR* 2299 at 2316. See for a similar application of the *per se* discrimination rule in the case law of the US Supreme Court in *Hughes* v. *Oklahoma*, 441 US 322 (1979) at 377 as referred to and documented by Geradin, n. 8 above, 157.

[119] See e.g. Case 788/79 *Criminal Proceedings against Gilli and Andres (Gilli and Andres)* [1980] *ECR* 2071 at 2078; Case 16/83 *Criminal Proceedings against K. Prantl (Bocksbeutel)* [1984] *ECR* 1299 at 1327; Case 177/83 *Theodor Kohl* v. *Ringelhan & Rennett* [1984] *ECR* 3651 at 3662.

[120] See e.g. E.-U. Petersmann, 'Freier Warenverkehr und nationaler Umweltschutz in EWG und EWR' [1993] *Aussenwirtschaft* 95 at 106.

[121] Kapteyn and VerLoren van Themaat, n. 1 above, 403. In a similar way the US Supreme Court has established the principle that if a state environmental law is in reality a 'simple economic protection' the Court applies 'a virtually *per se* rule of invalidity'; see *Philadelphia* v. *New Jersey*, 437 US 617 (1978) as referred to by Geradin, n. 8 above, 159.-

[122] See Ch. 2 for the different concepts of non-discrimination.

[123] Case 207/83 *Commission* v. *United Kingdom (Indications of Origin)* [1985] *ECR* 1201.

measure falls within the prohibition of Article 30 'if in practice it produces protective effects by favouring typical national products and, by the same token, operating to the detriment of certain types of products from other Member States.'[124]

In view of the Court's case law it seems, however, that the concept of discrimination because of the disparate effect of a national measure may not be extended.[125] It is an inherent effect of national product regulations that they bear less on domestic producers than on those from other Member States if the former have a larger share of their sales within the county of origin than nondomestic producers.[126]

Case: In Case 302/86 *Commission* v. *Denmark* (*Danish Bottles*)[127] the Commission had observed that the Danish requirement to set up a collection system for containers of beer and soft drinks for bottles bore more heavily on foreign producers than on domestic firms. Advocate General Sir Gordon Slynn shared this opinion. In his view the Danish measures were discriminatory even though on the surface indiscriminately applicable. In practice they bore much more heavily on foreign producers than on domestic firms. He therefore excluded the application of the rule of reason. The Court, however, applied the rule of reason with reference to the obviously equal application of the measure.

Ecological Differentiation

The main question in relation to the prohibition of discrimination under Article 36 and the rule of reason is, in my view, whether a specific differentiation is objectively and genuinely justified in the interest of a legitimate objective or whether it amounts to an arbitrary discrimination.[128] The distinction can be very difficult.[129]

In the field of health protection and environmental protection, a differentiation relating to the country of origin is most often not objectively justified, as the ecological risks of domestic goods and imports are equivalent. Such a differentiation can, however, be justified, for example, if phytosanitary control measures are taken at the point of entry into the country as a precaution against the trans-

---

[124] Case 16/83 *Bocksbeutel*, n. 119 above, 1327 (para. 21) as referred to by A. Furrer, 'Nationale Umweltschutzkompetenzen in der EG und im EWR' [1992] *AJP* 1517 at 1522.

[125] e.g. Case 302/86 *Danish Bottles*, n. 4 above, where the Court did not follow the AG's and the Commission's reasoning. See also Jadot, n. 40 above, 424, or Petersmann, n. 120 above, 120.

[126] It is, however, evident that the inherently protectionist effect of differing local standards is a preoccupation for every divided-power system which seeks integration through an open and undivided market; this is also the experience in federal states in general, see e.g. for Australia: C. Staker, 'Free Movement of Goods in the EEC and Australia: A Comparative Study' [1990] *YEL* 209 to 242 or for the United States: *State of Minnesota* v. *Clover Leaf Creamery Company et al.*, US Supreme Court, 21 Jan. 1981, reprinted in 101 SCt. 449 US 456, 715 to 737. See also Möschel, n. 98 above, 294.

[127] Case 302/86 *Danish Bottles*, n. 4 above.

[128] Even the very integration-oriented case law of the US Supreme Court accepts discriminatory measures if 'the discrimination [was] demonstrably justified by a valid factor unrelated to economic protectionism' see *Fort Gratiot Sanitary Landfill, Inc.* v. *Michigan Department of Natural Resources*, 112 SCt. 2019 (1992) at 2024, as referred to by Geradin, n. 8 above, 160.

[129] Case 40/82, n. 52 above.

mission of a destructive disease or pest which does not exist within the country of destination. The existence of complementary internal measures to prevent the distribution of contaminated products can be a clue for the genuineness of these measures.[130]

Proximity and Self-sufficiency

It seems reasonable to conclude that under the general system of the Community legal order, ecological reasons are also objective criteria for the differentiation between certain categories of products.[131] This derives from the Court's case law too. As in other areas, the Court and all Community actors should apply the general principles which govern the Community environmental policy.

In its recent judgment in Case C–2/90 *Commission* v. *Belgium (Walloon Waste Case)*[132] the Court gave an example of the consequences which the consideration of 'relatively new' ecological principles can have in the application of 'classical' Community principles. The Court accepted a regional rule applying only to non-domestic waste as justified under the rule of reason with reference to the principles of correction at source,[133] self sufficiency, and proximity.[134] It is a particularly interesting case, as here the mere fact that a product is imported and not locally produced leads to a differentiation of otherwise identical products. In the view of the Court, the ecological principles mentioned and the 'particular nature of waste' make such a differentiation lawful.[135]

---

[130] Case 4/75 *Phyto-Sanitary Examinations*, n. 115 above.

[131] See also the existing case law under Art. 95, described in Ch. 3.

[132] Case C–2/90 *Walloon Waste Case*, n. 7 above; for comments see P. v. Wilmowsky, 'Waste Disposal in the Internal Market: The State of the Play after the ECJ's ruling on the Walloon Import Ban' (1993) 30 *CMLRev.* 541 to 570 (in German: P. v. Wilmowsky, 'Abfall und freier Warenverkehr: Bestandesaufnahme nach dem EuGH-Urteil zum wallonischen Einfuhrverbot' [1992] *EuR* 414 to 433); W. Th. Douma, 'Walloon Waste Import Ban' [1993] *European Business Law Review* 32 to 34; D. Geradin, 'The Belgian Waste Case' (1993) 18 *ELRev.* 144 to 153; Geradin, n. 8 above, 185 to 190; S. Tostmann, 'EuGH-Verbot des Ablagerns von Abfall aus einem anderen Mitgliedstaat' [1992] *EuZW* 577 to 580; A. Epiney, 'Einbeziehung gemeinschaftlicher Umweltschutzprinzipien in die Bestimmungen mitgliedstaatlichen Handlungsspeilraums' [1993] *DVBl.* 93 to 100.

[133] Art. 130r(2) EC.

[134] Convention on the Control of Transboundary Movements of Hazardous Wastes and Their Disposal, signed in Basel on 22 Mar. 1989 (Basel Convention) reprinted in (1989) 28 *ILM* 657 and Dir. 91/156/EEC [1991] *OJ* L78/32. See for details A. Schmidt, 'Transboundary Movements of Waste under EC Law' [1992] *J Env. L* 57 at 72. Dir. 75/442/EEC [1975] *OJ* L194/39 and 91/156/EEC, see above, limit the principles of self-sufficiency and proximity to the disposal of waste and do not openly include the recovery of waste. Furthermore, it is not clear whether a Member State can rely on these principles against the Community. One might argue, however, that these principles are general principles of environmental law which are also applicable by the Member States when adopting domestic environmental laws infringing the general principles of the common market.

[135] See Case C–2/90 *Walloon Waste Case*, n. 7 above, 4480.

Case: In its decision in Case C–2/90 *Commission* v. *Belgium* (*Walloon Waste Case*)[136] the Court heard a case concerning an import restriction for waste established in the Belgian province of Wallonia. The Court held that waste, whether recyclable or not, was covered by the free movement of goods and that national measures had to be compatible with Article 30. As Wallonia was inundated by a heavy afflux of waste from other regions and Member States, the Court considered restrictions of the import as lawful, as the enormous afflux of waste constituted an environmental danger for the region. The restrictions, however, concerned only waste from other regions, while domestic waste was not concerned. The Commission argued that such a distinction between domestic and non-domestic waste was discriminatory and not compatible with the application of the rule of reason. The Court referred to the environmental principles of Community law, such as stated in Article 130r(2) that environmental damage should be rectified at source. From these principles the Court derived the principle that a differentiation on grounds of the origin of waste did not constitute an arbitrary discrimination.

From the Court's reasoning, however, it seems probable that an import restriction which applied to waste from other Member States rather than taking into account a concept of geographical or administrative regions or entities would have constituted an arbitrary discrimination.[137] The Court refers explicitly to the self-sufficiency of regions, communities, and other local entities. In my view, this might only coincide with the whole territory of a State in the case of a very small Member State, e.g. in the case of Luxembourg. Nevertheless, it is understandable that the Court rejected, in principle, any discrimination between the products of different Member States.[138] As the transport of waste over long distances is dangerous,[139] in principle the closest regenerating or disposal facility should be used[140] irrespective of any national borders.

While many authors recognize the principle of self-sufficiency as the 'best incentive to prevent the generation of waste, thereby attacking the problem at the source'[141] and minimizing the dangers involved in the transport of waste itself, they also argue that the national level of protection is not necessarily the optimal level for such measures. The concept of region or local entity, as used by the Court, seems to point to this conclusion. This interpretation alone makes it possible to reconcile the decision in the *Walloon Waste Case*[142] with the prior case law concerning waste exports[143] and the principles of secondary

---

[136] See Case C–2/90 *Walloon Waste Case*, n. 7 above, 4481.

[137] *Ibid.*, 4481; for comments see e.g. Tostmann, n. 132 above, 577 to 580.

[138] Krämer, n. 17 above, 128, refers to the German waste law (*Abfallgesetz*), s. 13, which provides for an authorization procedure for the import of waste into Germany.

[139] On the transport of waste within the Community see in general D. Laurence and B. Wynne, 'Transporting Waste in the European Community: A Free Market?' [1989] *Environment* (July/Aug.) 12 to 17 and 34 to 35 or Schmidt, n. 134 above, 57 to 80.

[140] Case C–2/90 *Walloon Waste Case*, n. 7 above, 4480 (para. 34).

[141] See e.g. A. Schmidt, 'Trade in Waste under Community Law' in Cameron, Demaret, and Geradin (eds.), n. 4 above, 184 at 197.

[142] Case C–2/90 *Walloon Waste Case*, n. 7 above.

[143] See above in this chapter on goegraphical scope of Article 36.

Community law, such as Directive 83/631/EEC[144] which indicates that, in some cases, it may be necessary to transport waste between Member States for its optimal disposal.[145]

Case: In earlier but similar proceedings the Commission started an action against Belgium because the Flanders Region prohibited *inter alia* the import of manure from its neighbour, The Netherlands. Flanders argued that the imported manure would be spread on the fields and could lead to excessive contamination of the soil and waters. On the other hand, the use of manure from Belgium was not regulated, although its spreading on the soil would have been as dangerous as in the case of manure from The Netherlands. The Commission held that the effective protection of the environment could not be obtained by a simple import ban, but had to be reached by a non-discriminatory measure such as the regulation of the use of manure in general. Therefore it considered the Flemish measure not to be justified on environmental grounds. The Court's reasoning in Case C–2/90 *Walloon Waste Case*[146] might have led to a different evaluation as far as regional measures are concerned which apply equally to all manure from outside the region or area.[147]

It is interesting to observe that the outcome of the decision in Case C–2/90 *Walloon Waste Case*[148] was by no means obvious. Similar cases arising in the United States were decided by the US Supreme Court restrictively. In two cases[149] in 1992 local waste bans were not approved by the Supreme Court in spite of the fact that they were equally applicable to waste from areas within the state or from other states. The Supreme Court argued on the basis of its settled case law that, in the absence of any justification apart from its origin, the differential treatment of waste coming from outside a region or local entity was discriminatory and not compatible with the commerce clause and the general principles governing the free movement of goods.[150]

While the Court of Justice of the European Community underlines the difference that lies in the non-local origin of waste, the US Supreme Court considers this an indication of the discriminatory and protectionist objective of a local measure.[151] The main difference between the decisions of the US Supreme Court and the Court of Justice lies in the way the two courts treat the place of origin of waste. While the Court of Justice accepts the unequal treatment of local waste and waste from other areas for environmental reasons, the US Supreme Court does not. The US approach seems to be more in favour of a common

[144] Council Dir. 84/631/EEC on the supervision and control within the European Community of transfrontier shipments of hazardous waste, several times amended [1984] *OJ* L326/31.

[145] See, on open questions with regard to the decision, Petersmann, n. 120 above, 121.

[146] Case C–2/90 *Walloon Waste Case*, n. 7 above.

[147] Unpublished proceedings reported by L. Krämer, *EEC Treaty and Environmental Protection* (Sweet & Maxwell, London, 1990), 37.

[148] Case C–2/90 *Walloon Waste Case*, n. 7 above.

[149] *Fort Gratiot Sanitary Landfill, Inc.* v. *Michigan Dept. of Natural Resources*, n. 128 above, and *Chemical Waste Management, Inc.* v. *Hunt*, 112 SCt. 2009 (1992), as referred to by Geradin, n. 8 above, 194.

[150] See n. 149 above.

[151] With reference to its decision in *Philadelphia* v. *New Jersey*, n. 121 above, as referred to by Geradin, n. 8 above, 194.

solution to the waste problem and rejects the possibility that one state could try 'to isolate itself from a problem common to many by erecting a barrier against the movement of interstate trade'.[152] In these cases the risk of a 'balkanization'[153] of a common market and the disintegrating effect of a measure have been considered more important than the possible environmental effects.

These environmental effects of the principle of correction at source, as it is explicitly set out in the EC Treaty, are by no means undisputed. Several authors argue that the principles of self-sufficiency and proximity are 'likely to distort commerce, interfere with economies of scale, divert waste to less protective facilities, have mischievous effects on efforts by responsible companies to internalize or otherwise closely control management of their hazardous waste'.[154] The mere reference by the Court to the principles of self-sufficiency and proximity, without further explanation, have rightly been criticized by several authors, especially because they are inherently contradictory to the general economic principles underlying trade and the theory of comparative advantage in general.[155]

Despite the possible positive effects of the principles referred to above, a more detailed analysis of their scope and their implications for legitimate differentiation between goods will be needed. The principles of self-sufficiency and proximity have also deeply influenced Community secondary legislation in recent years. Here some authors have criticized the Community for leaving Member States with too much discretion and competence to take key decisions and have argued that the Community thereby jeopardized its own harmonization.[156]

THE PROPORTIONALITY PRINCIPLE

General Observations

As has been noted, the Court has recognized that the protection of the environment can lead to situations where the free movement of goods has to be restricted by national measures. The Court recognizes both the protection of the environment and the free movement of goods as essential pillars of European integration. This may lead to situations where one has to be restricted in the interests of the other. The achievement of both may make it necessary to co-

---

[152] These are the words used by Justice Stewart in *Philadelphia* v. *New Jersey*, n. 121 above, also referred to by Geradin, n. 8 above, 193.

[153] D. Kommers and M. Waelbroeck, 'Legal Integration and the Free Movement of Goods: The American and European Experience' in M. Cappelletti, M. Seccombe and J. H. H. Weiler (eds.), *Integration through Law* (W. de Gruyter, New York, 1985), i, bk. 1, 165 at 221.

[154] e.g. T. Smith and V. Sarnoff, 'Free Commerce and Sound Waste Management: Some International Comparative Perspectives' [1992] *International Environmental Reporter* 207 at 214 as referred to by Geradin, n. 8 above, 196.

[155] See e.g. Petersmann, n. 120 above, 121 and 122; Geradin, n. 8 above, 196 and 197.

[156] See Schmidt, n. 141 above, 196 ff.

ordinate the two objectives. This, however, is not possible in an abstract and general way, but requires an evaluation of the interests concerned in a case-by-case analysis.

Like some national courts faced with the necessity of co-ordinating conflicting interests, the Court applies a proportionality test to decide whether a restriction on the free movement of goods is justified under the principles of Community law. Nevertheless, as always in Community law, national concepts of proportionality can only be used in a very cautious way, since Community law as a *ius sui generis* may follow different concepts from those used in one or several Member States.[157] From the existing case law, however, there seem to be similarities to the proportionality test as known in German administrative law.[158] Similar approaches are also used in international trade law and in other federal states with regard to inter-state trade.[159]

The Court views the application of the proportionality principle as an inherent consequence of Article 36, second sentence, of the Treaty.[160] Some legal writers, however, suggest the application of the proportionality test in the evaluation of the first sentence of Article 36.[161] A national environmental measure, although justified under Article 36, first sentence, can be prohibited if it is not proportionate and thus too onerous an interference with the principle of Article 30.

The Court itself has applied its proportionality test in different ways and does not always clearly distinguish all the elements of its test. The language of the Court is not always completely coherent and the variety of Community languages and legal traditions makes it difficult at times to recognize the proportionality test as applied by the Court.[162] For the purpose of this analysis the criteria for the proportionality of a measure may be distilled into the following three questions: (a) whether a measure is genuinely aimed at or reasonably justified for the attempted objective (suitability or reasonableness of a measure), (b) whether the measure is essential or necessary for the attainment of the objective, implying that it has to be the least trade-restrictive measure available among several alternatives (least trade-restrictive measure), and (c) whether the improve-

---

[157] See e.g. Case 283/81 *CILFIT* v. *Ministère de la Santé* [1982] *ECR* 3415 at 3430.

[158] See also the arguments of by J. Schwarze, *Europäisches Verwaltungsrecht* (Nomos, Baden-Baden, 1988) ii, 832 (in English: J. Schwarze, *European Administrative Law* (Sweet & Maxwell, London, 1992)); Henke, n. 40 above, 179; Becker, n. 40 above, 82 to 89. The perspective of these German authors might, however, be too biased because of their own experience with the German legal system. This may, however, also be true for the author of this study, writing from a Swiss perspective, where the proportionality principle is used in a similar way as in Germany. See. e.g. G. Häfelin and G. Müller, *Grundriss des allgemeinen Verwaltungsrechts* (Schulthess, Zürich, 1990), 104 to 108.

[159] See GATT: e.g. E.-U. Petersmann, 'International Trade Law and International Environmental Law—Prevention and Settlement of International Disputes in the GATT' [1993] *JWT* 45 to 81; for the United States see the detailed analysis by Geradin, n. 8 above, 146 to 155; for Australia see Staker, n. 1126 above, 229.

[160] Case 247/84, n. 15 above, 3905; see Becker, n. 40 above, 76.

[161] Kapteyn and VerLoren van Themaat, n. 1 above, 402.

[162] See for examples Becker, n. 40 above, 82, n. 82.

ment in environmental quality is proportionate to the restriction of trade resulting from this measure. This third aspect requires a sound relationship between
the restrictive character of a measure and its result (proportionality or prohibition of excessiveness[163]).

Reasonableness and Suitability

In its case law the Court has established that a national measure has to be reasonable[164] for the pursuit of a justified (environmental) objective.[165] Sometimes
the Court also refers to the capacity of a measure to in fact achieve the
attempted objective.[166] While the objective itself has to be sanctioned by the
Court's interpretation of Article 36 and the rule of reason[167] and the level of this
objective seems to lie in the discretion of the Member States,[168] a measure which
hinders trade among Member States must be in the genuine interest of the
objective indicated. The Member State must be able reasonably to justify the
use of a measure for environmental aims. The question to be asked is whether
the chosen measures are 'appropriate ways for achieving the desired results'[169]
or 'suitable for the purpose of achieving the desired objective'.[170]

As far as the suitability of domestic measures is concerned, the Court has
repeatedly held that Member States should have a relatively wide discretion in
the choice of the appropriate measures and that the test applied by the Court is
aimed mainly at eliminating obviously inappropriate measures.[171] This implies
that the Court will not assess whether the measure chosen is the most appropriate one, but rather whether there is an obvious and reasonable link[172]
between the measure used and the objective pursued.[173] Nevertheless, the Court

[163] See for details on the proportionality test as applied by the Court: Schwarze, n. 158 above,
661 ff. and Epiney and Möllers, n. 39 above, Part II.

[164] In German usually referred to as *geeignet/Geeignetheit*; in French referred to as *efficace/efficacité*;
see Jadot, n. 40 above, 419.

[165] See Case 25/70 *Einfuhr- und Vorratsstelle für Getreide und Futtermittel* v. *Köster et al.* [1970] *ECR*
1161 at 1175 (paras. 27 and 28); Case 808/79 *Criminal Proceedings against Pardini* [1980] *ECR* 2103 at
2120 (para. 17) where the measure is considered 'simple and effective' or Joined cases 279, 280, 285,
and 286/84 *Walter Rau* v. *Commission (Christmas Butter)* [1987] *ECR* 1069 at 1092 (para. 41). See e.g.
also Middeke, n. 40 above, 193.

[166] See e.g. Case 302/86 *Danish Bottles*, n. 4 above, 4632: 'the system for returning non-approved
containers is capable of protecting the environment'.   [167] See Ch. 4.

[168] See above in Ch. 5 on the remaining responsibility of the Member States.

[169] Lenz AG in Joined cases 279, 280, 285, and 286/84 *Christmas Butter*, n. 165 above, 1092.

[170] *Ibid.* 1125 (para. 34). See also the US Supreme Court's practice to ask for a 'reasonably effective measure' or 'reasonable means', see e.g. *Procter & Gamble* v. *Chicago*, 509 F2d 69 at 76 (7th Cir.),
cert. denied 421 US 978 (1975) as referred to by Geradin, n. 8 above, 159.

[171] See for details Schwarze, n. 158 above, 833 with reference to the Court's judgment in Case
40/72 *Schröder* v. *Germany* [1973] *ECR* 125 and 142 and Case 138/78 *Stölting* v. *Hauptzollamt Hamburg-
Jonas* [1979] *ECR* 713 at 722.

[172] This might go in the direction of the reasonableness test as known in English constitutional
law, but probably not as far as the similar concept in American constitutional law; for an appraisal
of the reasonableness test in Anglo-American law, see e.g. D. J. Galligan, *Discretionary Powers* (Oxford
University Press, Oxford, 1990), 323.

is prepared to eliminate the abuse of domestic measures for unjustified objectives if a measure seems predominantly to be adopted for other reasons.[174]

Case: In its decision in Case C–195/92 *Commission* v. *Germany* the Court did not accept the German argument that the introduction of a tax on heavy goods vehicles combined with a compensatory measure for domestic undertakings was justified for environmental reasons. In the view of the Court the domestic measures, in particular the quasi-compensation of domestic carriers, were rather intended at the protection of domestic carriers than at the protection of the environment. 'Dans ces conditions, il n'est pas établi qu'elle [la mesure allemande] soit apte à conduire à des transferts du trafic routier vers les moyens de transport ferroviaire et fluvial plutôt qu'à une augmentation des parts de marché des transporteurs allemends au détriment des transporteurs des autres Etats membres.'[175]

Least-restrictive Measure (Necessity)

A national measure may not hinder inter-state trade any more than is necessary for the attainment of the permitted objective.[176] While the decision about the level of protection falls within the discretion of Member States, the measure in question should be the least restrictive among the alternative measures[177] which can be used for the achievement of the national policy objective:[178] '[i]f a Member State has a choice between various measures for achieving the same aim, it should choose the means which least restrict the free movement of goods'.[179]

A domestic measure cannot be legitimated under the exceptions in Article 36 or the rule of reason if its aim can be achieved just as effectively by measures having effects which are less restrictive on intra-Community trade.[180] Sometimes this requirement is expressed by the simple wording that a measure must be essential or necessary for the attainment of the objective in question.[181] This is, however, slightly misleading, as sometimes the term 'necessary' is also used for the more comprehensive test of the justification of a measure in general. The test whether a measure could reasonably be replaced by another, less restrictive,

---

[173] See Case 2/78 *Commission* v. *Belgium* (*Certificates of Authenticity*) [1979] *ECR* 2555; see also Jadot, n. 40 above, 419.

[174] See e.g. Case 788/79 *Gilli and Andres*, n. 119 above, 2078.

[175] Case C–195/90 *Tax on Heavy Good Vehicles*, n. 38 above, 3184 (para. 31).

[176] e.g Case 8/74 *Dassonville*, n. 15 above, 852; Case 261/81 *Walter Rau* v. *P.V.B.A. De Smedt* [1982] *ECR* 3961 at 3973; Case 193/80 *Commission* v. *Italy* (*Vinegar*) [1981] *ECR* 3019 at 3035, referred to in Kapteyn and VerLoren van Themaat, n. 1 above, 387; see also Becker, n. 40 above, 82 to 88; Middeke, n. 40 above, 195.

[177] 'Le moindre obstacle pour la liberté des échanges', as referred to by Jadot, n. 40 above, 420.

[178] Case 240/83 *ADBHU*, n. 7 above, 549; Case 302/86 *Danish Bottles*, n. 4 above, 4629 (para. 6); see e.g. also Epiney and Möllers, n. 39 above, 85.

[179] Case 302/86 *Danish Bottles*, n. 4 above, 4629 (para. 6).

[180] See for a recent example the Court's reasoning in Case C–131/93 *Fresh-water Crayfish*, n. 41 above.

[181] See Kapteyn and VerLoren van Themaat, n. 1 above, 395, with reference to the abundant case law.

measure is often a rigorous one which frequently leads to the national measure being overturned.[182]

An important consequence of this principle is that a Member State must take into account the existing measures and safety controls in the country of origin of the imported goods. If the standards are considered equivalent, there is no need for a specific domestic measure, i.e. the measure is not necessary for the achievement of the national objective[183] as the environmental objective is already satisfied by equivalent standards in the exporting Member State.[184] The Commission bears the burden of proof that the measures applied in the State of origin ensure an equivalent level of protection.[185]

The comparison of different measures and the levels of protection achieved is a relatively difficult task.[186] Although the Court insists on the use of the measure which involves the least restriction on the free movement of goods, its case law suggests no intention to evaluate every measure in detail and to suggest other measures, as long as a Member State is able to justify its own measures in a reasonable and understandable way.[187] Some authors argue for a very high level of discretion for Member States as they believe this will guarantee the best protection of the environment.[188] Nevertheless, the Court has developed specific criteria for the evaluation of the necessity of a measure. The Court takes the view that a total ban on a product is often not necessary, and prefers to rely on declaration and information requirements.[189] In many cases therefore the Court of Justice has held a requirement of declaration about a product's contents and the production process undergone as sufficient and less trade restrictive than the

---

[182] See e.g. the analysis in Case 302/86 *Danish Bottles*, n. 4 above, 4629 (para. 12). The difficult problems which arise when evaluating the least trade-restrictive measure are set out in an analysis of a planned German measure to oblige car sellers to take back old cars by Möschel, n. 98 above, 293.

[183] See Case 104/75, n. 44 above, 636 to 638; Case 272/80, n. 41 above, 3291 and 3292; see also Kapteyn and VerLoren van Themaat, n. 1 above, 396.

[184] e.g. Case 188/84 *Commission* v. *France* (*Safety Requirements for Wood Manufacturing Equipment*) [1986] *ECR* 419 at 436 (para. 16); recently Case C–373/92 *Commission* v. *Belgium* (*Recognition of Foreign Standards*) [1993] *ECR* I–3107.

[185] Case 188/84, n. 184 above, 436 (para. 17).

[186] See Becker, n. 40 above, 87.

[187] See K. Hailbronner, 'Der "nationale Alleingang" im Gemeinschaftsrecht am Beispiel der Abgasstandards für PKWs' [1989] *EuGRZ* 101 at 119; E. Steindorff, 'Umweltschutz in Gemeinschaftshand?' [1984] *RIW* 767 at 769.

[188] Epiney and Möllers, n. 39 above, 85.

[189] Case 120/78 *Rewe Zentral AG* v. *Bundesmonopolverwaltung für Branntwein* (*Cassis de Dijon*) [1979] *ECR* 649; Case 788/79 *Gilli and Andres*, n. 119 above; Case 130/80 *Criminal Proceedings against Kelderman* [1981] *ECR* 527; Case 261/81, n. 176 above, 3973; Case 182/84 *Criminal Proceedings against Miro* [1985] *ECR* 3731; Case 179/85 *Commission* v. *Germany* (*Champagne Type Bottles*) [1986] *ECR* 3879; Case 176/84 *Commission* v. *Greece* (*Greek Beer Law*) [1987] *ECR* 1193; Case 178/84 *German Purity Law*, n. 48 above; Case 216/84 *Commission* v. *France* [1988] *ECR* 793; Case 298/87 *Criminal Proceedings against Smanor* [1988] *ECR* 4489; Case 407/85 *Drei Glocken et al.* v. *USL Centro Sud* [1988] *ECR* 4233; Case 286/86 *Criminal Proceedings against Deserbais* [1988] *ECR* 4907, as referred to in Jadot, n. 410 above, 421.

measure in question,[190] although this does not imply that such duties to declare are always justified.[191]

Disproportionality and Excessiveness

Even though most authors suggest that the level of protection on their territory falls completely within the discretion of Member States, the Court may reject a national measure as being disproportionate[192] 'or excessive in relation to the additional benefit to environmental quality.[193] This is the case, for example, if a very restrictive measure has a very small additional effect on the objective desired.[194] In these cases the relationship between the restriction on trade resulting from a measure and the environmental benefit it provides is considered to be unsound.[195]

In the landmark case for the admission of national environmental measures justified under the rule of reason, Case 302/86 *Commission v. Denmark*,[196] the Court held that the additional limitation on the number of containers which could be marketed was disproportionate to the objective pursued.[197]

---

[190] See Furrer, n. 124 above, 1522, referring to Case 178/84 *German Purity Law*, n. 48 above, 1235; Case 407/85, n. 189 above, para. 17; Case 788/79 *Gilli and Andres*, n. 119 above, para. 7 or recently Case C–17/93, n. 44 above.

[191] See e.g. the requirement of Flemish labels for bottles of mineral water imported from France into the Belgian province of Wallonia, Case C–369/89 *Piageme ASBL* v. *Peeters PVBA* [1991] *ECR* I–2971; or for the compulsory indication of the place of origin for chicken imported into Germany, the letter from the Commission to the German Government, reprinted in [1993] *EuZW* 126; see also Case C–317/92 *Commission* v. *Germany (Medical Products—Expiry Date)* [1994] *ECR* I–2039, concerning the lack of justification of a very elaborate declaration requirement for pharmaceuticals or Case C–144/93 *Pfanni* v. *Munich* [1994] *ECR* I–4605 relating to the listing of ingredients which do not serve a technological function in the finished product. Of course, one may argue that these general declaration principles do not satisfy the specific environmental needs, as the environment, in general, cannot be left to individual consumer choices.

[192] In German this criterion is referred to as *angemessen/Angemessenheit*, but certain authors also use the general term *Verhältnismäßigkeit* (proportionality) for this aspect, see Schwarze, n. 158 above, 677 ff. (English version); Jadot uses in French the term *adaptation*; see Jadot, n. 40 above, 418.

[193] See on the balancing test behind such a conclusion the general considerations in Ch. 12 and in detail Middeke, n. 40 above, 199 to 212.

[194] Referred to by the Court usually just as 'proportionality' (e.g. in Case 302/86 *Danish Bottles*, n. 4 above, 4632) while the German doctrine refers more specifically to *Angemessenheit* or *Übermaßverbot*, two descriptions for a concept developed in German administrative law, see e.g. Becker, n. 40 above, 89 to 91; Henke, n. 40 above, 186 to 187; Epiney and Möllers, n. 39 above, 87 to 89 and, in more detail, 90 to 124.

[195] See for the most detailed analysis of the proportionality principle in this context Epiney and Möllers, n. 39 above, 87 ff.

[196] Case 302/86 *Danish Bottles*, n. 4 above, 4632 (para. 21). For comments in English see e.g. P. Kromarek, 'Environmental Protection and Free Movement of Goods' [1990] *J Env. L* 87 to 107; L. Gormley, 'Recent Case Law on the Free Movement of Goods: Some Hot Potatoes' (1900) 27 *CMLRev.* 825 at 844; T. Sexton, 'Enacting National Environmental Laws More Stringent Than Other States' Laws' (1991) 24 *Cornell International LJ* 563 to 593; Geradin, n. 8 above, 183 to 185.

[197] See for a similar case under US law: *State of Minnesota* v. *Clover Leaf Creamery Co.*, n. 126 above,

Case: In the Court's judgment in Case 302/86 *Commission* v. *Denmark* (*Danish Bottles*),[198] the Court had to evaluate the compliance with the Treaty of a Danish system introducing a mandatory collection system for beer and soft drink containers. In the Court's view this system was justified in the interest of the protection of the environment and had to be considered necessary and proportionate. On the other hand the Court analysed the lawfulness of a complementary measure which obliged producers and importers to use only containers approved by the national authorities. The Danish Government had justified this additional licensing requirement by reference to the limited capacity of retailers to accept different types of bottles. In the Danish view the number of bottle types had to be restricted and controlled for the successful working of the collection system, but they were willing to allow an amount of 3,000 hectolitres of drinks per year to be sold in non-approved containers. The Court declared that such a measure undoubtedly ensured the functioning of the system and, to a very considerable degree, the protection of the environment. It continued, however, that the approved collection system itself already ensured a high degree of protection, and in the absence of a similar system for beverages other than beer and softdrinks, the limitation of the quantity to be bottled in non-approved containers was a disproportionate measure. 'In those circumstances, a restriction of the quantity of products which may be marketed by importers is disproportionate to the objective pursued.'[199]

In my view the Court's conclusion can only be interpreted as a rejection of a national measure because of its excessive character in relation to the consequent improvement of environmental protection. Although the Court indicates that the measure applied ensures the best level of protection it rejects the measure because of its restrictive character.[200] The Court does not say that another measure would produce exactly the same results but refers to the disproportionate relationship between the measure concerned and the additional benefit.[201]

Among the few environmental cases which have been decided under the rule of reason, the judgment in Case 302/86 *Danish Bottles*[202] is, for the time being, the only one in which a domestic measure was held to be unlawful by reason of its excessive character. Even if, in the future, the Court does not accept any

727 to 729 where the court held that in the absence of any discrimination and despite the environmental justification 'the controlling question is, whether the incidental burden imposed on interstate commerce by the Minnesota act is 'clearly' excessive to the local putative benefits'. The case concerned a local statute banning the retail sale of milk in non-returnable non-refillable containers. See for more examples J. Cameron and H. Ward, *The Uruguay Round's Technical Barriers to Trade Agreement* (WWF, Gland, 1992), 16.

[198] Case 302/86 *Danish Bottles*, n. 4 above, 4628 to 4632.
[199] Case 302/86 *Danish Bottles*, n. 4 above, 4632 (para. 21).
[200] Case 302/86 *Danish Bottles*, n. 4 above, 4632 (para. 20).
[201] Some authors consider this to be a declaration by the Court that the licensing measure is not necessary: Henke, n. 40 above, 186; probably also Becker, n. 40 above, 90, n. 346. In my view, however, the Court considered the measure necessary for the high-level objective but did not accept the unsound relationship between additional benefit and trade restriction. This is also the opinion of O. Brunetti, *EG-Rechtsverträglichkeit als Kriterium der nationalen Umweltpolitik* (Schulthess and Stämpfli, Zürich and Bern, 1993), 37 and H.-W. Rengeling and K. Heinz, 'Die dänische Pfandflaschenregelung' [1990] *JuS* 613 at 617.
[202] Case 302/86 *Danish Bottles*, n. 4 above.

national level of protection, no matter how high, it seems that it is willing to leave Member States a large sphere of discretion for the evaluation of the level of protection and adequate measures.[203] This corresponds to the Court's case law in the field of the protection of health of humans, animals, and plants under Article 36.[204] The precautionary principle and the Treaty's reference to a high level of protection seem to strengthen this approach.

[203] Epiney and Möllers, n. 39 above, 74, or Schutt and Steffens, n. 58 above, 449.

[204] Case 40/82 *Newcastle Disease*, n. 52 above, 295; Case 74/82 *Commission* v. *Ireland* (*Poultry and Eggs*) [1984] *ECR* 317 at 340; Case 94/83 *Pesticides on Apples*, n. 65 above, 3280. See for details Vorwerk, n. 65 above, 140.

6

Fair and Undistorted Competition and the Environment

INTRODUCTION

Besides the four freedoms and the approximation of laws, the Community's system ensuring fair and undistorted competition is a main pillar of the common market. The principles of Articles 85–90 primarily concern the distorting behaviour of private undertakings, but they apply by implication to Member States taking action to support, facilitate, or allow such private behaviour.

Agreements between undertakings and public authorities for the voluntary reduction of certain environmentally harmful behaviour or the co-ordination of environmental issues have become increasingly important in contemporary environmental policy. Nevertheless, such agreements defy, in principle, the prohibition contained in Article 85. The Commission may, however, concede exceptions to the prohibition under the relevant procedures. The importance of such voluntary agreements is recognized in principle as they can help to improve environmental quality and contribute to better solutions for current problems. The same applies to undertakings in a dominant position using their influence for specific environmental improvements as long as they do not abuse their position as prohibited under Article 86. Nevertheless, neither voluntary agreements nor the use of a dominant position may go beyond a necessary restriction of competition to achieve environmental goals. The strict application of the 'polluter pays principle' seems to be an important element in avoiding this effect.

Another important issue arising from national environmental policy which can distort competition is that of state aids for certain ecological behaviour. State aids which distort competition are prohibited under Article 92 EC. In principle, such subsidies are contrary to the 'polluter pays' principle. The Community does not permit the counter-balancing of stringent national environmental regulations by granting state aids in general. Certain kinds of state aids are, however, generally exempt from the application of Article 92.

Furthermore, the Commission recognizes the importance of financial incentives and the environmental benefit involved when deciding upon individual exemptions from the general prohibition. In cases where undertakings apply more stringent environmental standards than they are obliged to by existing Community and domestic standards or where transitional help is granted for adaptation to higher standards, green state aids may be acceptable under the existing Community system.

FAIR COMPETITION BETWEEN UNDERTAKINGS (ARTICLE 85)

General Observations

In a broad sense since the free movement of goods is considered to be a basic right that guarantees the individual the absence of trade-hindering measures not justified by the public interest, the competition rules of Articles 85–90 play an important complementary role.[1] In general, the possible interaction of national environmental policy and the competition provisions of the Treaty have been neglected by most authors. Only recently has this area started to attract the attention it deserves.[2]

The main areas of conflict to be analysed in this study arise when national policies which support or give incentives to concerted practices affect trade or when national regulations which leave certain regulatory power to private associations or groups of undertakings exclude certain market actors, possibly from other Member States. This 'private' aspect and the problems arising from this distortion of competition, in particular, need to be taken seriously.

In principle, agreements between private undertakings have limited relationship only with the shared regulatory competences between Community and Member States. The prohibition of Article 85 aims, in particular, at private market actors. Nevertheless, the Court draws from Article 85(1) in conjunction with Articles 3f and 5(2) EC the principle that Member States have an obligation under Community law to abstain from any action which favours, facilitates, or permits private behaviour which distorts competition.[3] Therefore the use of such agreements will be analysed in so far as their distorting effect falls within the responsibility of the Member States.[4]

[1] P. J. G. Kapteyn and P. VerLoren van Themaat, *Introduction to the Law of the European Communities* (2nd. edn,, Kluwer, Deventer, 1989), 356; U. Becker, *Der Gestaltungsspeilraum der EG-Mitgliedstaaten im Spannungsfeld zwischen Umweltschutz und freiem Warenverkehr* (Nomos, Baden-Baden, 1991), 63.

[2] See, in particular, T. Portwood, *Competition Law and the Environment* (Cameron May, London, 1994); L. Gyselen, 'The Emerging Interface between Competition Policy and Environmental Policy in the EC' in J. Cameron, P. Demaret, and D. Geradin (eds.), *Trade and the Environment: The Search for a Balance* (Cameron May, London, 1994), 242 to 259; some recent German articles have also drawn attention to the problem: I. Pernice, 'Rechtlicher Rahmen der europäischen Unternehmenskooperation im Umweltbereich unter besonderer Berücksichtigung von Art. 85 EWGV' [1992] *EuZW* 139 to 143; L. Krämer, 'Die Integrierung umweltpolitischer Erfordernisse in die gemeinschaftliche Wettbewerbspolitik' in H.-W. Rengeling (ed.), *Umweltschutz und andere Politiken der Europäischen Gemeinschaft* (Heymann, Köln, 1993), 47 to 83; M. Bock, 'Umweltrechtliche Prinzipien in der Wettbewerbsordnung der Europäischen Gemeinschaft' [1994] *EuZW* 47 to 52; to a limited extent also A. Furrer, 'Nationale Umweltschutzkompetenzen in der EG und im EWR' [1992] *AJP* 1517 at 1523. On the national level see for the case of Germany M. Kloepfer, 'Kartellrecht und Umweltrecht', in H. Gutzler (ed.), *Umweltpolitik und Wettbewerb* (Nomos, Baden-Baden, 1981), 57 to 102.

[3] Case 231/83 *Cullet* v. *Centre Leclerc* [1985] *ECR* 305 (para. 14) or Case 136/86 *BNIC* v. *Aubert* [1987] *ECR* 4789; more recently Case C-96/94 *Centro Servizi Spediporto Srl* v. *Spedizioni Marittima del Golfo*, judgment of 5 Oct. 1995. See also Bock, n. 2 above, 50.

[4] See on the responsibility of Member States under Arts. 85 and 86 H.-J. Niemeyer, 'Die Anwendbarkeit der Art. 85 und 86 EG-Vertrag auf staatliche Massnahmen' [1994] *WuW* 721 to

Environmental Agreements

Among modern instruments for environmental policy, voluntary agreements between undertakings (and perhaps the authorities) play an increasingly important role. While classical interventions by the State (prohibitions, limitations on use, product requirements, and corresponding controls and inspections) provide a legally stable framework, they often lack the necessary implementation and acceptance by the actors concerned. Such regulatory instruments often cannot follow the development of fields as dynamic as today's environmental problems.[5] The use of voluntary agreements between the State and the undertakings concerned or simply between undertakings with the object of effective implementation of environmentally friendly technologies or the substitution of certain harmful substances may, however, provide this dynamism and the necessary acceptance and implementation by the undertakings concerned.[6]

Such agreements between undertakings can have various forms and purposes.[7] One category may be the achievement of better co-operation in the production and distribution of goods. Common research programmes or the transfer of know-how in certain technical areas can also fall into this category.[8] Apart from 'economies of scale' such co-operation can involve opportunities for concentrating certain dangerous activities in a few production plants which are particularly well equipped and allow for an environmentally sound production process.[9] This is a development which the Community itself has favoured in specific regulations.

Example: Regulation 594/91/EEC provides for the phasing out of the production of CFCs and allows the transfer of existing quotas from one undertaking to another. This allows the undertakings concerned to concentrate the production of CFCs in very few production plants and facilitates the control of and safety checks on the process.[10]

Recently such voluntary co-operation agreements have evolved, in particular, in the area of waste recycling and processing.[11] As certain industrial sectors have very specific needs for the recycling and disposal of harmful substances or cer-

731 with reference to the relevant Court judgments. See also e.g. the survey of these agreements and their compatibility with Art. 30 EC given by A. Middeke, *Nationaler Umweltschutz und Binnenmarkt* (Heymann, Köln, 1994), 144 to 146.

    [5] Pernice, n. 2 above, 139.

    [6] See e.g. I. Pernice, 'Kompetenzordnung und Handlungsbefugnisse der Europäischen Gemeinschaft auf dem Gebiet des Umwelt- und Technikrechts' [1989] *DV* 1 at 29.

    [7] For environmental examples see e.g. Krämer, n. 2 above, 57.

    [8] See e.g. Pernice, n. 2 above, 140; a US example is antitrust proceedings against American car producers who had co-operated for the development of pollution control devices, see *US* v. *Automobile Manufacturers Association*, 307 F Supp. 617 (CD, Cal. 1969) as referred to by W. Zohlhöfer, 'Umweltschutz und Wettbewerb—Grundlegende Analyse' in Gutzler (ed.), n. 2 above, 15 at 46.

    [9] See for explanations and the following example Bock, n. 2 above, 48.

    [10] Reg. 594/91/EEC [1991] *OJ* L67/1 and London Amendment, Art. 5(2), [1991] *OJ* C11/22.

    [11] See also e.g. the most recent communications by the EC Commission, *XXIII Competition Report from the Commission: 1993* (EC, Brussels, 1994), also reprinted as COM(94)151 final, 82 ff.

tain materials, they are able to co-operate for the better organization of these activities.[12]

Example: An example is recent proceedings before the Commission in which two German companies had founded a joint-venture for the recycling of glass. The Commission considered the co-operation in recycling glass to be an essential element in the competitiveness of the two glass companies involved. Therefore, the co-operation agreement did not, in the Commission's view, qualify under the relevant prohibitions in the Community's merger control procedures,[13] and that the necessary level of competition within the market was still guaranteed.[14]

Another much more noted example is the German voluntary agreement between more than 400 undertakings for the recycling of packaging waste. In response to the new German legislation on the compulsory recycling of packaging materials[15] these companies founded a common undertaking ('Duales System Deutschland GmbH') for the fulfilment of their new obligations. The company awards the products of its members a 'green dot', printed on the product, which certifies that the products will be recycled and treated according to the German packaging ordinance. The member companies have to pay a fee per item. Such a system involves important questions concerning the admission of competing undertakings and possible competition effects from any kind of discrimination.[16]

Another important category of green voluntary agreements between undertakings is those leading to the voluntary limitation of certain dangerous activities or the voluntary use of more environmentally friendly production processes or materials.[17] Often such agreements are concluded to prevent state intervention and 'official' regulation of certain activities.[18] On the other hand, they often involve important competition issues. By limiting themselves, the undertakings

---

[12] See e.g. Pernice, n. 6 above, 29, who also points out that a new German plan (*Töpfer-Plan*) to facilitate the recycling and disposal of radioactive waste does not provide for the possibility to use non-domestic recycling facilities and thereby discriminate against such facilities..

[13] [1989] *OJ* L395/1.

[14] Decision by the Commission of 13 Apr. 1992, IV/M 168 [1992] *WuW* 1026, as referred to by Bock, n. 2 above, 49.

[15] Packaging Ordinance of 12 June 1991, BGBl. I 1234, § 6 III, reprinted in English in (1992) 31 *ILM* 1135, effective on 1 Jan. 1993; see Pernice, n. 2 above, 140.

[16] See for details J. Bongaerts, 'The German Packaging Ordinance' [1992] *Environmental Law Review* 53 to 57, or the considerations by the EC Commission in its XXIII Report on Competition Policy, n. 11 above; see also S. Thomé-Kozmiensky, *Die Verpackungsverordnung—Rechtmäßigkeit, 'Duales System', Europarecht* (Duncker & Humblot, Berlin, 1994).

[17] See e.g., Pernice, n. 6 above, 29, indicating a Danish agreement between the Ministry of Agriculture and farmer associations concerning the voluntary reduction of the use of pesticides; see also for an overview on German non-environmental cases C. Baudenbacher, 'Kartellrechtliche und verfassungsrechtliche Aspekte gesetzesvertretender Vereinbarungen zwischen Staat und Wirtschaft' [1988] *JZ* 689 ff.

[18] See e.g. Bock, n. 2 above, 48, and G. Gornig and M.Silagi, 'Vom Ökodumping zum Ökoprotektionismus—Umweltzeichen im Lichte des EWG-Vertrages und GATT' [1992] *EuZW* 753 at 756, referring to the pressure by the German Government on the German textile industry. They suggest that such pressure or incentives given by the State have to be considered as State action under Art. 30 of the Treaty; in my view, this could rather lead to the application of Art. 5 in conjunction with Art. 85(1) EC. See, however, also E. L. White, 'In Search of the Limits to Art. 30 of the EEC Treaty' (1989) 26 *CMLRev.* 235 at 264, or D. Schaefer, *Die unmittelbare Wirkung des Verbots*

concerned seek to ensure that potential competitors also apply the more stringent standards. Therefore such agreements often use quota systems and other mechanisms to exclude 'free riders'.

Member States and (Informal) Private Agreements

Such agreements between Member States and private undertakings exist in several Member States today, in particular on waste reduction,[19] and the Community itself seems to favour their introduction.[20] The Community has recommended the use of voluntary agreements for environmental purposes in several areas[21] and in Germany there are proposals to leave important parts of the implementation of Community Regulation 1836/93/EC on 'Eco-Auditing' to private organizations.[22]

Example: In Directive 85/339/EEC on containers of liquids for human consumption[23] Article 4(1) mentions, among the possible instruments for ecological policy and technology development, the use of 'voluntary agreements'. In its Decision 88/1988/EEC on the limitation of the use of CFCs and Halons[24] the Commission recommends that Member States establish voluntary agreements with the industries concerned.

In its proposal for a Directive on packaging,[25] such legitimate agreements are defined by the Commission as 'formal agreements concluded between the competent public authorities of the Member States and the economic sectors concerned, which have to be open to all partners who wish to meet the conditions of the agreement with a view towards the objectives of this Directive'.

This definition pointed to the sensitivity of such agreements from the point of view of the Member States' duties under the Treaty. For the first time, the

---

nichttarifärer Handelshemmnisse (Art. 30 EWGV) in den Rechtsbeziehungen zwischen Privaten: Probleme der horizontalen Wirkung des Gemeinschaftsrechts gezeigt am Beispiel des Art. 30 EWGV (Peter Lang, Frankfurt a.M., 1987), 63.

[19] e.g. the 'packaging covenant' between the Dutch Minister for the environment and the 'Stichting Verpakking en Milieu' of 6 June 1991 or the German concept of the 'Duales System Deutschland GmbH', the creation of which was mainly influenced by the new German waste legislation, see Pernice, n. 2 above, 140, or Thomé-Kozmiensky, n. 16 above.

[20] See Dir. 85/339/EEC [1985] *OJ* L176/18 and Council Dir. 94/62/EC [1994] *OJ* L365/31 or Council Recommendation 89/349/EEC [1989] *OJ* L144/56 for the voluntary reduction of CFCs; see also Council Reg. 1836/93/EC of 29 June 1993 allowing voluntary participation by companies in the industrial sector in a Community eco-management and audit scheme [1993] *OJ* L168/1; see on the latter e.g. A.v. Werder and A. Nestler, 'Grundsätze ordnungsgemässiger Umweltschutzorganisation als Maßstab des europäischen Umwelt-Audit' [1995] *RIW* 296 to 304 or K.-U. Marten and S. Schmid, 'Die EU-Öko-Audit-Verordnung und der British Standard' [1995] *RIW* 754 to 765; on the Community's earlier proposal see Gornig and Silagi, n. 18 above, 753.

[21] See for details Pernice, n. 2 above, 140.

[22] Council Reg. 1836/93/EC, n. 20 above; see also *Neue Zürcher Zeitung* (28 Oct. 1994, no. 252), 25 or e.g. Werder and Nestler, n. 20, above, or Marten and Schmid, n. 20 above.

[23] See n. 20 above.   [24] [1988] *OJ* C285/1.

[25] Dir. 94/62/EC, n. 20 above. See for the proposal also Pernice, n. 2 above, 140.

Commission, in its *XXII Report on Competition Policy*, dedicated a special paragraph to voluntary agreements between national authorities and undertakings for environmental purposes.[26] Although the prohibition of certain voluntary agreements which affect trade or distort competition under Article 85 applies first and foremost to private undertakings, the Member States have an obligation to observe and ensure the realization of the objectives of Article 85.[27]

The Commission also controls such action by the Member States in the area of environmental agreements. In its *XXII Report on Competition Policy* it declared:

Another problem arises where measures are taken by public authorities which might compromise the effect of the competition rules, for example by requiring firms to engage in behaviour which restricts competition and trade between Member States. In such cases the Court has held that Article 85 may apply, in conjunction with Articles 3f and 5 EC.'[28]

The Prohibition in Article 85

While voluntary agreements between private undertakings or between Member States and private undertakings may have positive effects on the protection of the environment,[29] they risk being incompatible with the general system provided under the Treaty ensuring undistorted competition within the common market.[30]

Article 85 prohibits all agreements between undertakings, decisions by associations of undertakings, and concerted practices which may affect trade between Member States and which have as their object or effect the prevention, restriction, or distortion of competition within the common market.'[31] This provision has direct effect.[32] The Treaty, however, provides general and special exceptions for certain categories of agreements.

Voluntary environmental agreements between undertakings may easily fall

---

[26] EC Commission, *XXII Report on Competition Policy 1992* (EC, Brussels, 1993) para. 75; see for comments Bock, n. 2 above, 48.

[27] See Case 231/83, n. 3 above; Case 311/85 *A.S.B.L. Vereniging van Vlaamse Reisebureaus* v. *A.S.B.L. Sociale Dienst van de Plaatselijke en Gewestelijke Overheidsdiensten* [1987] ECR 3801 at 3817; Case 136/86, n. 3 above; Case C–185/91 *Bundesanstalt für den Güterfernverkehr* v. *Gebrüder Reiff GmbH & Co. KG*, judgment of 17 Nov. 1993; see [1993] *EuZW* 769 and 770, concerning the interpretation of Arts. 5(2) and 85(1) EC with regard to a German system of compulsory minimum prices for the transportation of goods by road as laid down by the German 'Road Haulage Law'. See also most recently Niemeyer, n. 4 above, 724 ff.

[28] EC Commission, n. 20 above, 53.

[29] See e.g. D. Murswiek, 'Freiheit und Freiwilligkeit im Umweltrecht' [1988] *JZ* 985 at 988.

[30] For the most recent general description of the Community system under Arts. 85 and 86 EC and its functioning see R. Zäch, *Wettbewerbsrecht der Europäischen Union* (C. H. Beck, München, 1994), which, however, contains no special reference to environmental considerations or case law.

[31] See for details Kapteyn and VerLoren van Themaat, n. 1 above, 500 ff.

[32] See Gornig and Silagi, n. 18 above, 755.

within the scope of the general prohibition of this Article.[33] They may have the intention of fixing prices for certain products in order to cover the costs of environmentally friendly production methods or feed specific environmental funds for research or technology.[34] Other possible features of such agreements are the limitation on or control of the development of certain technologies which are considered dangerous for the environment, or the application of different conditions for the conclusion of contracts with suppliers or buyers of products, depending on their method of production or use and its impact on the environment. Such agreements may very easily distort competition and change the market situation to the detriment of consumers even if, in principle, they are open to all undertakings concerned.

A recent example from Germany of alleged discrimination shows the complexity of environmental co-operation between private undertakings and existing environmental rules. A group of German mineral water producers (*Genossenschaft Deutscher Brunnen (GDB)*) had established a well-organized recycling system for standardized refillable glass bottles and crates, which had been working satisfactorily for several years. In 1987 several French and Belgian mineral water producers had submitted a formal complaint against this as they had been denied access to this well-functioning and highly efficient system. At that time the Commission considered the agreement and the refusal of access to be lawful as the trade and competition effects were small and other packaging systems such as PVC or non-refillable glass bottles were available. After the introduction of the new German packaging and waste management legislation, the market situation had changed completely. The non-recyclable packaging methods were no longer valid alternatives to the existing GDB system. In the view of the Commission and several Member States, in this situation, the refusal of access to certain producers constituted an abuse of dominant position within the meaning of Article 86 EC as the establishment of a new pool of refillable bottles was not considered to be a realistic proposition. A complaint against GDB was only withdrawn after the GDB had stated its willingness to afford access to producers from other Member States.[35]

Another possible measure is the introduction of special labels which are awarded only under certain conditions.[36] Such measures may very easily have distorting effects on the competitive situation in the market.[37] Therefore all these

---

[33] For an analysis of the German packaging ordinance under German competition law see e.g. Thomé-Kozmiensky, n. 16 above, 98 to 122.

[34] See the examples below in this chapter, on state aids.

[35] *SPA Monopole* v. *GDB*, EC Commission, n. 11 above, 158 and 159.

[36] See e.g. Gornig and Silagi, n. 18 above, 753.

[37] See for considerations on a new eco-label by German textile undertakings Gornig and Silagi, n. 18 above, 757; see also T. Oppermann, *Europarecht* (C. H. Beck, München, 1991), para. 904; on the possible competition problems arising from the unlawful use of such labels see e.g. a German case decided by the OLG Köln, judgment of 21 Feb. 1992, 6 U 100/91, reprinted and commented on in [1993] *JZ* 100 to 102; the Community itself has introduced certain labels which, however, do not preclude the use of domestic labels, see G. Roller, 'Der "Blaue Engel" und die "Europäische Blume"' [1992] *EuZW* 499 to 505; L. Diederichsen, 'Ein neues Umweltzeichen für Europa' [1993] *RIW* 224 to 228; concerning the Council Reg. 880/92/EEC on the Community environmental labelling system [1992] *OJ* L99/1; see on the general development of such labels OECD, *Environmental Labelling in OECD Countries* (OECD, Paris, 1991).

measures taken by private undertakings would probably fall under the prohibition and the practices referred to under Article 85. Similar problems occur under Article 86. The only justification for such agreements would have to be found in one of the exceptions provided for in the Treaty and the relevant secondary legislation.[38]

Possible Exceptions under Article 85(3)

Article 85(3) EC provides for specific cases of agreements between undertakings, where the general prohibition of Article 85(1) is not applicable, either individually or generally. Thus, Article 85(3) allows for two categories of exemptions from the prohibitions of Article 85(1) and (2).

First, it allows for the general exemption of certain classes of voluntary agreements because of their generally positive effect. These have been qualified by the Commission in specific regulations.[39] Article 85(3) and the related secondary legislation provided for under Article 87 define groups of agreements to which the prohibition of Article 85 does not apply. They include, among others, the general exemption for voluntary agreements on common research and development[40] and the transfer of know-how.[41] Some environmental agreements fall into this category.[42]

Secondly, under Article 85(3), in conjunction with the relevant secondary legislation,[43] the Commission has the power to grant on request individual exemptions on a case-by-case basis for certain voluntary agreements. This is the case for any agreement or concerted practice 'which contributes to improving the production or distributing of goods or to promoting technical or economic progress'. The original objective of this Treaty provision was mainly economic; it aimed at a gain in efficiency and saving of resources on the quality and production of goods.[44] The term 'technological and economic progress' therefore covers situations where the economic advantages of co-operation between undertakings make these agreements economically beneficial. Purely subjective advantages for the undertakings involved, however, are not sufficient.[45]

Development of New Ecological Exceptions

In spite of this relatively narrow interpretation of the Treaty's objectives at the moment of its drafting, the modern understanding of technical and economic

---

[38] See, however, the interesting views by Pernice, n. 2 above, 141, on the application of a 'rule of reason' under Art. 85, also comprising the protection of the environment as under the *Cassis de Dijon* doctrine.

[39] Reg. 2349/84/EEC [1984] *OJ* L219/15; Reg. 41/85/EEC [1985] *OJ* L53/1; Reg. 418/85/EEC [1985] *OJ* L53/5; Reg. 556/89/EEC [1989] *OJ* L61/1.

[40] Reg. 418/85/EEC [1985] *OJ* L53/5.   [41] Reg. 556/89/EEC [1989] *OJ* L61/1.

[42] Pernice, n. 2 above, 141.   [43] Reg. 17/62/EEC [1962] *OJ* 13/204.

[44] Pernice, n. 2 above, 141.

[45] Joined cases 56 and 58/64 *Consten and Grundig* v. *Commission* [1966] *ECR* 429.

progress and, in particular, the introduction of the objectives found in the second sentence of Article 130r(2) raise new issues with regard to the Community legal order. In its *XXII Report on Competition Policy* the Commission underlined its intention to favour 'voluntary agreements to improve the environmental conditions in a given sector'. At the same time it declared its intention to 'ensure that undertakings competing in that sector do not resort to agreements which go beyond what is necessary to achieve that goal, to the detriment of competition'.[46] Therefore the Commission considers such agreements in principle to be prohibited by Article 85(1) but does not exclude the applicability of Article 85(3).[47]

An interpretation of the conditions of Article 85(3) in the light of Article 130r(2), i.e. the need to integrate environmental concerns in all Community policies, and the general environmental objective of the Community under Article 2 EC may lead to the acceptance of such voluntary agreements between undertakings.[48] Ecologically sound production methods must, in a qualitative way, be considered to be a production improvement in the sense of Article 85(3).[49] This view leads to the introduction of ecological consideration in the application of Article 85(3).[50] General environmental principles like the precautionary principle should be included in the evaluation process of agreements under Article 85(1) and their admissibility under Article 85(3).[51]

Currently there are few or no relevant decisions by the Commission or the Court,[52] but an 'environmentally friendly' interpretation of Article 85(3) may include the lawfulness of the agreements in question, with the proviso that they fulfil the other conditions of the provision.[53] A similar development has taken place in the Court's case law on the free movement of goods, where the restriction on trade has been justified by necessary environmental measures.[54]

Case: In recently reported proceedings *Vereniging van Onafhankelijke Tankopstang Bedrijven* (*VOTOB*)[55] for the obtaining of an exemption according to Regulation 17/62/EEC,[56] the Commission did not accept the applicants' environmental justifications. The procedure

---

[46] EC Commission, n. 26 above, 106.

[47] EC Commission, n. 26 above, 106, reads: '[t]he test it lays down, must of course be satisfied; in particular, sufficient competition must be maintained, and the restriction must be indispensable to the alleged economic benefit.'

[48] See e.g. the interesting views of Krämer, n. 2 above, 62 or Gyselen, n. 2 above, 243.

[49] See also Bock, n. 2 above, 49, and at an early stage M. Kloepfer, 'Umweltschutz als Kartell-privileg' [1990] *JZ* 781 at 783.

[50] See for considerations in this direction Pernice, n. 2 above, 141.

[51] See also e.g. Krämer, n. 2 above, 63.   [52] Pernice, n. 2 above, 142.

[53] That is in particular the mere application of indispensable restrictions and the maintenance of competition in respect of a substantial part of the products in question. (Art. 85(3) EC).

[54] See Chs. 4 and 5; While Case 302/86 *Commission* v. *Denmark* (*Danish Bottles*) [1988] *ECR* 4607 refers to measures taken by the Member States, Case 240/83 *Procureur de la République* v. *Association de Défense des Brûleurs d'Huiles Usagées* (*ADBHU*) [1985] *ECR* 531 refers to measures adopted by the Community.

[55] Reported in EC Commission, n. 26 above, 106 to 108; see also Gyselen, n. 2 above, 250; Bock, n. 2 above, 51.

[56] See n. 43 above.

involved an application by an association of six European undertakings offering bulk liquid tank storage facilities (land tanks) and maintaining a very important position on the Community market. They had concluded an internal agreement to raise prices and thereby impose a special fee for the installation of their tanks. This uniform 'environmental charge' was to cover the costs of investment required to reduce vapour emissions (volatile chemical and mineral oil products, VOCs) from members' storage tanks. Simultaneously, the association had concluded a covenant with the Dutch Government to reduce the emissions from their tank-storage facilities. Although the agreement with the authorities did not mention the introduction of a special duty and a consequent concerted rise in prices, consumers could easily gain the impression that this fee was backed by the Dutch authorities. As there was no differentiation between companies already applying higher standards and those which still used old technology, the system did not observe the 'polluter pays' principle. The Commission refused the required exemption for the agreement but indicated that it would perhaps have accepted a system whereby undertakings invoiced a total price, stating that it included the additional environmental investment cost.[57]

The future development of a justification of environmental or 'green' agreements despite the fact that they fall under the prohibition of Article 85(1) and are not explicitly referred to in Article 85(3) is therefore possible and, under certain circumstances, desirable.[58] On the basis of the Court's case law concerning the free movement of goods, however, one might expect that mere conformity with the objectives of national environmental policy is not enough for the justification of a 'green' agreement between undertakings. The objectives must also be viewed positively from a Community perspective,[59] that is, the protection of the environment may not be abused for measures which are unduly distorting.

Statements given by the Commission indicate that, like the problems arising from trade restrictions, the relationship between environmental benefit and the competition-distorting effect of voluntary agreements will have to be balanced. In order to achieve a satisfactory solution for both market integration and the protection of the environment,

the Commission will examine carefully all agreements between companies to see if they are indispensable to attain the environmental objectives. . . . The Commission in its analysis of individual cases will have to weigh the restrictions of competition in the agreement against the environmental objectives that the agreement will help attain, in order to determine whether, under this proportionality analysis, it can approve the agreement.[60]

It is particularly interesting in the context of this research to observe that the Community has elaborated certain conditions for the admissibility of

---

[57] See for details Bock, n. 2 above, 51 and 52. [58] Pernice, n. 2 above, 142.
[59] Kapteyn and VerLoren van Themaat, n. 1 above, 518.
[60] EC Commission, n. 11 above, 85.

environmental agreements which fall under Article 85(1) EC in order to balance economic interests and environmental needs. In the *VOTOB* decision, as well as in other similar decisions,[61] the Commission requires first that the agreement contribute to 'promoting technical or economic progress while allowing consumers a fair share of the resulting benefits', that is the environmental objectives.[62] Secondly, the Commission requires the agreements in question to be 'indispensable to the attainment of these objectives'.[63] Finally, the third requirement is comparable to the general proportionality test in the case law on Articles 30 and 36 including the rule of reason.[64] Thus, the test of whether or not Article 85(3) applies to agreements between undertakings in the sense of Article 85(1) is comparable, if not identical, to the one used under the provisions governing the free movement of goods, despite the specific characteristics of Community competition law which cannot be elaborated upon in this book.[65]

As far as the environmental objective is concerned, the general concepts of Community law imply the application of the general principles governing the Community's environmental policy and particularly the observation of the 'polluter pays principle'.[66] So far there are no guidelines concerning the application of Article 85 EC as they exist, for instance, in the field of state aids.[67] Some authors even suggest that a legally binding and explicit regulation at Community level under Article 87 EC might be helpful to determine the relation between Article 85 and environmental protection by informal means such as co-operation and agreements between undertakings and governmental authorities.[68]

---

[61] See, in particular, the following decisions of the Commission to exempt agreements under Art. 85(3) EC: [1992] *OJ* L3/7 (*Assurpol*) concerning an agreement between insurance companies to facilitate the co-reinsurance of environmental damage risks; [1991] *OJ* L19/25 (*KSB/Goulds/Lowara/ITT*) dealing with a joint 'research and development' and production agreement; [1988] *OJ* L301/68 (*BBC Brown Bovery*) concerning an agreement to facilitate the development of electrically driven vehicles; [1983] *OJ* L367/17 (*Carbon Gas Technology*) concerned an agreement to facilitate developing a process for coal gasification; all examples are described in Gyselen, n. 2 above, 255 and 256, or Portwood, n. 2 above, 153 ff.

[62] EC Commission, n. 11 above, 85.

[63] For a negative answer to this question see the Commission's decision in [1991] *OJ* L152/54 (*ANSAC*) where the Commission refused to consider the restrictions on competition used to favour the sales of natural soda instead of synthetic soda ash to be necessary or indispensable.

[64] See Ch. 5.

[65] For a very elaborate analysis of the case law and the emerging test see Portwood, n. 2 above, 132 to 163. He also shows the relevance of Art. 86 which cannot be discussed in the framework of this study.

[66] Art. 130r(2) EC, and more explicitly in Council Recommendation 75/436/EEC regarding cost-allocation and action by public authorities on environmental matters [1975] *OJ* L194/1; see also Bock, n. 2 above, 51, and the Commission's indications in EC Commission, n. 11 above, 82.

[67] See Ch. 6 the next section, on state aids.

[68] See also the suggestions by Krämer, n. 21 above, 64 or Pernice, n. 2 above, 143.

STATE AIDS (ARTICLE 92)

General Observations

Article 92, providing for a general prohibition on state aids, is an important element in the Community's concept of the common market. Apart from the efficiency losses through the State allocation of financial aids this prohibition is essential for the safeguard of the free movement of goods and undistorted trade.[69] The protection of inefficient domestic industry by state aids would hinder the effect intended by the abolition of protectionist barriers to trade in general.[70] Article 92 does not provide an explicit definition of the term 'state aids' but its broad wording ('any aid granted by a Member State') and the objective of protecting the free movement of goods against any competition-distorting national aid cover a broad range of state measures.[71] The Court argues that a financial aid, in whatever form, strengthens the position of a domestic company and thereby hinders the capacity of producers from other Member States to increase their market shares and exports.[72]

Article 92 EC provides a general prohibition against 'any aid granted by a Member State or through state resources in any form whatsoever which distorts or threatens to distort competition by favouring certain undertakings or the production of certain goods . . ., in so far as it affects trade between Member States.'

The Treaty itself however, provides exceptions (Articles 92(2) and (3) EC) and derogations under the specific provisions in Articles 42 agriculture, 77, and 80 (transport).[73] Furthermore there is special secondary legislation in various specific sectors which allows Member States to provide environmental subsidies.[74]

State aids normally favour particular national producers of goods and thereby distort trade as they interfere with the regular pricing mechanism. They could therefore in principle constitute state measures having an equivalent effect to trade restrictions as they are capable of hindering trade in the sense of the *Dassonville* formula. The Court, however, has declared the preferential applicability of the special rules under Articles 92–94 EC instead of Article 30 EC. Although state aids often have similar effects upon the market mechanism as

---

[69] See e.g. D. Ehle and G. Meier, *EWG-Warenverkehr* (O. Schmidt, Köln, 1971), as referred to by Becker, n. 1 above, 64.

[70] See Kapteyn and VerLoren van Themaat, n. 1 above, 487.

[71] See H.-J. Niemeyer, 'Recent Developments in EC State Aid Law' [1993] *EuZW* 273 to 279; see also O. Brunetti, *EG-Rechtsverträglichkeit als Kriterium der nationalen Umweltpolitik* (Schulthess and Stämpfli, Zürich and Bern, 1993), 79.

[72] Case 730/79 *Philip Morris Holland BV* v. *Commission* [1980] *ECR* 2671 (para. 11); Case 305/89 *Italy* v. *Commission* (*Capital Contributions in the Motor Vehicle Sector*) [1991] *ECR* I–1603 (para. 26).

[73] See G. von Wallenberg, Art. 92, para. 32 in E. Grabitz and M. Hilf (eds.), *Kommentar zur EU* (2nd edn., C. H. Beck, München, 1990 ff.).

[74] See E. Grabitz and C. Zacker, 'Scope for Action by EC Member States for the Improvement of Environmental Taxes and Subsidies' (1989) 26 *CMLRev.* 423 at 434, with reference to the legislation in question.

quantitative restrictions or measures having equivalent effect under Article 30, Article 92 is a special provision which prevails if the conditions for its application are established. It is, however, possible that certain parts of an integrative state-aid system are not necessary for the functioning of the latter and therefore have to be considered separately under the provisions of Article 30.[75]

Green State Aids

Member States may want to use financial incentives in the form of state aids for the promotion of environmentally sound behaviour in certain undertakings, in particular for investments in ecologically sound technology.[76] Such aids are often referred to as environmental or 'green' subsidies.[77] Apart from their questionable economic justification under the 'polluter pays' principle,[78] they may also have distorting effects prohibited by Article 92.[79] Each national environmental measure therefore has to be analysed step by step to establish whether (a) it falls after all under the prohibition of Article 92(1), and (b) whether it is eligible for the justified exceptions granted by the Treaty in Article 92(2) and (3).

In view of the growing importance and use of environmental subsidies by Member States, the Commission has, since 1974, regularly published guidelines concerning the applicability of Article 92 and, in particular, its own practice concerning the power to concede exceptions.[80] In spite of the validity of the 'polluter pays' principle in the Community, the Commission has, since the 1970s, followed an approach which tries to find a balance between environmental benefits which may arise from the pragmatic use of state aids and the distorting effects on competition and trade.[81]

---

[75] Case 74/76 *Ianelli and Volpi SpA* v. *Meroni* [1977] *ECR* 557 at 575; see also Becker, n. 1 above, 64; Kapteyn and VerLoren van Themaat, n. 1 above, 489, n. 77. The Court has applied the same reasoning in later cases e.g. Case 18/84 *Commission* v. *France (Tax Advantages for Newspaper Publishers)* [1985] *ECR* 1339 at 1345 or more recently in Case C–21/88 *Du Pont de Nemours Italiana SpA* v. *Unità Sanitaria* [1990] *ECR* I–889 at 916. For detailed accounts of the facts see White, n. 18 above, 272 or Brunetti, n. 71 above, 103.

[76] See for details Krämer, n. 2 above, 66 or Brunetti, n. 71 above, 77.

[77] See the detailed description of common forms of environmental subsidies in EC Commission, *Guidelines Concerning State Aids for Environmental Protection* [1994] *OJ* C72/3 ff. at 3 and 4; reprinted in Annex II of this book.

[78] Art. 130r(2) EC; see also L. Krämer, *Focus on European Environmental Law* (Sweet & Maxwell, London, 1993), 50.

[79] See for economic and theoretical considerations V. Strauch, 'Nationale Umweltschutzsubventionen als wettbewerbspolitisches Störpotential' in Gutzler (ed.), n. 2 above, 125 to 142.

[80] First published in part in EC Commission, *IV Report on Competition Policy* (EC, Brussels, 1975), para. 175 to 182; continued in *Xth Report on Competition Policy* (EC, Brussels, 1981), paras. 222 to 226; *XVIth Report on Competition Policy* (EC, Brussels, 1987), para. 259 and several times renewed. The guidelines have now been published as *Guidelines on State Aids for Environmental Protection*, n. 77 above. For a description and short, but critical, comment under competition policy considerations see R. Quick, 'Der Gemeinschaftsrahmen für staatliche Umweltschutzbeihilfen' [1994] *EuZW* 620 to 624.

[81] See the repetition of this statement in the *Guidelines on State Aids for Environmental Protection*, n. 77 above, 5 (para. 1.6).

Criteria for the Applicability of Article 92

The general prohibition of state aids which distort competition between under-takings within the common market includes specific exceptions. Nevertheless, the principles governing the admissibility of state aids in general also have an important impact on the use of such aids for environmental reasons.[82] Subsidies which do not fulfil all the criteria in Article 92 remain in general admissible. This applies, in particular, to state aids which do not distort competition as they are available either for the compensation of specific behaviour or for all competing market actors.[83]

Distortion and Hindrance of Trade

For the applicability of Article 92 a national aid must affect trade between Member States.[84] It is, however, sufficient if a measure is capable of affecting trade and if the circumstances make such an effect probable.[85] The same 'capability test' is applied to the competition distorting effects arising from domestic aids ('threatens to distort competition'[86]). General state promotion which does not distort competition[87] does not fall under Article 92. Article 92 applies only to state aids operating in specific sectors or industries, or selected enterprises within these industries. If a state aid applies to all sectors and enterprises to an equal extent, it does not fall foul of Article 92.[88] Similarly, general state aids for information campaigns or to raise consumer awareness of environmental degradation are normally not within the scope of Article 92.[89]

A general tax advantage for purchasers of 'clean' motor vehicles would therefore not fall under this provision.[90] If an aid is granted to the purchasers of a certain product, that is, a reduction in price for environmentally harmless products, one has to consider whether it provides indirect favours to specific

---

[82] See Becker, n. 1 above, 64.

[83] See e.g. Kapteyn and Verloren van Themaat, n. 1 above, 489.

[84] Art. 92 does not apply to aids distorting the trade with non-member countries, see H.-W. Rengeling, 'Das Beihilferecht der Europäischen Gemeinschaft' in B. Börner and K. Neudörfer (eds.), *Recht und Praxis der Beihilfen im Gemeinsamen Markt* (Heymann, Köln, 1984), 23 at 31 as referred to by Brunetti, n. 71 above, 83.

[85] See for details Brunetti, n. 71 above, 83.

[86] Rengeling, n. 84 above, 31.

[87] Rengeling, n. 84 above, 30.

[88] See e.g. Joined cases 6 and 11/69 *Commission* v. *France* (*Rediscount Rate For Export Claims*) [1969] ECR 523; see also Kapteyn and VerLoren van Themaat, n. 1 above, 489.

[89] See the Commission's view in the *Guidelines on State Aids for Environmental Protection*, n. 77 above, 7.

[90] See Grabitz and Zacker, n. 74 above, 429, setting out the German federal tax advantages for clean motor vehicles; see also [1992] *OJ* C160/5 concerning a carbon dioxide tax and energy conservation measure in Denmark with specific exemptions and refunds where the Commission required certain adaptations of the tax arrangements. Such tax grants for the purchase of a catalytic convertor, however, are no longer admissible under the Community secondary law adopted in the field of car emissions: Dir. 93/159/EC [1993] *OJ* L186/21.

producers and goods, in particular national producers.[91] Such national measures reducing the tax for purchasers can be considered as a kind of subsidy, as they give the favoured undertakings a financial advantage similar to the payment of a subsidy or state aid. It is generally recognized that even the granting of such advantages to the consumers of certain products would be considered as a favour granted to the relevant producers.[92]

Nevertheless such fiscal advantages are, generally, governed by the special provisions on taxes and in particular Article 95[93] EC so far as their discriminatory nature is concerned. In the event that they are compatible with Article 95, they still have to be lawful under Article 92.[94] In view of the current insecurity the Commission has declared such purchasing incentives outside the scope of the prohibition of Article 92, provided they do not grant specific advantages to certain undertakings. Such state aids, however, have to be applied in a non-discriminatory manner, may not be higher than the potential environmental cost and have to be compatible with the provisions on the free movement of goods.[95]

Case: In proceedings begun by the Commission in 1988, a Dutch fiscal measure for the purchase of certain types of cars was under question. The Dutch government provided a tax reduction for purchasers of cars with a catalytic convertor or with a cubic capacity of less than 1400 cubic centimetres, fulfilling the US exhausts standards of that period. The Commission initiated proceedings under Article 93(2) EC, considering the measure an infringement of Article 92 of the Treaty.[96] The Dutch authorities, however, declared that Article 92 was not applicable to such tax incentives.[97] The proceedings were finally terminated without any further investigation, the Commission conceding that Article 92 did not apply.[98]

No General Compensation for Comparative Disadvantages

A national subsidy granted to specific undertakings within the territory of a Member State to balance out the competitive disadvantage from a very ambitious national environmental legislation is not compatible with Article 92.[99] Such state aids change the competitive situation existing between Member States. The different regulatory systems governing production conditions in Member States are part of the existing competitive situation. The introduction of a subsidy to

---

[91] See Brunetti, n. 71 above, 89, referring to EC Commission, *XV Report on Competition Policy* (EC, Brussels, 1986), para. 224 and *XX Report on Competition Policy* (EC, Brussels, 1991), para. 288.

[92] See e.g. von Wallenberg, Art. 92, para. 8, in Grabitz and Hilf (eds.), n. 8 above, or Rengeling, n. 84 above, 27, as referred to by Brunetti, n. 71 above, 81; A. Duschanek, 'Umweltschutz-subventionen in der EG und in Österreich' in H.-P. Rill and S. Griller (eds.), *Europäischer Binnenmarkt und österreichisches Wirtschaftsverwaltungsrecht* (Orac, Wien, 1991), 355 at 361, is of the same view.

[93] See Becker, n. 1 above, 66, and Grabitz and Zacker, n. 74 above, 429. They also seem to favour this solution.

[94] See Brunetti, n. 71 above, 144.

[95] See the *Guidelines on State Aids for Environmental Protection*, n. 77 above, 8.

[96] See Becker, n. 1 above, 66, with reference to H. G. Sevenster, 'Van schone auto's EEG-dingen' [1989] *NJB* 556 at 558.

[97] [1988] *OJ* C80/5.   [98] Becker, n. 1 above, 66.

[99] Duschanek, n. 92 above, 362, who points out, however, a possible exemption.

balance out this difference affects the competitive conditions in relation to the situation as it existed before.[100] The different production conditions in Member States of the Community should not be equalized through competition-distorting state aids. Such different costs for production factors have to be accepted as long as they are not harmonized under the relevant Community procedures.[101] This does not preclude the Commission from granting exceptions for a limited adaptation period.[102]

Example: An example is a recent decision by the Commission concerning Dutch state aids linked to the action programme against chlorofluorocarbons (CFCs). In The Netherlands, the ban on the use of CFCs has been in force since 1993, whereas in the other Member States it has only been in force since 1 January 1995. In developing new production procedures, the Dutch firms concerned assumed a degree of technical and financial risk in that they had to innovate before firms in other Member States, and were thus not able to benefit from existing and tested technologies. The Commission therefore approved the Duth state aids granted to specific companies in this sector.[103]

Under the 'polluter pays' principle, Member States are encouraged to introduce environmental charges to internalize the external environmental costs of certain economic activities. If a Member State introduces such levies, it is bound to apply them in a non-discriminatory and even-handed way to all undertakings concerned. The exceptional non-application of such charges to certain industries or undertakings has to be considered an indirect state aid. While the Commission thus, in general, does not favour exceptions from such existing charges, it may eventually grant exceptions under Article 92(3). Such 'aids' may not go beyond the environmental cost and should retain a provisional character. The Commission will take into account the distorting effect and the putative environmental benefit.[104]

Case: In its decision in Case 173/73 *Italy* v. *Commission*[105] the Court considered an Italian state aid to specific textile undertakings to be distorting competition between the Member States. The Italian Government had tried to justify the aid with the argument that the Italian producers had to face much higher social security costs than producers from other Member States. The Court, however, held that such a unilateral change in the price of a production factor for national producers was capable of affecting competition. The

---

[100] Case 173/73 *Italy* v. *Commission* (*Family Allowances*) [1974] *ECR* 709 at 720.

[101] In Case 173/73 *Family Allowances*, n. 100 above, 720, the Court held that '[m]oreover Arts. 92 to 102 EC provide for detailed rules for the abolition of generic distortions resulting from differences between the tax and social security systems of the different Member States whilst taking account of structural difficulties in certain sectors of industry. . . . On the other hand, the unilateral modification of a particular factor of the cost of production in a given sector of the economy of a Member State may have the effect of disturbing the existing equilibrium.'

[102] See the considerations in the *Guidelines on State Aids for Environmental Protection*, n. 77 above, 6, and the very critical comments by Quick, n. 80 above, 622 to 624.

[103] Commission Decision [1994] *OJ* C72/1.

[104] See the *Guidelines on State Aids for Environmental Protection*, n. 77 above, 7 and 8; see for examples Chs. 3 and 10.

[105] Case 173/73 *Family Allowances*, n. 100 above, 720.

existing differences in the national regulatory system were part of the competitive differences existing among Member States.

Non-distortive Compensation of Voluntary Restrictions

The case, however, may be different where an aid is granted to all undertakings which voluntarily apply more stringent environmental standards than provided for by the national regulatory system. As such measures are not used to balance out the national regulatory difference and its competitive effect on the national undertakings, it will usually not fall under the prohibition of Article 92.[106] The state aids granted are only an incentive to help undertakings to apply more stringent environmental standards than the ones they are obliged to apply by law. The additional costs from such voluntary behaviour are recompensed by the state aid.[107] The aid is usually not used to balance out the different competitive situations.[108]

Nevertheless, in its most recent guidelines for the grant of environmental state aids by Member States, the Commission emphasizes the potentially competition-distorting character of such investment aids for voluntary pollution reductions. The Commission holds such aids eligible for the concession of an exception under Article 92(3) EC only if they do not amount to more than 30 per cent of the total environmentally relevant cost.[109]

Example: An application of this principle was published by the Commission in its *XVI Report on Competition Policy* in 1987.[110] The Commission had been confronted with aid granted by the German *Land* of Baden-Württemberg to all undertakings voluntarily applying more stringent environmental emission standards than prescribed by law. The Commission considered such measures compatible with Article 92. The main argument was that the aids were only granted for additional investments going beyond the compulsory legal requirements.

Similarly, state contributions which constitute a payment for services rendered[111] do not normally fall under Article 92.[112] The question to be asked, however, is not whether a state aid is linked to a specific service but whether the relationship between the service and the financial contribution corresponds to

---

[106] See e.g. the 1992 list established by the Commission on state aids where no objections were raised: Commission, n. 26 above, Annex referring to e.g. [1992] *OJ* C155/9 (loans for environmental aids programme in Baden-Württemberg); [1992] *OJ* C160/4 (investments in environmental protection: measures to control and treat industrial waste in Spain); [1991] *OJ* C298/7 (guidelines of *Land* Hessen on financial aid for the avoidance and reduction of waste including grants awarded for investments and research and development projects).

[107] See for an interesting list of examples EC Commission, n. 11 above, 273 to 275.

[108] See for details Brunetti, n. 71 above, 86.

[109] See the Commission's indications in the *Guidelines on State Aids for Environmental Protection*, n. 77 above, 7.

[110] EC Commission, *XVIth Report on Competition Policy*, n. 80 above, para. 260, as referred to by Brunetti, n. 71 above, 86.

[111] Wenig, n. 87 above, para. 5.

[112] See e.g. EC Commission, n. 11 above, para. 421.

the market situation. A disproportionate financial contribution for a minor service would have to be considered an aid under Article 92.[113]

Non-distortive Redistribution of Fund Contributions

State aids which are distributed indirectly through a national or semi-national[114] institution or fund which is fed by compulsory contributions from the importers, producers or sellers of certain products also have to be in conformity with the relevant Treaty provisions under Articles 9 and 12 on charges having equivalent effect to import duties and Article 95 on discriminatory taxation. As has been stated above, the feeding of a fund with parafiscal charges which are refunded mainly or exclusively to national producers is not compatible with the Treaty provisions.[115] In these situations foreign producers would be contributing to the subsidization of domestic producers without the chance of benefiting from the refund of these parafiscal charges.[116] Such charges have to be compatible with Article 95 as well as with Article 92 EC.[117]

Exceptions and their Environmental Benefit

The Treaty provides, however, for exceptions for state aids under certain conditions.[118] A very broad exception from the general prohibition of distorting state aids is provided by Article 92(3) subparagraph (b), which allows state aids which 'promote the execution of an important project of common European interest or to remedy a serious disturbance in the economy of a Member State'. The procedure requires a decision on their admissibility by the Commission under Article 93. Similarly, subparagraphs (a) and (c) provide for exceptions of a regional character or those concerning specific activities.

The Commission has elaborated a set of general rules which have to be fulfilled for the application of Article 92(3) EC:[119]

(a) the aid must be suitable for promoting an objective which is in the Community's interest as a whole;

(b) it must be necessary for the achievement of the legitimate objective, i.e. the aid must be indispensable for the achievement of the common European objective in question;

---

[113] See for details Kapteyn and VerLoren van Themaat, n. above, 488 or Brunetti, n. 71 above, 80.

[114] See Kapteyn and VerLoren van Themaat, n. 1 above, 489.   [115] See Ch. 3.

[116] Case 47/69 *France* v. *Commission (Union of Textile Industries)* [1970] *ECR* 487 at 495; Case 77/72 *Carmine Capolongo* v. *Azienda Agricola Maya* [1973] *ECR* 611; Case 78/76 *Steinike und Weinlig* v. *Germany* [1978] *ECR* 595 at 614; Case 105/76 *Interzuccheri* v. *Società Rezzano e Cavassa* [1977] *ECR* 1029 at 1042. See Kapteyn and VerLoren van Themaat, n. 1 above, 487 and 488, or Grabitz and Zacker, n. 74 above, 429.

[117] Case 73/79 *Commission* v. *Italy (Sovraprezzo)* [1980] *ECR* 1533 at 1544; see also the arguments on parafiscal charges in Ch. 3.

[118] See also Case 730/79, n. 72 above, 2691.

[119] On the considerable discretion the Commission is given in examining a case under Art. 92(3) see Kapteyn and VerLoren van Themaat, n. 1 above, 500, or Case 730/79, n. 72 above.

(c)   the aid must be proportionate to the importance of the objective achieved.[120]

Protecting the environment and fighting pollution may be 'projects of common European interest'.[121] The Commission itself has recognized that stricter national environmental standards are often feasible only if the undertakings concerned receive financial assistance as partial compensation for competitive disadvantages which they suffer in comparison with undertakings in other Member States.[122] In the field of environmental protection the possible conflict between the general prohibition in Article 92 and the desire to provide financial incentives for environmental reasons has been recognized as early as 1974, in a communication by the Commission.[123] Apart from national environmental subsidies the Community itself has introduced a set of financial incentives for the protection of the environment.[124]

In spite of the questionable economic reasoning behind this system,[125] the Commission subsequently published a communication on the Commissions approach to the admissibility of environmental state aids under Article 92.[126] In its own *Report* in 1975 the Commission announced that it would accept state aids under Article 93(3), subparagraphs (b) and (c), for a limited transitional period until 1980, if they were designed to facilitate the adaptation of enterprises to rules or regulations imposing on them important additional burdens in the field of environmental protection. The report set out the additional conditions that had to be fulfilled.[127]

Shortly before the end of the transitional period in 1980, the Commission extended its approach for another six years until 1986.[128] Despite the explicit introduction of the 'polluter pays' principle by the Single European Act in 1986 the Commission has adhered to the former guidelines of allowing environmental subsidies under Article 92(3) sub-paragraph (b), and in 1987 again extended the

---

[120]   See Case 730/79, n. 72 above, and Portwood, n. 2 above, 193.

[121]   See Joined cases 62 and 72/87 *Exécutif Régional Wallon* v. *Commission* [1988] *ECR* 1573 (paras. 22 to 25), as referred to by Niemeyer, n. 70 above, 274.

[122]   This, however, contradicts to a certain extent the Court's considerations in Case 173/73 *Family Allowances*, n. 100 above, 720.

[123]   Council Recommendation 75/436/Euratom/ECSC/EEC regarding the cost allocation and action by public authorities on environmental matters of 3 Mar. 1975 [1975] *OJ* L194/1. See also the corresponding reference in EC Commission, *IV Environmental Action Programme* [1987] *OJ* C328/1.

[124]   See E. Grabitz, 'Handlungsspielräume der EG-Mitgliedstaaten zur Verbesserung des Umweltschutzes—Das Beispiel der Umweltabgaben und -subventionen' [1989] *RIW* 623 at 625; see also Ch. 10.

[125]   See for economic considerations on the concession of state aids and the environmental behaviour of undertakings W. Baumol and W. E. Oates, *The Theory of Environmental Policy* (2nd edn., Cambridge University Press, Cambridge, 1988), 211 to 235.

[126]   EC Commission, *IV Report on Competition Policy*, n. 80 above, paras. 103 to 106 and 180. See on this report and the subsequent reports Krämer, n. 2 above, 48.

[127]   See for details Grabitz and Zacker, n. 74 above, 430.

[128]   EC Commission, *X Report on Competition Policy* (EC, Brussels, 1981), para. 224.

application of its *Guidelines* until 1992.[129] It reserved, however, the right to revise the necessary criteria on environmental and competition grounds. The existing framework guidelines were finally extended in view of the adoption of a new code in the course of 1993 or 1994.[130] In a communication in March 1994 the Commission published its currently applicable guidelines which generally follow the earlier approach.[131]

In the general recommendation, going back to 1975, the Commission had already established four basic principles which provide the Member States with guidelines concerning the Commission's policy on exceptions for environmental aids under Article 93(2), subparagraph (b) and (c), and thereby concretize the general rules applicable under Article 93(2):

(a) exceptions for environmental state aids were only granted to facilitate the adaptation to new and burdensome environmental obligations;

(b) such aids were granted only to undertakings which had had installations in operation for at least two years before the entry into force of new higher environmental standards;

(c) the aids granted should not exceed 15 per cent of the additional investments;

(d) Member States had to provide the Commission with detailed material about the aids granted and the necessary investments under their environmental programmes.[132]

The new guidelines confirm in principle the guidelines published since 1975.[133] They allow for minimal aids to accelerate adaptation to new standards and even provide for the possibility of granting higher state aids if undertakings exceed the legal requirements.[134] If used for accelerating the adaptation to new standards, however, the state aids may not amount to more than 15 per cent of the totally refundable cost. In the second case of undertakings going beyond legal requirements, the state aids granted may not amount to more than 30 per cent.[135] The guidelines include higher rates for small and medium-sized enterprises (SME). If investment aids are awarded under Article 92(3) subparagraph (b), in the European interest, the acceptable amounts may be higher.[136]

---

[129] EC Commission, *XVI Report on Competition Policy* (EC, Brussels, 1987), 171 and 172.

[130] See EC Commission, n. 26 above, 53.

[131] EC Commission, *Guidelines on State Aids for Environmental Protection*, n. 77 above.

[132] See e.g. EC Commission, *X Report on Competition Policy*, n. 80 above, paras. 224 ff.

[133] On these guidelines see also Gyselen, n. 2 above, 246, or Quick, n. 80 above.

[134] EC Commission, n. 26 above, 53.

[135] In this context it is important to mention the corresponding provisions on environmentally justified state aids under GATT law. The Agreement on Subsidies and Countervailing Duties included in GATT Secretariat (ed.), *The Results of the Uruguay Round of Multilateral Trade Negotiations—The Legal Texts* (GATT, Geneva. 1994), 264. It contains in its Art. 8(c) specific rules governing the admissibility of environmental state aids and their level in the industrial sector. It would have been advisable to include these worldwide regulations in the framework for Community guidelines, see also Quick, n. 80 above, 622.

[136] See the *Guidelines on State Aids for Environmental Protection*, n. 77 above, 8.

The provisions in the Community approach, namely the detailed conditions the Commission has communicated in its reports and guidelines, have, however, no binding legal force. They are part of Community Communications which should provide Member States with some guidelines on how Article 92(3), sub-paragraph (b), is to be understood. This is particularly important, as it gives Member States the opportunity to judge in advance the outcome of the compulsory procedure for the authorization of any kind of state aid, as it is provided for by Article 93(3) EC. Therefore the guidelines have the character of general administrative guidelines or advisory opinions.[137]

In its *XXII Report on Competition Policy* the Commission set out several examples where it had taken into consideration the environmental benefit of certain state aids when applying the procedure under Article 93(2).

Case: One case concerned a Dutch scheme to promote the recycling, storing, and disposal of manure in The Netherlands.[138] While the Commission had first initiated proceedings under Article 92(3) against this system in 1991, it reconsidered the case in 1992 and approved it on condition that the system would charge the farmers concerned with the variable costs of the system ('polluter pays' principle). The Commission declared that otherwise such a system would provide operating aid to the farmers concerned. This solution, however, seemed acceptable to the Commission as it took into account the environmental benefits of the system without distorting competition unduly.[139]

Other Exceptions

Apart from the exceptions admissible under Article 92(3), subparagraph (b), and more specifically defined by the Commission's guidelines, Article 92(3), sub-paragraph (c), provides a specific exception from the general prohibition on trade distorting state aids, allowing their application in cases where they serve the development of certain economic activities or economic areas. In the field of environmental subsidies the development of ecologically sound technologies and production methods, as well as assistance for afforestation projects, may fall under this provision.[140] These aids, however, may not adversely affect trading conditions to an extent contrary to the common interest. Similarly Article 92(3) subparagraph (a), allows specific exceptions for economically disadvantaged areas and regions.

The Community recommendation mentioned above on the environmental aspects of the exceptions under Article 93(3), subparagraph (b), also contain the conditions under which the Council should authorize national environmental

---

[137] For details on the guidelines see Brunetti, n. 71 above, 93 to 96, or Grabitz and Zacker, n. 74 above, 433.

[138] C/0025/91 IP (92) Aid for the ecologically acceptable disposal of manure of 11 Mar. 1992, as referred to by the EC Commission, n. 26 above, Annex II, 474, also reprinted in P. Sands and R. G. Tarasofsky (eds.), *Documents in European Community Environmental Law* (Manchester University Press, Manchester, 1995), 254 to 261.

[139] EC Commission, n. 26 above, 52.   [140] Grabitz and Zacker, n. 74 above, 429.

subsidies[141] according to the general procedural rules of Article 92(3) subparagraph (d), of the Treaty[142] which provides for special derogations in cases of exceptional circumstances.

Procedure

Article 93(3) requires any Member State to inform the Commission in due course[143] about its plans to grant or alter any kind of state aid.[144] The Commission must then in each individual case judge the compatibility of the state aids in question with the Treaty provisions.[145] This applies equally in the case of environmental state aids and investment aids.[146]

Member States have to observe this procedure very carefully, because otherwise the subsidies are considered illegal even though they would fall under the exceptions provided for in Article 92.[147] The Commission has determined[148] that under Community law all subsidies which violate the procedural rules of Article 93(3) are invalidly granted and may require, in some cases, Member States to withdraw the already distributed state aids.[149] These legal consequences are necessary to give Article 92 its effectiveness and to guarantee the observance of Article 93(3).[150] In many cases, however, Member States do not follow the procedure prescribed by Article 93 which makes the task of the Commission impossible in providing an efficient control of national measures in this field.[151]

A particular problem arises from the competition-distorting effect of certain state aids for market participants who do not receive subsidies or are not granted the same reduction of taxes as their competitors. The question of the admissibility of proceedings brought before the Court by a competing undertaking is a general problem of Community competition law[152] which may, in particular, arise in cases where certain undertakings are granted tax advantages or state aids for alleged environmental reasons or to facilitate the adaptation to higher environmental standards.[153]

[141] See e.g. Commission Decision 77/260/EEC of 22 Mar. 1977 concerning the aids planned by the Belgian Government for the extension of the capacity of a petroleum refinery in Antwerp [1977] OJ L80/23 ff.; see also Grabitz and Zacker, n. 74 above, 432.

[142] See Grabitz, n. 124 above, 628.

[143] Case 120/73 *Gebrüder Lorenz GmbH* v. *Germany et al.* [1973] *ECR* 1471 at 1478 gives no exact time limit, but holds that a two-month period is sufficient.

[144] On the procedure see also Portwood, n. 2 above, 195.

[145] Recent examples for (at least partly) environmentally justified state aids were: a British state aid for an undertaking specializing in recycling of newspapers and magazines, see [1993] *EuZW* 111 or a German state aid for undertakings specializing in recycling, see [1992] *EC Bulletin* (no. 4, 1 Feb.) 7 or [1993] *EuZW* 140.

[146] See the *Guidelines on Environmental State Aids*, n. 77 above, 9.

[147] For details on the procedure see Niemeyer, n. 70 above, 275.

[148] Communication of the Commission [1983] *OJ* C318/3.

[149] Grabitz and Zacker, n. 74 above, 437.

[150] Case 173/73 *Family Allowances*, n. 100 above, 717.   [151] See Furrer, n. 2 above, 1523.

[152] See for details N. Löw, *Der Rechtsschutz des Konkurrenten gegenüber Subventionen aus gemeinschaftsrechtlicher Sicht* (Nomos, Baden-Baden, 1992), 1 ff.

[153] See e.g. Case C–295/92 *Landbouwschap* v. *Commission*, judgment of 30 Sept. 1992.

Case: In January 1992 the Dutch Government had notified a change in its domestic environmental legislation (*Wet Algemene Bepalingen Milieuhygiëne*). The new law provided for the taxation of gas and fuels according to their carbon content. Nevertheless, it also provided for a tax reduction to consumers of very large amounts of natural gas (more than 10,000,000 cubic metres a year). The Commission considered the tax reduction a state aid in the sense of Article 92(1) EC. It was compatible with the common market, however, as it qualified for the exceptional application of Article 92(3)(c) EC. In response to the Commission's decision not to begin proceedings under Article 93(2) EC, a Dutch federation for the protection of the interests of farmers brought an action for annulment under Article 173(2) EC. It claimed that the preferential treatment of only those undertakings which consume very large amounts of natural gas was not justified. The federation represented mainly the interests of growers of greenhouse plants and flowers. The Court, however, did not enter into the merits of the case, considering the Commission's decision did not concern the plaintiffs individually as they were not in direct competition with the industrial undertakings favoured by the tax reduction.[154]

The 'Polluter Pays' Principle

Even before the coming into force of the Single European Act it was possible to interpret the general prohibition on competition-distorting subsidies, in the field of the protection of the environment, as an application of the 'polluter pays' principle,[155] which was adopted as early as 1973 in the First Environmental Action Programme.[156] The Commission views its guidelines as a compromise between the implications of the 'polluter pays' principle and the general wish to grant adaptation aids.[157]

According to the 'polluter pays' principle those who cause harm or pollute the environment are required to carry the costs of avoiding such action, to eliminate or compensate for such pollution. Nevertheless, the Community has always allowed exceptions to this principle and the provisions in Article 92(2) and (3), as well as Articles 42, 77, and 80 are the best examples of this. Here the cost of environmental protection becomes a common burden, which is carried by the general public, whereas the public authorities administer the allocation of the financial aids. Nevertheless, there have been recommendations by the Community to Member States to avoid these exceptions and to apply the 'polluter pays' principle in the field of environmental protection.[158]

The 'polluter pays' principle, as introduced explicitly in Article 130r(2) under the Single European Act, may have an impact on the lawfulness of national environmental subsidies apart from the non-discrimination requirement.[159] Its legal consequences are, however, difficult to imagine, as it is much more an eco-

---

[154] Case C–295/92, n. 153 above.   [155] See Grabitz and Zacker, n. 74 above, 426.
[156] [1973] *OJ* C112/1.   [157] See Grabitz and Zacker, n. 74 above, 433.
[158] Recommendation 75/436/Euratom/ECSC/EEC, n. 123 above.
[159] See, however, the Commission's guidelines for the acceptability of national environmental subsidies under Art. 93(3), sub-para. (b), n. 77 above.

nomic principle which lacks, for the moment, legal force. The main problem is that at the moment 'pollution' exists only if legal standards for limiting emission have not been respected. If there are no standards in force the fundamental legal principle in the Community and its Member States is that emissions into air, water, soil, and under the ground are lawful and therefore free of charge. Only some countries would require 'polluters' to buy an authorization for such emissions.

For the moment, the Community itself has not yet introduced any economic measures based on this principle. It did, however, as early as 1975 recommend that Member States adopt a policy dictating that costs of environmental pollution should be borne by the polluters and not by the taxpayers, even if in the form of grants or subsidies.[160] The Fifth Action Programme for the Environment contains further suggestions,[161] based mainly on the principle of sustainable development as understood by the Commission.[162] In its *XXII Report on Competition Policy* the Commission proposed, *inter alia*, a confirmation of the 'polluter pays' principle:[163] 'where additional environmental investment by firms was undertaken in order to meet legal requirements. . . . Thus the tightening of environmental standards should as far as possible be achieved without financial support from the governments'.[164]

Nevertheless, Member States should be capable of giving incentives to undertakings which are ahead of the prescribed standards.[165] This has been implemented through the Commission's guidelines concerning environmental state aids. They are based on the Fifth Action Programme and follow the ideas set out there.[166]

---

[160] See L. Krämer, 'Community Environmental Law—Towards a Systematic Approach' [1992] *YEL* 151 at 162 or B. Börner, 'Subventionen—unrichtiges Europarecht?' in B. Börner et al. (eds.), *Einigkeit und Recht und Freiheit—Festschrift Carl Carstens* (Heymann, Köln, 1984), 63.

[161] See Furrer, n. 2 above, 1523. [162] See EC Commission, n. 26 above, 53.

[163] See also Krämer, n. 77 above, 244 to 263.

[164] A different view is expressed by Quick, n. 80 above, 623.

[165] EC Commission, n. 26 above, 53.

[166] See EC Commission, *Guidelines on State Aids for Environmental Protection*, n. 77 above.

PART II
Community Environmental Law and Domestic Environmental Measures

7

The Environment-related Policy of the Community

INTRODUCTION

At the moment of its creation in 1957, the European Community was conceived of as a mainly economic organization. The original Treaty of Rome did not include the protection of the environment as a Community objective or an element of Community policy. Nevertheless, the establishment of the common market soon led to an urgent need for co-ordination between environmental protection and the intended elimination of obstacles to trade and national differences distorting competition. The first 'environmental measures' of the Community were adopted under the rubric of elimination of trade-hindering national standards. From the late 1960s until the middle of the 1980s the Community provisions for the harmonization of laws for the establishment of the common market were also used for the protection of the environment. This led to the extensive adoption of environment-related measures sometimes based additionally on Article 235. This practice was also supported by the Court of Justice which, however, established a detailed system for co-ordination between the objectives of the common market, Community environmental measures, and national environmental measures.

Only when the Single European Act came into force was the Community entrusted explicitly with the protection of the environment. Article 130r in particular gave the Community the authority for a comprehensive environmental policy. The protection of the environment has become an important element of all Community policies and also of the establishment of the common market. Article 130r(2) has integrated environmental protection into all areas of Community action. Nevertheless, the other Treaty provisions continued to be important for the adoption of specific environmental measures. The system elaborated by the Court for the co-ordination of environmental protection and trade has been institutionalized in the Treaty by specific mechanisms. Furthermore the existing Treaty is relatively open to the need for diverging national measures. The protection of the environment has been established as a common responsibility of the Community and its Member States.

THREE PERIODS OF COMMUNITY ENVIRONMENTAL POLICY

Several authors have tried to classify the Community's journey to its own environmental policy[1] into distinct periods.[2] They usually distinguish three periods related to the development of Community law in general.[3] In the field of the environment these periods are very closely linked to the growing awareness of the ecological problems which arise out of the establishment of the common market and the need for transnational co-operation in general. This process also had a significant influence on the establishment of environmental provisions in the Treaty and the use of the existing provisions for environmental measures[4] as well as their interpretation by the Court.[5]

The first period is usually described as a foundational period[6] where only a few Community acts with incidental environmental implications were adopted.[7] This period can be traced from the origins of the Community until the UN Conference on the Human Environment in Stockholm in 1972.[8] What can be considered as the environmental policy of the Community during this period was very much motivated by the strong desire to eliminate trade-distorting reg-

[1] See for details on the environmental policy of the EC: S. Johnson and G. Corcelle, *The Environmental Policy of the European Community* (Graham & Trotman, London, 1st edn., 1989 and 2nd edn., 1995); The American Chamber of Commerce in Belgium, *The EC Environment Guide 1994* (Catermill Publishing, London, 1995); E. Alonso García, *El Derecho Ambiental de las Comunidad Europea* (Civitas, Madrid, 1993); R. Romi, *L'Europe et la protection juridique de l'environnement* (Victoires Editions Litec, Paris, 1993); A. Kiss and D. Shelton, *Manual of European Environmental Law* (Grotius, Cambridge, 1993); P. Sands and R. G. Tarasofsky, *Documents in European Community Environmental Law* (Manchester University Press, Manchester, 1995); S. Hollins and R. Macrory, *A Source Book of European Community Environmental Law* (Oxford University Press, Oxford, 1995); E. Rehbinder and R. Stewart, *Environmental Protection Policy—Integration Through Law* (W. de Gruyter, New York, 1985), ii, 15; N. Haigh, *EEC Environmental Law and Policy and Britain* (2nd edn., Longman, Harlow (Essex), 1989); on the adopted acts in the different fields see L. Krämer, *EEC Treaty and Environmental Protection* (Sweet & Maxwell, London, 1990), 1 to 28; the author has published a second edition under a slightly different title: L. Krämer, *EC Treaty and Environmental Law* (2nd edn., Sweet & Maxwell London, 1995); several interesting contributions can be found in J. D. Liefferink *et al.* (eds.), *European Integration and Environmental Policy* (Belhaven Press, London, 1993).

[2] See P. M. Hildebrand, 'The European Community's Environmental Policy, 1957 to 1992: From Incidental Measures to an International Regime' [1992] *Environmental Politics* 13 to 44; P. Sands, 'European Community Environmental Law: The Evolution of a Regional Regime of International Environmental Protection' (1991) 100 *Yale Law Journal* 2511 to 2524; I. Koppen, *The European Community's Environmental Policy*, EUI Working Paper no. 88/238 (European University Institute, San Domenico di Fiesole, 1988).

[3] See the interesting contribution by J. H. H. Weiler, 'The Transformation of Europe' 100 (1991) *Yale Law Journal* 2403.

[4] See, in particular, the use of the provisions concerning the approximation of national laws for the establishment of the common market for environmental objectives; see Ch. 8.

[5] See e.g. the development of the Court's rulings from Joined cases 3, 4, and 6/76 *Criminal proceedings against Cornelis Kramer et al. (Biological Resources of the Sea)* [1976] *ECR* 1279 at 1313; Case 91/79 *Commission* v. *Italy (Detergents)* [1980] *ECR* 1099 at 1106; and Case 92/79 *Commission* v. *Italy (Maximum Supphur Content of Liquid Fuels)* [1980] *ECR* 1115 at 1122 to Case 240/83 *Procureur de la République* v. *Association de Défense des Brûleurs d'Huiles Usagées (ADBHU)* [1985] *ECR* 531.

[6] See Weiler, n. 3 above, 2403, as referred to by Sands, n. 2 above, 2511.

[7] See also Hildebrand, n. 2 above, 17 to 20.   [8] See e.g. Sands, n. 2 above, 2511.

ulatory differences in the national environmental regulations concerning product standards.

A second period dates from 1973 until the mid-1980s,[9] leading to the adoption of the Single European Act which established an authentic environmental policy in the Community. During this period the Community used the existing competences in the Treaty and the mechanism of filling *lacunae* under Article 235 for the extensive introduction of truly environmental measures. Apart from the fear of the distorting effect of diverging national environmental measures, which had dominated during the first period, the observation that the environment was a basis of further economic and social development[10] had led to a new interpretation of the Treaty leading ultimately to the introduction of an environmental chapter under the Single European Act.[11]

The third period is unanimously considered to start with the drafting and coming into effect of the Single European Act in the mid-1980s.[12] Only in this third period did the protection of the environment become an end in itself through the introduction of an explicit legal basis for environmental action by the Community. The Treaty on European Union continued the development started under the Single European Act by establishing the protection of the environment as an important factor of the Community's task to promote 'sustainable and non-inflationary growth'.[13] The Court has followed the development in its case law.[14]

THE PROTECTION OF THE ENVIRONMENT IN THE TREATY

General Conception of the Treaty of Rome

The Treaty of Rome, which established the European Economic Community (EEC Treaty) in 1957, did not mention the protection of the environment as an explicit objective of the Community. Vague mention was made of the environment in the Preamble and Article 2 EC. The Preamble spoke very generally of the quality of life in Member States. It referred to the 'constant improvement of the living and working conditions of their people' and even more generally to a 'harmonious development' of their economies.[15] Similarly, Article 2 EC referred as general objectives of the Community to the 'harmonious development', a 'balanced expansion', and 'the raising of the standard of living'.

[9] Referred to by Weiler as 'Mutational Period', see Weiler, n. 3 above, 2403.
[10] See e.g. also the Court's judgment in Joined cases 3, 4, and 6/76 *Biological Resources of the Sea*, n. 5 above, 1313.
[11] See e.g. Hildebrand, n. 2 above, 20 to 28.
[12] For the development of Community law in general see Weiler, n. 3 above; for the environment-related policy see Sands, n. 2 above, 2515; Hildebrand, n. 2 above, 28.
[13] Art. 2 EC after the coming into force of the Treaty on European Union.
[14] See Case 240/83 *ADBHU*, n. 5 above, 548.
[15] Preamble to the Treaty of Rome, fourth and sixth paras.

However, it remains arguable whether or not this included at the time of drafting a concern with the natural environment. It is interesting that, apart from these introductory statements, the only other reference to the environment was in the provisions referring to trade. Article 36 EC allows Member States to adopt certain trade restrictions 'for the protection of health and life of humans, animals or plants'.[16] Under the principle of attributed powers there was no explicit legal basis in the Treaty on which the Community could have based a proper environmental policy.[17] These attributed powers constitute the necessary basis for every Community action.[18] The framework of powers granted in the Treaty reflects the desire of Member States to restrict the transfer of national sovereignty to the Communities to the agreed areas.[19]

As the term 'environmental protection' does not appear in the Treaty of Rome of 1957,[20] it seems that the drafters of the Treaty did not consider the protection of the environment as a task of the European Community. At this time, in fact, most Member States did not yet have a proper environmental policy.[21] The concept of environmental protection and of the need for a coherent environmental policy, as we understand it today, simply did not yet exist.[22]

The Evolving Common Market and the Environment

In spite of the absence of an explicit Community competence it was realized soon after the Treaty entered into force that the creation of a common market might conflict with concern for the environment.[23] In particular, the harmonization of differing national laws and the elimination of extant obstacles to

[16] See Johnson and Corcelle, n. 1 above, 1, who consider this as a kind of 'negative reference'. See also Hildebrand, n. 2 above, 17.

[17] See P. J. G. Kapteyn and P. VerLoren van Themaat, *Introduction to the Law of the European Communities* (2nd edn., Kluwer, Deventer, 1989), 112.

[18] The principle of attributed powers is sometimes called principle of limited powers, in German *Prinzip der beschränkten Einzelermächtigung*, in French *principe des pouvoirs d'action limités*, but generally referred to as the *compétence d'attribution*, although there might exist a slight difference, as stated by: I. Schwartz, Art. 235, in H. v. d. Groeben, J. Thiesing, and C.-D. Ehlermann (eds.), *Kommentar zum EWG-Vertrag* (Nomos, Baden-Baden, 1983 ff.). See for a classical description H.-P. Ipsen, *Europäisches Gemeinschaftsrecht* (Mohr, Tübingen, 1972), 20 to 36.

[19] Kapteyn and VerLoren van Themaat, n. 17 above, 113.

[20] Nor do the terms 'environment' or 'pollution', as observed by Rehbinder and Stewart, n. 1 above, 15.

[21] H. Bungarten, *Umweltpolitik in Westeuropa* (Europa-Union, Bonn, 1978), 119; R. Kreutzberger, 'Der Umweltschutz als Aufgabe der Europäischen Gemeinschaften' [1986] *ZfU* 169; even today only a few Member States of the Community refer to the protection of the environment as a specific objective in their constitutions: Constitution of Greece of 1975 (Art. 24), Constitution of Spain of 1978 (Art. 45), Constitution of Portugal of 1975 (Arts. 9(e) and 66), Constitution of The Netherlands of 1982 (Art. 21), as reported by L. Krämer, 'Environmental Protection and Art. 30 EEC Treaty' (1993) 30 *CMLRev.* 111; see also Constitution of Italy (Art. 9(2)), for Austria, *Bundesverfassungsgesetz* of 27 Nov. 1984 (para. 1) or Germany (Art. 20(a) of the *Grundgesetz*); outside the EU see e.g. Switzerland (Art. 24 *septies* of the Federal Constitution).

[22] Johnson and Corcelle, n. 1 above, 1; Sands, n. 2 above, 2512.

[23] See Krämer, n. 1 above, 1.

trade to permit an accelerated exchange of goods was closely linked to the problem of different environmental standards and different national conceptions of how to safeguard the human environment. Thus the original incentive for implementing regulations concerning the environment was the implementation of common standards for the establishment of the common market itself rather than a real awareness of environmental problems.[24] There was a general fear that diverging national standards would hinder the free movement of goods and thus jeopardize one of the main mechanisms of the Community for the promotion of its objectives.

Despite the absence of an explicit competence for environmental measures, the Community adopted internal measures with the aim of ensuring the elimination of certain environment related technical trade barriers. Most of the relevant harmonizing instruments were adopted on the basis of the general competence under Article 100, and sometimes in conjunction with Article 235.[25]

Example: As early as 1967 the Council adopted a Directive on the classification, packaging, and labelling of dangerous substances.[26] This Directive was based on Article 100 EC and aimed at eliminating different national provisions which could hinder trade in these substances and thus directly affect the establishment and functioning of the common market. Although the Directive mentioned in its objectives 'the protection of the public' and 'in particular workers using such substances and preparations', it did not specifically refer to the protection of the environment. Its main focus was the establishment of the common market for goods, which obviously included the regulated dangerous substances. Subsequent directives implicitly concerning the human environment were also based on Article 100 EC and aimed at the approximation of diverging national provisions which directly affected the establishment or functioning of the common market.[27] Further examples were the Directives on noise levels[28] and pollutant emissions[29] for motor vehicles, both adopted in 1970. It is interesting to observe that these two Directives made no mention of the protection of the public or the protection of the environment. They were formulated purely to eliminate technical obstacles to trade, as provided for by Article 100. These Directives made clear reference to national measures previously introduced in France and Germany, which, it was considered, would hinder the establishment of the common market if no approximation of standards took place.[30]

---

[24] See A. Bleckmann, *Europarecht* (Heymann, Köln, 1990), 69.

[25] Rehbinder and Stewart, n. 1 above, 16. For examples see Ch. 8 and Hildebrand, n. 2 above, 19.

[26] Council Dir. 67/548/EEC of 27 June 1967 on the approximation of laws, regulations, and administrative provisions relating to the classification, packaging, and labelling of dangerous substances [1967] *OJ* L 196/1.

[27] See D. H. Scheuing, 'Umweltschutz auf Grundlage der Einheitlichen Europäischen Akte' [1989] *EuR* 152 at 154.

[28] Council Dir. 70/157/EEC of 6 Feb. 1970 on the approximation of the laws of the Member States relating to the permissible sound level and the exhaust system of motor vehicles [1970] *OJ* L42/16.

[29] Council Dir. 70/220/EEC of 20 Mar. 1970 on the approximation of the laws of the Member States relating to measures to be taken against air pollution by gases from positive ignition engines of motor vehicles [1970] *OJ* L76/1.

[30] See Krämer, n. 1 above, 1.

Although the first legislative instruments were aimed directly at the reduction of pollution and thereby at the protection of the human environment, this term was not mentioned in either their preambles or in any of their provisions. These Directives were strictly based on the approximation of laws for the establishment of the common market (as laid down in Article 100), although they did have an important environmental impact. The same is true for evolving environment-related regulations in other fields such as agriculture, the common commercial policy, etc., which were included under the more specific provisions of the Treaty.[31]

Paris Summit and Environmental Action Programmes

It was only fifteen years after the conclusion of the Treaty of Rome that the Community 'officially' started its own environmental policy at the 1972 Paris Summit.[32] The basic idea was that economic expansion should also result in an improvement of the quality of life and that this should include the protection of the environment. To bring the European Community closer to its citizens, the Heads of State and Government proposed[33] that the Community institutions should establish an Action Programme[34] for the environment, as well as similar programmes in other areas such as social and regional policy or consumer protection.[35] The first Community Environmental Action Programme was published in 1973.[36] It was followed by the programmes of 1977,[37] 1983,[38] 1988,[39] and most recently by the Fifth Action Programme 1992.[40]

The idea of an Environmental Action Programme was mentioned for the first time by the Commission in a memorandum to the Council in 1970, followed by an official communication in 1971.[41] This gave rise to an intense debate over the level at which environmental problems were best dealt with.[42] That there was a need for common action was not doubted. The question was rather

---

[31] See Ch. 9.

[32] The UN Environment Conference of 1972 in Stockholm must have had a substantial influence on the Paris summit, see L. Krämer, Artikel 130, 1610 in Groeben, Thiesing, and Ehlermann (eds.), n. 18 above; for more details on the development of the environmental policy of the Community see Hildebrand, n. 2 above; P. Sands, 'European Community Environmental Law: Legislation, the European Court of Justice and Common-Interest Groups' [1990] 53 *MLR* 685 to 698.

[33] Declaration of the Heads of State and Government of 19/20 Oct. 1972 at the Paris Summit about collaboration in environmental policy [1972] *EC Bulletin* (no. 10) 21.

[34] On the legal value of the Action Programmes see L. Krämer, *Focus on European Environmental Law* (Sweet & Maxwell, London, 1993), 64, and Krämer, n. 1 above, 2, although it seems arguable whether a mere statement by the Commission in its Environmental Action Programme that a certain environmental measure should be taken at Community level is a sufficient proof for the necessity of a Community action.

[35] Johnson and Corcelle, n. 1 above, 2.   [36] [1973] *OJ* C112/1.   [37] [1977] *OJ* C139/1.
[38] [1983] *OJ* C46/1.   [39] [1987] *OJ* C328/1.

[40] Presented by the Commission on 27 Mar. 1992, COM(92)23 (final), approved by the Council on 15 Dec. 1992 [1993] *OJ* C138/1; see e.g. R. Wägenbauer, 'Ein Programm für die Umwelt' [1993] *EuZW* 241 to 244.

[41] [1972] *OJ* C52/1.   [42] See Krämer, n. 1 above, 1.

whether there was a need for Community action or whether intergovernmental agreements and co-ordination of national environmental policies would be sufficient.[43] Finally, the Paris Summit set the basis for Community action although it would be another fifteen years before the environment was explicitly included in the Treaty.[44]

At the 1972 Paris Summit the Heads of Government and State showed no intention of officially amending the Treaty or including a special provision concerning the environment. They simply stated:

Economic expansion is not an aim in itself. Its firm aim should be to enable disparities in living conditions to be reduced. It must take place with the participation of all the social partners. It should result in an improvement in the quality of life as well as in standards of living. As benefits the genius of Europe, particular attention will be given to intangible values and to protecting the environment, so that progress may really be put at the service of mankind.[45]

It is interesting to observe that this statement of the Heads of State and Government led only to the relatively vague request that the Commission draw up an action programme on the environment. The declaration by the Heads of State and Government searches very carefully for terms close to the wording of the Treaty, 'improvement' in the 'living conditions' (Preamble to the Treaty) and 'standards of living' (Article 2 EC).

A more important step for the development of a Community environmental policy was that, at the same time, the participants in the summit recommended giving a more generous and broader meaning to Article 235 of the Treaty in order to take action in the field of the environment. The interpretation of the Preamble and Article 2 EC in conjunction with Article 235 could provide the legal basis for further Community regulations on the basis of Article 100 of the Treaty.[46] One can therefore view this summit as the official beginning of the Community's environmental policy.[47] In spite of the missing explicit competence, the Community was invited to adopt environmental provisions in the application of Article 235.

According to legal teaching, Article 235 EC allows the Community to act where the Contracting Parties wanted it to be empowered to act.[48] After the end of the transitional period, the European Communities were more often confronted with problems which were not explicitly covered by a corresponding competence in the Treaty. Therefore at the 1972 Paris Summit, the Heads of State and Government of the Member States recommended a fairly loose interpretation of Article 235 to allow the existing Treaties to deal with the new

[43] Krämer, n. 1 above, 2.
[44] With the introduction of the new Art. 130s by the Single European Act 1987.
[45] EC Commission, *Sixth General Report* (EC, Brussels, 1972), 8.   [46] See Ch. 8.
[47] See Johnson and Corcelle, n. 1 above, 2.
[48] See for details Kapteyn and VerLoren van Themaat, n. 17 above, 1; Schwartz, n. 18 above.

problem areas,[49] but the scope of Article 235 is very limited.[50] It does not provide a general competence for new areas of Community action which might seem useful in the framework of the Treaty. It allows the Community to act only where the mentioned objectives of the Treaty make such an action necessary.[51]

Between 1973 and 1983 over seventy legislative texts on environment-related areas were adopted and several international agreements concluded on the basis of Article 100[52] and/or 235.[53] The legal basis for this important legislation in the field of the environment[54] was, however, considered by most legal writers to be relatively weak.[55]

This policy was considerably strengthened by the case law of the Court of Justice.[56] While it had usually legitimized environment-related measures under Article 100 by referring to the possible trade effects of diverging national standards,[57] it later considered the protection of the environment to be an essential objective of the Community which legitimized Community measures and even certain restrictions on the free movement of goods.[58] This reasoning allowed the Court, in the context of the implied powers theory, to accept a Community competence for measures concerning the environment. Although there was no explicit competence, the general objectives of the Treaty enabled the Community to take measures for their safeguard. Article 100 and eventually Article 235 (for the filling of *lacunae*) were possible provisions for such action.[59]

Case: Case 240/83 *ADBHU*[60] was concerned with a request for a preliminary ruling by a French court on the lawfulness of Directive 75/439/EEC on the disposal of waste oil

[49] See U. Everling, I. Schwartz, and C. Tomuschat, 'Die Rechtsetzungsbefugnisse der EWG in Generalermächtigungen, insbesondere Art. 235 EWGV' [1976] *EuR* (special issue) 1 to 73.

[50] See e.g. Case 45/86 *Commission* v. *Council* (*General Customs Preferences–GCPI*) [1987] *ECR* 1493 which limits the use of Art. 235 EC in comparison to the former view expressed e.g. in Case 8/73 *Hauptzollamt Bremerhaven* v. *Massey Ferguson GmbH* [1973] *ECR* 897.

[51] In German this Art. is often referred to as *Vertragsabrundungsklausel*, see e.g. T. Oppermann, *Europarecht* (C. H. Beck, München, 1991), 169.

[52] At the same time the Community continued to adopt environment-related regs. under the specific Treaty provisions for certain fields such as agriculture (Art. 43) or transport policy (Arts. 75 and 84 (2)); see Ch. 9.

[53] F. Behrens, 'Die Umweltpolitik der Europäischen Gemeinschaft und Art. 235 EWGV' [1978] *DVBl.* 462 to 469.

[54] See Oppermann, n. 51 above, 741 and 742; for a list see: [German] Umweltbundesamt (ed.), *Rechtsakte der EG auf dem Gebiet des Umweltschutzes* (Umweltbundesamt, Berlin, 1991). On the relevant case law see Krämer, n. 21 above, 112.

[55] For details see Ch. 8, and Rehbinder and Stewart, n. 1 above, 18; D. Geradin, 'Free Trade and Environmental Protection in an Integrated Market: A Survey of the Case Law of the United States Sureme Court and the European Court of Justice' (1993) 2 *Journal of Transnational Law and Policy* 141 at 163 to 165.

[56] A fact that is still true for the most recent developments, see e.g. L. Krämer, 'Die Rechtsprechung des Gerichtshofs der Europäischen Gemeinschaften zum Umweltrecht 1992–1994' [1995] *EuGRZ* 45 to 53.

[57] See Ch. 8.   [58] Case 240/83 *ADBHU*, n. 5 above, 548.

[59] On the role of the Court in the development of European environmental policy see I. Koppen, *The Role of the European Court of Justice in the Development of the European Community Environmental Policy* EUI *Working Paper 92/18* (European University Institute, San Domenico di Fiesole, 1992), 12 ff.

[60] Case 240/83 *ADBHU*, n. 5 above.

and a related French national measure. France implemented the Directive by setting up a system of districts and the compulsory authorization of recycling undertakings. The plaintiffs argued this was an infringement of the free movement of goods (Articles 30 and 34). The Court, however, held that the principle of free movement of goods was not absolute and that the other objectives of the Community had to be observed as well and could therefore lead to a lawful restriction of the free movement of goods. It considered the protection of the environment to be such an essential objective: '[t]he directive must be seen in the perspective of environmental protection which is one of the Community's essential objectives.'

The Single European Act and the Environment

In 1983 the Stuttgart European Council stressed the urgent need to speed up and reinforce the action carried out at all levels against the pollution of the environment and decided that environmental protection policy should be given more priority within the Community. In March 1985, at its Brussels session, the European Council judged that environmental policy should become a fundamental part of the policies set up by the Community and its Member States.[61] In particular, the difficulties concerning the implementation of environmental measures at a national level led to 'the Environment' being introduced as a part of the Community constitution.[62]

With the coming into force of the Single European Act (SEA) in 1987, the European Community obtained an explicit basis for its own environmental actions.[63] The provisions under the new title VII, Environment, provided a framework for the environmental policy of the Community. Article 130r sets out in a relatively detailed way the principles of the Community's environmental policy including its objectives and instruments.[64] The environment also became a general objective of the Community in all its activities (Article 130r(2) EC[65]).

---

[61] See Johnson and Corcelle, n. 1 above, 2 and 3.

[62] D. Vandermeersch, 'The Single European Act and the Environmental Policy of the EC' (1987) 12 *ELRev.* 407.

[63] On the general environmental concept of the EEA see e.g. K. Heinz and A. Körte, 'Die Ziele Umweltschutz und Binnenmarkt zwischen gemeinschaftlicher Kompetenz und nationaler Verantwortung—Zu den neuen Umweltvorschriften im EWG-Vertrag' [1991] *JA* 41 to 48; C. Binder, 'Wege der Rechtsangleichung am Beispiel des Umweltschutzrechts' in K. Korinek and H.-P. Rill (eds.), *Österreichisches Wirtschaftsrecht und das Recht der EG* (Orac, Wien, 1990) 163 to 187; I. Pernice, 'Auswirkungen des europäischen Binnenmarktes auf das Umweltrecht—Gemeinschafts(verfassungs)rechtliche Grundlagen' [1990] *NVwZ* 201 to 210; T. C. W. Beyer, 'Europa 1992: Gemeinschaftsrecht und Umweltschutz nach der Einheitlichen Europäischen Akte' [1990] *JuS* 962 to 967; U. Beyerlin, 'Die "neue" Umweltpolitik der Europäischen Gemeinschaft' [1989] *UPR* 361 to 364.

[64] See for details Vandermeersch, n. 62 above, 415; E. Grabitz and C. Zacker, 'Die neuen Umweltkompetenzen der EWG' [1989] *NVwZ* 297 at 299; for recent examples of the fast growing environmental legislation see L. Krämer, 'L'environnement et le marché unique européen' [1993] *RMC* 45 at 63.

[65] In German referred to as *Querschnittklausel*, see Oppermann, n. 51 above, 744; J. Jahns-Böhm, 'Die umweltrechtliche Querschnittklausel des Art. 130r II (2) EWGV' [1992] *EuZW* 49.

Particularly interesting for the relationship between national environmental policy and Community environmental policy was the inclusion of a provision concerning diverging national measures (Article 130t). This provision allows, subject to certain conditions, the systematic introduction and application of more stringent national measures after a harmonization has taken place.[66]

The case law of the Court concerning the restriction of the free movement of goods for environmental reasons[67] was institutionalized by recognizing the protection of the environment as a main objective of the Community and by introducing a specific exception clause. Unlike the Treaty of Rome the Single European Act includes 'the protection of the environment' as a public interest in addition to the areas mentioned in Article 36 EC. This is evident in the case of Article 100a(4) EC, which allows diverging national measures in areas where an approximation of laws in the interest of the internal market has taken place.[68]

Even if the concrete meaning of Article 100a(4) has given rise to much controversy, in my view it shows the particular focus on regulatory co-operation in this field. Furthermore Member States wanted the protection of the environment to be given a fundamental place in the Community constitutional framework and the Community to be given the competence to continue its environmental policy on an explicit legal basis: Article 130r. At the same time the Member States should take part in the protection of the environment in those fields where a harmonization at Community level is not necessary or is politically not possible at the desired level. Both the Community and the Member States are competent to regulate the protection of the environment and the Community should only act when the objectives can be better attained at Community level.[69] Even in the case of harmonization, the Member States, under certain conditions, retain the regulatory power to improve the quality of their national environment.

Articles 130r–t do not exclude the use of other provisions of the Treaty as a legal basis for the adoption of environmental measures. In the fields of agriculture, transport, tax harmonization, and commercial policy the relevant provisions remain important for the Community's environmental policy. Article 130r(2) explicitly allows all these provisions to be handled in an ecological way and for environmental purposes.[70]

The European Union and the Environment

The Treaty on European Union signed at Maastricht on 7 February 1992 came into force on 1 November 1993. Its impact on the Community's environmental policy[71] is therefore still difficult to evaluate. It seems, however, that the current

---

[66] See for details Ch. 9.
[67] Case 240/83 *ADBHU*, n. 5 above, 548.
[68] See for details Ch. 8.
[69] Art. 130r(4), first sentence.
[70] For the conditions see the relevant sections, mainly in Chs. 8 and 9.
[71] See D. Wilkinson, 'Maastricht and the Environment: The Implications for the EC's

understanding of the Community's environmental policy is a broad continuation of that begun with the Single European Act.

On the one hand the revised text of the Treaty now includes as one of the Community's basic tasks the promotion of 'sustainable and non-inflationary growth respecting the environment' (amendment of Article 2). The requirement that environmental protection should be integrated into other Community policies has been reinforced: new Article 130r(2), third sentence. On the other hand the procedural requirements for the adoption of new measures have been radically changed, which might cause delay and confusion in the adoption of new environmental measures.[72]

On the whole it seems, however, that the protection of the environment is now definitely an established Community objective.[73] Several provisions indicate that the level of protection is intended to be high.[74] The Maastricht Treaty also includes a new provision for the establishment of a cohesion fund.[75] It should help the less developed member countries pay the often substantial costs of introducing the higher environmental standards required by Community legislation. This might indicate the willingness of the environmentally advanced Member States to contribute financially to guaranteeing a high standard of environmental protection in the Community as a whole.

SHARED COMPETENCE, SHARED RESPONSIBILITY AND SUBSIDIARITY

Pre-emption and Precedence

As was noted in Part I, the Community's environmental policy restricts Member States who adopt environmental measures.[76] As for Community secondary law in general, the adoption of exhaustive measures at Community level precludes the Member States in principle from adopting their own measures in the field or from introducing any supplementary requirements.[77] This is sometimes

Environmental Policy of the Treaty on European Union' [1992] *J Env. L* 221 to 239; A. Epiney and A. Furrer, 'Umweltschutz nach Maastricht' [1992] *EuR* 369 to 408; L. M. Falomo, 'L'incidenza del Trattato di Maastricht sul Diritto Comunitario Ambientale' [1992] *Rivista di Diritto Europeo* 701 to 716.

[72] Wilkinson, n. 71 above, 222.

[73] See e.g. a survey on the Community's policy in the field of clean air: J. Jahns-Böhm, *Umweltschutz durch Europäisches Gemeinschaftsrecht am Beispiel der Luftreinhaltung* (Duncker & Humblot, Berlin, 1994).

[74] See e.g. the 'principle of optimal protection of the environment', as developed by M. Zuleeg, 'Vorbehaltene Kompetenzen der Mitgliedstaaten der Europäischen Gemeinschaft auf dem Gebiet des Umweltschutzes' [1987] *NVwZ* 280 at 283.

[75] Art. 130s(5) EC.

[76] See in particular the conditions for the application of Art. 36 and the rule of reason, Ch. 5.

[77] See for details concerning the application of Art. 36 in Ch. 5; in general, see the detailed analysis by A. Furrer, *Die Sperrwirkung des sekundärrechtlichen Gemeinschaftsrecht auf die nationalen Rechtsordnungen* (Nomos, Baden-Baden, 1994), 9 ff.; with reference to environmental law see also the detailed reference to the case law in A. Middeke, *Nationaler Umweltschutz und Binnenmarkt* (Heymann, Köln, 1994), 23 to 39.

referred to as pre-emption by analogy to American constitutional law[78] or more generally as a consequence of the precedence of Community law.[79]

Under the general system of the Treaty the Member States no longer have the right to regulate an area when it has been regulated exhaustively at Community level[80] or if the regulation is 'otherwise incompatible with the provisions of Community law'.[81] National law which contradicts Community law is inapplicable.[82] All domestic authorities are obliged to guarantee full compliance with Community environmental law and courts[83] and administrators have the duty to interpret national law in conformity with Community law.[84] The general system of the Treaty and the jurisdiction of the Court have elaborated the governing principles to guarantee the effectiveness of Community law and in particular its relationship to national law.[85]

It must, however, be underlined that the pre-emption principle of American constitutional law cannot be applied to European Community law without taking into consideration the specific historic and legal differences between the two systems.[86] Pre-emption in the American sense basically includes two elements:[87] (1) the pre-emptive effect of an existing harmonization which excludes any circumventive or incompatible regulations by states; and (2) the pre-emptive effect

---

[78] See for a comparison e.g. T. Sandalow and E. Stein, 'On the two Systems—Chapter 1' in T. Sandalow and E. Stein (eds.), *Courts and Free Markets* (Oxford University Press, Oxford, 1982), 3 ff.; R. Bieber, 'On the Mutual Completion of Overlapping Legal Systems' (1988) 13 *ELRev.* 147 at 155; see the very instructive analysis by E. D. Cross, 'Pre-emption of Member State Law in the European Economic Community: A Framework for Analysis' (1992) 29 *CMLRev.* 447 ff. For the US model of pre-emption and the environmental case law see Geradin, n. 55 above, 146.

[79] See e.g. Case 106/77 *Administration des Finances* v. *SA Simmenthal* [1978] *ECR* 629 at 643 and 644.

[80] See, however, the interesting observations by Cross, n. 78 above, 469. In German, this effect is sometimes referred to as *Sperrwirkung*, a term introduced very early by Ipsen, n. 18 above, 701 ff.; see, however, recently Furrer, n. 77 above, on the criteria for the interpretation of the exhaustive nature of a Community act, in particular, under Art. 36 and the rule of reason. He speaks even of the 'myth of the pre-emptive effect of Community law' at 90 ff.

[81] Case 106/77 n. 79 above, 643.

[82] Referred to by Cross, n. 78 above, 463 as 'direct conflict pre-emption', generally, however, considered as a consequence of the primacy of Community law, see e.g. Case 218/85 *CERAFEL* v. *Le Campion* [1986] *ECR* 3513 at 3532.

[83] See e.g. Case C–106/89 *Marleasing SA* v. *Comercial Internacional de Alimentación SA* [1990] *ECR* I–4135.

[84] See for detail L. Krämer, 'Community Environmental Law—Towards a Systematic Approach' [1992] *YEL* 151 at 163.

[85] See among the abundant literature on this topic e.g. F. Snyder, 'The Effectiveness of European Community Law' [1993] *MLR* 19 to 54.

[86] See e.g. U. Everling, 'Zur föderalen Struktur der Europäischen Gemeinschaft' in K. Hailbronner, G. Ress, and T. Stein (eds.), *Staat und Völkerrechtsordnung—Festschrift K. Doehring* (Duncker & Humblot, Berlin, 1989), 179 at 186 ff. or J. M. Bergmann, *'Principle of Preemption' versus 'Nationaler Alleingang'—Eine Erörterung am Beispiel der Umweltpolitik, Vorträge, Reden und Berichte aus dem Europainstitut* Nr. 251 (Europainstitut der Universität des Saarlandes, Saarbrücken, 1993), 18 and 19.

[87] For this differentiation see also: G. Ress, 'Luftreinhaltung als Problem des Verhältnisses zwischen Europäischem Gemeinschaftsrecht und nationalem Recht' in *150 Jahre Landgericht Saarbrücken* (Heymann, Köln, 1985), 255 at 357, n. 9, as referred to by Bergmann, n. 86 above, 16.

of federal competence in a specific field of law which precludes the states from any regulatory activity in this field.

As far as the effect of existing Community legislation in a specific field is concerned, Article 189(3) EC makes Community secondary legislation binding for the Member States and thereby pre-empts their sovereignty to regulate a field where exhaustive Community regulation has taken place.[88] In Community law this is generally discussed under the rubric of 'precedence of Community law'.[89] The second element of pre-emption is basically concerned with the question of competence to adopt regulatory legal acts. Here the situation in Community law is much more complicated than in the American doctrine and depends very much on the field of regulation concerned.[90]

Shared Competence

As will be shown, the Community has no exclusive competence for the protection of the environment.[91] The Community should only act where the interest concerned, that is the protection of the environment, can be better protected at Community level. This was particularly expressed through Article 130(4) under the Single European Act[92] and is considered to be strengthened by the elevation of the subsidiarity principle to Article 3a of the Treaty after the coming into force of the Treaty on European Union.[93] The Fifth Environmental Action Programme elaborates in detail on the principle of subsidiarity and shared

---

[88] Ipsen, n. 18 above, 701 ff.; see, however, Furrer, n. 77 above, 15 to 42 and 90 to 160. An overview is also given by Bergmann, n. 86 above, 14 to 16.

[89] See the section on pre-emption above.

[90] See for the external and environmental competences e.g. the development of the case law of the Court of Justice in Case 22/70 *Commission* v. *Council (ERTA)* [1971] *ECR* 263, Joined cases 3, 4, and 6/76 *Biological Resources of the Sea*, n. 5 above, and Opinion 1/78 *International Rubber Agreement* [1979] *ECR* 2871 as demonstrated by J. H. H. Weiler, 'The Community System: The Dual Character of Supranationalism' [1981] *YEL* 267 at 277 or Bergmann, n. 86 above, 17.

[91] See e.g. Krämer, n. 21 above, 113; for details see also Middeke, n. 77 above, 39 to 46 or I. Pernice, 'Kompetenzordnung und Handlungsbefugnisse der Europäischen Gemeinschaft auf dem Gebiete des Umwelt- und Technikrechts' [1989] *DV* 1 to 54; A. Vorwerk, *Die umweltpolitischen Kompetenzen der Europäischen Gemeinschaft und ihrer Mitgliedstaaten nach Inkrafttreten der EEA* (VVF, München, 1990); F. Hochleitner, *Die Kompetenzen der Europäischen Wirtschaftsgemeinschaft auf dem Gebiet des Umweltschutzes* (VWGO, Wien, 1990); T. Schröer, *Die Kompetenzverteilung zwischen der Europäischen Wirtschaftsgemeinschaft und ihren Mitgliedstaaten auf dem Gebiet des Umweltschutzes* (Duncker & Humblot, Berlin, 1992) with many references to the abundant German literature.

[92] Art. 130r(4) reads: 'The Community shall take action relating to the environment to the extent to which the objectives referred to in paragraph I can be attained better at Community level than at the level of the individual Member State . . .'

[93] Art. 3b, second sentence, now reads: 'In areas which do not fall within its exclusive competence, the Community shall take action, in accordance with the principle of subsidiarity, only if and in so far as the objectives of the proposed action cannot be sufficiently achieved by the member states and can therefore, by reason of the scale or the effects of the proposed action, be better achieved by the Community.' It is therefore also valid for Community measures with environmental aspects adopted under legal provisions other than Art. 130s.

responsibility for the protection of the environment within the European Community.[94]

Shared Responsibility

The existence of a shared competence[95] for the protection of the environment has, in the principle of subsidiarity and the case law of the Court, three main aspects. First, Member States are allowed to adopt measures for the protection of the environment when there is no exhaustive Community law in the area or when the pre-emptive effect of Community law in general does not preclude them from adopting measures. Secondly, even in the case of harmonization of measures at Community level there are several mechanisms which allow for divergent national standards, and, thirdly, the principle of subsidiarity will have an influence on the adoption of measures by the relevant entities and the interpretation of their pre-emptive effect.[96]

So, the Member States are responsible for taking action for the protection of the environment as long as there is no exhaustive Community law which ensures the ecological aims. The Court has stated this on several occasions, underlining that in the absence of exhaustive[97] Community law it is the Member States' responsibility to satisfy mandatory requirements such as the protection of the environment.[98] The pre-emptive effect of a Community measure has therefore to be interpreted in the light of the scope and nature of the relevant Community act.[99]

However, the Community has always established mechanisms in its secondary acts which allow for the co-operation of the Member States in the application and introduction of specific national standards and environmental objectives.[100] Apart from specific escape and safeguard clauses in Community secondary law[101] this has also been established through the use of directives instead of reg-

---

[94] See Ch. 12 for details of the principles of subsidiarity and shared responsibility in Community environmental law in general; see also EC Commission, *V Environmental Action Programme—Towards Sustainability*, n. 40 above. See for comments Wägenbauer, n. 40 above, 243.

[95] See e.g. the explanations of Middeke, n. 77 above, 42 on the distinction between *parallele Kompetenzen* und *konkurrierende Kompetenzen* influenced by the German federal system.

[96] See for general considerations K. Hailbronner, *Der nationale Alleingang im EG-Binnenmarkt: Vortrag gehalten vor der Juristischen Gesellschaft zu Berlin, 17. Mai 1989, Heft 116* (Schriftenreihe der Juristischen Gesellschaft zu Berlin, Berlin, 1989).

[97] Whether a Community measure is exhaustive has to be decided according to the nature and scope of the act; see e.g. Case 31/74 *Criminal Proceedings against Filippo Galli* [1975] *ECR* 47 or Case 51/74 *Van den Hulst's Zonen* v. *Produktschap voor Siergewassen* [1975] *ECR* 79; see Bieber, n. 78 above, 155.

[98] See Ch. 5 and e.g. Case 302/86 *Commission* v. *Denmark (Danish Bottles)* [1988] *ECR* 4607 at 4608.

[99] See also Ch. 5 and e.g. Case 255/86 *Commission* v. *Belgium (Bulk Fruit)* [1988] *ECR* 693 at 708; on the question of the occupation of a certain field by Community law see e.g. Cross, n. 78 above, 459.

[100] See also Krämer, n. 84 above, 164; Cross, n. 78 above, 456, who refers to these provisions as express savings against pre-emption.

[101] They will be described in Chs. 8 to 11.

ulations and, in particular through framework regulation[102] and minimum standards which allow diverging national standards.[103] Under the Single European Act and the Treaty on European Union these principles have been established in particular Treaty provisions[104] which allow for national diverging measures in spite of an existing Community harmonization.[105]

Subsidiarity

Finally, while it is generally recognized that the responsibility for environmental protection lies with both the Community and the Member States, it is not so easy to evaluate where the demarcation line between the relevant competences lies.[106] In general, Brinkhorst noted that '[the a]llocation of responsibilities between the Community and the Member States tends to be not so much a separation but rather an intermingling of powers'.[107] As Bieber shows in an interesting contribution[108] the relationship between a supranational legal system and its components is never static.[109] While the Community has very few exclusive powers,[110] the exercise of a parallel or concurrent competence or power can lead to a transformation of the respective powers in the regulated area.[111]

After the establishment of subsidiarity as a basic principle of all Community law under the Treaty of European Union,[112] the exhaustive character of Community acts will also have to be interpreted under this principle. The Community will have to justify why certain measures should be taken exhaustively at Community level and whether subsidiarity will not lead to the acceptance of locally desirable adjustments which do not jeopardize the Community system or the established system in a certain field.[113] In this sense it is desirable

---

[102] See L. Brinkhorst, 'Subsidiarity and European Community Environmental Policy A Pandora's Box?' [1991] *European Environmental Law Review* 16 at 20.

[103] See also the principle of co-operative federalism as is it applied in the United States, see the Popham Haik Law Firm, 'Subsidiarity and the Environment—US Lessons' [1993] *European Environmental Law Review* 15.

[104] e.g. Arts. 100a(4) and 130t for general exceptions and Arts. 100a(5) and 130r(2), second sub-para., for a preferential inclusion of such clauses in secondary law.

[105] See the following Chs.

[106] See, however, the attempts by several German authors, e.g. Pernice, n. 91 above; Vorwerk, n. 91 above; Hochleitner, n. 91 above; Schröer, n. 91 above.

[107] See Brinkhorst, n. 102 above, 17.

[108] Bieber, n. 78 above, 147 to 158.

[109] See also J. H. H. Weiler, *Il sistema comunitario europeo* (Molino, Bologna, 1985), 130 to 167.

[110] Recognized by the Court e.g. in the area of the common commercial policy, Case 8/73, n. 50 above, 908 or Case 41/76 *Donckerwolcke* v. *Procureur de la République* [1976] *ECR* 1921; see also Ch. 11.

[111] This effect is described as 'pre-emption' in American constitutional law, see e.g Bieber, n. 78 above, 149.

[112] Art. 3b EC.

[113] See, for example, Cross, n. 78 above, 454. He even argues in favour of a presumption of the validity of local or domestic measures. This would lead to the burden of proof lying with the Commission when attacking national measures..

that the Court takes subsidiarity into consideration when interpreting the exhaustive character of Community law and the precluding effect on domestic law.[114]

For the adoption of Community environmental law the principle of subsidiarity implies in each case an analysis of whether an environmental problem should be tackled exhaustively at Community level, whether the measure should include specific provisions to allow different protection levels according to differing national preferences, or whether the area should be left completely in the ambit of the Member States. In particular, economists refer to the possible efficiency gains arising from the competition of legal or regulatory systems and its advantages in comparison to all-over harmonization.[115] Without going into economic and conceptual details, it will be shown, however, that this development has already taken place in the implementation and development of the Community environmental law over the last two decades at least. How far the established principle of subsidiarity will influence future Community action in the area of the environment has still to be evaluated.[116]

---

[114] See, however, the Court's ruling in Case 302/86 *Danish Bottles*, n. 98 above, where the Court did not even mention the possible pre-emptive effect of existing Community law on food containers which is described by Cross, n. 78 above, 469 as 'a judicial effort to preserve a Member State law in the face of conflicting Community legislation'.

[115] See e.g. H. Hauser and M. Hösli, 'Harmonization of Regulatory Competition in the EC (and the EEA)?' [1991] *Aussenwirtschaft* 497 at 507 or N. Reich, 'Competition Between Legal Orders: A Paradigm of EC Law' (1992) 29 *CMLRev.* 861 to 896; H. Siebert, *Umweltpolitik in der Europäischen Gemeinschaft—Zentralisierung oder Dezentralisierung*, Kieler Reprints (Institut für Weltwirtschaft an der Universität Kiel, Kiel, 1991), 13; H. Giersch, 'Subsidiarität statt Vereinheitlichung von oben' in *Neue Zücher Zeitung* (28/29 Mar. 1992, no. 74), 85. See also M. E. Streit, *Systemwettbewerb und Harmonisierung im europäischen Integrationsprozess*, *Diskussionsbeitrag 09/95* (Max-Planck-Institut zur Erforschung von Wirtschaftssystemen, Jena, 1995); H. Karl, 'Europäische Umweltpolitik im Spannungsfeld zwischen Zentralität und Dezentralität' in K. W. Zimmermann et al. (eds.), *Umwelt und Umweltpolitik in Europa* (Heymann, Köln, 1995), 139 at 181; G. Kirchgässner, 'Ansatzmöglichkeiten zur Lösung europäischer Umweltprobleme' [1992] *Aussenwirtschaft* 55 to 77; S. Sinn, *The Taming of Leviathan: Competition among Governments—Constitutional Political Economy* (Institut für Weltwirtschaft an der Universität Kiel, Kiel, 1992), 177 to 196; S. Woolcock, *The Single European Market: Centralization or Competition among National Rules* (The Royal institute of International Affairs, London, 1994).

[116] See Brinkhorst, n. 102 above, 17 and 22, who indicates in particular the Community's interest in a stronger presence on the international level. See also the Popham Haik Law Firm, n. 103 above, 15, which indicates the importance of federal solutions for the guarantee of a high level of environmental protection.

8

The General Approximation of Laws

The main legal basis for the harmonization of national rules which hinder the establishment and the functioning of the common market was, until 1987, Article 100 EC. In the field of the environment the Community sometimes used additionally Article 235. In harmonized fields Member States kept regulatory power only if a Community measure provided for specific safeguard clauses or did not completely cover an area. In the absence of Community measures the Member States were, however, responsible for the adoption of environmental measures. These had to be compatible with the other Treaty obligations and the procedural information duties in drafting had to be observed by the Member States.

With the entry into force of the Single European Act, Article 100a EC has become pre-eminent for the general harmonization of laws. In the interest of the establishment of the internal market it allows the adoption of new measures by majority vote and allows diverging national measures. In spite of controversy over its appropriateness as a legal basis for environmental secondary legislation, Article 100a is considered to be an important basis for such action. In spite of existing harmonization it allows Member States to adopt their own measures under specific safeguard clauses (Article 100a (5)) or under the general provision of Article 100a(4). The Member States must observe the relevant information procedures of Article 100a(4) and (5).

THE COMMON MARKET (ARTICLES 100 AND 235 EC)

General Observations

The harmonization of laws has always been considered important for the establishment of the common market.[1] As long as national exceptions are necessary to safeguard certain public interests, then, by definition, obstacles to trade remain. While classical trade agreements accept such restraints provided they

---

[1] See for economic considerations on diverging product and production standards H. Bartling, 'National unterschiedliche Produktstandards und Produkthaftung unter aussenwirtschaftlichem Aspekt' (1988) 39 *Jahrbuch für Sozialwissenschaften* 145 ff. or H. Hauser, 'Harmonisierung oder Wettbewerb nationaler Regulierungssysteme in einem integrierten Wirtschaftsraum' [1993] *Aussenwirtschaft* 459 at 470.

are not used to discriminate against foreign producers,[2] the Community has more far-reaching objectives. The general harmonization of laws under Articles 100 and 100a EC[3] is continuously used for the elimination of existing trade obstacles, such as technical rules, quality requirements, production and process measures, administrative testing requirements etc.[4]

From 1967[5] until the entry into force of the Single European Act the Community based most of its environment-related secondary legislation on Article 100 EC and sometimes additionally on Article 235 EC.[6] Article 100 EC entrusts the Community with the task of issuing 'directives for the approximation of such provisions laid down by law, regulation or administrative action in Member States as directly affect the establishment or functioning of the common market.'

In a first phase the Community adopted directives to harmonize existing national environmental laws only in order to abolish obstacles to trade consisting in different environmental standards between Member States. They were all proposed in the framework of the General Programme for the Elimination of Technical Obstacles to Trade.[7] Later, however, the Community also adopted measures in fields where no regulation had previously been made by the Member States.

The Appropriateness of Article 100

Before the entry into force of the Single European Act in 1987, the legal basis of almost all the directives was Articles 100 and 235 EC, sometimes combined,[8] while certain measures were adopted under special provisions concerning special fields (agriculture, traffic, common commercial policy etc.[9]). In spite of the large number of environment-related measures based on Articles 100 and 235

---

[2] See the case law under the General Agreement on Tariffs and Trade (GATT) or the Free Trade Agreements between the EFTA Member States and the European Community, see e.g. E.-U. Petersmann, 'Umweltschutz und Welthandelsordnung im GATT-, OECD- und EWG-Rahmen' [1992] *EA* 257 ff.

[3] The term 'general harmonization' is used to mark the difference from special harmonization provisions for certain areas such as Arts. 43 (agriculture), 75, and 84(2) (transport), 99 (indirect taxes), 118a (social policy), 130s (environment) etc.

[4] See P. J. G. Kapteyn and P. VerLoren van Themaat, *Introduction to the Law of the European Communities* (2nd. edn., Kluwer, Deventer, 1989), 467 to 469. In its 'White Paper to complete the Internal Market by January 1, 1993' the Commission had set out a detailed scheme of some 300 legislative proposals to remove remaining barriers, many of which concerned environment-related standards, see COM(85)310 final.

[5] See Ch. 7 for the first relevant examples.

[6] See e.g. Kapteyn and VerLoren van Themaat, n. 4 above, 655, or D. Vandermeersch, 'Twintig jaar EG milieurecht in retrospectief: van casuïstik naar modern beleid' [1992] *SEW* 532 at 534; see also E. Grabitz and C. Zacker, 'Die neuen Umweltkompetenzen der EWG' [1989] *NVwZ* 297.

[7] [1969] *OJ* C76/1; updated version [1973] *OJ* C117/1.

[8] See S. Johnson and G. Corcelle, *The Environmental Policy of the European Community* (Graham & Trotman, London, 1989), 3 ff.

[9] See Ch. 9.

EC, the question whether these articles used together[10] or used separately were a sufficient legal basis for environmental action remained controversial.[11]

In several cases the European Court of Justice, however, had the opportunity of expressing its opinion on whether these Articles were appropriate as a basis for Community action in the field of environmental protection. In view of the development of the Community environmental policy it is interesting to observe how carefully the Court in its reasoning kept to the terms of the Treaty of Rome, provided environmental protection was not mentioned there explicitly. Initially the European Court of Justice held, in two cases concerned with the Community legislation in the field of waste oil, that in principle Article 100 could serve as a legal basis for the approximation of laws necessary for the functioning and the establishment of the common market even if it included an approximation of laws on environment related topics:

Furthermore it is by no means ruled out that provisions on the environment may be based upon Article 100 EC. Provisions which are made necessary by considerations relating to the environment and health may be a burden for the undertakings to which they apply and if there is no harmonization of national provisions on the matter competition may be appreciably distorted.[12]

Case: In Cases 91/79 and 92/79 *Commission* v. *Italy*[13] the Court was asked in a preliminary ruling *inter alia* whether Article 100 EC was a sufficient basis for a Council directive concerning the biodegradability of detergents and the sulphur content of liquid fuels respectively.[14] The Court took into consideration that these Directives had been passed in the light of the Environmental Action Programme but also adopted in the framework of the General Programme in order to eliminate the technical barriers to trade which result from disparities between the provisions laid down by law, regulation, or administrative action in Member States. The Court held that the directives were validly founded on Article 100 EC.

In these cases the Court based its reasoning and its decision completely on the competitive effects of diverging environmental standards.[15] Although the

---

[10] See D. Vandermeersch, 'The Single European Act and the Environmental Policy of the EC' (1987) 12 *ELRev.* 407 at 412; E. Rehbinder and R. Stewart, *Environmental Protection Policy—Integration through Law* (W. de Gruyter, New York, 1985), ii, 245 ff.

[11] For critical comments see: E. Grabitz and C. Sasse, *Umweltkompetenz der Europäischen Gemeinschaften* (E. Schmidt, Berlin, 1977), 93 and 96 ff.

[12] Case 91/79 *Commission* v. *Italy* (*Detergents*) [1980] *ECR* 1099 at 1106 and Case 92/79 *Commission* v. *Italy* (*Maximum Sulphur Content of Liquid Fuels*) [1980] *ECR* 1115 at 1122. See, however, for very similar developments in the United States, where the commerce clause was interpreted in a similar way, D. Geradin, 'Free Trade and Environmental Protection in an Integrated Market: A Survey of the Case Law of the United States Supreme Court and the European Court of Justice' (1993) 2 *Journal of Transnational Law and Policy* 141 at 144 with reference to US writers.

[13] Case 91/79 *Detergents*, n. 12 above, 1106, and Case 92/79 *Maximum Sulphur Content of Liquid Fuels*, n. 12 above, 1122.

[14] Adopted by the Council on 28 May 1969 [1969] *OJ* C76/1.

[15] An argument that is still used in the Court's recent case law: e.g Case C–300/89 *Commission* v. *Council* (*Titanium Dioxide*) [1991] *ECR* I–2867, see for this aspect: U. Everling, 'Durchführung und Umsetzung des Europäischen Gemeinschaftsrechts im Bereich des Umweltschutzes unter

Environmental Action Programme showed the importance of the Community objective of 'environmental protection' in itself, the latter was not mentioned as an important justification for Community action. The Court avoided mentioning the Community interest in environmental protection in general and stressed the general aim of measures based on Article 100 EC—the elimination of trade-distorting regulative differences between the Member States of the Community.[16] It was only much later that the Court referred to the protection of the environment as an essential objective of the Community.

Case: In 1985, in its judgment in Case 240/83 *ADBHU*[17] the Court again had the opportunity of judging the validity of an environment-related directive based on Article 100 EC. The Court maintained its reasoning from the earlier cases[18] but went further in its considerations. Apart from the reference to possible trade effects the Court also stated that the adoption of measures for the protection of the environment itself was an essential objective of the Community.[19]

Article 235 as a Complementary Legal Basis

The application of Article 100 alone to introduce environmental directives was, however, always problematical. Therefore, Article 235 EC was regarded as an important additional legal basis for environment oriented measures.[20] This provision gives the Community the power to adopt the necessary measures for the pursuit of Community objectives in fields where no explicit or implicit Community competence exists. Referring to the Preamble to and Article 2 of the EEC Treaty, the Community considered the protection of the environment to be an essential objective and therefore an area where the Community can take action. While most product-related measures were taken on the basis of Article 100, certain measures, more generally concerned with the environment, were adopted on the basis of Article 100 in conjunction with Article 235. This was considered to allow the adoption of environment-related directives, which

---

Berücksichtigung der Rechtsprechung des EuGH' [1993] *NVwZ* 209 at 211. A very similar reasoning was used by the US Congress when using its power under the commerce clause to harmonize environmental controls, see e.g. Geradin, n. 12 above, 145, or R. Stewart, 'Pyramids of Sacrifice? Problems of Federalism in Mandating State Implementation of National Environmental Policy' (1977) 86 *Yale Law Journal* 1196 at 1222.

[16] See Kapteyn and VerLoren van Themaat, n. 4 above, 656; also D. Kupfer, 'Rechtsschöpfung oder Rechtsharmonisierung? Tendenzen des europäischen Umweltrechts' [1989] *Agrarrecht* 57 ff.

[17] Case 240/83 *Procureur de la République* v. *Association de Défense des Brûleurs d'Huiles Usagées (ADBHU)* [1985] *ECR* 531.

[18] See Case 91/79 *Detergents*, n. 12 above.   [19] Case 240/83 *ADBHU*, n. 17 above, 548.

[20] Particularly since the recommendation of the Heads of Government and State at the Paris Summit, see Ch. 7; in the framework of the use of Art. 235 for the filling of *lacunae*, see Kapteyn and VerLoren van Themaat, n. 4 above, 113; see also T. Oppermann, *Europarecht* (C. H. Beck, München, 1991), 740; F. Behrens, 'Die Umweltpolitik der Europäischen Gemeinschaften und Art. 235 EWGV' [1978] *DVBl.* 462 to 469. This was strengthened by the Court's view of the environment as an essential objective of the Community: Case 240/83 *ADBHU*, n. 17 above, 548.

were not provided for by Article 100 on its own. Reliance on Article 235 alone has always been very unusual.[21]

The Degree of Harmonization

Once an area has been completely harmonized by secondary legislation on the basis of Article 100 and/or Article 235 respectively,[22] a Member State is no longer able to introduce more stringent environmental regulation in this field,[23] except for particular safeguard clauses[24] or minimum requirements in the relevant Community legislation itself. A Member State cannot, for example, invoke the provisions of Article 36 or the rule of reason, thereby creating new obstacles to trade.[25] This applies, however, only where a Community measure under Article 100 entirely covers the relevant area.[26] As all the measures based on Article 100 must be adopted with unanimity in the Council, a Member State is supposed to integrate from the beginning its own view of the needs for environmental protection within the framework of the directive to be adopted.[27]

Provided an area is not regulated by the Community or the measures adopted do not lead to full harmonization of a certain field, the Member States remain responsible for the adoption of measures to safeguard their environment.[28] These must, however, be compatible with the other provisions of the Treaty. A Member State may take environment related-measures[29] provided they do not 'jeopardize the objectives and the proper functioning of the system established

---

[21] See Rehbinder and Stewart, n. 10 above, 18; Vandermeersch, n. 10 above, 411; Oppermann, n. 20 above, 740.

[22] The same is true for the other EC provisions such as Arts. 43, 99, 113 etc., apart from the few provisions which provide explicitly for the opportunity to introduce or maintain higher national standards such as, e.g., Art. 130t or 100a(4).

[23] See Everling, n. 15 above, 211.

[24] See the section on safeguard clauses below in this chapter.

[25] See Case C–169/89 *Criminal Proceedings against Gourmetterie Van den Burg (Scottish Red Grouse)* [1990] *ECR* I–2143; Case 172/82 *Syndicat National des Fabricants Raffineurs d'Huiles de Graissage et al.* v. *Groupement d'Intérêt Economique 'Inter-Huiles' (Inter-Huiles)* [1983] *ECR* 555, see also A. Furrer, 'Nationale Umweltschutzkompetenzen in der EWG und im EWR' [1992] *AJP* 1517 at 1525 or L. Krämer, 'Environmental Protection and Art. 30 EEC Treaty' (1993) 30 *CMLRev.* 111 at 117; but restricting this principle M. Zuleeg, 'Umweltschutz in der Rechtsprechung des Europäischen Gerichtshofes' [1993] *NJW* 31 at 34.

[26] See Case 5/77 *Carlo Tedeschi* v. *Denkavit (Tedeschi/Denkavit)* [1977] *ECR* 1555 at 1576 and Case 251/78 *Denkavit Futtermittel* v. *Minister of Food, Agriculture and Forests (Denkavit)* [1979] *ECR* 3369 at 3388.

[27] See the different procedure under the new Art. 100a EC.

[28] See e.g. L. Krämer, 'L'environnement et le marché unique européen' [1993] *RMC* 45 at 47. See e.g. the limitation of a Community measure to certain substances by means of a detailed annex of the substances included: Joined cases C–54/94 and C–74/94 *Criminal Proceedings against Ulderico* [1995] *ECR* I–391 *Cacchiarelli and others*, [1995] *ECR* I-391, regarding Council Dir. 90/642/EEC.

[29] See Joined cases 3, 4, and 6/76 *Criminal Proceedings against Cornelis Kramer et al. (Biological Resources of the Sea)* [1976] *ECR* 1273 at 1276.

by the regulations' of the Community.[30] This derives from the general principle of shared competence for environmental protection.[31]

The Use of Directives

As Article 100 only allows the adoption of directives,[32] the Member States always retain a certain autonomy when implementing Community measures. Thus, there remains a limited discretion here for national needs and choices of methods and instruments.[33] This is particularly so if a regulation does not prescribe exact standards but rather qualitative objectives such as 'the best available technology not entailing excessive costs' or uses terms like 'significant disturbance', or 'major risk'.[34]

Under not only Article 100, but under all Treaty provisions which allow the adoption of Community legal acts,[35] the use of directives can be a means to achieve an equalized protection of the environment throughout the Community by giving the Member States options for the implementation of the objectives prescribed.[36] This is particularly true in environmental law, where the often technical character of the obligations arising from a directive leave the Member States with a relatively large discretion.[37] This is often considered as an important element for the adequate evaluation of the local situation and decision-making by local and regional authorities.[38]

At the same time, this very flexible nature of directives entails the danger of

[30] See Case 788/79 *Criminal Procedure against Gilli and Andres (Gilli and Andres)* [1980] *ECR* 2071 at 2078 or Case 216/84 *Commission* v. *France (Milk Powder)* [1988] *ECR* 793 at 811; for more environmental examples see Zuleeg, n. 25 above, 34.

[31] See e.g. B. Jadot, 'Mesures nationales de police de l'environnement, libre circulation des marchandises et proportionnalité' [1990] *CDE* 403 at 409.

[32] For the use of regulations under Art. 235 see L. Krämer, 'Community Environmental Law— Towards a Systematic Approach' [1992] *YEL* 151 at 157.

[33] See e.g. the case study on the implementation of the groundwater directive in C. Demmke, *Die Implementation von EG-Umweltpolitik in den Mitgliedstaaten—Die Umsetzung der Trinkwasserrichtlinie* (Nomos, Baden-Baden, 1994); see, however, for the minimum requirements for the implementation of a dir. in the field of the environment, e.g. the Court's qualification of the German implementation of certain Dirs.: Case C-361/88 *Commission* v. *Germany (TA Luft)* [1991] *ECR* I-2567 at 2609; Case C-131/88 *Commission* v. *Germany (Groundwater Directive)* [1991] *ECR* I-825 at 866; details given by Everling, n. 15 above, 209 at 213, or Zuleeg, n. 25 above, 35; for details of the recent case law see A. Middeke, *Nationaler Umweltschutz und Binnenmarkt* (Heymann, Köln, 1994), 48 to 60. For the effect of Community law on national legislation and national enforcement see F. Snyder, 'The Effectiveness of European Community Law' [1993] 53 *MLR* 19 to 54.

[34] Examples taken from Krämer, n. 32 above, 151 at 159 and 160.

[35] See below, for the statement by the Heads of States and Governments relating to Art. 100a and the preferential use of directives, Ch. 8.

[36] L. J. Brinkhorst, 'Subsidiarity and EC Environment Law—A Pandora's Box? [1993] *European Environmental Law Review* 16 at 20 shows that more than 90% of all Community environmental measures are taken in the form of dirs. and refers to the underlying principle of subsidiarity.

[37] See on this issue J.-G. Huglo, 'L'application par les Etats membres des normes communautaires en matière d'environnement' [1994] *RTDE* 451 at 452.

[38] See e.g. the Court's reasoning in Case C-334/89 *Commission* v. *Italy (Regional Environmental Competence)* [1991] *ECR* 93 at 105.

a heterogeneous realization of Community objectives and the misuse by Member States' authorities. The Commission and the Court have to ensure the enforcement of Community environmental acts,[39] in particular, where Member States neglect the agreed level of protection throughout the Community and the common heritage of the Community.[40] Certain authors state emphatically that the lax implementation of Community directives by the Member States is the major problem of today's Community environmental law.[41]

Example: An interesting example of a Community directive which leaves the Member States with important discretion is the 1979 Community Directive on the protection of wild birds.[42] The Directive stipulates that the Member States retain the power to decide on the classification of certain areas as protection zones for wild birds under the Community Directive. The Court has reaffirmed in Case C–334/89 *Commission* v. *Italy* and Case C–57/89 *Commission* v. *Germany*[43] that the margin of evaluation of the Member States was relatively large and was only reduced once a chosen protection zone was to be reduced in size. Still the implementation of the directive's objectives is controlled by the Commission and the Court has underlined that the Member States' discretion does not cover cases of obvious non-implementation, as decided in Case C–355/90 *Commission* v. *Spain*,[44] where the criteria of the Directive were arbitrarily not applied.

Safeguard Clauses

The measures under Article 100 may, however, even if there is complete harmonization, provide special safeguard clauses or minimum standards[45] which explicitly allow the Member States to apply more stringent measures.[46] Many of

---

[39] See e.g. L. Krämer, 'The Implementation of Environmental Laws by the European Economic Community' [1991] *GYIL* 9 to 53; R. Macrory, 'The Enforcement of Community Environmental Law: Some Critical Issues' (1992) 29 *CMLRev.* 347 to 369; recent cases included Case C–13/90 *Commission* v. *France* (*Limit Lead Value in the Air*) [1991] *ECR* I–4327; Case C–64/90 *Commission* v. *France* (*Sulfer Dioxide*) [1991] *ECR* I–4335; Case C–361/88 n. 33 above; Case–59/89 *Commission* v. *Germany* (*Air Pollution—Lead*) [1991] *ECR* I–2607; more recently e.g. Case C–255/93 *Commission* v. *France* (*Containers for Liquids for Human Consumption*) [1994] *ECR* I–4949 or Case C–422/92 *Commission* v. *Germany*, judgment of 10 May 1995 (1995) 13 *Proceedings of the Court* 4. For a systematic survey see I. Pernice, 'Kriterien der normativen Umsetzung von Umweltrichtlinien der EG im Lichte der Rechtsprechung des EuGH' [1994] *EuR* 325 to 341.

[40] See for this terminology e.g. Case 252/85 *Commission* v. *France* [1988] *ECR* 2243 referring to Council Dir. 79/409/EEC on the conservation of wild birds [1979] *OJ* L103/1, preamble.

[41] See e.g. L. Krämer, *Focus on European Environmental Law* (Sweet & Maxwell, London, 1993), 194 ff. and the compilation of cases in L. Krämer, *European Environmental Law—Casebook* (Sweet & Maxwell, London, 1993) or L. Krämer, 'Die Rechtsprechung des Gerichtshofes der EG zum Umweltrecht 1992 bis 1994' [1995] *EuGRZ* 45 to 53.

[42] Dir. 79/409/EEC on the protection of wild birds, n. 40 above, amended by Dir. 85/411/EEC [1985] *OJ* L233/33. The series of cases for this example is taken from Huglo, n. 37 above, 452.

[43] Case C–334/89, n. 38 above, and Case C–59/89, n. 39 above.

[44] Case C–355/90 *Commission* v. *Spain* (*Implementation of Directive*) [1993] *ECR* I–4221.

[45] Sometimes referred to as minimum harmonization, see e.g. D. Wyatt and A. Dashwood, *European Community Law* (3rd edn., Sweet & Maxwell, London, 1993), 367. See for the many names given to these provisions e.g. in German Middeke, n. 33 above, 64.

[46] See L. Krämer, 'EWG-Umweltrecht und nationale Alleingänge' [1990] *UTR* 437 at 447 or C. E. Palme, *Nationale Umweltpolitik in der EG—Zur Rolle des Art. 100a IV im Rahmen der Europäischen Umweltgemeinschaft* (Duncker & Humblot, Berlin, 1992), 56.

the regulations based on Article 100 contain such clauses.[47] They often allow Member States provisionally to ban or restrict the use of certain products. The application of such rules must, however, be environmentally justified and non-discriminatory.

The General Notification Procedure

The notification to the Commission of planned national measures is an essential element for the co-ordination of national and Community measures in these cases.[48] Member States are not generally required to notify the Commission when they intend to enact new environmental measures. However, because of the trade effects such measures can have on the common market there are certain notification rules within the Community.

In 1973 the Member States adopted an agreement to inform the Commission of any draft environmental legislation.[49] This agreement was intended to allow the Commission to take action for the prevention of any new technical barriers to trade which would jeopardize the establishment and functioning of the common market. The non-mandatory character and the short time limits for notification of this gentlemen's agreement mean that it has, however, little effect.[50]

As a result, in 1983, the Community adopted a directive on the notification of draft national legislation for product specifications.[51] It provides for compulsory notification[52] and a standstill period for national measures of between three and twelve months.[53] The Commission's broad interpretation of this Directive leads to the compulsory notification of almost all draft national environmental legislation.[54] The failure to communicate new or extended national measures leads to a breach of Community law as has been held by the Court of Justice in several cases.[55]

---

[47] See Furrer, n. 25 above, 1525, referring to certain rules adopted under Art. 100 as minimal requirements.

[48] See for details Krämer, n. 32 above, 179.

[49] Agreement of 5 Mar. 1973 [1973] *OJ* C9/1; see Oppermann, n. 20 above, 740.

[50] Krämer, n. 32 above, 172.

[51] Dir. 83/189/EEC [1983] *OJ* L109/8, amended by Dir. 88/182/EEC; on the effect see Krämer, n. 32 above, 172.

[52] For the failure to notify see e.g. Case C–139/92 *Commission v. Italy (Notification Requirements)*, judgment of 2 Aug. 1993.

[53] The principle of notification of national environmental legislation corresponds to the newly introduced specific Treaty provisions under Art. 100a(4) and (5), and since the coming into force of the Treaty on European Union also in Art. 130t.

[54] See Krämer, n. 32 above, 173, referring to the exceptions of nature-protection laws and packaging regulations; see for details also Middeke, n. 33 above, 214.

[55] Also the extension of an existing and notified national measure on more or new products has to be notified to the Commission under Art. 8 of Dir. 83/189/EEC, n. 51 above; see Case C–317/92 *Commission v. Germany (Medical Products—Expiry Date)* [1994] *ECR* I–2039; Case C–52/93 *Commission v. The Netherlands (Obligation to give Prior Notification)* [1994] *ECR* I–3591; Case C–61/93 *Commission v. The Netherlands (Obligation to give Prior Notification)* [1994] *ECR* I–3607.

Articles 100 and 235 after the Single European Act

While most environmental Community measures were initially based on Article 100 (sometimes in connection with Article 235) the entry into force of the Single European Act has substantially changed the application of these articles as a legal basis for the harmonization of laws. Article 100a in particular provides a new, much more flexible way of approximating diverging national rules and laws.[56] As it allows by simple majority vote the adoption of regulations as well as other measures, it has definitely replaced Article 100 as an overall legal basis for the harmonization of laws.[57] Nevertheless, it remains possible to adopt environment-related directives under Article 100, if their objectives fall under the concept of the common market. Although this may be exceptional,[58] its application is undoubtedly appropriate for the areas mentioned in Article 100a(2).[59] These, however, do not directly concern the environment, apart from possible fiscal provisions.[60]

Article 235, since the introduction of the specific environment-related Article 130s, is no longer an appropriate basis for the adoption of environment-related Community measures.[61] This new provision provides the Community with the explicit competence and sets out the instruments to be used to achieve the environmental objectives of the European Community.[62]

---

[56] See J. De Ruyt, *L'acte unique européen—Commentaire* (2nd edn., Editions de l'Université de Bruxelles, Bruxelles, 1989), 167, who lists 17 proposals for noise protection which could not be adopted or at least only after long negotiations.

[57] This does not preclude the use of Art. 100 for appropriate cases. Art. 100a is a special provision in relation to Art. 100; see Middeke, n. 33 above, 236.

[58] See M. Zuleeg, 'Vorbehaltene Kompetenzen der Mitgliedstaaten der Europäischen Gemeinschaft auf dem Gebiet des Umweltschutzes' [1987] *NVwZ* 280 at 281. Relevant in this context might be the distinction between Internal Market (Art. 100a) and common market (Art. 100). See e.g. T. Schröer, *Die Kompetenzverteilung zwischen der Europäischen Wirtschaftsgemeinschaft und ihren Mitgliedstaaten auf dem Gebiet des Umweltschutzes* (Duncker & Humblot, Berlin, 1992) 170.

[59] For details see Schröer, n. 58 above, 167 to 170; U. Becker, *Der Gestaltungsspielraum der EG-Mitgliedstaaten im Spannungsfeld zwischen Umweltschutz und freiem Warenverkehr* (Nomos, Baden-Baden, 1991), 93 to 95; J. Henke, *EuGH und Umweltschutz* (VVF, München, 1992), 83 to 90; U. Everling, 'Abgrenzung der Rechtsangleichung zur Verwirklichung des Binnenmarktes nach Art. 100a EWGV durch den Gerichtshof' [1991] *EuR* 179 at 181.

[60] Henke, n. 59 above, 90; I. Pernice, 'Auswirkungen des europäischen Binnenmarktes auf das Umweltrecht—Gemeinschafts(verfassungs-)rechtliche Grundlagen' [1990] *NVwZ* 201 at 203.

[61] See A. Epiney and T. M. J. Möllers, *Freier Warenverkehr und nationaler Umweltschutz* (Heymann, Köln, 1992), 6; Schröer, n. 58 above, 193 to 195.

[62] See the case law of the Court: e.g. Case 45/86 *Commission* v. *Council (General Customs Preferences)* [1987] *ECR* 1493 at 1520; Case 242/87 *Commission* v. *Council (Erasmus)* [1989] *ECR* 1425 at 1452; Case C–62/88 *Greece* v. *Council (Chernobyl I)* [1990] *ECR* I–1527. See Henke, n. 90 above, 99, with many references to mainly German legal writers.

THE INTERNAL MARKET (ARTICLE 100A EC)

General Observations

By derogation from Article 100 the Single European Act introduced the new Article 100a for the 'approximation of the provisions laid down by law, regulation or administrative action in Member States which have as their object the establishment and the functioning of the internal market'.[63]

As one of the main purposes of Article 100a EC is the accelerated elimination of diverging technical rules and requirements between the Member States, this provision is very important for environmental product standards as well as any kind of production and process requirement. In relation to these possible trade obstacles the exception clause of Article 36 and the case law of the European Court of Justice allow certain national requirements to products because of environmental reasons.[64] These national rules and regulations can likewise be removed by an extensive harmonization of laws under Article 100a of the Treaty.[65] In respect of the protection of the environment, consumer protection and health safety the Community shall integrate high-levelled protection requirements (Article 100a(3)).

Article 100a and Other Specific Treaty Provisions

The use of Article 100a and its relationship with the other provisions of the Treaty have been controversial since its introduction.[66] As it provides a very flexible instrument for the approximation of national rules by majority vote there have been many fears that its use would lead to an accelerated approximation of laws against the will of outvoted minorities in the Council. As it provides for different procedural requirements and particularly because of the majority vote, the Council might choose Article 100a instead of another, more appropriate legal basis for political considerations.[67] Furthermore, it has been suggested that almost every approximation of diverging national rules fits into the broad scope

---

[63] As a special provision in relation to Art. 100 this replaces the application of the latter in most cases.

[64] See Case 240/83 *ADBHU*, n. 17 above, 548, or Case 302/86 *Commission* v. *Denmark* (*Danish Bottles*) [1988] *ECR* 4607.

[65] An example is Dir. 99/220/EEC on the deliberate release of genetically modified organisms [1990] *OJ* L117/15.

[66] For the field of protection of health and nuclear radiation see: T. Schröer, 'Abgrenzung der Gemeinschaftskompetenzen zum Schutze der Gesundheit vor radioaktiver Strahlung, Anmerkungen zum Urteil des EuGH vom 4.10.1991 in Rs C–70/88' [1992] *EuZW* 207 to 210. For general views on the Court's case law on the legal basis of a Community measure see N. Emiliou, 'Opening Pandora's Box: The Legal Basis of Community Measures before the Court of Justice' (1994) 19 *ELRev.* 488 to 507.

[67] For the consequences of the choice of an incorrect legal basis see: M. Röttinger, 'Bedeutung der Rechtsgrundlage einer EG-Richtlinie und Folgen einer Nichtigkeit' [1993] *EuZW* 117 to 121.

of Article 100a, in order to eliminate the use of other more appropriate specific Treaty provisions.[68]

Particularly controversial in the field of environmental protection has been the discussion concerning the different application of Article 100a and Article 130s for the approximation of environment-related rules.[69] Apart from their different objectives these provisions differ mainly in the procedural requirements for the adoption of measures. Before the entry into force of the Treaty on the European Union, Article 100a EC required for the adoption of a Community measure a Parliament co-operation procedure and a qualified majority within the Council. Article 130s EC, on the other hand, requires only the consultation of the Parliament but unanimity within the Council.[70]

The procedural requirements for Articles 100a and 130s have been changed by the Treaty on the European Union. The Treaty now permits a majority vote in both cases, but still requires different procedures. While measures under Article 100a follow the procedure of Article 189b, the Treaty requires for measures under Article 130s the procedure set out in Article 189c. As there are different procedural requirements depending on the legal basis chosen they must also lead to a difference in the appropriateness of the two provisions.[71] Both allow in principle all possible legal instruments of Article 189 EC,[72] but a declaration of the Member State governments[73] indicates that in the framework of

---

[68] See also Gilsdorf and Priebe, Art. 38, para. 18, in E. Grabitz and M. Hilf (eds.), *Kommentar zur EU* (2nd edn., C. H. Beck, München, 1990 ff.); V. Goetz, 'Anmerkungen zu den Gerichtsurteilen des Europäischen Gerichtshofs Rs 68/86 und 131/86 vom 23.2.1988' [1988] *EuR* 298 at 299.

[69] For examples see R. Barents, 'Milieu en interne markt' [1993] *SEW* 5 to 29; Everling, n. 15 above, 209; Zuleeg, n. 25 above, 31; C.-O. Lenz, 'Immanente Grenzen des Gemeinschaftsrecht' [1993] *EuGRZ* 57 to 64; A. Epiney, 'Gemeinschaftsrechtlicher Umweltschutz und Verwirklichung des Binnenmarktes—"Harmonisierung" auch der Rechtsgrundlagen?' [1992] *JZ* 564 to 570; Everling, n. 59 above, 179; H.D. Jarass, 'Binnenmarktrichtlinien und Umweltschutzrichtlinien' [1991] *EuZW* 530 at 531; L. Krämer, 'The Single European Act and Environmental Protection' (1987) 24 *CMLRev.* 659 at 682; Middeke, n. 33 above, 223 to 229. A very brilliant analysis is also made by D. Geradin, 'Trade and Environmental Protection: Community Harmonization and National Environmental Standards' [1993] *YEL* 151 to 199.

[70] See, in particular, the most recent cases before the Court: Case C–70/88 *Parliament v. Council (Radioactive Contamination)* [1991] *ECR* I–4529; Case C–300/89 *Commission v. Council (Titanium Dioxide)* [1991] *ECR* I–2867; Case C–155/91 *Commission v. Council (Waste Directive)* [1993] *ECR* I–939; Case C–187/93 *Parliament v. Council (Regulation of Shipments of Waste)*; see S. Breier, 'Ausgewählte Probleme' [1994] *RIW* 584 at 585; for the impact of the new provisions in the Treaty on European Union see e.g. Krämer, n. 32 above, 168.

[71] See Epiney and Möllers, n. 61 above, 6; D. H. Scheuing, 'Umweltschutz auf Grundlage der Einheitlichen Europäischen Akte' [1989] *EuR* 152 at 185, L. Krämer, 'Einheitliche Europäische Akte und Umweltschutz: Überlegungen zu einigen neuen Bestimmungen im Gemeinschaftsrecht' in H.-W. Rengeling (ed.), *Europäisches Umweltrecht und europäische Umweltpolitik* (Heymann, Köln, 1988), 137 at 157. K. Lietzmann, 'Einheitliche Europäische Akte und Umweltschutz: Die neuen Umweltbestimmungen im EWG-Vertrag' in H.-W. Rengeling (ed.), *Europäisches Umweltrecht und europäische Umweltpolitik* (Heymann, Köln, 1988), 163 at 178 and Everling, n. 59 above, 181 think otherwise; see also Middeke, n. 33 above, 229.

[72] Unlike Art. 100 EC which only refers to dirs.

[73] See Vandermeersch, n. 10 above, 424.

Article 100a there will be a preference for directives.[74] The Court has twice had
the opportunity of declaring its view on the appropriate legal basis for measures[75] which concern the approximation of environmental rules having at the
same time an impact on the internal market.[76]

Its reasoning can be divided into two stages: first, the question whether a measure relates to the protection of the environment (Article 130s) or the establishment of the internal market (Article 100a) is to be determined by reference to
its purpose and content. The purpose of such a measure is, however, not to be
interpreted subjectively by the institution adopting it. If a measure falls, *prima
facie*, under both provisions, the decision on which legal basis a measure is to be
adopted depends on various objective criteria established by the Court.

Secondly, Article 100a EC must be chosen in those cases where a measure is
specifically devoted to the completion of the internal market.[77] It could be held
that the Court sees in Article 100a the *lex specialis* for the adoption of measures
related to the establishment of the internal market, while under Article 130s EC
all kinds of environmental measures can be adopted.[78] Article 130s remains the
appropriate legal basis if the measure in question aims mainly at the protection
of the environment and has only a secondary effect of harmonizing certain conditions of the internal market.[79] In practice, it seems that the Court allows product-related measures to be adopted under Article 100a or 130s according to their
impact on the environment.[80]

This very broad understanding of the application of Article 100a as a legal
basis for Community measures must also include regulations concerning prod-

[74] As mandatory under Art. 100; see also U. Everling, 'Probleme der Rechtsangleichung zur
Verwirklichung des Europäischen Binnenmarktes' in J. Baur, K. J. Hopt, and P. Mailänder (eds.),
Festschrift für Ernst Steindorff zum 70. Geburtstag (Duncker & Humblot, Berlin, 1990), 1155 to 1173 at
1166.

[75] On the consequence of the choice of the wrong legal basis see Röttinger, n. 67 above.

[76] Case C–300/89 *Titanium Dioxide*, n. 70 above; Case C–155/91 *Waste Directive*, n. 70 above. For
a discussion of the *Titanium Dioxide* Case see e.g. H. Somsen, 'Comments on Case C–300/89' (1992)
29 *CMLRev.* 140 to 151; S. A. Pappas, 'The Legal Basis for Action to be Taken by the European
Community in the Field of the Environment' in *Subsidiarity: The Challenge of Change, Working Document,
Proceedings of the Jacques Delors Colloquium* (European Institute for Public Administration, Maastricht,
1991), 119 to 125; Geradin, n. 12 above, 168 to 170; U. Voss and G. Wenner, 'Der EuGH und die
gemeinschaftliche Kompetenzordnung—Kontinuität oder Neuorientierung?' [1994] *NVwZ* 332 to
337; S. Breier, 'Das Schicksal der Titaniumdioxid-Richtlinie' [1993] *EuZW* 315 to 319; Everling, n.
15 above, 211; Zuleeg, n. 25 above, 32; Barents, n. 69 above; Epiney, n. 69 above, 564 to 570.

[77] See e.g. O. Brunetti, *EG-Verträglichkeit als Kriterium der nationalen Umweltpolitik* (Schulthess and
Stämpfli, Zürich and Bern, 1993), 51 and 52.

[78] See the explicit reference by the Court to the case law on the adoption of environmental measures under Art. 100 in Case 91/79 *Detergents*, n. 12 above, and Case 92/79 *Maximum Sulphur Content
of Liquid Fuels*, n. 12 above, now under Art. 100a: Case C–300/89 *Titanium Dioxide*, n. 70 above; for
comments Everling, n. 15 above, 211, and Zuleeg, n. 25 above, 32.

[79] Case C–155/91 *Waste Directive*, n. 70 above, 939, uses the term 'ancillary effect'; see for comments Voss and Wenner, n. 76 above, 336; for a similar constellation between Art. 100a and Art.
31 of the Euratom Treaty, see Case C–70/88, n. 70 above ; Schröer, n. 66 above, 207 to 210;
Zuleeg, n. 25 above, 33.

[80] See L. Krämer, *EC Treaty and Environmental Law* (2nd edn., Sweet & Maxwell, London, 1995),
89 to 97.

ucts whose production in one Member State is submitted to less stringent environmental requirements than in another. This can lead to a distortion of the competitive situation in the internal market.[81] Most legal writers thus argue that
product-related measures fall in any case under Article 100a.[82]

Case: In its decision in Case C-300/89 *Titanium Dioxide*[83] in 1991 the Court had to adjudicate on the appropriateness of the legal basis for a Council directive on procedures for
the harmonization of programmes on pollution reduction and improvement of the conditions of competition in the titanium dioxide industry. While the Commission had proposed Article 100a EC,[84] the Council adopted the Directive on the basis of Article 130s.
The Commission, supported by the Parliament, brought the case before the Court of
Justice. The Court followed two steps in its reasoning: first it held that in principle the
measure in question could, *prima facie*, be adopted under both provisions. Secondly, with
reference to the general principle that, under Article 130s(2) EC, the protection of the
environment should be a component of the Community's other policies and the measure's important impact on the internal market held Article 100a to be the
appropriate legal basis for the measure.[85]

This principle was upheld in the more recent decision in Case C-155/91 *Waste
Directive*.[86] Here the Court had to give its opinion on the appropriateness of Article 130s
as the legal basis for a Council Directive on waste management.[87] Here again the Council
had based the Directive on Article 130s in spite of the Commission proposing Article
100a as the appropriate legal basis. The Court held that the Directive was validly based
on Article 130s as it touched the harmonization of laws only accidentally and was on the
contrary concerned with the limitation of the free movement of goods for environmental
requirements rather than with the complete approximation of national laws for the establishment of the internal market.[88] In the Court's view the very weak harmonizing effect
did not allow for an adoption under Article 100a. Article 130s was the appropriate basis
for such a measure introducing environmental principles explicitly justifying exceptions
from the free movement of goods.[89]

Possible Safeguard Clauses (Article 100a(5))

Article 100a(5) EC provides for the general possibility of including specific safeguard clauses in harmonization measures adopted under Article 100a(1) EC.[90]

---

[81] See Furrer, n. 25 above, 1521.

[82] See Becker, n. 59 above, 43; see H. Soell, 'Überlegungen zum europäischen Umweltrecht'
[1990] *NuR* 158 ff. and A. Vorwerk, *Die umweltpolitischen Kompetenzen der Europäischen Gemeinschaft und
ihrer Mitgliedstaaten nach Inkrafttreten der EEA* (VVF, München, 1990) 67, for a different view.

[83] Case C-300/89 *Titanium Dioxide*, n. 70 above; see Brunetti, n. 77 above, 52.

[84] In the early stage of the proposal the Commission had applied Arts. 100 and 235 EC, as this
was before the coming into force of the Single European Act.

[85] For a detailed commentary on the decision see e.g. J. Robinson, 'The Legal Basis of EC
Environmental Law' [1992] *J Env. L* 109 to 120; Somsen, n. 76 above, 140 to 151.

[86] Case C-155/91 *Waste Directive*, n. 70 above.

[87] Dir. 91/156/EEC on waste modifying Dir. 75/442/EEC [1991] *OJ* L78/32.

[88] Case C-155/91 *Waste Directive*, n. 70 above, para. 15.

[89] See also the Court's reference to this judgment in Case C-2/90 *Commission* v. *Belgium* (*Walloon
Waste Case*) [1992] *ECR* I-4431.

[90] See also for details Middeke, n. 33 above, 307 to 333.

According to Article 100a(5) such measures shall in appropriate cases include 'a safeguard clause authorizing the Member State to take, for one or more of the non-economic reasons referred to in Article 36, provisional measures subject to a Community control procedure'.

Environmental measures raise the disputed question whether the environment is included amongst the reasons referred to in Article 36.[91] Even when applying a narrow interpretation[92] of Article 36 many measures may fall under this provision, as concerning 'the protection of health and life of humans, animals or plants'.[93]

This new provision is a continuation of the practice under Article 100,[94] where most directives contained safeguard clauses for special situations.[95] Such clauses usually allow Member States to take provisional measures if they think that a product which conforms in general to Community rules, presents a risk to man or the environment.[96] The Member States must, however, inform the Commission, which will start a procedure by which either the national measure is made generally applicable or the Member State is asked to withdraw its measure. Until the Community decision is taken, the provisional national measure may remain in force.[97]

Example: An example is Directive 75/716 modified by Directive 87/219 fixing the maximum content of sulphur for liquid fuels. The maximum level is 0.3 per cent but the Directive allows Member States to apply a maximum level of up to 0.2 per cent if this is required for reasons of environmental protection or protection of the cultural heritage.[98] Another example is Directive 91/414/EEC on car emissions,[99] based on Article 100a containing specific provisions on national fiscal incentives for equipment for 'clean cars'. It allows Member States to apply fiscal incentives for compliance with the prescribed Community standards. The incentives must be significantly lower than the real cost of the pollution reduction equipment and its installation. Once the Community introduces its own fiscal standards they must cease to exist.[100]

---

[91] Becker, n. 59 above, 71, with many references.

[92] As indicated by the Court e.g. in Case 113/80 *Commission* v. *Ireland* (*Buy Irish Case*) [1981] *ECR* 1625.   [93] See Ch. 4.

[94] See above in this chapter the section on Article 100 EC

[95] On the character of Art. 100a(5) EC as a legal basis for the relevant provisions in the dirs. concerned see most recently the Court's reasoning in Case C–359/92 *Germany* v. *Council* [1994] *ECR* I–3681.

[96] A possible example could be a safeguard clause for the outbreak of disease in animals; see Kapteyn and VerLoren van Themaat, n. 4 above, 475; see for problems with regard to fish movements W. Howarth, 'The Single European Market and the Problem of Fish Movements' (1990) 15 *ELRev.* 34 at 36.

[97] See Krämer, n. 32 above, 180, with reference e.g. to Art. 16 of Dir. 90/220/EEC on the deliberate release of genetically modified organisms, n. 65 above.

[98] Dir. 75/716 on the approximation of laws of the Member States relating to the sulphur content of certain liquid fuels [1975] *OJ* L307/22, based on Art. 100, modified by Dir. 87/219 [1987] *OJ* L91/19, based on Arts. 100 and 235.

[99] Dir. 91/414/EEC [1991] *OJ* L242/1.

[100] For details and on the question whether this dir. should rather have been based on Art. 99 see Krämer, n. 25 above, 141 and 142.

Article 100a(4): Systematic Diverging Measures

Article 100a(4) EC allows Member States 'to apply national provisions on grounds of major needs referred to in Article 36, or relating to the protection of the environment or the working environment', despite existing harmonization under Article 100a(1) EC[101] and the absence of a specific safeguard clause.[102] If a Member State deems such provisions necessary it shall notify these provisions to the Commission. The notion of 'complete harmonization' of an area, which is very important under Article 100,[103] is less important under Article 100a as it provides explicitly for the application of diverging national measures.[104] Nevertheless, it remains important to know whether a domestic measure falls after all within the scope of existing harmonization under Article 100a because of the procedural requirements.[105]

This new concept, which allows diverging national measures after a comprehensive harmonization of rules,[106] has been widely criticized. Certain legal writers consider it to be a retreat from the former legal situation in the Community[107] and therefore that it seriously endangers the common market.[108] While the complete harmonization of environmental rules on the basis of Article 100 EC did not, in principle, permit any differing national provisions, the new Article 100a EC allows them explicitly under certain conditions. The reasons laid down in Article 36 as well as the national protection of the environment and the working environment are explicitly recognized as being permanent even after harmonization.[109] These legitimate exceptions coincide, however, with the principles established by the Court in its case law on Article 30 in conjunction with Article 36 EC and the rule of reason.[110]

---

[101] Compare the similar provisions of Art. 118a(3) and Art. 130t EC.

[102] See for the specific differences between paras. (4) and (5) of Art. 100a: Middeke, n. 33 above, 327 to 333.

[103] See above in this chapter the section on Article 100.

[104] See for details Wyatt and Dashwood, n. 45 above, 363 to 368; J. Flynn, 'How will Article 100a(4) work? A Comparison with Article 93' (1987) 24 *CMLRev.* 689 to 707; Krämer, n. 69, 659 to 688; Scheuing, n. 71 above, 167; D. Vignes, 'Le rapprochement des législations mérite-t-il encore son nom?' in *Mélanges pour J. Boulouis, L'Europe et le Droit* (Dalloz, Paris, 1991) 533 to 546.

[105] See e.g. Middeke, n. 33 above, 250.

[106] See the case law of the Court of Justice concerning national measures harmonized under Art. 100 of the Treaty, e.g. Case 5/77 *Tedeschi/Denkavit*, n. 26 above, 1576 (para. 35); Case 251/78 *Denkavit*, n. 26 above, 3388.

[107] See Kapteyn and VerLoren van Themaat, n. 4 above, 474; J. Mertens de Wilmars, 'Het Hof van Justitie van de Europese Gemeenschappen na de Eurpese Akte' [1986] *SEW* 601 to 619.

[108] See P. Pescatore, 'Die "Einheitliche Europäische Akte"—Eine ernste Gefahr für den europäischen Markt' [1986] *EuR* 153 to 169.

[109] On the compatibility with existing primary and secondary law see the corresponding comments on Art. 130t in Ch. 9. See also B. Langeheine, Art. 100a, para. 76, in Grabitz and Hilf (eds.), n. 68 above.

[110] Compare the explicit reference to Art. 36 in Art. 100a(4) EC; on the relevance of the case law on Art. 100a(4) see Krämer, n. 25 above, 124; P.-C. Müller-Graff, 'Die Rechtsangleichung zur Verwirklichung des Binnenmarktes' [1989] *EuR* 107 at 147; H.-J. Glaesner, 'Die Einheitliche Europäische Akte' [1986] *EuR* 119 to 152; B. Langeheine, 'Rechtsangleichung unter Art. 100a

The Controversial Application of Article 100a(4)

In view of the current discussion in the Community of terms such as subsidiarity, competition of regulatory systems, decentralization, harmonization versus pluralism, etc. the interpretation of the substantive elements of Article 100a(4) is still very controversial.[111] There are several open questions about the limits and the scope of this provision.[112] The main problem areas can be summarized as follows:

The Application of More Stringent National Measures

The wording of Article 100a(4) refers to 'grounds of major needs referred to in Article 36, or relating to the protection of the environment or the working environment'. It seems therefore to indicate a clear link with the principles developed by the European Court of Justice concerning measures justified under Articles 30 (rule of reason) and 36 concerning the protection of the environment.[113] By reference to Article 36 it is also intended that the diverging national measures comply with the other requirements of Article 36; that is, mainly, that they are justified in the public interest, may not be taken as disguised protectionist measures, and must not be applied in a discriminatory manner.[114]

This indicates that diverging national measures for the protection of the environment must be more stringent than those introduced by the Community under Article 100a EC.[115] Another consequence of the reference to Article 36 is that the measures under Article 100a(4) have to be proportionate in the sense of the case law of the Court of Justice. As in the case of national measures under the rule of reason or Article 36 EC, diverging national measures in the sense of Article 100a(4) EC must correspond to the requirements of the proportionality test as applied by the Court.[116]

The Introduction of New Diverging National Measures

Another fundamental question concerning the limits of Article 100a(4) is whether it allows Member States to introduce new measures once an area has

EWGV' [1988] *EuR* 235 at 252; and F. Montag, 'Umweltschutz, Freier Warenverkehr und Einheitliche Europäische Akte' [1987] *RIW* 935 at 942.

[111] See for an extensive discussion: Wyatt and Dashwood, n. 45 above, 364 to 368; Geradin, n. 12 above, 175 to 177; Flynn, n. 104 above; A. Furrer, *Die Sperrwirkung des sekundärrechtlichen Gemeinschaftsrechts auf die nationalen Rechtsordnungen* (Nomos, Baden-Baden, 1994), 234 to 247; Palme, n. 46 above, 96 to 175; Schröer, n. 58 above, 226 to 245; Epiney and Möllers, n. 61 above, 51 to 60; Becker, n. 59 above, 109 to 118; Vorwerk, n. 82 above, 108 to 145. In my view the Court's decision in Case 41/93 *France* v. *Commission* (*PCP Decision*) [1994] *ECR* I–1829, does not give any guidance on the substantive elements of the application of Art. 100a(4).

[112] For a detailed discussion see Schröer, n. 58 above, 226 to 245.

[113] See Epiney and Möllers, n. 61 above, 58, with many references.

[114] See Zuleeg, n. 58 above, 284, and Scheuing, n. 71 above, 170.

[115] See also Middeke, n. 33 above, 270 and 312.

[116] See Epiney and Möllers, n. 61 above, 58 and 59, with many references.

been harmonized under Article 100a(1) or whether this Article covers only the maintenance of already existing legislation.[117] The term 'to apply' and its literal meaning have been invoked by certain authors to underline that Article 100a(4) EC allows existing diverging national measures but does not allow the adoption of new ones after the harmonization.[118] This limitation on the introduction of new measures has been rejected by many others.[119] They declare that the wording 'to apply'[120] can be interpreted as maintaining existing rules and introducing new measures.[121] A survey of the wording in other official languages does not, however, provide a concrete solution.[122] It can only be concluded that the term 'to apply' might theoretically include 'to maintain' and 'to introduce',[123] so the wording gives no clear indication of the correct interpretation. An analysis of the use of the term 'apply' by the Court might eventually strengthen the arguments of a broad interpretation.[124]

Others argue that the objective of an internal market as mentioned in Article 8a EC would be jeopardized if the Member States could introduce new and permanent diverging measures for the protection of the environment and the other stated grounds.[125] Several authors see in the historical development of Article 100a another reason for the prohibition of new measures or at least for a limited transitional period.[126]

Another argument arises in an analogy to Article 130t, which states that in the field of the environment 'the protective measures adopted in common pursuant to Article 130s shall not prevent any Member State from maintaining or

[117] See for an extensive overview Middeke, n. 33 above, 266 to 272.

[118] See Krämer, n. 41 above, 78 ff.; Langeheine, n. 110 above, 235; C.-D. Ehlermann, 'The Internal Market Following the Single European Act' (1987) 24 *CMLRev.* 360 at 392; E. Grabitz and C. Zacker, 'Die neuen Umweltkompetenzen der EWG' [1989] *NVwZ* 297 at 300.

[119] See for details: K. Hailbronner, 'Der "nationale Alleingang" im Gemeinschaftsrecht am Beispiel der Abgasstandards für PKW' [1989] *EuGRZ* 101 at 108 ff.; also N. Forwood and M. Clough, 'The Single European Act and Free Movement' (1986) 11 *ELRev.* 383 at 389 ff.; Epiney and Möllers, n. 61 above, 52; Vorwerk, n. 82 above, 115 ff.; Scheuing, n. 73 above, 170 ff.; De Ruyt, n. 56 above, 171; I. Pernice, 'Kompetenzordnung und Handlungsbefugnisse der Europäischen Gemeinschaft auf dem Gebiet des Umwelt- und Technikrechts' [1989] *DV* 1 at 10; Ø. Møller, 'Binnenmarkt und Umweltschutz, Artikel 100a der Einheitlichen Europäischen Akte' [1987] *EA* 497 at 503; Zuleeg, n. 58 above, 284.

[120] In French: *appliquer*, in German: *anwenden*, in Italian: *applicare*, in Spanish: *aplicar* etc.

[121] See Hailbronner, n. 119 above, 109 ff.; De Ruyt, n. 56 above, 171.

[122] See Palme, n. 46 above, 126 to 128.

[123] See Becker, n. 59 above, 114; Hailbronner, n. 119 above, 109; Müller-Graff, n. 110 above, 148, or J. M. Bergmann, *'Principle of Preemption' versus 'Nationaler Alleingang'—Eine Erörterung am Beispiel der Umweltpolitik, Vorträge, Reden und Berichte aus dem Europainstitut* (Europainstitut der Universität des Saarlandes, Saarbrücken, 1993), 22.

[124] See Furrer, n. 111 above, 240 and 241, with reference to Case 53/86 *Officier van Justitie* v. *L. Romkes et al.* [1987] *ECR* 2691, para. 5.

[125] See Krämer, n. 71 above, 155; Langeheine, n. 110 above, 249; the same tendency M. Dauses, 'Die rechtliche Dimension des Binnenmarktes' [1991] *EuZW* 8 at 9.

[126] See Krämer, n. 69 above; Krämer, n. 32 above, 164; B. Langeheine, Art. 100a, para. 65 in Grabitz and Hilf (eds.), n. 68 above; B. Langeheine, n. 110 above, 248, more balanced, J. Pipkorn, Art. 100a, 110 ff. in H. v.d. Groeben, J. Thiesing, and C.-D. Ehlermann (eds.), *Kommentar zum EWG-Vertrag* (Nomos, Baden-Baden, 1983 ff.)

introducing more stringent protective measures'. The supporters of a broad interpretation state that Article 100a(4) has to be interpreted in the light of Article 130s, as the drafters did not want to exclude the adoption of new diverging protection measures in the framework of the important Article 100a(4) if they stated this possibility explicitly in Article 130t in the field of environmental policy.[127] On the other hand those authors who object to such an interpretation invoke the different wording of Article 130t and 118a(3) EC[128] as proving the different intention of the drafters.[129]

Probably the most striking argument in favour of a competence without any time limit for the introduction of new protection measures is interpretation in the light of the general objectives of the Single European Act. Considering the lack of explicit references to the protection of the environment in the Treaty of Rome, the Single European Act has introduced several provisions to implement a far-reaching environmental policy of the European Community. Articles 100a(3)—a high level of protection for Community environmental measures—, 130r(1)—the objectives of the Community environmental policy—and Article 130r(2) EC—principles of the Community environmental policy—indicate the general desire for high-standards of effective protection of the environment.[130]

Certain authors derive from the above set of environmental provisions of the Single European Act the 'principle of the best possible environmental protection'.[131] It is, however, arguable whether this high level of protection provides only a guideline for the environmental measures taken by the Community or whether it implicitly justifies the introduction of new diverging domestic measures. Only if the introduction of diverging national measures is considered to be an incentive for an efficient Community environmental policy and necessary in order to reach a high level of protection in general is this solution preferable with respect to environmental protection.[132] Such an interpretation undoubtedly allows the introduction of new measures only if they are more stringent than the Community standard. A further argument in favour of the introduction of new more stringent measures might be that only the introduction of new national measures allows a Member State to react to new scientific evidence or a change

---

[127] See Hailbronner, n. 119 above, 112.

[128] Art. 118a(3) EEC Treaty states: 'The provisions adopted pursuant to this Article shall not prevent any Member State from maintaining or introducing more stringent measures for the protection of working conditions compatible with this Treaty.'

[129] Krämer, n. 25 above, 111; Ehlermann, n. 118 above, 392.

[130] See Epiney and Möllers, n. 61 above, 53 ff.; Pernice, n. 60, above, 201; Hailbronner, n. 119 above, 113 ff.; Scheuing, n. 71 above, 170; L. Krämer, 'Grundrecht auf Umwelt und Gemeinschaftsrecht' [1988] *EuGRZ* 285 at 288, Bergmann, n. 123 above, 30.

[131] '*Grundsatz des bestmöglichen Umweltschutzes*'; see Zuleeg, n. 58 above, 283. This view is supported by Vorwerk, n. 82 above, 33; Pernice, n. 60 above, 203; Scheuing, n. 71 above, 176; Hailbronner, n. 119 above, 104; Krämer, n. 130 above, 288; L. Krämer, 'Das Verursacherprinzip im Gemeinschaftsrecht' [1989] *EuGRZ* 353 at 356.

[132] See Hailbronner, n. 119 above, 115; also Epiney and Möllers, n. 61 above, 54.

in its regional or national conditions[133] by introducing appropriate new measures.[134]

On the whole, it seems to me that only an interpretation of Article 100a(4) which also permits the introduction of new more stringent measures complies with the spirit of the Single European Act and, in particular, with its new approach to environmental problems. The conceptual problem that such an interpretation is in opposition to the establishment of the common market and the final harmonization of standards at a Community-wide level is a problem of all mechanisms which allow for domestic diverging measures (specific derogations in secondary law, minimal standards, national freedom when implementing directives, Article 130t, 118a etc.[135]).

As Article 100a(4) allows the application of diverging domestic standards the principle of the establishment of the Internal Market through the introduction of harmonized standards has been essentially replaced by a principle of high standards for protection of the environment with acceptance of diverging domestic needs and preferences. Thus, the old concept of the harmonization of standards at a Community-wide level has been modified by the changes under the Single European Act. The reconciliation of diverging local needs and the efficient protection of the environment on one side and the establishment of the Internal Market on the other can be found throughout the Treaty[136] and in the practice of the Council.[137] In my view, the narrow interpretation of Article 100a(4) is no remedy for saving and re-establishing the harmonizing approach in its old form.

No Limited Period for Application

Most authors argue that the application of diverging national measures under Article 100a(4) is not subject to a limited period of application.[138] Although Article 100a EC was introduced for the accomplishment of the Internal Market as mentioned in Article 7a EC, this did not prevent the further application after January 1st 1993 of the exceptions specifically provided for. Although the application of diverging national measures can hinder the establishment of a homogeneous internal market,[139] Article 100a(4) provides a legal basis for the unlimited application of diverging national measures after 1993.[140]

---

[133] Apart from possible specific safeguard clauses as provided for e.g. in Art. 100a (5) EC.

[134] See Epiney and Möllers, n. 61 above, 56; Becker, n. 59 above, 115; Zuleeg, n. 58 above, 280 at 284.

[135] See the strong criticism in Pescatore, n. 108 above, or P. Pescatore, 'Some Critical Remarks on the "Single European Act" ' (1987) 24 *CMLRev.* 9 at 12.

[136] Arts. 130t and 118a.

[137] Derogations in Community acts under Arts. 43, 75, 84(2), 99, 113 etc. EC.

[138] See Becker, n. 59 above, 116, with more references.

[139] See Krämer, n. 41 above, 77 and 78.

[140] See also C. Guhlmann, 'The Single European Act—Some Remarks from a Danish Perspective' (1987) 24 *CMLRev.* 31 at 36; Langeheine, n. 110 above, 256.

Application in spite of Non-objection on Occasion of the Adoption

Very controversial is the question of who may apply divergent measures according to Article 100a(4).[141] Some legal writers have suggested that the logic of this provision allows only those Member States which have been outvoted on the adoption of a measure under Article 100a(1) to invoke Article 100a(4) EC. They interpret Article 100a(4) as a necessary safeguard clause for the outvoted Member States and as a consequence of the newly-introduced qualified majority requirement.[142] Voting in favour of the adoption of a measure under Article 100a or abstention would thus preclude the invocation of Article 100a(4).[143] The same reasoning lies behind the opinion that the unanimous adoption of a measure under Article 100a EC prevents any Member State from relying on the provision of Article 100a(4) EC.[144]

Others argue that Article 100a EC has been introduced to make decision-making in the Community easier.[145] Concerning the safeguard clause of Article 100a(4) they refer to the possible situation where a Member State prefers the proposed new Community legislation to the existing rules but would still like to apply higher standards in its own territory. A country in this situation would vote in favour of the new legislation, knowing that Article 100a(4) EC will then allow it to apply more stringent national rules. If this country were not allowed to apply its higher standard if it consented to the relevant measure it would never consent, since consent would mean being unable to apply higher standards. This could mean the paralysing of the harmonization of environment-related rules.[146] Referring again to the objective of a generally high level of environmental protection within the Community as a whole, in my view, the second interpretation seems to be more in the interest of the efficient protection of the environment and the spirit of the Single European Act.[147]

[141] See for a detailed survey of the literature Middeke, n. 33 above, 262 to 266.

[142] See Mertens de Wilmars, n. 107 above, 601; see also Kapteyn and VerLoren van Themaat, n. 4 above, 475; Krämer, n. 71 above, 154, Langeheine, n. 126 above, para. 65; G. Meier, 'Einheitliche Europäische Akte und freier EG-Warenverkehr' [1987] *NJW* 537 at 540; Dauses, n. 125 above, 9; Pipkorn, Art. 100a, 98 ff. in: Groeben, Thiesing, and Ehlermann (eds.), n. 126 above.

[143] See J.-P. Jacqué, 'L'acte unique européen' [1986] *RTDE* 575 at 600; Ehlermann, n. 118 above, 394.

[144] See Krämer, n. 41 above, 76; Geradin, n. 12 above, 176; Meier, n. 142 above, 539; Langeheine, n. 110 above, 246; Dauses, n. 125 above, 9; Pipkorn, n. 142 above, 98.

[145] Hailbronner, n. 119 above, 109, considers such an interpretation to be a consequence of the general principle governing the interpretation of Community law, the *effet utile*—interpretation. In his view even a unanimous decision can be reached although certain countries want to apply higher national standards; see also Epiney and Möllers, n. 61 above, 57; Becker, n. 59 above, 111 ff.

[146] See E. Klein, Art. 100a, para. 14, in K. Hailbronner, E. Klein, S. Magiera, and P.-C. Müller-Graff, *Handkommentar zum EWG-Vertrag* (Heymann, Köln, 1991); Becker, n. 59 above, 109; Scheuing, n. 71 above, n. 82 above, 108; Bergmann, n. 123 above, 30 to 32.

[147] See Epiney and Möllers, n. 61 above, 55; Becker, n. 59 above, 110 and 112; Soell, n. 82 above, 160; Hailbronner, n. 119 above, 117; Scheuing, n. 71 above, 171; Grabitz and Zacker, n. 118 above, 300; Pernice, n. 119 above, 11; Montag, n. 110 above, 942; C. Joerges, J. Falke, H.-W. Micklitz and G. Brüggemeier, *Die Sicherheit von Konsumgütern und die Entwicklung der Europäischen Gemeinschaft* (Nomos, Baden-Baden, 1988), 369 ff.

Procedural Requirements

Once a State has notified a divergent measure,[148] according to the second paragraph of Article 100a(4) EC, the Commission may only check whether it is compatible with the general conditions of Article 36 and the rule of reason.[149] If the Commission or another Member State consider that a Member State has made improper use of this provision it may bring the matter directly before the Court without the necessity of observing the procedural requirements of Articles 169 and 170 EC.

It has been suggested that the judicial control over whether a Member State makes 'improper use' of Article 100a(4) should include an evaluation of the objective involved (in the sense of a broad interpretation of Article 100a(4), paragraph 3[150]). It seems, however, better to follow the approach used by the Court for the application of Article 36 and the rule of reason, where the level of protection is not under review provided the objective is covered by Community law and the national measure fulfils the other requirements developed by the Court. In my view and that of several other authors, the Commission is not able to examine the justification of the level of protection.[151]

The Court has confirmed that the Commission is obliged to explain the reasons which lead to the acceptance or rejection of a national measure.[152] From the only case decided so far it seems that the Court requires a high standard in the arguments put forward for the justification of national derogations. As in other cases,[153] the Court has underlined in this case the exceptional nature of such national measures in application of Article 100a(4) which hinder trade.[154] It will be interesting to see whether the high level of procedural correctness the Court demands is a consequence of the broad interpretation of Article 100a(4) and is thus an instrument to prevent abuse or whether it derives from the narrowness of Article 100a(4). The Court's decision in Case C–41/93 *France* v. *Commission*[155] does not yet give a decisive answer to all the open questions with regard to Article 100a(4).

Case: The only reported example to date of a proceedings under Article 100a(4) is the 1992 German ban on pentachlorophenol (PCP), a chemical substance principally used as a wood preservative and considered dangerous for man and the environment. In 1987,

---

[148] See on the notification procedure Middeke, n. 33 above, 278 to 305.

[149] Art. 100a(4) second sentence, referring to Art. 36, second sentence.

[150] See Kapteyn and VerLoren van Themaat, n. 4 above, 475.

[151] Kapteyn and VerLoren van Themaat, n. 4 above, 475; probably also supported by Bergmann, n. 123 above, 34 referring to Hailbronner, n. 119 above, 108.

[152] On the nature of this decision see e.g Bergmann, n. 123 above, 37 with many references.

[153] See the Court's narrow interpretation of Art. 36 and the oft-repeated argument that national derogations must be profoundly justified because of their derogation from the principles underlying the establishment of the common market; see Chs. 4 and 5.

[154] See Case C–41/93 *PCP Decision*, n. 111 above, paras. 24 ff.

[155] *Ibid.* for comments see H. Keller and C. Tobler, 'PCP-Verbot im Gemeinschaftsrecht' [1995] *AJP* 1562 to 1569.

Germany had notified the Commission of its intention severely to restrict the use of PCP. Since the Community itself intended to introduce regulations on this substance, it asked Germany to withhold its bill for twelve months, as it is provided for by Directive 83/189.[156] In 1989, however, Germany adopted the national regulation in question,[157] which contained a very restrictive ban of PCP (0.01 per cent). In 1991 the Community, in Directive 91/173/EEC,[158] adopted provisions concerning the use of PCP (now providing for a maximum content of PCP of 0.1 per cent). In the same year Germany notified the Commission under Article 100a(4) EC that it intended to maintain its more restrictive regulation. This decision was confirmed by the Commission on 2 December 1992, as provided for by Article 100a(4).[159] This decision by the Commission has been taken to the Court by France asking for an annulment of the decision by reason of the Commission's insufficient statement of reasons according to Article 190 EC. The Court shared the French view and asked the Commission for a better explanation of its reasoning. The French argument that the restrictive nature of the German measure was not justified, under Article 100a(4) and Article 36 respectively, was not addressed by the Court. Furthermore, the Court did not give any further indications of the exact interpretation of the conditions of application of Article 100a(4).[160] In the meantime the Commission reconfirmed its decision on the lawfulness of the German measure under Article 100a(4) and gave a sufficient statement of reasons.[161]

MUTUAL RECOGNITION OF STANDARDS (ARTICLE 100B)

Under Article 100b EC the Council is empowered to require the mutual recognition of national environmental rules and standards provided they have not been harmonized under Article 100a EC.[162] The Commission was entrusted with establishing a list of the relevant domestic laws, regulations, and administrative provisions until the end of 1992. There has, however, so far been no proposal by the Commission for the national standards eligible for mutual recognition.[163] Certain authors suggest even that Article 100b might possibly never be of any practical use.[164] In 1990 the Commission sent out a letter to the Member States asking them to prepare the implementation of Article 100b EC but as a result of the responses of the Member States the Commission came to the conclusion that most barriers to trade fell under Article 100a or were cov-

---

[156] Dir. 83/189/EEC, n. 51 above; see the section on Article 100 EC above in this chapter.

[157] Reg. of 12 Dec. 1989 (Germany), BGBl. I of 22 Apr. 1989.

[158] Dir. 91/173/EEC [1991] *OJ* L85/34 amending Dir. 76/769/EEC.

[159] Communication by the Commission [1992] *OJ* C334/4, reported by Furrer, n. 111 above, 267; Krämer, n. 25 above, 125 and 133; Geradin, n. 12 above, 177; see also [1992] *OJ* C250/38 at 40, [1992] *OJ* C245/13, and questions by the Members of the European Parliament [1992] *OJ* C345/1.

[160] Case C–41/93 *PCP Decision*, n. 111 above; see also Wyatt and Dashwood, n. 45 above, 367, or Furrer, n. 11 above, 267.

[161] See the Commission's decision of 14 Sept. 1994 [1994] *OJ* L316/43, also reprinted in [1994] *EuZW* 642.

[162] See for a more detailed description Becker, n. 59 above, 152 to 155.

[163] See Wyatt and Dashwood, n. 45 above, 368.   [164] See Vignes, n. 104 above, 544.

ered by Article 30 in conjunction with Article 169 EC. Thus the Commission never established a list of national standards eligible for mutual recognition.[165]

The concept of mutual recognition follows, however, the general idea proposed by the Commission in its White Paper of 1985.[166] Referring to the Court's reasoning under the rule of reason or *Cassis de Dijon* doctrine, there was not always a need for positive harmonization of national laws as Member States were obliged to recognize the safety measures and controls applied by other Member States if they were equivalent to domestic measures.[167] The Community would only adopt directives which regulated the minimum standards which had to be observed and would leave more detailed regulation to private organizations and institutions.[168]

As Article 100a(4) remains applicable, however, the Member States are allowed to take their own measures and are permitted not to recognize standards and controls which do not ensure an equivalent level of protection. Thus, the implications of Article 100b are the same as those deriving from the Court's rule of reason: as long as product standards and control measures applied by other Member States ensure an equivalent level of protection, additional domestic requirements and measures are not justified because they are not necessary for the achievement of the desired level of protection. If the level is not equivalent, Member States may apply more stringent measures and controls under Article 100a(4) or the general principles developed by the Court.

---

[165] [1994] *OJ* C18/23, see for details T. D. Winkler, *Wo kein Kläger, da kein Richter—Die Verwirklichung der gegenseitigen Anerkennung von Produktregulierungen in der Europäischen Union, Diskussionsbeitrag 07/95* (Max-Planck-Institut zur Erforschung von Wirtschaftssystemen, Jena, 1995), 18.

[166] EC Commission, *White Paper on Completing the Internal Market* (EC, Brussels, 1985), paras. 65 ff.

[167] See Case 120/78 *Rewe Zentral AG* v. *Bundesmonopolverwaltung für Branntwein* (*Cassis de Dijon*) [1979] *ECR* 649; EC Commission, n. 165 above, para. 77.

[168] See Brunetti, n. 77 above, 71.

9

Selected Community Policies and the Environment

Since the entry into force of the Single European Act Articles 130r to 130t have finally introduced an explicit environmental policy into the Treaty. In spite of the harmonization of environmental measures under Article 130s the Member States may apply or introduce more stringent national measures under Article 130t. These must be notified to the Commission. If deemed appropriate Community measures under Article 130s include specific safeguard clauses allowing diverging national measures, subject to a Community inspection procedure: Article 130r(2).

Article 43 is the appropriate legal basis for environment-related Community measures concerning the production and marketing of agricultural products. The creation of a uniform agricultural policy also has effects on the national regulation of product and production requirements. If a Community measure adopted under Article 43 does not exhaustively regulate a certain area the Member States retain the competence to introduce national measures compatible with the Treaty. Specific safeguard clauses and minimum requirements are possible means of enacting the participation of Member States in Community acts under Article 43.

The common transport policy under Article 75 and 84(2) EC includes certain measures regulating environmental aspects of traffic. As long as an area is not completely covered by Community measures the Member States remain free to adopt their own measures, including prohibitions and restrictions on use, charges, and subsidies. The measures must respect the general rules of the Treaty and must not operate to the detriment of foreign carriers in a discriminatory manner, prior to the introduction of Community measures (Article 76).

Measures taken for the improvement of the working environment under Article 118a EC are not to be considered environmental measures but rather as serving objectives of social policy. The Community research policy (Article 130o) has practically no impact on the Member States' competence in relation to environmental programmes and state aids in the field.

COMMUNITY ENVIRONMENTAL POLICY (ARTICLES 130R TO 130T)

General Observations

While Articles 100 and 100a provide for the possibility of eliminating step by step diverging national rules and regulations which might hinder the establishment of the common market and the internal market respectively,[1] the Treaty contains certain provisions which allow the Community to develop a common policy in specific areas. In the field of environmentally relevant policies these are mainly the protection of the environment itself (Article 130r to 130t), the common agricultural policy (Articles 38–47), and the common transport policy (Articles 74–84). While the general approximation of laws allows the establishment of a single market and thereby integration through economic factors, the establishment of common policies in certain particularly important areas of regulation can be seen as an additional element to complement the general establishment of the common market. The legal acts to embody these common policies are based on special provisions in relation to Articles 100 and 100a. The application of these special provisions prevails for the adoption of specific regulations related to the common policies. The case law of the European Court of Justice, however, shows that the distinction can be rather difficult and is not always clear.[2]

Since the entry into force of the Single European Act (SEA) in 1987, the Community has been entrusted, under the general system of the Treaty, with the protection of the environment.[3] Its objectives closely resemble the Community practice developed since the UN Environment Conference in Stockholm 1972.[4] Article 130r(2) sets out the principles upon which Community action is to be based. These principles are: the principle of preventive action, the principle of rectification of environmental damage at the source, and the polluter pays principle. The second sentence of Article 130r(2) states that environmental protection requirements shall be a component of the other Community policies.[5] These principles shall dictate the environmental policy of the Community in general.[6] Article 130r(4) provides that within their relevant

---

[1] See for the different concepts Ch. 8 above.

[2] See for a survey I. Pernice, 'Kompetenzordnung und Handlungsbefugnisse der Europäischen Gemeinschaft auf dem Gebiet des Umwelt- und Technikrechts' [1989] *DV* 1 at 23 to 30.

[3] For a detailed description of Arts. 130r to 130t and their origins see L. Krämer, *EEC Treaty and Environmental Protection* (Sweet & Maxwell, London, 1990), 31 to 97 and more recently H. Matuschak, 'Die Bedeutung des neuen Art. 130s(2) EGV im Rahmen des EG-vertraglichen Umweltrechts' [1995] *DVBl.* 81 to 88.

[4] See P. J. G. Kapteyn and P. VerLoren van Themaat, *Introduction to the Law of the European Communities* (2nd edn., Kluwer, Deventer, 1989), 650.

[5] Referred to as integration clause, in German, as *Querschnittklausel*. See for its direct implications on the Community policies J. Jahns-Böhm, 'Die umweltrechtliche Querschnittklausel des Art. 130r II(2) EWGV' [1992] *EuZW* 49 to 55.

[6] See Kapteyn and VerLoren van Themaat, n. 4 above, 651; a possible consequence could

spheres of competence the Community and the individual Member States shall co-operate with non-member countries and with the relevant international organizations.[7]

While Articles 130r to 130t were introduced in the Treaty only with the entry into force of the Single European Act, the Treaty on the European Union has not substantially changed the framework of the Community's environmental policy under these provisions.[8] The main changes are the new procedural requirements in Article 130s for the adoption of measures.[9] Furthermore, the Treaty in the new Article 130r(2) now explicitly states the objective of a high level of protection and the importance of taking into account the diversity of situations in the various regions of the Community.[10]

Article 130s and Other Provisions

On the whole it seems that Articles 130r to 130t EC provide the Community with a very extensive and explicit power to regulate environmental areas.[11] Nevertheless, its introduction does not preclude the adoption of Community legislation under other relevant provisions of the Treaty. This follows in particular from the principle of Article 130r(2), the so-called 'integration clause', which states that the protection of the environment shall be a component of the Community's other policies. That which has been discussed with regard to the relationship between Articles 130r and 100a[12] is also relevant for the relationship between Article 130r and the other possible provisions entailing environmental effects.

In cases where the content of a legal action can find its legal basis in two different provisions of the Treaty, the Court demands that in principle the corre-

therefore be that the Community does not approve certain state aids for environmental purposes if the 'polluter pays' principle is not observed (see for details Ch. 6) or that a differentiation between imported waste and local waste is justified under the principle of correction at source: see Case C–2/90 *Commission* v. *Belgium* (*Walloon Waste Case*) [1992] *ECR* I–4431, see Chs. 4 and 5.

[7] See for details Ch. 11.

[8] See for details D. Wilkinson, 'Maastricht and the Environment: The Implications for the EC's Environment Policy of the Treaty on European Union' [1993] *J Env. L* 221 to 239 and A. Epiney and A. Furrer, 'Umweltschutz nach Maastricht' [1992] *EuR* 369 to 408.

[9] Art. 130s EC now provides for an adoption of legislation by majority vote; U. Everling, 'Durchführung und Umsetzung des Europäischen Gemeinschaftsrechts im Bereich des Umweltschutzes unter Berücksichtigung der Rechtsprechung des EuGH' [1993] *NVwZ* 209 at 216 indicates the possible development for the choice of the legal basis (Art. 100a or 130s).

[10] The requirement of a high level of environmental protection, first included in Art. 100a(3), is thereby extended to all aspects of Community policy because of the horizontal effect of Art. 130r(2) on all Community policies: see Wilkinson, n. 8 above, 223.

[11] See L. Krämer, 'Environmental Protection and Art. 30 EEC Treaty' (1993) 30 *CMLRev.* 111 at 112 and Cases C–300/89 *Commission* v. *Council* (*Titanium Dioxide*) [1991] *ECR* I–2867 and C–155/91 *Commission* v. *Council* (*Waste Directive*) [1993] *ECR* I–939; for a detailed analysis see A. Epiney and T. M. J. Möllers, *Freier Warenverkehr und nationaler Umweltschutz* (Heymann, Köln, 1992), 7; see also Ch. 8 on Article 100a EC.

[12] See Ch. 8 and Case C–300/89 *Titanium Dioxide*, n. 11 above, and Case C–155/91 *Waste Directive*, n. 11 above.

sponding act be based on both provisions.[13] This is not possible if these provisions provide for different procedures, such as do Articles 130s and 100a.

The Court of Justice has therefore stated that the mere fact that a Community measure is aimed at the protection of the environment does not automatically lead to the application of Article 130s.[14] The Court initially declared that a regulation was to be based on Article 100a instead of Article 130s whenever it had any impact on the Internal Market, e.g. the establishment of uniform conditions for production and competition.[15] In a subsequent decision[16] the Court added, however, that Article 130r was to be chosen whenever the harmonization of competition conditions within the internal market was only of accessory importance in relation to the environmental objective of a regulation.[17]

Thus, the Court treats Articles 130r and 130s as specific provisions which leave intact the Community powers under other provisions of the Treaty. The Court refers particularly to Article 130r(2).[18] This supports the Community's practice under the SEA of basing environment-related measures on other Treaty provisions if they are considered to be more specific[24]: Article 100a (internal market),[19] Article 43 (Agriculture),[20] Article 75 and 84(2) (transport),[21] Article 99 (fiscal measures),[22] 113 (common commercial policy),[23] or 130o (research).[25]

Case: A recent example for the distinction between the use of Article 130s in relation to Articles 100a or 113 of the Treaty is the Court's decision in Case C–187/93 *European Parliament* v. *Council*. The European Parliament had brought an action for the annulment of Council Regulation 259/93/EEC on the shipment of wastes. The Regulation was mainly concerned with the organization of movements of waste within the Community and foreign trade in waste between the Community and non-member countries. While the Council

---

[13] Case 165/87 *Commission* v. *Council* (*International Convention on the Harmonized Commodity Description and Coding*) [1988] *ECR* 5545.

[14] Case C–300/89 *Titanium Dioxide*, n. 11 above; see L. Krämer, 'Community Environmental Law—Towards a Systematic Approach' [1992] *YEL* 151 at 154.

[15] Case C–300/89 *Titanium Dioxide*, n. 11 above, para. 15.

[16] Case C–155/91 *Waste Directive*, n. 11 above, para. 19.

[17] For a detailed discussion of the question see H. Somsen, 'Comments on Case C–300/89' (1992) 29 *CMLRev.* 140 to 151; A. Epiney, 'Gemeinschaftsrechtlicher Umweltschutz und Verwirklichung des Binnenmarktes—"Harmonisierung" auch der Rechtsgrundlagen?' [1992] *JZ* 564; Epiney and Möllers, n. 11 above, 7 ff.

[18] Case C–62/88 *Greece* v. *Council* (*Chernobyl I*) [1990] *ECR* I–1527 at 1545, which concerned the different application of Arts. 113 and 130r(5) of the SEA, now 130r(4). See for details Ch. 11.

[19] e.g. Dir. 91/441/EEC on the limitation of air pollution from motor vehicles [1991] *OJ* L241/1.

[20] e.g. Dir. 91/414/EEC on the putting into circulation of pesticides [1991] *OJ* L230/1.

[21] e.g. Dir. 89/629/EEC on the limitation of noise emissions from subsonic aircraft [1989] *OJ* L363/27.

[22] e.g. Proposal for a Dir. on the introduction of an energy tax in order to limit carbon dioxide emissions [1992] *OJ* C216/4; for details see Ch. 10.

[23] e.g. Proposal for a regulation on the transport including export and import of dangerous waste (also based on Art. 100a) [1990] *OJ* C289/9, still based on Art. 130q.

[24] e.g. Decision of 7 June 1991 to adopt a specific programme on research and technological development in environmental measures [1991] *OJ* L192/29.

[25] All references from Krämer, n. 14 above, 155.

had based the regulation on Article 130s (environmental policy, the Parliament considered Articles 100a and 113 EC as the correct legal basis. The Court did not enter into the facts concerning the use of Article 113 because at the time of adoption of the Regulation concerned the Parliament had no right to be involved in the drawing up of legal acts under this Article. For the remaining points the Court considered that the Regulation had been adopted with a view to ensuring the protection of the environment, taking account of objectives falling within the scope of environmental policy such as the principles of proximity, priority for recovery, and self-sufficiency at Community and national levels. The Court considered Article 130s the correct legal basis of the Regulation as it was taken within the framework of the environmental policy pursued by the Community and not in view of implementing the free movement of waste within the Community.

The main area in which Article 130s is to be applied in the adoption of Community actions might therefore be defined, as where the protection of the environment is so predominant over the other effects of a regulation that these others become secondary and do not call for adoption under any of the other more specific provisions.[26] This is normally the case for those areas whose regulation was based on Article 235 before the introduction of the SEA.[27] The exact definition of such areas remains difficult, even considering the principles of jurisdiction described above.[28] There are, however, important consequences, as the procedures for the adoption differ. The same is true for the possibilities for the Member States to apply diverging national measures.

Non-harmonized Areas and Safeguard Clauses

As shown in the context of Articles 100 and 100a EC the Member States remain free to adopt their own environmental measures in areas which have not been completely harmonized by Community law. Furthermore, in many cases where harmonization has taken place the specific Community measure itself provides for national safeguard clauses for the application of diverging measures. Under the Single European Act (SEA) Article 130r did not mention such specific safeguard measures. Now, after the coming into force of the Treaty on European Union, the new version of Article 130r(2), second subparagraph, introduces the general inclusion of specific safeguard measures, as mentioned before under Article 100a(5) and in practice existing for all Community harmonization.[29] It states: '[i]n this context, harmonization measures answering these requirements shall include, where appropriate, a safeguard clause allowing Member States to take provisional measures, for non-economic environmental reasons, subject to a Community inspection procedure.'

Article 130r(2), second sub-paragraph, corresponds in most aspects to the pro-

---

[26] See J. Henke, *EuGH und Umweltschutz* (VVF, München, 1992), 97, referring to specific examples.
[27] Henke, n. 26 above, 97.
[28] Case C–300/89 *Titanium Dioxide*, n. 11 above, at para. 15, and Case C–155/91 *Waste Directive*, n. 11 above, para. 19.
[29] See, in particular, the sections on safeguard clauses in Ch. 8.

vision of Article 100a(5).[30] It differs, however, by mentioning environmental reasons instead of 'major needs referred to in Article 36'. From a functional point of view this provision institutionalizes Community practice in the field of harmonization of laws to include safeguard clauses in specific measures if deemed appropriate.[31]

This widening of the possibilities for diverging national measures might be a further consequence cf the procedural changes.[32] While Article 130s EEC under the Single European Act provided for unanimous adoption, after the entry into force of the Treaty on European Union, the newly drafted Article 130r EC allows for adoption with qualified majority.[33] This leads to a similar situation to that of Article 100a where individual Member States can be obliged to accept and implement EC environmental measures which they consider insufficient.

The new Article 130s(5) provides for temporary derogations and/or financial support from a new cohesion fund. This should allow the Member States with a lower environmental level to incorporate the minimum standards of the Community, while more progressive countries remain capable of adopting more stringent measures.

Systematic Diverging Measures (Article 130t)

The mere existence of Article 130r to 130t does not preclude the Member States from taking legal action related to the environment. The adoption of Community action is restricted by the subsidiarity principle as provided for by Article 130r(4). Not even the adoption of exhaustively harmonizing measures in a particular field excludes the Member States from taking their own measures in the regulated field.[34] Similarly to the provision in Article 100a(4) EC, Article 130t provides that the protective measures of the Community based on Article 130s EC 'shall not prevent any Member State from maintaining or introducing more stringent protective measures compatible with the Treaty'. This specific Treaty provision allows Member States to take more stringent action without the need to refer to a specific derogation in secondary law.[35] It thus reverses the principle that Member States are prevented from taking domestic action in harmonized fields[36] and replaces it by the general lawfulness of such action in the field of environmental policy.[37]

---

[30] See for a detailed comparison A. Middeke, *Nationaler Umweltschutz und Binnenmarkt* (Heymann, Köln, 1994), 357 to 368.

[31] See the relevant section on Articles 100 and 100a(5) in Ch. 8, on Articles 43, 75, and 84 in Ch. 9, and on Article 113 in Ch. 11.   [32] See Wilkinson, n. 8 above, 231.

[33] See, however, the different procedure under Art. 130s(2) EC and its application; for comments see e.g. Matuschak, n. 3 above.

[34] See for details Krämer, n. 3 above, 91.

[35] See for details Middeke, n. 30 above, 335 to 356.   [36] See Chs. 5 and 7.

[37] This does not imply that there are no limits to such domestic action, but in my view the introduction of Art. 130t is much more than a mere codification of the earlier Community practice to include specific derogations in Community secondary law, such as considered e.g. by D. Geradin,

In comparison with Article 100a(4) this provision is much less controversial. It is clearly stated that the Member States are also allowed to introduce new measures and that these have to be more stringent to be legitimate under Article 130t.[38] The only limit to diverging national measures under Article 130t, apart from their necessarily more stringent character, is the obligation to observe the Treaty as a whole. This is explicitly repeated in Article 130t, second sentence, but is also a general EC principle.[39] This relates only to the provisions of the Treaty and not to secondary legislation.[40] Apart from the basic freedoms, the Treaty principles to be observed are first and foremost the general principle of non-discrimination and the principle of proportionality in cases where the domestic measures adopted fall within the scope of Article 36 or the rule of reason.[41]

Only few authors argue that the application of Article 130t is not lawful in cases where the relevant Community act was adopted in view of the elimination of obstacles to the free movement of goods and therefore divergent national measures would jeopardize the objectives of such directives.[42] In my view only a deeply incorrect conception of the new character of Community harmonization after the introduction of Articles 100a(4) and 130t explains this opinion. It is explicitly their scope and nature to introduce environmental concerns into Community law and this may in certain cases lead to the maintenance or even recreation of obstacles if this is justified under the conditions of Article 130t. Any other interpretation would undermine the scope of Articles 100a(4) and 130t.[43]

The additional argument that in these cases the introduction of more stringent environmental measures would lead to an infringement of Article 5 EC[44] cannot be upheld either. Member States have the explicit right and responsibility to introduce divergent measures if the conditions of Article 130t

---

'Free Trade and Environmental Protection in an Integrated market: A Survey of the Case Law of the United States Supreme Court and the European Court of Justice' (1993) 2 *Journal of Transnational Law and Policy* 141 at 175.

[38] See the different wording of Arts. 130t and 118a in comparison to Art. 100a(4); on the conditions underlying Art. 130t see Krämer, n. 3 above, 95.

[39] Art. 5 EC.

[40] See Epiney and Möllers, n. 11 above, 59; M. Zuleeg, 'Vorbehaltene Kompetenzen der Mitgliedstaaten der Europäischen Gemeinschaft auf dem Gebiet des Umweltschutzes' [1987] *NVwZ* 280 at 284; E. Grabitz and M. Nettesheim, Art. 130t, para. 8, in E. Grabitz and M. Hilf (eds.) *Kommentar zur EU* (2nd edn., C. H. Beck, München, 1990 ff.).

[41] See Ch. 5.

[42] See in particular S. Breier, 'Verbesserung der Kraftstoffqualität im Wege des nationalen Alleingangs?' [1994] *EuZW* 624 at 626, with reference to T. Schröer, *Die Kompetenzverteilung zwischen der Europäischen Gemeinschaft und ihren Mitgliedstaaten auf dem Gebiet des Umweltschutzes* (Duncker & Humblot, Berlin, 1991), 224; see also S. Breier, 'Ausgewählte Probleme des gemeinschaftlichen Umweltrechts' [1994] *RIW* 584 at 587. Despite the reference made by Breier, I cannot find any arguments in this sense in W. Kahl, *Umweltprinzip und Gemeinschaftsrecht* (Müller Juristischer Verlag, Heidelberg, 1993), 43.

[43] See for the same opinion Epiney and Möllers, n. 11 above, 59, with reference to Zuleeg, n. 40 above, 280; Grabitz and Nettesheim, n. 40 above, para. 14, now consider that other secondary law apart from the legal act in question has to be observed.

[44] Breier, n. 42 above, EuZW 626; Breier, n. 42 above, RIW 587.

are given.[45] Thus it cannot be argued that it puts Community law in jeopardy when a Member State applies the specific provisions of Articles 130t or 100a(4).[46] The general argument that Article 5 EC prevents Member States from adopting more stringent measures under Article 130t cannot be upheld, as it would completely undermine the objective of this provision.[47]

Example: An interesting example is the current discussion in Germany on the introduction of a more stringent maximum limit on the lead and benzol content of petrol.[48] Lead content of petrol is regulated by Community Directive 85/210/EEC, modified by Directive 87/102/EEC, which provides for a maximum benzol content of 5 per cent (Article 4). It was adopted in 1985 and is based on Article 100, but the modifying Directive 87/102/EEC was based on the new Article 130s EC. It seems therefore reasonable to apply the provisions of Article 130 for the question whether Member States may take more stringent measures or are bound by Community law.[49] The Community rules were adopted to safeguard the common market for petrol and to allow petrol which corresponds to the provisions of the Directive to circulate freely within the Community. The 1987 amendment makes clear reference to the environmental concerns at stake. Article 7 of the original Directive pre-empts Member States from limiting or preventing the free movement of petrol because of its lead or benzol content. Some authors argue that this prevents Member States from applying Article 130t EC, as they would not comply with their obligations under Article 7 of the Directive or in any case with Article 5 EC.[50] This argument is not convincing. Article 130t permits adoption of more stringent measures under the conditions mentioned therein, including general observance of the Treaty, but for logical reasons cannot refer to provisions of the Directive based on Article 130s EC that leads to the adoption of higher domestic standards as this would preclude diverging national standards in any case.

Some authors fear that the explicit provisions for diverging domestic environmental measures, Article 130t and 100a(4) EC respectively, may lead to a circumvention of these mechanisms by the Community by simply choosing a different legal basis which does not provide for the possibility of adopting diverging national measures.[51] A possible solution, it has been suggested, would be to give Article 130t a general character which allows Member States to take more

[45] See also Kahl, n. 42 above, 43, with reference to J. Glaesner, 'Die Einheitliche Europäische Akte' [1986] *EuR* 119 at 142; E. Grabitz, 'Handlungsspielräume der EG-Mitgliedstaaten zur Verbesserung des Umweltschutzes—Das Beispiel der Umweltabgaben und -subventionen' [1989] *RIW* 623 at 624; Kapteyn and VerLoren van Themaat, n. 4 above, 403; J. Mertens de Wilmars, 'Het Hof van Justitie van de Europese Gemeenschappen en de Europese Akte' [1986] *SEW* 601 at 610 and many others.

[46] These authors also apply this reasoning to Art. 100a(4) see in particular Breier, n. 42 above, EuZW 624 at 626, with reference to Schröer, n. 42 above, 224; see also Breier, n. 42 above (RIW), 587.

[47] See also Kahl, n. 42 above, 43.

[48] The example is taken from Breier, n. 42 above (EuZW), 626 and Breier, n. 42 above (RIW), 587. I do not agree, however, with his findings and conclusions.

[49] Grabitz and Nettesheim, n. 40 above, para. 8; Breier, n. 42 above (EuZW), 626 and Breier, n. 42 above (RIW), 587.

[50] See in particular Breier, n. 42 above (EuZW), 626, with reference to Schröer, n. 42 above, 224; see also Breier, n. 42 above (RIW), 587.

[51] See Krämer, n. 3 above, 93 ff.; Epiney and Möllers, n. 11 above, 61.

stringent national measures whenever the environment is concerned.[52] This should be rejected,[53] as Article 130t concerns only measures adopted under Article 130s EC,[54] while Article 100a(4) is applicable for measures adopted under Article 100a EC. The risk that the Community may circumvent the provisions of Article 130t and 100a(4) EC by choosing a different legal basis has to be dealt with under the legal procedures provided for by the Treaty.[55] The case law of the Court has developed the principles for the choice of the correct legal basis.[56]

Notification Requirements

Since the entry into force of the Treaty on European Union Article 130t, second sentence, provides for a specific mandatory procedure of notifying diverging national measures by the Member States to the Commission.[57] In a similar way the introduction of more stringent measures under specific safeguard clauses (Article 130r(2), second subparagraph) is subject to a Community inspection procedure. This development follows the general Community system of notification[58] of national draft legislation, as under Article 100a(4) and (5) and more generally under Directive 83/189/EEC.[59]

THE COMMON AGRICULTURAL POLICY (ARTICLE 43)

General Observations

Under Articles 38 to 47 EC, the Community has hitherto had general competence to regulate areas concerning agriculture and trade in agricultural products.[60] Article 43 provides a sufficient legal basis for the development of a proper Community agricultural policy as well as for the approximation of rules concerning production and product requirements. As the notion 'agricultural products' is supposed also to include products of fisheries,[61] the Community bases its legal acts concerning the common fishery policy on Article 43.[62] In doing so the Community has to observe the general objectives of Article 39 of the Treaty.

---

[52] See Epiney and Möllers, n. 11 above, 61.

[53] See for details Epiney and Möllers, n. 11 above, 60 ff.

[54] See Krämer, n. 14 above, 164.   [55] First and foremost Art. 173 EC.

[56] See Case C–300/89 *Titanium Dioxide*, n. 11 above; Case C–155/91 *Waste Directive*, n. 11 above.

[57] See e.g. Middeke, n. 30 above, 354 to 356.

[58] See Ch. 8 on the notification procedure and its role in the system of the Treaty.

[59] See e.g. the considerations by Krämer, n. 3 above, 39 and 40.

[60] For a general survey on the Community's agricultural policy see F. Snyder, *Law of the Common Agricultural Policy* (Sweet & Maxwell, London, 1985).

[61] Art. 38(1), second sentence, EC; Case 185/73 *Hauptzollamt Bielefeld* v. *König* [1974] ECR 607; see F. Snyder, 'The Common Agricultural Policy in the Single European Market', in Academy of European Law (ed.), *Collected Courses of the Academy of European Law* (Martinus Nijhof, Dordrecht, 1992), 303 at 315.

Agricultural measures can have enormous environmental impact.[63] This is mainly the case when production and process standards as well as product standards for agricultural products are defined.[64] It is also true for the regulation of products which are used in agricultural production, such as pesticides[65] or hormones,[66] which directly affect the environment and animals. In its decision on the first Community directives on pesticides and foodstuff containing residues of pesticides the Court stated, '[i]t is not disputed that pesticides constitute a major risk to human and animal health and to the 'environment; this has moreover been recognized at Community level'.[67]

Community regulations under Articles 38–47 also have a very important environmental effect in the field of the common fishery policy. A basic element of the management of fisheries is the preservation of the existing fishery resources.[68] This is governed by purely internal regulations[69] as well as by the conclusion of international agreements on the preservation of fishery resources.[70]

The Appropriateness of Article 43

The close link between certain agricultural harmonization measures and protection of the environment also raises the question of the appropriateness of Article 43 for such legal acts. The approximation of laws concerning the common agricultural policy finds a sufficient legal basis in Article 43, even if such approximation covers environmentally important aspects which have a certain relationship with Article 130s. Article 43 no longer needs to rely on the more general Article 100 EC, as has, in the meantime, been confirmed by the Court

---

[62] See e.g. G. Schneider, 'Die Erhaltung und Bewirtschaftung der Fischereiressourcen im Rahmen der Gemeinsamen Fischereipolitik der EG' [1989] *RIW* 873 to 879.

[63] See e.g. Schröer, n. 42 above, 140, and W. Howarth, 'The Single European Market and Problems of Fish Movements' (1990) 15 *ELRev.* 34 at 35.

[64] See Henke, n. 26 above, 73; Pernice, n. 2 above, 23; R. Breuer, 'Die internationale Orientierung von Umwelt- und Technikstandards im deutschen und europäischen Recht' [1989] *UTR* 43 at 101; Krämer, Artikel 130r, para. 77 ff., in H. v. d. Groeben, J. Thiesing, and C.-D. Ehlermann (eds.), *Kommentar zum EWG-Vertag* (Nomos, Baden-Baden, 1983 ff).

[65] e.g. Dir. 91/414/EEC concerning the authorization of pesticides, n. 20 above.

[66] e.g. Dir. 85/358/EEC concerning the prohibition of certain substances with hormonal effect [1985] *OJ* L362/8 or Dir. 79/117/EEC prohibiting the placing on the market and use of plant protection products containing certain active substances [1979] *OJ* L33/36, amended in [1987] *OJ* L71/33.

[67] Case 94/83 *Criminal Proceedings against Hejin (Pesticides on Apples)* [1984] *ECR* 3263 at 3280.

[68] See Schneider, n. 62 above, 874.

[69] e.g. Reg. 170/83/EEC on the introduction of a common regulation for the preservation and management of fishery resources [1983] *OJ* L24/1 or Commission Reg. 93/25/EEC on the issuing of import documents for preserved tuna and bonito of certain species from certain non-member countries [1993] *OJ* L5/7.

[70] See Convention on the conservation of salmon in the North Atlantic [1982] *OJ* L378/25 or Convention on fishing and conservation of the living resources in the Baltic Sea [1983] *OJ* L237/5; see also the Court's decision in Joined cases 3, 4, and 6/76 *Criminal Proceedings against Cornelis Kramer et al. (Biological Resources of the Sea)* [1976] *ECR* 1279 at 1311.

of Justice[71] in spite of the former EC practice[72] and the Court's own earlier case law[73] to the contrary.[74]

'Article 43 of the Treaty is the appropriate legal basis for any legislation concerning the production and the marketing of agricultural products listed in Annex II to the Treaty which contributes to the achievement of one or more of the objectives of the common agricultural policy set out in Article 39 of the Treaty.'[75]

It seems that in these cases the primary purpose or main objective of the Directive was of little relevance, although it dealt first with the protection of human health (substances having a hormonal action) and secondly with the protection of the well-being of animals (protection of laying hens kept in battery cages). It therefore seems from the Court's case law that Article 43 is a perfectly appropriate legal basis for environmental regulations provided they cover the products and areas mentioned in Article 39 EC.[76] In a recent decision the Court has reaffirmed that Article 43 rather than Article 100 is the more specific provision (*lex specialis*) for the approximation of laws in the area of the common agricultural policy.[77] Academic thinking now shares this view.[78] The same principle governs the relationship between Articles 43 and 100a after the introduction of the latter in the framework of the Single European Act.[79]

Case: In Case 68/86 *United Kingdom* v. *Council (Hormone Case)*[80] the Court was concerned with the validity of Council Directive 81/102 prohibiting the use of hormonal and thyrostatic substances in livestock farming. In the parallel Case 131/86 *United Kingdom* v. *Council (Laying Hens)*[81] the United Kingdom challenged the validity of Directive 86/113 which had been adopted to comply with the Council of Europe's Convention for the Protection of Animals Kept for Farming Purposes.[82] In both cases the Council had

---

[71] Case 68/86 *United Kingdom* v. *Council (Substances Having Hormonal Action)* [1988] *ECR* 855 at 896 and Case 131/86 *United Kingdom* v. *Council (Laying Hens)* [1988] *ECR* 905 at 930.

[72] See e.g. C. Offermann-Clas, 'Die Kompetenzen der Europäischen Gemeinschaft im Umweltschutz' [1983] *ZfU* 56 at 58.

[73] Case 5/77 *Carlo Tedeschi* v. *Denkavit (Tedeschi/Denkavit)* [1977] *ECR* 1555.

[74] See also Snyder, n. 61 above, 324 ff.

[75] Case 68/86 *Substances Having a Hormonal Action*, n. 71 above, 896, and Case 131/86 *Laying Hens*, n. 71 above, 930; for comments see J. Bridge, 'Case 68/89 UK v. Council' (1988) 25 *CMLRev.* 723 to 742 or V. Goetz, 'Anmerkungen zu den Gerichtsurteilen dess Europäischen Gerichtshofs Rs 68/86 und 131/86 vom 23.12.1988' [1988] *EuR* 298 to 301.

[76] Krämer, n. 14 above, 151 at 153, referring to a Commission proposal on animal welfare in zoos [1991] *OJ* C300/7.

[77] Case 131/87 *Commission* v. *Council (Trade in Animal Glands)* [1989] *ECR* 3743 at 3770; for the *lex specialis* argument see Case 83/78 *Pigs Marketing Board* v. *Redmond* [1978] *ECR* 2347.

[78] See U. Becker, *Der Gestaltungsspielraum der der EG-Mitgliedstaaten im Spannungsfeld zwischen Umweltschutz und freiem Warenverkehr* (Nomos, Baden-Baden, 1991), 100; Epiney and Möllers, n. 11 above, 20; T. Oppermann, *Europarecht* (C. H. Beck, München, 1991), 420 and 492; E. Rehbinder and R. Stewart, *Environmental Protection Policy—Integration Through Law* (W. de Gruyter, New York, 1985), 19.

[79] Epiney and Möllers, n. 11 above, 20; Becker, n. 78 above, 100; Henke, n. 26 above, 75.

[80] Case 68/86 *Substances Having a Hormonal Action*, n. 71 above; for comments Bridge, n. 75 above, 733 to 742.

[81] Case 131/86 *Laying Hens*, n. 71 above; for comments see Bridge, n. 75 above.

adopted the Directives on the basis of Article 43 by qualified majority. The United Kingdom supported by Denmark sought the annulment of this Directive on grounds of insufficient legal basis and procedural irregularities. It was suggested that the contested Directives should have been based on Article 100 in addition to Article 43. They argued that the primary purpose of these Directives was the approximation of laws to safeguard health and consumer interests.[83] In both cases, however, the Court held Article 43 to be the appropriate legal basis as the Directives concerned the regulation of production and marketing of agricultural products in the sense of the Treaty.

There is no case law on Article 130s but it again seems appropriate to consider Article 43 to be applicable in cases where the purely ecological aspect of a measure is secondary to the objective of harmonization.[84] Some authors suggest that the introduction of Article 130r(2), second sentence (integration clause), leads to integration of environmental concerns into all the relevant Treaty provisions and therefore definitively renders Article 43 appropriate for environmental purposes.[85]

Article 43 and the Preservation of Fishery Resources

In the field of the common fisheries policy the Community has adopted several measures for the protection of fishery resources. The main instruments used are: (a) the creation of special zones where fishing is prohibited or restricted, (b) the regulation of fishing methods, (c) the regulation of the minimal size and weight for specific fish species, and (d) a quota system for the total allowable catch (TAC).[86] The relevant legal acts are based on Article 43 although it does not explicitly mention the field of a common fisheries policy.[87]

It seems that the original purpose of the introduction of such measures was mainly the economic fear that the constant over-fishing of the Community waters would endanger the prosperity of the European fishing industry. Therefore a Community regulation was supposed to be in the interest of the industries concerned.[88] Nevertheless, today these measures are considered to have a very important environmental effect. The preservation of fishery

---

[82] Approved by the Council on behalf of the Community by a Decision of 19 June 1978 [1978] *OJ* L323/12.

[83] For comments on these two cases see Bridge, n. 75 above, or Goetz, n. 75 above.

[84] See also Schröer, n. 42 above, 143.

[85] See Snyder, n. 61 above, 332, referring to the 'Reflection Paper', presented by the Commission on 31 January 1991: EC Commission, *Communication of the Commission to the Council on the Development and Future of the CAP*, COM(91)100 (EC, Brussels, 1991); see also Pernice, n. 2 above, 15; followed by Henke, n. 26 above, 75.

[86] Art. 2 of Reg. 170/83, n. 69 above.

[87] See, however, also Art. 103 of the Act of Accession of the United Kingdom [1972] *OJ* L73/1; for details see Schneider, n. 62 above, 873 ff.

[88] See Joined cases 3, 4, and 6/76 *Biological Resources of the Sea*, n. 70 above, 1311, and e.g. Art. 1 of Reg. 170/83/EEC, n. 69 above; see for comments A. T. Koers, 'The External Authority of the EEC in Regard to Marine Fisheries' (1977) 14 *CMLRev*. 269 to 301.

resources is also regulated in international environmental agreements[89] to which the Community is a party.

Diverging National Measures

The approximation of rules based on Article 43 can lead to a complete regulation in certain areas. This means that measures can be adopted with a qualified majority and there is no possible application of any general safeguard provision such as in Article 100a(4) or Article 130t. If a legal act based on Article 43 regulates a specific area exhaustively the Member States retain no power to apply diverging national measures.[90] As in other areas it is, however, possible that the Community acts based on Article 43 provide only for minimum standards or list only a basic set of products whose commercialisation may not be hindered.[91]

Example: An interesting example is Directive 91/414/EEC on the authorization of pesticides. It is based on Article 43 EC, as it was suggested that the trade in pesticides and their use mainly concerns the competitive situation in agriculture. In Annex A it provides for the elaboration of a list containing all the permitted effective substances which may form pesticides in the Community. If such a list contained, for example, atrazina, a substance currently forbidden in Germany and The Netherlands, these countries would have to allow this substance back on to the market.[92]

If the legislation in question provides explicitly for options for the Member States,[93] the latter remain free to take their own measures. They must, however, keep in mind the other Treaty obligations. This also applies in the absence of any relevant Community regulation.[94] In relation to Article 43 this has been repeatedly stated by the Court in several cases[95] concerning pesticides and agricultural products containing residues of pesticides.[96]

---

[89] Convention for the protection of the Mediterranean against pollution (Barcelona Convention) [1977] *OJ* L240/3, Convention on fishing and conservation of the living resources in the Baltic Sea and the Belts [1983] OJ L237/5 or, Agreement for co-operation in dealing with the pollution of the North Sea by oil and other harmful substances (Bonn Agreement) [1984] OJ L188/9.

[90] Henke, n. 26 above, 76; P. Gilsdorf and D. Boos, Art. 43, para. 37, in Grabitz and Hilf (eds.), n. 40 above, referring to the relevant case law.

[91] e.g. Dir. 91/414/EEC on the authorization of pesticides, n. 20 above.

[92] See n. 20 above and Krämer, n. 11 above, 134.

[93] See e.g. Dir. 76/895/EEC on the fixing of maximum levels of pesticide residues in and on fruit and vegetables [1976] *OJ* L340/26 and Dir. 79/117/EEC prohibiting the placing on the market and use of plant products containing certain active substances, n. 66 above.

[94] Case 272/80 *Criminal Procedure against FNMBP (Plant Protection Products)* [1981] *ECR* 3277 at 3290.

[95] Case 94/83 *Pesticides on Apples*, n. 67 above, 3279; Case 54/85 *Ministère Public* v. *Xavier Mirepoix (Pesticides on Fruits)* [1985] *ECR* 1067; Case 125/88 *Criminal Proceedings against Nijman (Pesticide Residues on Apples)* [1989] *ECR* 3533.

[96] See e.g. Krämer, n. 11 above, 115, referring to possible restrictions in use of pesticides under Dir. 91/414/ EEC, n. 20 above.

THE COMMON TRANSPORT POLICY (ARTICLES 75 AND 84 (2))

General Observations

Article 75 explicitly provides the Community with competence to enact a common transport policy. According to Article 84(1) EC the common transport policy includes transport by rail, road, and inland waterway. Nevertheless Article 84(2) EC allows for the widening of competence to cover sea and air transport. In spite of its general competence the Community has not yet adopted a coherent transport policy[97] but has, rather, taken some specific measures in certain areas.[98] It is clear that transport measures can have important environmental effects, as can easily be seen in the field of car traffic and air pollution.[99] Traffic and transport issues in general have become one of today's main factors in environmental policy. In particular, the introduction of tax incentives and related economic instruments for the reduction of air pollution, noise emissions, or environmental harm in general have given the transport issue a special weight in today's discussion.[100]

The Appropriateness of Articles 75 and 84(2)

Over the past few years traffic regulation for environmental reasons has indeed become increasingly important in the Community and its Member States.[101] Community measures to regulate transport issues[102] in most cases involve environment-related aspects. In the framework of the common transport policy the Community pursues the objectives of the Treaty in general[103] (Article 74) which obviously include the adequate protection of the environment[104]

In relation to Articles 100, 100a, and 130s EC, Article 75 is the more specific provision (*lex specialis*) in those cases where a measure aims mainly at the

---

[97] See, however, the programme presented by the Commission as 'the future development of the Common Transport Policy', COM(92)494 final, suppl. to [1993] *EC Bulletin* (no. 3).

[98] In spite of the judgment in Case 13/83 *Parliament* v. *Council* (*Common Transport Policy*) [1985] *ECR* 1513; see also Oppermann, n. 78 above, 531, or e.g. Dir. 89/629/EEC on the limitation of noise emissions from subsonic aircraft [1989] *OJ* L363/27.

[99] See Schröer, n. 42 above, 151.

[100] See for the environmental impact of transport, EC Commission, *A Community Strategy for Sustainable Mobility*, COM(92)46 (final) of 20 Feb. 1992.

[101] e.g. Council Dir. 80/51/EEC on noise levels of certain airplanes [1980] *OJ* L18/26 or Council Dir. 79/116/EEC concerning minimum requirements for certain tankers entering or leaving Community ports [1979] *OJ* L33/33.

[102] For a discussion on the effective competence see S. Lütkes, 'Kompetenz der EG für Geschwindigkeitsbeschränkungen für PKW auf Autobahnen' [1991] *EuZW* 277 to 281.

[103] Henke, n. 26 above, 76, Becker, n. 78 above, 101; and Pernice, n. 2 above, 25, are of the same opinion.

[104] e.g. Case 240/83 *Procureur de la République* v. *Association de Défense des Brûleurs d'Huiles Usagées* (*ADBHU*) [1985] *ECR* 531.

regulation of transport issues in the sense of Article 75.[105] Yet as far as the harmonization of technical standards and norms in the transport sector is concerned the Community has based certain directives on Article 100 and 100a respectively.[106] The Commission has also for some time been seeking a regulation for a community-wide speed limit on motorways, but so far without success.[107] The legal basis for such a regulation is disputed, as several options seem possible.[108] The recent Directive for the harmonization of heavy motor-vehicle taxes and charges for the use of motorways was based on Articles 75 and 99 EC taken together because of the important fiscal issues at stake.[109]

The use of economic incentives and disincentives for the promotion of certain means of transport or specific technical equipment which help to reduce energy consumption or noise and pollution have become very important in the discussion among economists and politicians.[110] The harmonization of car taxes or other tax instruments in the transport area for a coherent application of the 'polluter-pays' principle might be based (additionally) on Article 75 in spite of the specific tax provisions under Article 99.[111] On the whole, Articles 75 and 84(2) will probably become increasingly important for the adoption of environment-related measures of the Community. Provided that these measures aim principally at the regulation of traffic issues, Article 84 is the correct legal basis even if they also have an important environmental impact.[112]

---

[105] Compare the Court's case law on the relationship between Art. 100 and Art. 43, Ch. 8, and Henke, n. 26 above, 77; B. Langeheine, Art. 100a, para. 15, in Grabitz, n. 40 above.

[106] See e.g. Dir. 70/157/EEC on the approximation of laws of the Member States relating to type-approval of motor vehicles and their trailers (exhaust systems) [1970] *OJ* L42/16 or Dir. 71/320/EEC on the approximation of laws of the Member States relating to the breaking devices of certain categories of motor vehicles and of their trailers (Brake Dir.) [1971] *OJ* L202/37.

[107] See for details S. Lütkes, *Zulässigkeit von Geschwindigkeitsbeschränkungen auf Autobahnen nach dem EWG-Vertrag—insbesondere unter Berücksichtigung der gemeinschaftsrechtlichen Verkehrs- und Umweltpolitik sowie des freien Warenverkehrs in der EG* (Kommentator-Verlag, Neuwied and Frankfurt a.M., 1990), 27 ff.; also Lütkes, n. 102 above, 277 ff.

[108] Lütkes, n. 107 above, 89 ff., and also Lütkes, n. 102 above, 277. He argues mainly for Art. 130s, while Henke, n. 26 above, 77, or P. Behrens, *Rechtsgrundlagen der Umweltpolitik der Europäischen Gemeinschaften Heft 55 A* (Beiträge zur Umweltgestaltung, Berlin, 1976), 125, could imagine such measures under Arts. 75 ff.

[109] Dir. 93/89/EEC [1993] *OJ* L279/32. This Dir. was annulled, however, by the Court at the request of the European Parliament which felt its rights of participation had been circumvented, but its effects are preserved until new legislation is adopted in the matter: see Case C–21/94 *Parliament v. Council*, judgment of 5 July 1995 [1995] *OJ* C229/8 and 9. For comments see P. Mückenhausen, 'Die Harmonisierung der Abgaben auf den Strassengüterverkehr in der Europäischen Gemeinschaft' [1994] *EuZW* 519 to 528.

[110] e.g. F. Stähler, 'Eine Analyse möglicher Instrumente zur Reduktion von CO_2-Emissionen in der Bundesrepublik Deutschland' [1990] *Zeitschrift für Energiewirtschaft* 273 to 284 or J. Heister, P. Michaelis and E. Mohr, 'The Use of Tradable Emission Permits For Limiting CO_2-Emissions' [1992] *European Economy*, spec. edn., 'The Economics of Limiting CO_2-Emissions', 27 to 61.

[111] Dir. 93/89/EEC, n. 109 above, was based on both provisions. The contents of the Dir. remain in force despite its annulment by the Court: see Case C–21/94, n. 109 above ; see also Henke, n. 26 above, 78, who refers to Behrens, n. 108 above, 122 ff.

[112] See Pernice, n. 2 above, 25. See, however, for the limitations as far as environmental issues are concerned: Lütkes, n. 102 above, 278.

National Transport Measures

As described above, the Community has adopted only very few specific regulations in the field of transport. Therefore, inspired by the current discussion, many Member States have introduced or are trying to introduce specific duties, taxes, and subsidies for the promotion of environmentally friendly means of transport and technical equipment such as catalytic converters or certain types of fuel. Here again, in principle, such measures are lawful if they respect the obligations of the Treaty and do not interfere with any Community regulation that exhaustively covers the field and does not provide specific options for the Member States.[113]

As far as the use of economic instruments in transport/environment issues is concerned a close link exists between the provisions of Articles 92 (state aids) and 95 (taxes) and the specific transport provisions of Articles 75 and 84(2). As far as subsidies are concerned, Article 77 amends the general rules of Article 92 on state aids. It explicitly allows state aids to be granted for the purpose of the co-ordination of transport policy or as a reimbursement for the discharge of certain obligations, inherent in the concept of public service. This obviously also includes subsidies for public transport for environmental considerations.[114] Nevertheless, the general provisions of Articles 92–94 EC. and, in particular, the procedural requirements and the non-discrimination principle remain applicable.[115]

The introduction of particular duties and taxes for cars according to their technical equipment or pollution levels as well as tolls for the use of particular roads[116] remains within the competence of the Member States provided they comply with the existing Community acts under Articles 99, 75, and 84(2).[117] In particular, they have to observe the rules of Article 95 and, possibly, Article 30. The same is true for product standards and production or process measures as well as related regulations concerning means of transport.[118]

---

[113] Dir. 93/89/EEC, n. 109 above, leaves the domestic authorities with a relatively wide discretion; see, however, Case C–21/94, n. 109 above; for more examples, see Krämer, n. 11 above, 114.

[114] Henke, n. 26 above, 79; Behrens, n. 108 above, 123; Frohmeyer, Art. 77, paras. 4 and 9, in Grabitz, n. 40 above.

[115] Case 156/77 *Commission* v. *Belgium (Transport Aid)* [1978] *ECR* 1881 at 1895; see: Henke, n. 26 above, 78; G. von Wallenberg, Art. 92, para. 34, in Grabitz and Hilf (eds.), n. 40 above.

[116] Such as motorways or urban traffic ways.

[117] See, however, the recently adopted Council Dir. 93/89/EEC, n. 109 above, based on Arts. 75 and 99; the Dir. has been annulled but its contents remain in force: Case C–21/94, n. 109 above; for purely internal taxes for car owners see M. Jachmann, 'Die Einführung einer Nahverkehrsabgabe durch Landesgesetz' [1992] *NVwZ* 932 to 939.

[118] Such as national speed limits or a temporary prohibition of certain transport means on grounds of smog, for details: C. Moench, 'Die Fahrverbotsregelungen der Smog-Verordnungen auf dem Prüfstand des EG-Rechts' [1989] *NVwZ* 335 ff.; K. Heinz, 'Nochmals: Die Fahrverbotsregelungen der Smog-Verordnungen auf dem Prüfstand des EG-Rechts' [1989] *NVwZ* 1035 ff.; K. Hailbronner, 'Der "nationale Alleingang" im Gemeinschaftsrecht am Beispiel der Abgasstandards für PKW' [1989] *EuGRZ* 101 ff.; see also Chs. 3 and 5.

Example: Most countries now differentiate between taxes on different types of fuel, usually favouring lead-free fuel and diesel. It is also lawful to introduce different taxes for cars according to ecological evaluations, such as lower taxes for diesel cars[119] and small cars[120] or tax incentives for cars with catalytic converters.[121] So far the introduction of such instruments for ecological reasons has caused problems only because of its allegedly discriminatory treatment of domestic and foreign car-owners or producers under Article 76 or Article 95.[122]

The Stand-still Obligation (Article 76)

The Member States thus remain relatively free to adopt their own measures as long as the Community has not adopted any comprehensive transport measures. For the time prior to the adoption of such measures Article 76 contains a stand-still requirement for national measures.[123] It prohibits the introduction of discriminatory[124] transport regulations,[125] which are in contradiction with the various provisions governing the transport policy between the Member States before the coming into force of the Treaty. National transport measures become unlawful if the existing situation is changed in a way which makes it less favourable for carriers from other Member States than for nationals.[126] It becomes clear, however, from the case law that Article 76 does not preclude national measures justified for the protection of the environment and applied in a non-discriminatory way.

Article 76 seeks to avoid any deterioration of the situation for non-domestic carriers in comparison to domestic carriers. While certain legal authors favour the interpretation of Article 76 as a non-discrimination principle which would allow a change in the existing legal framework in a Member State[127] if it leads

---

[119] Case 200/85 *Commission* v. *Italy* (*Diesel Engines*) [1986] *ECR* 3953, commented on in [1987] *RIW* 633; see the relevant case law on Art. 95 in Ch. 3.

[120] Case C–132/88 *Commission* v. *Greece* (*Taxation of Motor Cars*) [1990] *ECR* I–1567 at 1591 and 1592.

[121] See e.g. Case C–105/91 *Commission* v. *Greece* (*Automobile Taxes*) [1992] *ECR* I–5871 at 5897.

[122] All three quoted national regs. have been attacked by the Commission on grounds of a presumed discriminatory application.

[123] For details: A. Bleckmann, *Europarecht* (Heymann, Köln, 1990), paras. 1730 ff.

[124] Apart from the general non-discrimination requirements of Arts. 5, 30 ff., 92, and 95 EC.

[125] This also covers a stricter application of existing regulations or a change in the administrative practice. See Joined cases C–184 and C–221/91 *Criminal Proceedings against Christof Oorburg and Serge van Meesem*, judgment of 31 Mar. 1993.

[126] Case C–195/90 *Commission* v. *Germany* (*Tax on Heavy Goods Vehicles*) [1992] *ECR* I–3141 at 3183. For comments: J. Basedow, 'Besprechung zum EuGH-Urteil C–195/90' [1992] *JZ* 868 ff.; for a critical approach and the relationship between Arts. 76 and 95 see S. Heselhaus, 'Gemeinschaftsrechtliche Vorgaben für Strassenbenützungsgebühren für den Schwerverkehr' [1993] *EuZW* 311 at 312.

[127] C. T. Ebenroth *et al.*, 'Vereinbarkeit des Strassenbenützungsgebührengesetzes mit dem EWG-Vertrag' [1990] *BB* 2125 to 2135; A. Frohnmeyer, Art. 76, para. 6, in Grabitz and Hilf (eds.), n. 40 above; R. Breuer, 'Umweltrechtliche und wirtschaftslenkende Abgaben im europäischen Binnenmarkt' [1992] *DVBl.* 485 at 496.

to a situation which disadvantages domestic car owners, this does not seem to be the Court's interpretation.[128]

Case: In Case C–196/90 *Commission* v. *Germany (Charge on Heavy Goods Vehicles)* the Commission claimed that Germany had neglected its Treaty obligations by introducing a special charge for heavy goods vehicles using federal roads and motorways. This charge was to be paid by all heavy goods vehicles regardless of their place of registration. Simultaneously, the German law governing the general motor vehicle tax for German vehicles was changed in a way which entailed a reduction of the tax for certain heavy goods vehicles.[129] The German government justified its new legislation *inter alia* by the environmental effect which a general charge on trucks using the motorways would have, as this led to more frequent use of other, more ecological, means of transport. The Court held that the combination of the two measures (new charge and reduction of taxes of domestic car owners) had the effect of giving rise to a discriminatory change in the existing situation contrary to Article 76 EC between carriers registered in Germany and those from other Member States,[130] which would make it more difficult for the Council to introduce a common transport policy (Article 76). The Court underlined that the protection of the environment was one of the main objectives of the Community but that the quasi-compensation of German carriers was not justified for ecological reasons.[131] Consequently, Germany cancelled the reduction of the domestic car-owner tax.[132]

Such discrimination may also be created by new duties or requirements which indirectly burden non-domestic car-owners more than domestic car-owners.[133] This may be the case if, for example, they very seldom use a foreign motorway system and still have to pay the same amount as a national.[134] This is not the case , however, if the toll or duty is in strict relation to the use of the motorway system[135] or the pollution produced.[136] Measures that have an influence on the

---

[128] See for criticism: H. J. Brauns and J. Riedel, 'EG-Verträglichkeit von Autobahn-Gebühren' [1991] *RIW* 224 to 228; Basedow, n. 126 above; Heselhaus, n. 126 above.

[129] In the meantime, Council Dir. 93/89/EEC, n. 109 above, was adopted; see, however, Case C–21/94, n. 109 above. [130] Case C–195/90 *Tax on Heavy Goods Vehicles*, n. 126 above, 3183.

[131] Case C–195/90 *Tax on Heavy Goods Vehicles*, n. 126 above, comments in [1992] *EuZW* 390 to 392. See also Ebenroth *et al.*, n. 127 above, 2126 ff., who argue that the reimbursement of the duty by lowering the applicable tax rate was not discriminatory as it reflected the result of the existing tax differences within the Community.

[132] See on the domestic (German) legal problems which resulted from the retroactive annulment of the administrative act, Case 292015 K5 before the Finanzgericht Bremen, judgment of 20 Oct. 1992 [1993] *RIW* 156 to 161; the introduction of Dir. 93/89/EEC, n. 109 above, has introduced a Community system which allows Germany to adopt measures equivalent to the originally envisaged solution under the domestic system. See Mückenhausen, n. 109 above, 520. See also Case C–21/94, n. 109 above.

[133] For general considerations on the harmonization of the competitive situation in the EC transport sector see V. Schmitt, 'Die Harmonisierung der Wettbewerbsbedingungen in der EG-Binnenverkehrspolitik' [1993] *EuZW* 305 to 310.

[134] This is discussed in detail by Brauns and Riedel, n. 128 above, 226.

[135] Such as the duties for the use of certain motorways in Spain, France, or Italy. The new Art. 7g of the Community Dir. allowing the facultative introduction of motorway tolls states: 'User charges rates shall be in proportion to the duration of the use made of the infrastructure.' Dir. 93/89/EEC, n. 109 above, was formally annulled in Case C–21/94, n. 109 above; see also COM (92)405 final, or [1992] *OJ* C311/63; see Schmitt, n. 133 above, 309.

[136] Such as specific duties on petrol or a tax differentiation between different car types on the basis of their emissions.

use of certain vehicles may, apart from their non-discriminatory application under Article 76 and 95,[137] pose certain problems under Article 30 to 36.[138]

Case: The Belgian Government had already in 1967 proposed to introduce a special duty in the form of a particular car sticker (vignette) for the use of its motorways. Instead of such a sticker the Belgian government in 1973 introduced a special tax on petrol of one Belgian Franc and in 1979 raised general car taxes. In 1987, it was proposed that a special sticker be introduced for the use of Belgian motorways. It was planned that Belgian car-owners should receive it without any further payment as they paid car taxes in Belgium.[139] Foreign car-owners would have had to buy it. After heavy criticism from the other Member States and the initiation of an inquiry procedure by the Commission the sticker proposal was abandoned. The Commission had warned that it discriminated against non-nationals and jeopardized the free movement of goods and persons.[140]

ENVIRONMENT-RELATED SOCIAL POLICY (ARTICLE 118A)

The Single European Act introduced a new specific legal basis for the harmonization of laws concerning the health and safety of workers. Article 118a refers to the improvement of the 'working environment' as an objective which shall be attained by adopting Community measures. The working environment could be considered to be a particular, more specific aspect of the protection of the environment in general. But Article 118a aims more specifically at the improvement of working conditions in the framework of the Community social policy.[141] In spite of the existing connection between the two areas Article 118a has a different objective from Article 130s and is more specific than Article 100a.[142] It is, however, possible to conceive of certain measures adopted under Article 118a aiming at the protection of the health and safety of workers as environmental measures.[143] This seems, however, only to be useful for a legal analysis of the Treaty and not very helpful in practice.

If the Community adopts a measure under Article 118a the Member States

---

[137] See for considerations on tolls under Art. 95, Heselhaus, n. 126 above, 313, Brauns and Riedel, n. 128 above, 227, and Ebenroth *et al.*, n. 127 above 2130.

[138] e.g. the prohibition on the use of certain vehicles which do not fulfil national requirements in spite of existing Community legislation, such as the German prohibition on the use of cars without catalytic convertors in smog, see Moench, n. 118 above, 335, and Heinz, n. 118 above.

[139] Switzerland has had such a motorway duty in the form of a special sticker (*vignette*) since 1985, but all users have to buy it, i.e. Swiss car-owners and foreigners, irrespective of the total use of the motorway system.

[140] See Brauns and Riedel, n. 128 above, 226 with more references.

[141] Krämer, n. 14 above, 153, stresses that measures concerning noise level at work places etc. should be considered rather as social policy measures than as environmental measures in the Commission's view.

[142] For a detailed study of the differences between the application of Arts. 130s and 118a see Schröer, n. 42 above, 249.

[143] e.g Dir. 80/1107/EEC concerning the protection of workers against certain dangerous substances [1980] *OJ* L327/8 or the proposal for a new dir. on dangerous biological substances at work [1989] *OJ* L183/1.

are still able to maintain or introduce their own national measures in the field (Article 118 a(3)). As with Articles 100a(4) and 130t, the only requirements under the Treaty are that they must be more stringent and that they must be compatible with the other Treaty provisions. Their more stringent character is a logical consequence of the Community competence to elaborate minimum requirements (standards) under this provision: Article 118a(2). As has been shown before, the compatibility of national measures with the Treaty is a systematic requirement for all national measures under the law of the Treaty.

ENVIRONMENTAL RESEARCH POLICY (ARTICLE 130o)

Article 130o EC introduced under the Treaty of European Union systematically replaces Article 130q(2), introduced under the Single European Act (SEA). It aims roughly at the establishment of a Community research policy consisting mainly of the establishment of joint undertakings and other structures for Community research and technical development (Article 130n). Environmental research has been part of the Community's policies since the early 1970s.[144] Before the coming into force of the Treaty on European Union, certain environmental research programmes[145] with environmental objectives were based on the old Article 130q(2).[146]

In the framework of the present analysis Article 130o will not be dealt with in detail, as it does not lead to any restriction of the Member States concerning their own environmental policy.[147] In the field of environmental research the Community as well as the Member States has its own policies which may lead to a certain level of co-ordination of programmes and projects.

---

[144] Schröer, n. 42 above, 191; G. Fülgraff, 'Forschung für die Umwelt' in L. Gündling and B. Weber (eds.), *Dicke Luft in Europa* (Müller Juristischer Verlag, Heidelberg, 1988), 95 at 99.

[145] Council Decision 89/625/EEC on two specific programmes related to research and technological development in the field of the environment: STEP and EPOCH (1989 to 1992) [1989] *OJ* L359/9.

[146] At the same time Art. 130r may include environmental research, see e.g. Krämer, n. 3 above, 49. For discussion on the use of the appropriate legal basis see Schröer, n. 42 above, 191.

[147] See, however, the implications from the Community provisions on competition, as described in Ch. 6.

10

Economic Pricing Instruments at Community Level

INTRODUCTION

Pricing instruments for the establishment of incentives and disincentives concerning ecological behaviour are increasingly important elements of environmental policy. Economic literature recommends the use of such instruments, while it is sometimes rather sceptical of the use of prohibitions, restrictions, and fixed standards. In the current discussion the proposed instruments are mainly taxes and emission charges, while state aids do infringe to a certain extent the 'polluter pays' principle. The Community itself may take such measures under several Treaty provisions.

Article 99 provides the Community with the competence to harmonize indirect taxation. The Community has recently achieved a harmonization of the minimum standards for value added tax (VAT). Apart from this there are harmonized minimum standards for excise duties on alcohol, tobacco, and mineral oils. The Member States may introduce other excise duties if they do not lead to any border formalities which would hinder the establishment of the internal market. As Article 99 does not apply to direct taxation and to production charges the Member States maintain the right to introduce emission charges, environmental taxes, or pollution duties. The other Treaty provisions which have to be observed are in particular Articles 9, 12, 30, and 95.

The existence of Community subsidies in certain environmentally relevant areas does not preclude the Member States from granting their own state aids. Nevertheless, the provisions of Articles 92–94 EC also limit the Member States' use of environmental subsidies. The Community has adopted certain programmes for environmentally justified regional subsidies under Article 130e(1) apart from research programmes under Article 130r–t EC.

INDIRECT TAXATION AND THE ENVIRONMENT (ARTICLE 99)

General Observations

Environmental taxes or 'green taxes'[1] have been promoted vigorously during the last few years.[2] Economic theory shows that these pricing instruments for envir-

---

[1] e.g. higher taxes for goods not produced in an environmentally friendly manner or special tax incentives for those that have been so produced.

[2] See for general considerations on environmental taxes and charges E. Grabitz and C. Zacker,

onmental behaviour are often more effective than prohibitions or technical product or production requirements.[3] Furthermore, they correspond to the 'polluter
pays' principle.[4] The general principles of non-discrimination and non-
protectionist use of internal taxes under Article 95 EC also apply to environmentally justified domestic taxes.[5]

On the occasion of a meeting of the Ministers of the Environment and Energy
in 1990 the European Council encouraged the Member States to adopt economic and fiscal instruments for the protection of the environment which are
compatible with the Treaty.[6] In the same year the European Parliament adopted
a decision which urged the Commission to submit a proposal for a tax related
to the use of primary energy in the framework of global climate protection.[7] In
general such Community environmental taxes are discussed under the Articles
99, 100, 100a, and 130s, to a lesser extent also under the specific chapters on
the common agricultural policy (Article 43), the common transport policy, and
the Community budget (Article 201).[8] In this Chapter I will look at the system
of Article 99, its use by the Community, and the scope for action by Member
States after the introduction of measures under Article 99 EC.[9]

Article 99 and Indirect Taxation

Since the coming into force of the Single European Act the newly formulated
Article 99 EC entrusts the Community with the task of adopting 'provisions for
the harmonization of legislation concerning turnover taxes, excise duties and
other forms of indirect taxation'. These provisions shall, however, only be taken
'to the extent that such harmonization is necessary to ensure the establishment
and the functioning of the internal market'.

'Scope for Action by EC Member States for the Improvement of Environmental Protection Under
EEC Law: The Example of Environmental Taxes and Subsidies' (1989) 26 *CMLRev.* 423 to 447;
R. Breuer, 'Umweltrechtliche und wirtschaftslenkende Abgaben im europäischen Binnenmarkt'
[1992] *DVBl.* 485 to 496; M. Kloepfer, 'Rechtsprobleme einer CO_2-Abgabe' [1992] *DVBl.* 195 to
204; M. Hilf, 'Umweltabgaben als Gegenstand von Gemeinschaftsrecht und -politik' [1992] *NVwZ*
105 to 111.

[3] See e.g. F. Stähler, 'Eine Analyse möglicher Instrumente zur Reduktion von CO_2-Emissionen
in der Bundesrepublik Deutschland' [1990] *Zeitschrift für Energiewirtschaft* 273 to 284, J. Heister,
P. Michaelis, and E. Mohr, 'The Use of Tradable Emission Permits for Limiting CO_2-Emissions'
[1992] *European Economy*, spec. edn., 'The Economics of Limiting CO_2-Emissions', 27 to 61.

[4] Such as referred to in Art. 130r(2) EC.

[5] Most cases of disputed environmental taxes before the Court of Justice concerned their
discriminatory application. The Court supported them when they were applied in a non-
discriminatory way and did not infringe other provisions of the Treaty. See e.g. Case 200/85 *Commission
v. Italy (Diesel Vehicles)* [1986] *ECR* 3953 at 3971; Joined cases 78 to 83/90 *Compagnie Commerciale de l'Ouest
et al.* v. *Receveur principal des douanes de La Pallice Port* [1992] *ECR* I–1847. See in general Ch. 3.

[6] See [1990] *EC Bulletin* (no. 6), para. 1.17 and [1990] *EC Bulletin* (no. 10), para. 1.3.78; see also
Hilf, n. 2 above, 106.

[7] Decision on economic and fiscal instruments of environmental policy [1991] *OJ* C183/296.

[8] See for details Hilf, n. 2 above, 105 ff.; Breuer, n. 2 above, 485 ff.

[9] For fiscal measures under the other provisions of the Treaty see the relevant chs.

Article 99 was introduced under the Single European Act to ensure the abolition of borders and border controls within the Community also with respect to fiscal aspects. Before the accomplishment of the harmonization of indirect taxation on products the fiscal treatment of imported goods follows the 'destination principle'.[10] This implies that the Community system allows for the reimbursement of domestic indirect taxes and taxation at the border of the importing country with a border tax adjustment when goods are imported. Article 95 provides that the imported goods shall not be more heavily taxed than domestic products.[11] Additionally, Article 96 provides that any reimbursement of internal taxation should not exceed the internal taxation imposed on them whether directly or indirectly.[12] Taxes which are not imposed on products but 'upon the producing undertaking in the very varied aspects of its general commercial and financial activity' cannot be reimbursed under Article 96.[13]

As long as taxes differ, the application of this system makes border controls necessary, while the internal market as described in Article 7a EC aims at the elimination of such controls and the establishment of an area without internal frontiers. Under the premise that differing indirect taxation without the existing system of tax adjustments would lead to competitive distortions, the harmonization of indirect taxation seems to be the necessary complement of the abolition of border controls and readjustments.[14]

In the field of 'green taxes' Article 99 applies mainly to consumer taxes, that is, taxes levied on products while taxes on the production[15] itself should rather be based on Articles 100, 100a,[16] or even 130s EC as they concern the competitive conditions of the production of goods.[17] Similarly, the imposition of spe-

---

[10] As in international trade in general; see e.g. in GATT Art. III:2 in conjunction with Art. III:8 (b) as exemplified in GATT, *Basic Instruments and Selected Decisions*, 23rd suppl. (GATT, Geneva, 1977), 98, and GATT, *Basic Instruments and Selected Decisions*, 28th suppl. (GATT, Geneva, 1982), 114; for comments see J. H. Jackson, *The World Trading System* (MIT Press, Cambridge, Mass., 1989), 194.

[11] See also Ch. 3; Art. 95 applies also to discrimination on exported goods, see Case 142/77 *Statens Kontrol med Œdle Metaller* v. *Larsen* [1978] *ECR* 1543 at 1553.

[12] The term 'directly' does not imply that direct taxes can always be reimbursed but merely relates to taxes levied on final products. 'Indirectly' relates to raw materials and semi-finished goods used in the manufacture of exported goods; see Case 45/64 *Commission* v. *Italy* [1965] *ECR* 1057; see also D. Wyatt and A. Dashwood, *European Community Law* (3rd edn., Sweet & Maxwell, London, 1993), 203 and 204.

[13] Case 45/64, n. 12 above, 1066.

[14] See also T. Oppermann, *Europarecht* (C. H. Beck, München, 1992), 402; O. Brunetti, *EG-Rechtsverträglichkeit als Kriterium der nationalen Umweltpolitik* (Schulthess and Stämpfli, Zürich and Bern, 1993), 148.

[15] Such as duties or levies for the production of sewage or waste, pollution, use of herbicides, or fertilizers etc.

[16] It is disputed whether the term 'fiscal provisions' which is explicitly excluded from the application of Art. 100a also comprises environmental charges, see Hilf, n. 2 above, 105; Brunetti, n. 14 above, 149 argues that this is not the case.

[17] P. J. G. Kapteyn and P. VerLoren van Themaat, *Introduction to the Law of the European Communities* (2nd edn., Kluwer, Deventer, 1989), 474; Breuer, n. 2 above, 495; I. Pernice, 'Auswirkungen des europäischen Binnenmarktes auf das Umweltrecht—Gemeinschafts(verfassungs-)rechtliche Grundlagen [1990] *NVwZ* 201 at 204.

cific taxes in certain sectors, such as the introduction of tolls for the use of certain motorways or roads falls usually under the application of the special provisions of the Treaty.[18] The appropriate legal basis of Community measures may, however, be disputed.[19]

Existing 'Environmental' Taxes under Article 99

Apart from the introduction of a uniform system of value added tax (VAT) and the general harmonization of the minimum VAT rates only the harmonization[20] of certain specific consumer taxes has been achieved.[21] The Community has adopted a directive which limits the application of excise duties to three categories of products.[22] The harmonization comprises excise duties on alcohol and alcoholic beverages, tobacco, and cigarettes as well as mineral oils.[23]

The most interesting area of excise duties for the protection of the environment is thus the existing system for the harmonization of the tax levels on mineral oils. The recently adopted Directive 92/82/EEC[24] sets the minimum level of taxation for certain mineral oils, while Directive 92/80/EEC[25] basically concerns the harmonization of the tax structure. Both are based on Article 99 alone. The Community Directive leaves the Member States with a relatively wide discretion to implement higher taxes, as it only provides for minimum standards and a common system for the structure of the taxation.

The second, very interesting example of a harmonized tax with an important environmental impact is the recently adopted harmonization of the minimum standards for heavy goods vehicles and tolls and charges for the use of motorways

---

[18] See e.g. J. Henke, *EuGH und Umweltschutz* (VVF, München, 1992), 78.

[19] See for Dir. 91/414/EEC on car emissions and possible fiscal incentives [1993] *OJ* L242/1, in L. Krämer, 'Environmental Protection and Art. 30 EEC Treaty' (1993) 30 *CMLRev.* 111 at 143 and also L. Krämer, 'L'environnement et le marché unique européen' [1993] *RMC* 45 at 60.

[20] See for details Reicherts, Art. 99, paragraph 31, in H. v. d. Groeben, J. Thiesing, and C.-D. Ehlermann (eds.), *Kommentar zum EWG-Vertrag* (Nomos, Baden-Baden, 1983 ff.).

[21] See on the problems during the negotiations: Kapteyn and VerLoren van Themaat, n. 17 above, 373.

[22] Dir. 92/12/EEC on the general arrangements for products subject to excise duty and on the holding, movement, and monitoring of such products [1992] *OJ* L76/1.

[23] e.g. for alcohol: Dir. 92/83/EEC on the harmonization of the structure of consumer taxes on alcohol and alcoholic beverages [1992] *OJ* L316/21 and Dir. 92/84/EEC on the approximation of the level of consumer taxes on alcohol and alcoholic beverages [1992] *OJ* L316/29 or, in the case of tobacco, Dir. 92/79/EEC on the approximation of consumer taxes on cigarettes [1992] *OJ* L316/8 and Dir. 92/80/EEC on the approximation of consumer taxes on tobaccos other than cigarettes [1992] *OJ* L316/10.

[24] Dir. 92/82/EEC of 19 Oct. 1992 on the approximation of the tax levels on mineral oils [1992] *OJ* L316/19.

[25] Dir. 92/81/EEC on the approximation of the structure of consumer taxes on mineral oils [1992] *OJ* L 316/12. See also the Commission's proposal for a dir. on fiscal marking of gas oil containing measures to control the use of gas oil for which the full rate of duty has not yet been paid, COM(93)352 fin.

and certain infrastructures.[26] It is based on Articles 75 and 99 jointly. The Directive contains only minimum standards.[27] The application of different rates remains possible. The existing differences and the opposition of the Member States to a strict harmonization seemed to exclude a harmonization which did not provide the Member States with considerable discretion.[28]

The Planned Carbon Dioxide Charge

Projects exist in the Community for further tax harmonization, for example the proposal for a directive on the introduction of an energy tax in order to limit carbon dioxide emissions.[29] In its proposal for an energy tax the Commission based its directive on both Article 99 and 130s.[30] This might pose some problems as far as the application of the provision of Article 130t is concerned. The proposal intends the introduction of a tax on carbon dioxide in order to rectify damage at its source and to encourage the use of ecologically sound production methods.[31]

While certain Member States already have specific taxes or duties on environmental emissions (such as sewage, waste, air pollution emissions, or energy) most countries are reluctant to introduce a carbon dioxide tax without general harmonization by the EC or even among industrialized countries.[32] The differences the unilateral introduction of such a tax would create in the competitive conditions between the Member States seem to prevent the national govern-

---

[26] Council Dir. 93/89/EEC on the application by Member States of taxes on certain vehicles used for the carriage of goods by road and tolls and charges for the use of certain infrastructures [1993] *OJ* L279/32. See, however, Case C-21/94 *Parliament* v. *Council*, judgment of 5 July 1995, see [1995] *OJ* C228/8 to 9 or (1995) 20 *Proceedings of Court* 1. For details refer to Ch. 9.

[27] See for critical comments on their ecological aspects see K. Hailbronner, 'EG-Verkehrspolitik und Umweltschutz' in H.-W. Rengeling (ed.), *Umweltschutz und andere Politiken der Europäischen Gemeinschaft* (Heymann, Köln, 1993), 149 at 162.

[28] For details see V. Schmitt, 'Die Harmonisierung der Wettbewerbsbedingungen in der EG-Binnenverkehrspolitik' [1993] *EuZW* 305 at 309. Only recently Germany, the Benelux countries, and Denmark introduced a common 'euro vignette' for the use of public motorways by lorries, effective from 1 Jan. 1995: see e.g. N. Eickhof and M. Franke, 'Die Autobahngebühr für Lastkraftwagen' [1994] *Wirtschaftsdienst* 244 to 247. See also P. Mückenhausen, 'Die Harmonisierung der Strassenbenutzungsgebühren in der Europäischen Gemeinschaft' [1994] *EuZW* 519 to 526.

[29] Proposal for a Council dir. introducing a tax on carbon dioxide emissions and energy [1992] *OJ* C196/1. For details on the introduction of the planned carbon dioxide tax or duty see Breuer, n. 2 above, 485 to 496; Hilf, n. 2 above, 105; Kloepfer, n. 2 above, 195.

[30] Other possible provisions for the adoption might have been Art. 100a, 130s, or 201, dependent on the actual formulation of such a charge.

[31] See EC Commission, *V Environmental Action Programme* (EC, Brussels, 1992), i, 71 or COM(92)23 final (27 Mar. 1992); for details of the proposal for a tax on carbon dioxide see P. Thieffry, 'Les nouveaux instruments juridiques de la politique communautaire de l'environnemnt' [1992] *RTDE* 669 at 676.

[32] See, however, the existing projects in Denmark and The Netherlands combined with certain exemptions for the most concerned undertakings, see [1992] *OJ* L223/28; The Netherlands had, however, originally postponed the introduction until later in 1994, see *Neue Zürcher Zeitung* (23 Dec. 1993), 25.

ments from taking any major individual step.[33] This also reflects the heavy opposition of European industry to the Commission's proposal for the introduction of a carbon dioxide tax, as most non-EC countries do not have such taxes.[34] The proposal for a directive is therefore subject to the condition that other OECD countries take similar measures.[35]

National Environmental Taxes

For the moment the limited extent of fiscal harmonization of indirect taxes under Article 99 leaves the Member States with a relatively wide discretion to introduce their own environmental taxes.[36] This applies in particular for production- and emission-related duties and taxes as long as they are not harmonized under the other relevant provisions of the Treaty.[37] But also in the area of consumption-related indirect taxation the relevance of Article 99 is still relatively limited. Member States are explicitly granted the opportunity to introduce or maintain taxes which are levied on products other than those already harmonized. They must, however, not give rise to any border-crossing formalities.[38] This makes any reimbursement or border tax-adjustment impossible.[39]

In the regulated areas, however, the Member States are bound to the existing minimum standards.[40] Additionally, it is generally disputed whether the Member States are obliged under the principles of Article 5 EC to abstain from the introduction of any new indirect taxation in a field if they know that the Community is planning to adopt measures in a specific area.[41]

---

[33] See e.g. the declaration of the former Dutch Minister for Economics Andriessen as reported in *Neue Zürcher Zeitung* (1/2 Feb. 1992, no. 26), 35.

[34] As reported in [1992] *EuZW* 192. On 10 May 1995 the Commission presented a new modified version of its proposal, see COM(95)172 or [1995] *EU Bulletin* (no. 5) 39 or [1995] *EU Magazin* (no. 6) 44. It seems that the Essen Summit of the Heads of Governments of the Member States in autumn 1994 proved that there was no way to introduce a harmonized system. The new proposal delegates the ability to introduce a tax basically to the Member States.

[35] Art. 1 of Proposal, n. 29 above. In a later communication the Commission hoped, however, to be able to introduce, during a first stage, certain 'environmental taxes' on a broader range of energy products such as natural gas, coal, and electricity, which were not subject to the initial proposal. Furthermore, the Commission considers the introduction of lower levels of taxation than originally planned and even to abandon the requirement of 'conditionality', i.e. the introduction of similar measures by non-member countries; see *EUR-OP News* (Spring 1994, no. 1) 5 or *Neue Zürcher Zeitung* (26/27 Mar. 1994, no. 72), 35. It has been rightly suggested that the proposed dir. might also pose certain problems under the international obligations of the Community, i.e. GATT; see for details Ch. 11 and M. Düerkop, 'International Trade Aspects of the Proposed EC Directive Introducing a Tax on Carbon Dioxide Emissions and Energy' (1994) 31 *CMLRev.* 807 to 844.

[36] See for details Krämer, n. 19 above (RMC), 60.

[37] See for examples Breuer, n. 2 above, 495.

[38] Art. 3 of Dir. 92/12/EEC [1992] *OJ* L76/1; see for considerations on the German project for the introduction of a CO_2-input levy, Breuer, n. 2 above, 495.

[39] e.g. The Netherlands have abolished their existing excise duties on sugar and goods containing sugar, see e.g. A. Lier (ed.), *Tax and Legal Aspects of EC Harmonisation* (Kluwer, Deventer, 1993), 146.

[40] See Breuer, n. 2 above, 495.

[41] This is, in particular, the opinion of E. Grabitz, *Stillhalte-Verpflichtungen vor dem Binnenmarkt-Unvereinbarkeit der Edgassteuer mit Gemeinschaftsrecht* (Engel, Kehl am Rhein, 1988), 13; see for further

Apart from a possible restriction resulting from the existing harmonization under Article 99, national fiscal measures have to be compatible with the other provisions of the Treaty. This is particularly important as far as the non-discrimination principle of Article 6 EC on European Union[42] is concerned, particularly established for domestic taxation under Article 95 and for duties and charges under Article 12. Further problems may arise under Article 30 when such charges or taxes are considered 'measures having equivalent effect as quantitative restrictions' on trade.[43]

Minimum Standards

Article 99 does not provide for a general safeguard clause allowing for more stringent national measures in the interest of the environment in general, neither is there a general safeguard clause comparable to Article 36.[44] Nevertheless, in the case of the taxation of mineral oils the Directive indicates only minimum standards and leaves the Member States free to introduce higher tax rates for environmental reasons. The Commission's proposal for the introduction of a carbon dioxide tax allows Member States to apply higher rates.[45]

As far as the recently adopted directive on vehicle taxes and tolls is concerned, it provides similarly for minimum standards of vehicle taxes.[46] The introduction of tolls and user charges is not compulsory; the Directive establishes, however, a maximum which shall not be exceeded and certain rules on the application of tools and user charges.[47] Among these principles is the rule that user charges should be in proportion to the duration of the use made of the infrastructure, which corresponds to the 'polluter' or 'user pays' principle.[48]

In general, the application of minimum standards for indirect taxes serves the principles of subsidiarity and allows differing preferences among the Member States. It reduces, however, the harmonization effects on the competitive situation and the elimination of fiscal differences in general. Nevertheless, this minimum standard in the field of taxation seems to be the only way to reach consensus in the current situation of the Community.

references M. Kloepfer and R. Thull, 'Rechtsprobleme einer CO_2-Abgabe' [1992] *DVBl.* 195 at 200; see also Ch. 9 on the common transport policy.

[42] Before the introduction of the Treaty of the European Union: Art. 7 EEC.

[43] For the case law see Ch. 3; also U. Becker, *Der Gestaltungsspielraum der EG-Mitgliedstaaten im Spannungsfeld zwischen Umweltschutz und freiem Warenverkehr* (Nomos, Baden-Baden, 1991), 68; Krämer, n. 19 above (*CMLRev*), 141 and L. Krämer, 'Community Environmental Law—Towards a Systematic Approach' [1992] *YEL* 151 at 162.

[44] See also Pernice, n. 17 above, 204, and Hilf, n. 2 above, 109.

[45] Art. 2 (c) of the Commission Proposal, n. 29 above.

[46] Art. 6.   [47] Art. 7.   [48] Art. 7(g).

THE USE OF ENVIRONMENTAL SUBSIDIES

Environmental Subsidies at Community Level

As has been shown in the discussion of the Community's environmental policy under Article 130r, the Community is authorized to use different instruments and measures to attain the environmental objectives set out by the Treaty.[49] Whether this includes environmental aids for the development of certain activities is, however, disputed.[50] From the 'polluter pays' principle, as referred to in Article 130r, it follows, in principle, that the Community should only use instruments which leave the burden of environmental degradation with the polluters responsible. Subsidies financed from the general funding of the Community, however, allocate the costs of environmental protection among all contributors to the Community income and do not directly affect the polluters.[51]

The Community has introduced environmental subsidies[52] but only to a very limited extent.[53] Regulation 2242/87/EEC on Community environmental action[54] based on Article 130s has introduced a programme for the financing of measures for the protection of the environment. With Directive 1973/92/EEC the Community introduced its LIFE programme for the financing of specific action for the protection of the environment.[55] Another mechanism is the funding of environmental investment measures in certain regions, as established by the Community programme ENVIREG.[56] The programme aims at facilitating the implementation of Community environmental policy at regional level and includes loans and non-refundable subsidies.[57]

---

[49] See T. Schröer, *Die Kompetenzverteilung zwischen der Europäischen Wirtschaftsgemeinschaft und ihren Mitgliedstaaten auf dem Gebiet des Umweltschutzes* (Duncker & Humblot, Berlin, 1992), 157.

[50] See Schröer, n. 49 above, 188.

[51] See also the report prepared by an expert panel of the Member States concerning the use of economic and fiscal instruments in EC environmental policy of 5 Sept. 1990; XI/185/90–EN, 11. The current situation in the Community limits the application of the 'polluter pays' principle: see L. Krämer, 'Die Integrierung umweltpolitischer Erfordernisse in die gemeinschaftliche Wettbewerbspolitik' in H.-W. Rengeling (ed.), *Umweltschutz und andere Politiken der Europäischen Gemeinschaft* (Heymann, Köln, 1993), 47 at 79 to 81.

[52] See for a survey Krämer, n. 51 above, 73.

[53] Which may mainly be caused by the limited financial possibilities, as Schröer argues, n. 49 above, 186 with reference to U. Weinstock, 'Nur eine europäische Umwelt? Europäische Umweltpolitik im Spannungsfeld von ökologischer Vielfalt und ökonomischer Einheit' [1983] *ZfU* 1 at 31; H.-J. Glaesner, 'Die Einheitliche Europäische Akte' [1986] *EuR* 119 at 144; see, however, the strong criticism by the Court of Auditors concerning the irresponsible assignment of such funding irrespective of the 'polluter pays' principle, as referred to in *Neue Zürcher Zeitung* (24 Sept. 1992, no. 222), 33.

[54] [1987] *OJ* L207/8.

[55] Dir. 1973/92/EEC [1992] *OJ* L206/1. For a proposed renewal see IP/95/367 of 12 Apr. 1995.

[56] Programme adopted by the Commission on 2 May 1990 according to Art. 11 of Council Reg. 4253/88/EEC [1990] *OJ* C115/3.

[57] For details see L. Krämer, 'Das Verursacherprinzip im Gemeinschaftsrecht' [1989] *EuGRZ* 353 at 358, and Krämer, n. 43 above, 163.

The second sentence of Article 130r(4) sets out the way in which the burden is to be shared for the financing of environmental measures. National measures should, in principle, be financed by the Member States. Nevertheless, the range of environmental projects which are eligible under Article 2 of Regulation 2242/87/EEC is quite broadly drawn and allows the co-funding of all projects which are of interest to the Community in terms of protection of the environment and/or the management of natural resources. The purely national character of an environmental project is therefore not a bar to Community financing.[58]

National Measures

National subsidies or investment measures for the protection of the environment are not influenced by existing Community measures in this field. Much more important in this field is the general prohibition of certain state aids under Article 92 EC.[59] There is case law in abundance on the lawfulness of state aids and subsidies, which applies in principle also to environmental aids.[60] Nevertheless, their specific character has led to clarification by the Commission concerning environmentally justified state aids and their compatibility with the Treaty.[61] In all these cases, however, the restriction of national measures results not from pursuit of Community harmonization but from the basic competition rules of the Treaty.

[58] See Kapteyn and VerLoren van Themaat, n. 17 above, 652.
[59] See for details Ch. 6.   [60] Becker, n. 43 above, 64 to 67.
[61] See communication by the Commission in its *XXII Report on Competition Policy 1992* (EC, Brussels, 1993); see Ch. 6.

11

External Relations and Environmental Protection

Environmental protection in many cases requires multilateral co-operation and negotiations within international bodies. This co-operation can lead to multilateral environmental agreements (MEAs). The Community has concluded many of these MEAs, usually together with the Member States as so-called 'mixed agreements'. Before the coming into force of the Single European Act all Council decisions to conclude international environmental agreements were based on Article 235 EC. Now Article 130r(4) EC provides specific Community competence for international co-operation for the protection of the environment.

International agreements are usually implemented internally by Community regulations to ensure a homogeneous application. Most of these agreements or the respective implementing regulations allow Member States to adopt more stringent measures. If such measures are adopted under Article 130s the application of Article 130t is possible. On the other hand, there are certain international agreements or unilateral action by the Community falling primarily in other areas, which have an important impact on national or Community environmental policy. Apart from international fishery conventions (Article 43) and transport conventions (Articles 75 and 84 (2)) they exist particularly in the fields of trade (Article 113) or general co-operation with non-member countries (Article 228). Under Articles 113 and 130s EC trade restrictions for environmental reasons have become increasingly important. They are often referred to as trade related environmental measures (TREMs).

While the exclusive external competence of the Community for the common commercial policy usually precludes the Member States from taking their own measures, many Community regulations implementing MEAs provide only for minimum requirements or allow for more stringent measures. In the field of autonomous measures there is specific Community secondary legislation which entitles the Member States to take their own action subject to a particular notification procedure and conditions similar to those under Article 36 EC. The co-operation agreements concluded by the Community on the basis of Article 238 also involve environmental obligations.

MULTILATERAL ENVIRONMENTAL AGREEMENTS (MEAS)

General Observations

Before the coming into force of the Single European Act the Community had already concluded several multilateral environmental agreements (MEAs). Their conclusion was mainly based on Article 235.[1] As the Community's competence for nature conservation in general was controversial,[2] the conclusion of these agreements was also criticized.[3] Apart from the specific competence for external relations in certain fields provided for by the Treaty itself, the general competence for the conclusion of international agreements was very controversial until the decision of the Court in the *ERTA* Case in 1971.[4] Here the Court stated that the Community had the power to conclude agreements if a Treaty provision explicitly[5] or implicitly provided such a power. Therefore, using the implied power theory:[6]

'The Court has concluded *inter alia* that whenever Community law has created for the institutions of the Community powers within its internal system for the purpose of attaining a specific objective, the Community has the authority to enter into the international commitments necessary for the attainment of that objective even in the absence of an express provision in that connection.'[7]

Later the ERTA judgment was developed by the Court in several judgments.[8] Particularly important was the extension of its principle to areas where the

---

[1] See L. Krämer, 'Community Environmental Law—Towards a Systematic Approach' [1992] *YEL* 151 at 156.

[2] See above Ch. 7. A survey of the whole issue is undertaken by J. A. Usher, 'Protection of the Environment through Trade Restrictions and the Community's Internal Relations: The Respective Competence of the Community and its Member States' in J. Cameron, P. Demaret, and D. Geradin (eds.), *Trade and the Environment: The Search for Balance* (Cameron May, London, 1994), 261 to 276.

[3] See for Denmark: L. Krämer, *EEC Treaty and Environmental Protection* (Sweet & Maxwell, London, 1990), 83 or I. Pernice, 'Kompetenzordnung und Handlungsbefugnisse der Europäischen Gemeinschaft auf dem Gebiet des Umwelt- und Technikrechts' [1989] *DV* 1 at 35.

[4] Case 22/70 *Commission* v. *Council (ERTA)* [1971] *ECR* 263; for comments see e.g. J. Temple Lang, 'ERTA Judgment and Court's Case Law' [1986] *YEL* 183 to 218; see in general for the EC's external relations E. L. M. Völker, *Leading Cases and Materials on the External Relations Law of the European Community (with Emphasis on the Common Commercial Policy)* (Kluwer, Deventer, 1985) or J. Rideau, 'Les accords internationaux dans la jurisprudence de la Cour de justice des Communautées européennes' [1990] *Revue Générale de Droit International Public* 289 to 418.

[5] See Art. 228 in conjunction with Arts. 113, 229, and 238. Now see also Art. 130r(4). See, however, on the limits of e.g. Art. 228 Case C–327/91 *France* v. *Commission (Competition Law Agreements)*, 9 Aug. 1994.

[6] See P. J. G Kapteyn and P. VerLoren van Themaat, *Introduction to the Law of the European Communities* (2nd edn., Kluwer, Deventer, 1989), 772.

[7] Opinion 1/76 *European Laying-up Fund For Inland Waterway Vessels* [1977] *ECR* 741 at 755, referring to the previous judgment in Case 22/70 *ERTA*, n. 4 above, 275.

[8] Joined cases 3, 4, and 6/76 *Criminal proceedings against Cornelis Kramer et al. (Biological Resources of the Sea)* [1976] *ECR* 1279; Opinion 1/78 *International Rubber Agreement* [1975] *ECR* 1355; Opinion 1/76 *European Laying-up Fund for Inland Waterway Vessels*, n. 7 above. See most recently the Court's Opinion 1/94 *Uruguay Round Agreements* [1994] *ECR* I–5267 concerning the Community's competence to conclude the Uruguay Round Agreements or Opinion 2/92 *OECD Decision* [1995] *ECR* I–521 concerning the shared competence with regard to the revised decision on national treatment of the Council of the OECD.

Community had not yet made any internal regulations but was allowed to adopt external regulations which seemed necessary to achieve an objective of the Community.[9] Despite the existence of such an external competence, it was by no means conferred exclusively on the Community.[10] A consequence of the rule described is, however, that the

EC's external powers expand without the express approval of the Member States simply in the course of developing the EC's internal policies. An extra constraint has therefore been added to EC internal policy-making, since the member States should now always consider whether the adoption of some desirable item of EC legislation might not result in the undesirable (to them) loss of external competence'.[11]

Community Participation in MEAs

In the field of the environment the Community started very early to co-operate in the framework of multilateral environmental agreements (MEAs), although its own competence to do so and the autonomous possibilities for its Member States were clarified only later by the case law of the Court of Justice. The Court found that the international conclusion of MEAs was necessary for the effective protection of the environment as this is sometimes best reached through the establishment of a 'set of rules binding on all the States concerned, including non-Member States'.[12] While most environmental agreements were concluded on the basis of Article 235, some were agreed under more specific provisions.[13]

The most important multilateral environmental agreements, still based on Article 235, to which the Community and its Member States are parties, are:

- Paris Convention of 4 June 1974 for the prevention of marine pollution from land-based sources;[14]

[9] Opinion 1/76 *European Laying-up Fund For Inland Waterway Vessels*, n. 7 above, 756, or Joined cases 3, 4, and 6/76 *Kramer*, n. 8 above, 1311 or Opinion 1/94, n. 8 above, concerning the Uruguay Round Agreements or Opinion 2/92, n. 8 above. For details on the development see also T. Schröer, *Die Kompetenzverteilung zwischen der Europäischen Wirtschaftsgemeinschaft und ihren Mitgliedstaaten auf dem Gebiet des Umweltschutzes* (Duncker & Humblot, Berlin, 1992), 278.

[10] Kapteyn and VerLoren van Themaat, n. 6 above, 773. An example of exclusive Community competence is the common commercial policy, where the Court has confirmed the exclusiveness see e.g. Case C–62/88 *Greece* v. *Council (Chernobyl I)* [1990] *ECR* I–1527 at 1545. See, in the field of services and intellectual property rights, however, Opinion 1/94, n. 8 above, concerning the Uruguay Round Agreements. The Court considered the competence for the conclusion of the GATS (General Agreement on Trade in Services) and the TRIPs Agreement (Trade Related Intellectual Property Rights Agreement) 'a shared competence'. See for comments e.g. M. Hilf, 'EG-Aussenkompetenzen in Grenzen' [1995] *EuZW* 7 and 8. Most recently see also Opinion 2/92, n. 8 above, with regard to the revised decision on national treatment by the OECD Council.

[11] N. Haigh, 'The European Community and International Environmental Policy' in A. Hurrell and B. Kingsbury (eds.), *The International Politics of the Environment* (Clarendon Press, Oxford, 1994), 228 at 239.

[12] Joined cases 3, 4, and 6/76 *Kramer*, n. 8 above, 1311; commented on by D. Wyatt in 'European Court Judgment of 14 July 1976, Cases 3, 4 and 6/76' (1977) 2 *ELRev.* 41 to 45 and 47 to 51.

[13] Krämer, n. 1 above, 156.

[14] Decision of 3 Mar. 1975 [1975] *OJ* L194/5.

- Barcelona Convention of 16 February 1976, for the protection of the Mediterranean Sea against pollution;[15]
- Bonn Convention of 3 December 1976, for the protection of the Rhine against chemical pollution;[16]
- Bonn Convention of 23 June 1979, on the conservation of migratory species of wild animals;[17]
- Bern Convention of 19 September 1979 on the conservation of European wild life and natural habitats;[18]
- Geneva Convention of 13 November 1979, on long-range transboundary air-pollution.[19]

The Community's competence for the conclusion of external fishery agreements on basis of the Article 43 and the effect such agreements would have on the position of the Member States was initially disputed. In its decision in Joined cases 3, 4, and 6/76 *Criminal Proceedings against Cornelis Kramer et al.*[20] in 1976 the Court of Justice declared that on the basis of Article 43[21] the Community had the power to take measures for the protection of the Community fishery resources. It underlined the fact that this competence also included the High Seas and that therefore the Community was also competent to conclude agreements with third parties if this served the interest of the common fishery policy.[22]

Case: In Joined cases 3, 4, and 6/76 *Kramer*[23] the Court of Justice had to evaluate the validity of certain Dutch penal provisions concerning the protection of fishery resources in the North Sea. Several Dutch fishermen had been accused before a Dutch court of having offended against the Dutch implementation measures of the Agreement on Fishery in the North Atlantic. The agreement aims at the conservation of fish stocks and the rational exploitation of fisheries in the North Sea. The establishment of a Fishery Commission and its recommendation to introduce catch quotas led to the introduction of implementing legislation in The Netherlands. The fishermen argued that The Netherlands were no longer competent under the EC Treaty to conclude international agreements on fisheries or fishery resources protection. The Court of Justice confirmed *inter alia*, that Article 43 entrusted the Community with the conclusion of external agreements on fisheries. Nevertheless, as the Community had taken no measures at that time the Member States were still competent to conclude agreements for the protection of the

---

[15] Decision of 27 July 1977 [1977] *OJ* L240/1.
[16] Decision of 27 July 1977 [1977] *OJ* L240/37.
[17] Decision of 3 Dec.
[18] Decision of 24 June 1982 [1982] *OJ* L210/10.
[19] Decision of 11 June 1981 [1981] *OJ* L171/11.
[20] N. 8 above; for comments see Wyatt, n. 12 above, or A. T. Koers, 'The External Authority of the EEC in Regard to Marine Fisheries' (1977) 14 *CMLRev.* 269 to 301.
[21] The Court also referred to Art. 102 of the Act of Accession of the United Kingdom and Denmark in 1973.
[22] See Ch. 9 on the common agricultural policy.
[23] N. 8 above.

biological resources of the sea. They were lawful if they were necessary for this purpose even if they interfered with the provisions of Articles 30–37 of the Treaty.[24]

Since the coming into force of the Single European Act, its Article 130r(5)—now Article 130r(4) EC, after the coming into force of Treaty on European Union—states that '[w]ithin their respective spheres of competence, the Community and the Member States shall co-operate with third countries and with the relevant international organizations'.[25] It now provides the Community with an explicit basis for its negotiations and the ratification of multilateral and bilateral environmental agreements.[26] This is more or less a restatement of the relevant case law by the Court of Justice.[27] It therefore seems adequate[28] to conclude new environmental agreements on the basis of Article 130r(4) and no longer on the basis of Article 235 EC.[29]

The wording of this provision, however, does not provide clear guidelines on the distribution of competences between the Community and the Member States. In a protocol adopted on the occasion of the closing conference on the Single European Act the following declaration[30] was given by the Heads of State and Government: '[t]he Conference considers that the provisions of Article 130r(5), second subparagraph do not affect the principles resulting from the judgment handed down by the Court of Justice in the ERTA Case.'

This declaration together with the wording of Article 130r(4) EC makes clear that there is still no intention to confer an exclusive external competence for MEAs on the Community.[31] The principle of subsidiarity, as once stated in Article 130r(4) of the SEA and now in Article 3b, underlines the fact that the Community has the power to act internally and externally only if the objectives

---

[24] This is one of the first decisions of the Court concerning the relationship between environmental protection measures and the Treaty provisions on the free movement of goods. For details F. Montag, 'Umweltschutz, Freier Warenverkehr und Einheitliche Europäische Akte' [1987] *RIW* 935 to 943; I. Pernice, 'Auswirkungen des europäischen Binnenmarktes auf das Umweltrecht-Gemeinschafts(verfassungs-)rechtliche Grundlagen'[1990] *NVwZ* 201 to 211; U. Becker, *Der Gestaltungsspielraum der der EG-Mitgliedstaaten im Spannungsfeld zwischen Umweltschutz und freiem Warenverkehr* (Nomos, Baden-Baden, 1991), 77; A. Epiney and T. M. J. Möllers, *Freier Warenverkehr und nationaler Umweltschutz* (Heymann, Köln, 1992), 22; J. Henke, *EuGH und Umweltschutz* (VVF, München, 1992), 170, and many others.

[25] See for a detailed analysis see Krämer, n. 3 above, 81 to 86, or A. Middeke, *Nationaler Umweltschutz und Binnenmarkt* (Heymann, Köln, 1993), 369 to 380.

[26] See for details Henke, n. 24 above, 117 to 120.

[27] Case 22/70 *ERTA*, n. 4 above; Joined cases 3, 4, and 6/76 *Kramer*, n. 8 above; see also Temple Lang, n. 4 above, 210.

[28] Krämer, n. 3 above, 82; Schröer, n. 9 above, 229 to 299; Henke, n. 24 above, 110 to 115; e.g. the Council Decision for the ratification and implementation of the Vienna Convention for the Protection of the Ozone Layer in 1988 has been based on Art. 130s [1980] *OJ* L297/8.

[29] This has happened even after the coming into force of the Single European Act. A few measures have still been adopted under this provision, e.g. Decision 89/557/EEC [1989] *OJ* L304/1 or Decision 89/558/EEC [1989] *OJ* L304/8; for details see E. Grabitz, Art. 130s, para. 26, in E. Grabitz and M. Hilf (eds.), *Kommentar zur EU* (2nd edn., C. H. Beck, München, 1990 ff.).

[30] See Krämer, n. 3 above, 82.

[31] This is indicated in the same way by Schröer, n. 9 above, 276; Henke, n. 24 above, 119.

can be better attained at Community level.[32] Whether this ultimately means that leadership in international environmental issues should always lie with the Community may, however, be disputed.[33]

Member States' Participation in MEAs

Whenever the Community has no exclusive power in a field, or has not yet used its power to conclude an international agreement the Member States are free to do so.[34] If the Community, however, decides to use its competence in the field of the environment to conclude international agreements the Member States are limited in their autonomy.[35] The existing information procedure between the Community and the Member States may facilitate co-operation and even induce the Community itself to conclude an agreement instead of the Member States.[36] The latter are able to conclude agreements themselves only under the condition of the general compliance with their Treaty obligations. This is especially important for the duties deriving from a Member State's accession to such international agreements which could jeopardize the objectives of the Community, particularly the establishment of the common market.[37]

As in other fields of external relations of the Community most MEAs have been concluded as mixed agreements.[38] This allows both the Member States and the Community to negotiate and ratify international conventions. This is possible even if the Community has already taken internal measures in a relevant area.[39] This practice has been continued since the coming into force of the Single European Act. Examples of the use of mixed agreements are the Montreal Protocol on substances depleting the ozone layer,[40] the Vienna Convention[41] and the London adjustments to the Montreal Protocol.[42] Since then the Member States have also taken part in the drafting of the UNEP

[32] See Kapteyn and VerLoren van Themaat, n. 6 above, 786.

[33] This is the view expressed by L. Brinkhorst, 'Subsidiarity and European Community Environment Policy' [1993] *European Environmental Law Review* 16 at 23.

[34] This derives from the delegation doctrine, see Kapteyn and VerLoren van Themaat, 775. Member States have, however, to observe their obligations under the Treaty in general.

[35] See Schröer, n. 9 above, 283.   [36] [1973] *OJ* C9/1.

[37] Joined cases 3, 4, and 6/76 *Kramer*, n. 8 above, 1312; see Schröer, n. 9 above, 284.

[38] See Kapteyn and VerLoren van Themaat, n. 6 above, 775; for the environment see Schröer, n. 9 above, 285; see generally D. O'Keefe and H. G. Schermers (eds.), *Mixed Agreements* (Kluwer, Deventer, 1983). On the few agreements concluded by the Community alone see J. Groux and P. Manin, *The European Communities in the International Order* (EC Commission, Brussels, 1985), 61 to 62. On the political problems in the negotiation of such mixed agreements see Haigh, n. 11 above, 240 ff.

[39] See Krämer, n. 1 above, 165.

[40] Signed on 16 Sept. 1987 and approved on 16 Dec. 1988, entered into force on 16 Mar. 1989: Council Decision 88/540/EEC [1988] *OJ* L297/8.

[41] Decision of 14 Oct. 1988 [1988] *OJ* L297/8.

[42] Approved on 20 Dec. 1991, entered into force 10 Aug. 1992: Council Decision 91/690/EEC [1991] *OJ* L377/28.

Convention on the transport of waste,[43] although the Community had already adopted measures in this field.[44] Nevertheless, the acceptance of the Community as a signatory to these conventions was often disputed, particularly by third parties.[45]

Member States' Obligations under MEAs

Once the Community has ratified international conventions or treaties, they become part of Community law[46] and have to be observed by the Member States as such.[47] Although they rank below primary Community law they are above secondary legislation and therefore prevail over conflicting environmental directives.[48] In the case where both the Community and the Member States are parties to an agreement, the observation of such an international treaty can also be derived from national law.[49]

The case may, however, be different when an environmental convention is not directly applied in a Member State or if certain Member States have not yet ratified a Convention which is already part of the Community legal order.[50] In general, the Community does not supervise the implementation of international conventions or environmental treaties by the Member States, even if the Community is a party to them.[51] If the Community, however, has adopted secondary law for the implementation of environmental treaties in the internal legal order of the Community, these acts have to be observed by the Member States as normal Community law and the Community will control

[43] Basel Convention on the Control of Transboundary Movements of Hazardous Wastes and their Disposal, reprinted e.g. in (1989) 28 *ILM* 657 ff.

[44] Krämer, n. 3 above, 85, cites Dir. 84/631/EEC on the movement of waste within the Community and Dir. 86/279/EEC on the export of waste from the Community; see also Kapteyn and VerLoren van Themaat, n. 6 above, 653 and 656.

[45] See on the difficult negotiation leading to the 'ozone regime' the descriptions by M. Jachtenfuchs, 'The European Community and the Protection of the Ozone Layer' [1990] *JCMS* 261 ff. or in general A. Nollkaemper, 'The European Community and International Environmental Co-operation: Legal Aspects of External Community Powers' [1987] *LIEI* 55 at 72; also Haigh, n. 11 above, 243 ff.

[46] See Krämer, n. 1 above, 165.

[47] Art. 228 EC.

[48] Certain commercial conventions also contain environmental provisions, see Krämer, n. 1 above, 155. On the general relation between Community law and international agreements and judgments by international judicial bodies see e.g. I. Cheyne, 'International Agreements and the European Community Legal System' (1994) 19 *ELRev.* 581 to 598; critical of the Court's case law is E.-U. Petersmann, 'International and European Trade and Environmental Law after the Uruguay Round' in Academy of European Law (ed.), *Collected Courses of the Academy of European Law* (Martinus Nijhoff, Dordrecht, 1995), 1 at 63.

[49] The problems arising from direct applicability, precedence, and the ability to invoke international law within the different national legal orders cannot be elaborated on here.

[50] By 1989 two Member States, Ireland and Greece, had not yet ratified CITES.

[51] See for justified criticism of this attitude L. Krämer, 'The Implementation of Environmental Laws by the European Economic Communities' [1991] *GYIL* 9 at 44.

their implementation.[52] As a general rule the Community and the Member States are responsible for the implementation of an international agreement.[53]

While in general the Community introduces its environmental measures in the form of directives it mostly uses the form of regulations for the implementation of environmental conventions.[54] The reason may be the need for a homogeneous application of these international rules within the territory of the common market.[55] Many of these regulations require the Member States to take appropriate legal or administrative measures internally where they find a breach of a treaty obligation implemented by an appropriate regulation.[56] A new development seems to be the introduction of sanctions against breaches of the relevant regulations.[57]

The general Community principle that the Member States have to guarantee their compliance with Community rules implementing international law within their national jurisdiction[58] has seldom led to Commission proceedings against a Member State. For a long time the question whether the obligations arising from environmental agreements were part of national law or of Community law was thus insignificant as the Community did not try to enforce Member States' compliance with those parts of international conventions which came within Community competence.[59] Recently, however, there have been proceedings against Member States which did not comply with their obligations under Community law implementing international environmental agreements.[60] Both instances concerned the Community regulations for the implementation of the Convention on International Trade in Endangered Species of wild fauna and flora (CITES). Although the Community had not been allowed to become a signatory of the CITES Convention, it had adopted detailed regulations for its implementation.[61] The main reasons for their adoption were the problems which could have arisen for the common commercial policy from a non-uniform implementation of the trade instruments upon which CITES relies. Furthermore, at the time of its coming into force, the accession of only certain Member States (Greece and Ireland were not yet parties) could have posed prob-

---

[52] See Krämer, n. 51 above, 45, and Krämer, n. 1 above, 165.

[53] Noellkaemper, n. 45 above, 78.

[54] e.g. Reg. 3322/88/EEC on substances which affect the ozone layer [1988] *OJ* L297/1; Reg. 594/91/EEC on substances which affect the ozone layer [1991] *OJ* L67/1; Reg. 1734/88/EEC on the export of chemicals [1988] *OJ* L152/2; Reg. 348/81/EEC on the import of whales and certain cetacean products [1981] *OJ* L39/1; Reg. 3626/82/EEC on trade with endangered species [1982] *OJ* L384/1; all these references can be found in Krämer, n. 1 above, 157.

[55] Krämer, n. 1 above, 157; Jachtenfuchs, n. 45 above, 269.

[56] e.g. Reg. 3322/88/EEC on substances which affect the ozone layer, n. 54 above.

[57] Krämer, n. 1 above, 157, with reference to a Commission proposal for a new reg. replacing Reg. 3626/82/EEC on the implementation of the CITES convention, n. 54 above.

[58] Which is also derived from Art. 5 EC.   [59] Krämer, n. 1 above, 156 and 167.

[60] See, in particular, Case C–182/89 *Commission* v. *France (CITES—Feline Skins from Bolivia)* [1990] *ECR* I–4337.

[61] See below and also the annual reports on the international trade in endangered flora and fauna, i.e. the 7th Annual Report (EC, Brussels, 1990), also in: COM(94)104 final.

lems in intra-Community trade. The implementation of CITES by a Community regulation allowed the Member States to avoid the controls which parties to CITES are normally bound to implement at their national borders.[62]

Case: One case concerned the Spanish system with regard to penal and administrative sanctions for the breach of rules deriving from the Community regulation on the implementation of the CITES Convention into the Community order.[63] The proceedings against Spain concerned the illegal import and use of chimpanzees, a protected species under the relevant Community regulation. The Commission raised the question whether the Spanish customs legislation was a sufficient deterrent, but finally decided not to submit the case to the European Court of Justice because it felt that it would be difficult to prove a breach of obligations by the Spanish Government.[64]

Case C-182/89 *Commission v. France (CITES)*[65] is the only case which has ever come before the European Court of Justice concerned with the Community regulations for the implementation of the CITES Convention. The Commission brought an action before the Court asking for a declaration that, by issuing import permits for more than 6,000 wild-cat skins of an endangered species under the CITES Convention, France had failed to fulfil its obligations under the Council regulation concerning the implementation of this Convention. The wild cats were listed in Appendix II of the Convention. The Community regulation went even further than the provisions of the CITES Convention. The Court decided that France had failed to fulfil its obligations as the permits were not issued in accordance with all the requirements of the Community Regulation.

Autonomous Application of MEAs

There remains, however, the problem arising from conventions which have been ratified by certain Member States but not (or not yet) ratified or implemented by the Community. Apart from the question of competence, this raises the question of the application of the convention's obligations among Member States and their compatibility with the other Treaty obligations.[66] Many conventions require trade restrictions with countries which are not parties to the convention. In the framework of the Community such discriminatory treatment would clearly contradict the obligations arising from the Treaty.[67] The general

---

[62] P. Demaret, 'Environmental Policy and Commercial Policy: The Emergence of Trade-Related Environmental Measures (TREMs) in the External Relations of the European Community' in M. Maresceau (ed.), *The European Community's Commercial Policy after 1992: The Legal Dimension* (Kluwer, Deventer, 1993), 315 at 323; see also preamble to Reg. 3626/82/EEC, n. 54 above.

[63] Reg. 3626/82, n. 54 above.

[64] Unpublished proceedings, reported by Krämer, n. 1 above, 151 at 170.

[65] Case C-182/89 *CITES—Feline Skins from Bolivia*, n. 60 above.

[66] See e.g. the dispute which arose out of the fact of the membership of certain Member States of the International Rhine Commission (IRC). While higher standards for e.g. cadmium seemed desirable, the Member States were prevented from adopting them by existing Community legislation on maximum levels in this field. See R. Kamminga, 'Who Can Clean Up the Rhine: The European Community or the International Rhine Commission?' [1978] *NILR* 63 at 74; Noellkaemper, n. 45, 73.

[67] The general non-discrimination principle as incorporated in e.g. Arts. 6, 9, 12, 30, 34, 36, 95, and others of the Treaty.

principle, as developed by the Court of Justice, that a Member State may not use its obligations arising out of a subsequent international treaty as a reason for the non-fulfilment of its Treaty obligations[68] applies. The adherence to an MEA which entails trade restrictions against other Member States or non-member countries which are not lawful under the general EC provisions is incompatible with the obligations arising from the EC framework and in particular from Article 5.[69]

Example: The Basel Convention, for example, was signed by the Community and the Member States. In the framework of the Community it was intended to become a mixed agreement.[70] For a while, however, only France had ratified this Convention while the other Member States and the Community itself had not yet ratified the Convention. One of the most significant aspects of the Convention, however, is that it prohibits any movement of hazardous waste between parties and non-parties.[71] In this case France is, in principle, obliged to apply the Convention's provisions also in relation to its Community partners. As shown above, however, such discrimination against other Member States is not lawful under the Treaty.[72] If the Community and the Member States were all parties to this agreement the question would be dealt with in the relevant Community regulations concerning the application of the Convention between the Community members. In the absence of such Community legislation on the application of the Basel Convention the general Treaty obligations and the Community secondary legislation have to be observed. Directive 84/631, which deals with external and internal movement of hazardous waste, pre-empts the unilateral application of the Basel Convention by France. The jurisdiction of the Court of Justice concerning import and export restrictions on waste remained applicable and France would have been obliged to fulfil its Community obligations.[73] In the meantime, however, the Community itself has signed the Convention and adopted the relevant Community measures.[74]

ENVIRONMENTAL MEASURES AND EXTERNAL TRADE (ARTICLE 113)

Trade-related Environmental Measures (TREMs)

The system of the Treaty and in particular Article 130r(4) does not limit the Community in its scope for environmental protection measures for the Community environment. Attempts to insert a relevant clause into Article 130r(1) limiting Community action to the Community environment failed.[75]

---

[68] The same is true for treaties which oblige the signatories to take certain measures which are not compatible with other basic principles of the EEC Treaty, such as e.g. the French prohibition of night work for women deriving from an ILO Convention, which was considered not to be compatible with the Community legislation in force: see Case C–345/89 *Criminal Proceedings against Alfred Stoeckel* [1991] *ECR* I–4047.   [69] Demaret, n. 62 above, 377.

[70] Demaret, n. 62 above, 380.   [71] Art. 4(5) of the Basel Convention, n. 43 above.

[72] See also Case C–2/90 *Commission* v. *Belgium* (*Walloon Waste Case*) [1992] *ECR* 4431.

[73] See only Krämer, n. 1 above, 158.   [74] [1993] *OJ* L30/1.

[75] Krämer, n. 1 above, 153; J. De Ruyt, *L'acte unique européen—Commentaire* (2nd edn., Editions de l'Université de Bruxelles, Bruxelles, 1989), 214.

The Community has, therefore, in its international environmental agreements and through unilateral measures, adopted a great number of measures to preserve the non-domestic environment.[76] Most of these measures involve important commercial issues, mainly import or export restrictions to non-member countries. In this field Community action is closely linked to its exclusive competence[77] for a common commercial policy, as provided for under Article 113 EC. Such trade measures for the purpose of environmental protection, also referred to as trade related environmental measures (TREMs),[78] have an important impact on both the Community's trade relations with non-member countries and international environmental policy.

Today, measures restricting the Community's external trade for the purpose of protecting the environment concern trade in wildlife,[79] waste and dangerous substances,[80] and products which deplete the ozone layer.[81] The Community is party to several international agreements using trade measures[82] and has usually implemented the consequent obligations on the Community through its own legal acts. In most cases the Community and the Member States are parties to the relevant conventions, but there are cases where certain Member States or even the Community itself are not (yet) parties.[83]

The Appropriateness of Article 113 for TREMs

If the Community wants to implement autonomous measures or obligations deriving from a multilateral agreement using trade related environmental measures (TREMs) the question remains whether the implementing regulation should be based on Article 130r(4) or on the competence for the common commercial policy (Article 113). The survey of TREMS adopted by the Community

---

[76] See Krämer, n. 1 above, 153.

[77] e.g. Case 41/76 *Suzanne Donckerwolcke épouse Criel et al.* v. *Procureur de la République et al.* [1976] *ECR* 1921 at 1937; see e.g. Kapteyn and VerLoren van Themaat, n. 6 above, 791.

[78] See Demaret, n. 62 above, 319.

[79] Reg. 3626/82/EEC on the implementation in the Community of the Convention on International Trade in Species of wild fauna and flora, n. 54 above, modified by several Council regs.; specifically for certain species see Reg. 348/81 on the trade in whales, n. 54 above; Dir. 83/129 on the trade in seals [1983] *OJ* L91/30; Reg. 3254/91 on the trade in fur-bearing mammals [1991] *OJ* L308/1; for the prohibition of imports of ivory into the Community in order to protect the African elephant, see Reg. 2496/89/EEC [1989] *OJ* L240/5.

[80] e.g. the ban on exports of dangerous wastes to non-member countries which do not guarantee the disposal of such waste in an environmentally sound manner, see Dir. 86/279/EEC amending Dir. 84/631/EEC on the trans-frontier shipment of toxic and dangerous waste [1986] *OJ* L181/13.

[81] e.g. the ban on CFCs which might harm the ozone layer: Council Reg. 3322/88/EEC of 14 Oct. 1988 on certain chlorofluorocarbons and halons which deplete the ozone layer, n. 54 above; Reg. 594/91/EEC, n. 54 above; and Council Reg. 3952/92 of 30 Dec. 1992 amending Reg. 594/91 in order to speed up the phasing-out of substances that deplete the ozone layer, n. 54 above.

[82] e.g. Art. 4 of the Montreal Protocol on substances that deplete the ozone layer, reprinted e.g. in UNEP, *Selected Multilateral Treaties in the Field of the Environment* (Grotius, Cambridge, 1991).

[83] The Community was not yet allowed to sign CITES (Convention on International Trade in Endangered Species of wild fauna and flora) reprinted e.g. in UNEP, n. 82 above. Now all Member States have ratified CITES, but for a long time Greece and Ireland were not signatories.

in the past indicates that most measures were based on Article 235 EC before the Single European Act and on Article 130s thereafter.[84] This legal basis is very controversial,[85] especially as the Commission has most often proposed to base the measures in question on Article 113. This, however, has only twice been accepted by the Council, in 1991 for the Community's leghold trap regulation[86] and in 1989 for the regulation on the export of certain chemicals.[87]

The legal basis for these agreements however, again has an important impact on national possibilities for diverging measures. Where an agreement has been based on Article 130s EC, the Member States are in principle able to adopt more stringent measures under Article 130t EC. This possibility for more stringent national measures is also provided for in most of the agreements in question.[88] This is not possible, however, or requires a special Community safeguard clause where agreements are based on the exclusive competence of Article 113 EC.

The Court has held in its decision in Case 45/86 that, in principle, Article 113 is the appropriate legal basis for Community acts regulating trade between the Community and non-member countries even if the objective of the regulation is part of another policy of the Community.[89] The fact that a regulation uses the establishment of uniform import rules to avoid heterogeneous rules adopted by the Member States makes Article 113 applicable even if the rules in question are made for a specific policy objective such as the protection of the health of consumers, an objective expressly included in Article 130r(1).[90]

In its case law on Article 113 EC the Court held that the commercial policy of the Community had to take into account the other objectives of the Community and that Article 130r(2) in particular justified the pursuit of environmental aims with trade instruments. Article 130s was treated as a special provision which leaves intact the powers held by the Community under other provisions of the Treaty. The reasoning is astonishingly close to that in Case

---

[84] See Demaret, n. 62 above, 361; E.-U. Petersmann, 'Freier Warenverkehr und nationaler Umweltschutz in EWG und EWR' [1993] *Aussenwirtschaft* 95 at 123; the first legislation on CITES and the protection of whales was adopted under Art. 235 while the more recent modifying legislation was based on Art. 130s.

[85] Demaret, n. 62 above, 361.

[86] Reg. 3254/91/EEC prohibiting the use of leghold traps in the Community and the introduction into the Community of pelts and manufactured goods of certain wild animal species originating in countries which catch them by means of leghold traps or trapping methods which do not meet international human trapping standards, n. 79 above. The Reg. makes reference to both Arts. 113 and 130s.

[87] Reg. 428/89/EEC concerning the export of certain chemical products [1989] *OJ* L50/1. It makes, however, no reference to the protection of the environment but only to the Paris conference on chemical weapons (7–11 Jan. 1989).

[88] See Ch. 9 on the Community's environmental policy.

[89] See Case 45/86 *Commission* v. *Council (GSP I)* [1987] *ECR* 1493 at 1517 and Case C–62/88 *Chernobyl I*, n. 10 above, 1545; see for general comments on the Court's case law on the Community's commercial policy e.g. E.-U. Petersmann, 'Constitutional Principles Governing the EEC's Commercial Policy' in Maresceau (ed.), n. 62 above, 21 to 62.

[90] Case C–62/88 *Chernobyl I*, n. 10 above, 1545.

C–300/89 *Titanium Dioxide* on the relationship between Article 100a and the other provisions of the Treaty. Thus, one should probably also take into consideration the reasoning of the Court in Case C–155/91 *Waste Directive* which precludes the application of the more general provisions in cases where the harmonizing economic effect is negligible in comparison to the environmental effects at stake.[91]

Case: In its judgment in Case C–62/88 *Greece* v. *Council (Chernobyl I)*[92] the Court had to decide on the appropriate legal basis of trade restrictions which were taken *inter alia* for the protection of human health. After the nuclear accident at Chernobyl in the former Soviet Union, the Community had adopted a regulation to regulate the import of contaminated agricultural products. This regulation prescribed the maximum acceptable levels of radioactive contamination for agricultural products imported from non-member countries into the Community and required Member States to make appropriate verifications at its borders, and, if necessary, to prohibit the importation of the products in question. This regulation had been adopted by the Council on the basis of Article 113 by majority vote. Greece brought an action before the Court for the annulment of the regulation in question, pleading that the wrong legal basis had been chosen, as the regulation dealt mainly with the protection of health. The Court, however, dismissed the action holding that the regulation was mainly intended to regulate trade between the Community and non-member countries. The legal basis had therefore been chosen correctly.

The reasoning behind this judgment was that if the Community had not intervened with Community action, the Member States would have taken their own measures to restrict imports of agricultural products from non-member countries, as they are entitled to, under secondary legislation.[93] These measures could eventually have serious implications for the Community's internal trade which, however, could be justified under Article 36 EC. To prevent such additional obstacles to trade within the common market TREMs should, in general, be based on Article 113 EC.[94] This also applies to commodity agreements which sometimes may have an important environmental impact, such as in the case of tropical timber.[95]

---

[91] See Ch. 8.   [92] Case C–62/88 *Chernobyl I*, n. 10 above, 1545.

[93] See Reg. 288/82/EEC on common rules for imports [1982] *OJ* L35/1 and Reg. 1765/82 on common rules for imports from state-trading countries [1982] *OJ* L195/1.

[94] This argument is uphold by Demaret, n. 62 above, 363, who indicates the analogy to Art. 100a in its relation to Art. 130s and the relevant case law; see also Schröer, n. 9 above, 290. See also the next section.

[95] Council Decision of 26 Mar. 1985 on the application of the International Agreement on Tropical Timber 1983 [1985] *OJ* L236/8. The text can be found in UNEP, n. 82 above, vol. II, 271. See also Opinion 1/78 *International Rubber Agreement* [1979] *ECR* 2871 at 2915.

DIVERGING NATIONAL MEASURES UNDER MEAS

Specific Derogations and Safeguard Clauses

Apart from the question whether the Member State, the Community, or both, should conclude an international agreement under Article 130r(4) there may be options for a national environmental policy in spite of existing external obligations. As in the case of the internal harmonization of laws, the international treaty itself or the implementing Community regulation may allow Member States to adopt more stringent measures or to provide only for minimum standards.[96] Thus, Member States are able in many cases to adopt more stringent measures. This is, for example, the case of the 1981 Whales Regulation[97] and the 1982 CITES Regulation.[98] In both Regulations specific provisions allow Member States to take more stringent national measures concerning trade with non-member countries *and* intra-community trade.[99]

In 1989 several Member States introduced measures restricting the imports of ivory in order to protect the African elephant. They invoked Article 15 of Regulation 3626/82/EEC implementing the CITES Convention which allowed for more stringent restrictions by parties provided they comply with their other obligations under the Treaty. Later, however, the Community itself adopted measures in the field and the existing measures by Member States underlie now the specific Community legislation under Regulation 2496/89/EEC.[100]

---

[96] e.g. Art. 10 of Dir. 76/464/EEC [1976] *OJ* L129/23 concerning the protection of the aquatic environment of the Community; see Schröer, n. 9 above, 285, with reference to C. Mastellone, 'The External Relations of the E.E.C. in the Field of Environmental Protection' [1981] *ICLQ* 106 at 113; Noellkaemper, n. 45 above, 73; H. U. J. d'Oliveira, 'Das Rheinchloridabkommen und die EWG' [1983] *RIW* 322 at 328 and others.

[97] Council Reg. 348/81/EEC on common rules for imports of whales and other cetacean products, n. 54 above, implementing (and applying more stringent rules than) the International Convention for the Reg. of Whaling, reprinted in UNEP, n. 82 above, 67. The Community is not a party to the convention, but several Member States are; the Reg. was adopted under Art. 235; see for details Demaret, n. 62 above, 325.

[98] Art. 3 of Reg. 3626/82/EEC, n. 54 above, implementing the Convention on International Trade in Endangered Species of wild fauna and flora (CITES), reprinted in UNEP, n. 82 above. The Community was never allowed to become a party to CITES. The Reg. was adopted under Art. 235; see Demaret, n. 62 above, 374; L. Krämer, 'Environmental Protection and Art. 30 EEC Treaty' (1993) 30 *CMLRev.* 111 at 137.

[99] See also Case C-169/89 *Criminal Proceedings against Gourmetterie Van den Burg (Scottish Red Grouse)* [1990] *ECR* I-2143; for a survey of the State practice under Art. 15 of Dir. 3626/82, n. 54 above, which allows a Member State to adopt more stringent measures concerning the trade in wild life see A. Schmidt-Räntsch, 'Besitz und Vermarktung von geschützten Tieren und Pflanzen nach der Vollendung des EG-Binnenmarktes' [1992] *NuR* 49 at 50.

[100] Reg. 2496/89/EEC on a prohibition on importing raw and worked ivory derived from the African elephant into the Community, n. 79 above. See also Krämer, n. 98 above, 137.

Article 130t and External Relations

In the specific case of the adoption of an international obligation under Article 130s the special provision of Article 130t remains applicable in principle.[101] This allows the identical application of the rules governing the use of more stringent national measures under Article 130s within the Community.[102] From a theoretical point of view the homogeneity in the Community's external relations implied by the compulsory character of Article 228 is corrected by the principle of diverging national measures in the interest of the optimal protection of the environment.[103] It is particularly interesting that the original proposal for Article 130t included an express derogation for external affairs ('external competences apart') which was no longer part of the final version.[104]

Case: Regulation 594/91 on the production and consumption of CFCs was based on Article 130s EC although it deals mainly with trade matters.[105] This legal basis led Germany and Denmark to introduce more stringent national measures by invoking Article 130t. They restricted the use of CFCs even further than was laid down in the Regulation. Denmark limited the import of certain products containing CFCs and Germany started to prohibit certain substitutes for CFCs. The Commission did not take any action in these cases.[106] The Netherlands and Luxembourg have also taken measures to prohibit products containing CFCs or substitute substances.[107]

Article 113 and Safeguard Measures

Where a Community measure has been adopted under Article 113, it has been taken with the objective of eliminating intra-Community obstacles to trade, and therefore the Member States no longer have the option of taking diverging national measures.[108] Most legal writers hold that the safeguard clause of Article

---

[101] This becomes particularly clear if one takes into account that the provisional version of Art. 130t included an amendment 'external competences apart' to exclude diverging national measures in the field of external relations. It was later omitted. See D. H. Scheuing, 'Umweltschutz auf Grundlage der Einheitlichen Europäischen Akte' [1989] *EuR* 152 at 173, n. 127; Henke, n. 214 above, 120; Schröer, n. 9 above, 285; Middeke, n. 25 above, 379.

[102] See also Demaret, n. 62 above, 373; Krämer, n. 98 above, 136.

[103] See for this implication Schröer, n. 9 above, 285, referring also to K. Lietzmann, 'Einheitliche Europäische Akte und Umweltschutz: Die neuen Umweltbestimmungen im EWG-Vertrag' in H.-W. Rengeling (ed.), *Europäisches Umweltrecht und europäische Umweltpolitik* (Heymann, Köln, 1988), 163 at 177; L. Krämer, 'Einheitliche Europäische Akte und Umweltschutz: Überlegungen zu einigen neuen Bestimmungen im Gemeinschaftsrecht' in Rengeling (ed.), above, 137 at 153; to avoid problems, Demaret, n. 62 above, 363 suggests a preferential use of Art. 113 for such measures.

[104] See for details Henke, n. 24 above, 120; Scheuing, n. 101 above, 173, n. 127.

[105] See Krämer, n. 1 above, 158, with reference to Reg. 594/91/EEC on the production and consumption of CFCs, n. 54 above.

[106] See Krämer, n. 1 above, 158.

[107] See Krämer, n. 98 above, 135, who argues that even if Art. 130t did not apply such a prohibition would be lawful under Art. 36 or the rule of reason.

[108] See above Case C–62/88 *Chernobyl I*, n. 10 above, 1545; see, however, for domestic case law on the question whether a national measure falls within the scope of Art. 113 *R.* v. *Her Majesty's Treasury and the Bank of England, ex parte CENTRO-COM srl*, QBD, 6 Sept. 1993 [1994] 1 *CMLR* 109.

115 is not applicable in the field of environmental measures.[109] The case law of the Court is very restrictive when the interference of Member States' action with the common commercial policy under Article 113 is concerned.[110]

Nevertheless, as submitted before, also in Community regulations adopted under Article 113 the Member States could be expressly endowed with the power to adopt more stringent environmental requirements. However, the two existing environmental regulations adopted under Article 113, the leghold trap Regulation of 1991[111] and the Regulation on the export of certain chemicals of 1989,[112] are both silent on the powers retained by the Member States.[113]

Intra-Community Trade and Stricter Measures

TREMs can have an important impact on the internal market. One of the main reasons for the explicit implementation of MEAs in the Community legal order by secondary legislation is therefore the prevention the heterogeneous application of MEAs by the Member States which would hinder intra-Community trade.[114] Only by implementing the MEAs directly can the Community guarantee the functioning of the internal market. Normally these agreements would provide for strict border controls and trade restrictions towards non-parties.[115] Any national ban on imports from non-member countries which is not applied homogeneously in all the Member States results in new trade barriers erected between Member States.[116] The implementation of the agreements in question on the Community level avoids this danger.

Some of the Community regulations which implement international environmental agreements are also applicable between Member States. They regulate in detail when a Member State may rely on the provisions for the protection of its own territory or certain species within its territory against dangers arising from trade with other Member States. They generally follow the principles developed by the Court under Articles 30 and 36 in its *Cassis de Dijon* doctrine. They may, however, include specific derogations for protection measures for the

---

[109] Schröer, n. 9 above, 295.

[110] See e.g. Case C–62/88 *Chernobyl I*, n. 10 above, 1545; see also more recent proceedings by the Commission against Greece concerning the Greek trade embargo against Macedonia, reported in *Neue Zürcher Zeitung* (14 Apr. 1994, no. 86), 3.

[111] Council Reg. 3254/91/EEC prohibiting the use of leghold traps in the Community and the introduction into the Community of pelts and manufactured goods of certain wild animal species originating in countries which catch them by means of leghold traps or trapping methods which do not meet international humane trapping standards, n. 79 above.

[112] Reg. 428/89 concerning the export of certain chemical products, n. 87 above.

[113] See in detail Demaret, n. 62 above, 369.

[114] See the preamble to Council Reg. 3626/82/EEC on the implementation in the Community of the Convention on International Trade in Endangered Species of wild fauna and flora, n. 54 above.

[115] e.g. Art. 4(5) of the Basel Convention on Transboundary Movements of Hazardous Wastes and their Disposal, n. 43 above, or Arts. II, III, IV, and XIV of the CITES Convention, n. 98 above.

[116] Demaret, n. 62 above, 375.

non-domestic environment in accordance with the objectives agreed upon under the international agreements.[117]

Case: Germany introduced an import ban against products made from *corallum rubrum* which is a coral occurring in the Mediterranean Sea and used for the production of jewellery. It is not covered by Community secondary law and lawfully used and exported from Italy. Germany invoked Article 15 of Regulation 3626/82 implementing the CITES convention which allows for more stringent domestic measures for the species regulated in this regulation. It allows *inter alia* the adoption of more stringent domestic measures for the conservation of an endangered species in the country of origin. The Commission did not take any steps to challenge the German measure.[118]

Autonomous Domestic Trade Measures

Whenever the Community has not adopted any measures under Article 113 EC the Member States are authorized under the delegation doctrine[119] to adopt trade measures against non-member countries. This is explicitly provided for by Regulation 288/82 on common import rules[120] which authorizes Member States to adopt or maintain TREMs against non-member countries as long as the Community does not act, provided the measures are notified to the Commission.[121] They allow the restriction of imports and exports to non-member countries under similar grounds as provided for by Article 36 EC.[122] *Demaret* holds correctly that the grounds under the rule of reason should also be included.[123]

The main problem in such a case, however, might be the implications for trade within the Community, as a Member State must also ban trade with the other Member States to prevent any circumvention of these regulations. This, however, implies that the Member State must justify the trade restrictions towards other Member States as lawful under Article 36 or possibly the rule of reason. Keeping in mind the broad interpretation of Article 30 in the *Dassonville*

---

[117] See e.g. Art. 14 of Council Dir. 79/409/EEC on the conservation of wild birds [1979] *OJ* L103/1 which allows also stricter measures for the protection of migratory birds and seriously endangered birds in relation to other countries. See for details also J. Temple Lang, 'The European Community Dir. on Bird Conservation' [1982] *Biological Conservation* 11 to 25. See also Case C–169/89 *Van den Burg*, n. 99 above.

[118] See for details of this unpublished case Krämer, n. 98 above, 151 at 166; see also Case C–169/89 *Van den Burg*, n. 99 above, 2164.

[119] See e.g. Case C–62/88 *Chernobyl I*, n. 10 above, 1545; Case 41/76, n. 77 above; or Case 174/84 *Bulk Oil (Zug) AG* v. *Sun Ltd. and Sun Oil Trading Company (Sun Oil)* [1986] *ECR* 559.

[120] Council Reg. 288/82/EEC on common rules for imports, n. 93 above; Reg. 1765/82/EEC on common rules of imports from state-trading countries, n. 93 above; and Reg. 1766/82 on common rule for imports from the People's Republic of China, all amended by Council Reg. 1243/86/EEC [1986] *OJ* L113/1.

[121] Art. 21; see for the system concerning the notification of environmental measures also the relevant provisions and secondary legislation under Arts. 100, 100a(4), 100a(5), and 130r.

[122] See also Schröer, n. 9 above, 295, with reference to P. Gilsdorf, 'Die Grenzen der gemeinsamen Handelspolitik' in G. Ress (ed.), *Rechtsprobleme der Rechtsangleichung. Vorträge, Reden und Berichte aus dem Europainstitut, Nr. 137* (Europainstitut der Universität des Saarlandes, Saarbrücken, 1988), 44.

[123] Demaret, n. 62 above, 358.

formula and the questionable justification of Article 36 for the protection of the non-domestic environment, this can lead to serious problems. In this case the products originating in a non-member country but legally brought into commerce in another Member State are covered by the provisions of Article 30 EC.[124] Any national measure has to be compatible with the relevant Treaty obligations even if the products' country of origin is a non-member country. The provision of Article 9(2) EC prevents the application of more stringent measures outside Article 36 or the rule of reason.

Example: A fictitious example would be Germany's restriction on the import of beer not produced according to the German standard of the 'Reinheitsgebot' (purity law).[125] In its 1987 judgment[126] the Court of Justice decided that Germany could no longer restrict the import of beer from other Member States on the ground that it did not conform to its own norms. Germany had not been able to demonstrate that the justification needed under Article 36 EC. Germany remained, however, free to restrict the import of such beer from non-member countries as external trade restrictions are not normally subject to the broad prohibition of the *Dassonville* formula. The problem arising for Germany, however, in this situation would be that it is not allowed to ban the import of such beer from another Member State even if it originates from a non-member country but is in free circulation in another Member State.

INTERNATIONAL TRADE AND COMMODITY AGREEMENTS

Articles 113 and 114 EC provide the Community with an explicit and exclusive[127] competence to regulate commercial policy relations. This power includes, apart from the regulation by unilateral measures concerning imports and exports (autonomous commercial policy), the conclusion of agreements with non-member countries (conventional commercial policy).[128]

Many of the commercial agreements concluded by the Community on the basis of Article 113 include certain environmental provisions which limit or authorize the Community and its Member States to take trade measures for the protection of the environment.[129] They are usually rather difficult to interpret as the main objective of the concluded treaties is the promotion of trade and not the protection of the environment. Nevertheless, there is a growing awareness of the importance of such environmental escape clauses or minimum standards.

---

[124] There may, however, be specific Community regs. in order to co-ordinate such import restrictions against goods originating in non-member countries.

[125] This example is given by Demaret, n. 62 above, 378.

[126] Case 178/84 *Commission* v. *Germany (German Purity Law)* [1987] *ECR* 1227.

[127] See Case 41/76, n. 77 above, 1937.

[128] Kapteyn and VerLoren van Themaat, n. 6 above, 788.

[129] e.g. Art. XX GATT; see for details E.-U. Petersmann, 'International Trade Law and International Environment Law—Prevention and Settlement of International Disputes in GATT' [1993] *JWT* 45 to 81. See, however, the Court's case law on the direct applicability of GATT law, e.g. most recently in Case C–280/93 *Germany* v. *Commission (Bananas)* [1994] *ECR* I–4973.

They seek a symbiosis between environment and trade and should not be interpreted as eliminating national environmental measures to a maximal extent. Still, the impact of these provisions can be particularly far-reaching and has not yet been sufficiently analysed.[130] A particularly important issue at the global level is the integration of domestic environmental rules under the common trade system of the General Agreement on Tariffs and Trade (GATT) and the newly created World Trade Organization (WTO). Environmental measures which differentiate according to not commonly recognized 'environmental criteria' may very easily interfere with the obligations arising out of the international trade order. The developments in this area show, however, that the international conception of the relationship between 'trade and environment' are changing fast.[131] Unilateral measures to influence another State's environmental policy or to counterbalance any existing cost disadvantage of national producers resulting from higher domestic environmental standards[132] remain, however, highly controversial.[133] Specific commodity agreements may sometimes also have an important environmental impact (e.g. tropical timber[134]). They are usually based on Article 113 in spite of their importance for the international environmental policy of the Community.[135] Many of the more recent trade agreements between the EC and non-member countries contain specific provisions on economic co-operation in the area of the environment. The recently concluded trade and co-operation agreements between the former COME-CON countries and the EC contain important provisions on economic and environmental co-operation.[136] The free-trade agreements between the EFTA countries and the

[130] See e.g. for the compatibility of EC law, in particular environmental standards, with GATT S. Woolcock, 'The European *Acquis* and Multilateral Trade Rules: Are they Compatible?' [1993] *JCMS* 540 at 546, or for unilateral trade restrictions for environmental reasons see H. Grossmann, 'Einseitige Schutzmassnahmen der EG gegenüber unfairen Handelspraktiken' [1993] *Wirtschaftsdienst* 487 at 491.

[131] See e.g. D. Esty, *Greening the GATT—Trade, Environment and the Future* (Institute for International Economics, Washington, DC, 1994) or D. Zaelke, P. Orbuch, and R. F. Housman (eds.), *Trade and Environment—Law, Economics and Policy* (Island Press, Washington, DC, 1993). For a comparative aspect of GATT rules and the Community conception see e.g. Petersmann, n. 48 above.

[132] A particularly interesting example for a domestic environmental measure with potential trade effects is the Commission's proposal for a CO_2 dir.; see for a hypothetical analysis of the current proposal M. Düerkop, 'Trade and Environment: International Trade Law Aspects of the Proposed EC Dir. Introducing a Tax on Carbon Dioxide Emissions and Energy' (1994) 31 *CMLRev.* 807 at 820 ff.

[133] See in particular the panel reports of two disputes arising in GATT on trade restrictions against 'non-dolphin-friendly' fished tuna; see for a comprehensive analysis Petersmann, n. 48 above. On the EC's approach to the use of trade measures for international environmental policy see: e.g. C. Bail, 'The Promotion of Policy Coherence on Trade and Environment: A Role for the European Community' in Cameron, Demaret, and Geradin (eds.), n. 2 above, 333 at 335 ff.

[134] The Community is a party to the International Tropical Timber Agreement: Council Decision of 26 Mar. 1985 on the application of the International Agreement on Tropical Timber 1983, n. 95 above; see for details of the Community's timber trade policy: P. Demaret, 'Trade-Related Environmental Measures (TREMs) in the External Relations of the European Community' in Cameron, Demaret, and Geradin (eds.), n. 2 above, 277 at 282 to 285.

[135] See the section on external trade (Art. 113 EC) above.

[136] See e.g. the new trade and co-operation agreements between the Community and most Eastern European countries, based on Arts. 113 and 235: Albania [1992] *OJ* L343/1; Estonia [1992]

EC[137] include similar provisions to Article 30 and 36[138] which allow also for domestic protection measures on established grounds[139] provided the non-discrimination requirement is fulfilled.[140] The EEA Agreement incorporates a large amount of the secondary environmental law of the EC and the Agreement itself corresponds in large parts to the EC Treaty.[141]

Case: In Case 125/88 *Criminal Proceedings against Nijman*[142] a Dutch prohibition on certain pesticides was challenged before the Court. Besides the application of Article 30 EC[143] the plaintiffs invoked also the corresponding provision of the free-trade agreement between the EC and Sweden,[144] as the prohibited substance had been imported from Sweden. The Court accepted the application of Article 13(1) (prohibition of quantitative restrictions and measures having equivalent effect) of the free-trade agreement but concerned the measures to be justified under Article 20, which, in the same way as Article 36 within the Community, allows Member States to take their own protection measures under the established conditions.

ASSOCIATION AGREEMENTS UNDER ARTICLE 238

Association agreements under Article 238 may also include environmental provisions which lead to common rules at Community level and thereby restrict the Member States in their national environmental policy towards the associated countries. In certain cases association agreements also provide for specific trade

OJ L403/1; Romania [1991] *OJ* L79/1 and[1993] *OJ* L81/1; former Soviet Union/CIS [1990] *OJ* L291/1; Czech Republic [1990] *OJ* L291/1; Slovakia [1990] *OJ* L291/1; Bulgaria [1990] *OJ* L291/1; Poland [1989] *OJ* L339/1; Hungary [1988] *OJ* L327/1; Slovenia [1993] *OJ* L189/1; for a survey and the references to the agreements concluded see [1993] *EUR–OP News* (no. 3) 4.

[137] See e.g. H.-P. Duric, *Die Freihandelsabkommen EG-EFTA: Die rechtliche Problematik* (Nomos, Baden-Baden, 1991) or S. Griller, *Europäische Normung und Rechtsangleichung—Der Abbau technischer Handelshemmnisse in Europa unter besonderer Berücksichtigung Österreichs* (Signum-Verlag, Wien, 1990) or A. Oehmichen, *Die unmittelbare Anwendbarkeit der völkerrechtlichen Verträge der EG: Die Freihandels- und Assoziierungsabkommen* (Diss., Saarbrücken, 1992).

[138] See e.g. Case 125/88 *Ministère Public* v. *Nijman* [1989] *ECR* 3533 concerning pesticides from Sweden or Case C–228/91 *Commission* v. *Italy* (*Nematode Larvae*) [1993] *ECR* I–2701, concerning fish imports from Norway containing nematode larvae.

[139] For a detailed analysis see J. Borer, *Massnahmen gleicher Wirkung wie mengenmässige Beschränkungen im im Freihandelsabkommen Schweiz–EWG* (Stämpfli, Bern, 1988); for a survey of the EEA provisions and measures for the protection of the environment see A. Furrer, 'Nationale Umweltschutzkompetenzen in der EWG und im EWR' [1992] *AJP* 1517 at 1527 to 1531 or Petersmann, n. 84 above, 126.

[140] See e.g. Case C–312/91 *Criminal Proceedings against Metalsa Srl*, judgment of 1 July 1993 (*discrimination in tax matters—EC-Austria free trade agreement*) or Case C–125/94 *Aprile Srl* v. *Amministrazione delle Finanze dello Stato*, judgment of 5 Oct. 1995; see also for an environmental case involving the relevant provisions of the free trade agreement between Switzerland and the Community: BGE 118 Ib 367 (*prohibition of importations of PVC bottles from France into Switzerland*) and the comments e.g. by O. Jacot-Guillarmod, *Le juge national face au droit européen* (Bruylant, Basel and Bruxelles, 1993); C. Bovet, 'Concurrence et environnement' [1995] *SZW/RSDA* 169 at 171.

[141] See e.g. Petersmann, n. 84 above, 126 to 128, or Furrer, n. 139 above.

[142] Case C–125/88, n. 138 above.   [143] See Ch. 4.

[144] [1972] *JO* L300/185 or English Special Edition, 99.

rules between the Community and its associated partners which may also include certain restrictions concerning the adoption of environmental control measures and licensing procedures.[145] Legal literature maintains that Article 238 is the correct basis in these cases, as association agreements may cover all areas referred to in the Treaty.[146] Considering the effect of Article 130r(2) the protection of the environment will also be taken into consideration in the association policy of the Community. In the Lomé Conventions, in particular, the Community has over time incorporated more and more environmental aspects with direct effect on the Member States.

Example: While the Lomé II Convention contained only a declaration on environmental desirability of certain objectives,[147] the Lomé III Convention contained an entire chapter on drought and desertification control.[148] The Lomé IV Convention contains a specific chapter on the environment including a prohibition on exporting dangerous waste from the Community to Lomé countries.[149] The most important provision here is Article 39. It provides that the Community shall prohibit all direct or indirect export of such waste to the ACP countries.[150]

---

[145] See e.g. Case C–432/92 *The Queen* v. *Ministry of Agriculture, Fisheries and Food, ex parte S. P. Anastasiou (Pissouri) Ltd. et al.* [1994] *ECR* I–3087, which concerned the Association Agreement between the Community and the Republic of Cyprus, annexed to Council Reg. 1246/73/EEC of 14 May 1973.

[146] Schröer, n. 9 above, 296; Vedder, Art. 234, in Grabitz and Hilf (eds.), n. 29 above. See also Case 12/86 *Meryem Demirel* v. *Stadt Schwäbisch Gmünd* [1987] *ECR* 3719 at 3751.

[147] [1980] *OJ* L347/2, Arts. 83, 84g, and 93c.

[148] [1986] *OJ* L86/3 and L292/52; Ch. 2, Arts. 38 to 43, also in Council of Ministers, *The Third ACP-EEC Convention* (EC, Brussels, 1985).

[149] See Krämer, n. 1 above, 156, referring to the Fourth ACP–EEC Convention, signed at Lomé on 15 Dec. 1989, Part 2, Title 1, Arts. 33 to 44, and Council of Ministers, *Fourth AC–EEC Convention* (EC, Brussels, 1992).

[150] See Demaret, n. 62 above, 345; H.-D. Kuschel, 'Das neue Lomé-Abkommen zwischen der EG und den AKP-Ländern' [1981] *EA* 333 at 335; C. Cova, 'Lomé IV: Une convention pour 10 ans' [1990] *RMC* 1. Similar provisions have been adopted by the parties to the Basel Convention on Transboundary Transport of Hazardous Wastes and their Disposal, n. 43 above, see *Neue Zürcher Zeitung* (26/27 Mar. 1994, no. 72), 35.

12

Integration of the Common Market and the Environment

THE ENVIRONMENT: SHARED RESPONSIBILITY AND COMPETENCE

On Competence and Responsibilities

Common Market and Environment

The establishment of a common market and the elimination of national borders for the exchange of goods has been one of the pillars of the European Community since its inception.[1] However, the protection of the environment was given little attention during the first period of European integration.[2] Nevertheless, since the early 1970s and particularly since the coming into force of the Single European Act the Community has been entrusted with the effective protection of the environment.[3]

Today both the establishment of one market and the efficient protection of the environment are equally important objectives of the Community.[4] Nevertheless, the pursuit of these two objectives simultaneously can cause problems. They are not *per se* contradictory but they do require some co-ordination. Apart from the relevant sections of the Treaty[5] this also has important implications for the work of the Court[6] and the Commission.[7] The two main means used by the Community to establish the common market without jeopardizing the state of the environment are the limited national autonomy to adopt environmental measures[8] and the adoption of harmonized Community environmental rules and standards[9] which sometimes provide for specific opportunities for Member States to adopt more stringent measures.[10]

---

[1] See Chs. 1 and 8.   [2] See Ch. 7 for these early stages.
[3] See Ch. 7 on the SEA and TEU.
[4] Although the establishment of the common market is not an aim in itself but much more the essential means for the achievement of many other Community objectives, see Art. 2 EC.
[5] Arts. 2, 130r(2), 100a(4) and (5), 130t etc.
[6] See e.g. Joined cases 3, 4, and 6/76 *Criminal Proceedings against Cornelis Kramer* (*Biological Resources of the Sea*) [1976] *ECR* 1279; Case 240/83 *Procureur de la République* v. *Association de Défense des Brûleurs d'Huiles Usagées* (*ADBHU*) [1985] *ECR* 531; Case 302/86 *Commission* v. *Denmark* (*Danish Bottles*) [1988] *ECR* 4607; Case C–2/90 *Commission* v. *Belgium* (*Walloon Waste Case*) [1992] *ECR* I–4431. See the section below on finding a balance.
[7] See EC Commission, *V Environmental Action Programme 'Towards Sustainability'*, COM(92)23 final, Vol. ii, 113, also at [1993] *OJ* C138/1; EC Commission, *XXII Report on Competition Policy* (EC, Brussels, 1993), 52 and 251.   [8] See Pt. I.   [9] See Pt. II.
[10] See also D. Geradin, 'Free Trade and Environmental Protection in an Integrated Market: A Survey of the Case Law of the United States Supreme Court and the European Court of Justice' (1993) 2 *Journal of Transnational Law and Policy* 141 at 162 to 197; U. Becker, *Der Gestaltungsspielraum der Mitgliedstaaten der EG-Mitgliedstaaten im Spannungsfeld zwischen Umweltschutz und freiem Warenverkehr*

Relevant Competences

The Community has no exclusive competence over the protection of the environment. The Community and the Member States share responsibility for the protection of the environment within the Community[11] and for global co-operation,[12] despite the fact that the Community's own environmental policy is limited by the principle of subsidiarity.[13] From the common responsibility derives the shared competence for the adoption of measures to safeguard the environment.[14] The system developed by the Community and its Member States includes various instruments or mechanisms for the co-ordination of national environmental measures, Community environmental measures, and rules and principles for the establishment and functioning of the common market.[15]

Community Competence and Domestic Measures

Before the coming into force of the Single European Act the Community based its environmental policy mainly on Article 100 and/or possibly on Article 235 EC.[16] As long as the Community had not adopted any measures in a specific field, Member States remained free to adopt their own measures provided they did not interfere with the obligations arising from the Treaty.[17] Once the Community had adopted harmonization measures, Member States were no longer able to adopt their own measures. Under the principle of supremacy of Community law over domestic law, exhaustive regulation at Community level precluded the Member States from the adoption of any additional measures.[18]

The quasi-pre-emptive effect[19] of Community secondary law under Articles 100 and 235 could only be moderated by specific exceptions in the secondary acts. This was, however, in common use, not only under Articles 100 and 235 but also when secondary environmental acts were adopted under the special provisions of Articles 43, 75, 84(2) etc.[20] With the rapid growth of Community

---

(Nomos, Baden-Baden, 1991), 17; A. Middeke, *Nationaler Umweltschutz und Binnenmarkt* (Heymann, Köln, 1993), 39 to 42.

[11] See Ch. 7 on shared responsibility and in general L. Krämer, 'Environmental Protection and Art. 30 EEC Treaty' (1993) 30 *CMLRev.* 111 at 114; M. Zuleeg, 'Vorbehaltene Kompetenzen der Mitgliedstaaten der Europäischen Gemeinschaft auf dem Gebiet des Umweltschutzes' [1987] *NVwZ* 280 at 281; I. Pernice, 'Kompetenzordnung und Handlungsbefugnisse der Europäischen Gemeinschaft auf dem Gebiet des Umwelt- und Technikrechts' [1989] *DV* 1 at 42.

[12] See Ch. 11.

[13] See Ch. 7 on subsidiarity and below 4.1; also e.g. A. G. Toth, 'The Principle of Subsidiarity in the Maastricht Treaty' (1992) 29 *CMLRev.* 1179 to 1106.

[14] See Chs. 7 on shared competences and 9 on environmental policy.

[15] See the detailed conclusions below.

[16] See Chs. 7 and 8 on Arts. 100 and 235 EC.   [17] See Chs. 8, 9, and 10.

[18] See Ch. 7 and Ch. 5 on Art. 36 and the rule of reason.

[19] See Ch. 7 on pre-emption and the most interesting contribution by E. D. Cross, 'Pre-emption of Member State Law in the European Economic Community: A Framework for Analysis' (1992) 29 *CMLRev.* 447 to 472.   [20] See Ch. 9.

environmental law the need for an institutionalized system for domestic divergent measures became evident.

The Institutionalization of Shared Responsibility

Under the Treaty on European Union a system of rules has been further institutionalized which allows for different degrees of harmonization and a complex set of Community measures and national measures for the protection of the environment.[21] In view of the principles of subsidiarity[22] and the commitment to a high level of environmental protection at a locally adequate level,[23] this system allows the Member States, in most cases, to adopt more stringent environmental measures if they are justified in the interests of the environment and do not jeopardize the other Community objectives. Apart from the explicit Treaty provisions on domestic environmental measures in fields where harmonized Community measures exist, the Court's and the Commission's practice with regard to the use of the Treaty's exception clauses, such as Articles 36, 85(3), or 92(3), provides important opportunities for the application of diversified economic and legal instruments at national and regional levels.[24]

Thus, the principle of 'quasi-pre-emption' and incidental derogations has been complemented by a general co-operation principle which allows the Member States to adopt measures after the harmonization of an environmentally relevant field.[25] The implementation of Community directives, the use of specific derogation in secondary law and minimum standards, as well as the general capacity to adopt more stringent measures under the systematic derogations of Articles 100a(4) and 130t, create a system which follows the idea of a common responsibility through a common competence for the environment.[26] Thus the Community has created a unique set of instruments to co-ordinate domestic and Community action for the efficient protection of the environment at both Community and domestic level.

---

[21] See Ch. 7 on subsidiarity.

[22] Art. 3b; the particular importance for the environment is stressed by the fact that the subsidiarity principle was referred to in Art. 130r(4) under the Single European Act, exclusively for actions related to the protection of the environment.

[23] See for details Zuleeg, n. 11 above, 280 to 286, and W. Kahl, *Umweltprinzip und Gemeinschaftsrecht* (Müller Juristischer Verlag, Heidelberg, 1993), 10 to 91.

[24] See Chs. 5 and 6.

[25] In particular Art. 100a(4) and 130t as described in Chs. 8 and 9; see the harsh criticism of this rupture in the Community's legal order by P. Pescatore, 'Some Critical Remarks on the Single European Act' (1987) 24 *CMLRev.* 9 at 12, or P. Pescatore, 'Die "Einheitliche Europäische Akte" ' [1986] *EuR* 153 to 169. See also Ch. 8.3.5.

[26] See also the equivalent approach by Pernice, n. 11 above, 42, or Krämer, n. 11 above, 114 and 143, or L. Krämer, 'Community Environmental Law—Towards a Sustematic Approach' [1992] *YEL* 151 at 163 to 165; D. H. Scheuing, 'Umweltschutz auf Grundlage der Einheitlichen Europäischen Akte' [1989] *EuR* 152 at 164 to 173.

Mutual Recognition and Loyalty

The existence of shared responsibility for the protection of the environment is essentially based on the principles of co-operation within the Community.[27] Article 5[28] in conjunction with the specified, environmentally important provisions such as Articles 130r(3), 130r(4), 130t, 100a(4) and (5) etc. codifies the co-operative element which is necessary for co-ordina tion and collaboration in the protection of the environment at different levels.[29] The shared competence and shared responsibility rely on the co-operative sharing of tasks and the mutual co-ordination of environmental measures through the established mechanisms.

The Court derives from Article 5 the principles of loyalty[30] and solidarity[31] between Member States and between Member States and the Community. For the protection of the environment mutual co-operation and solidarity are particularly important. In this field the Community system incorporates the general principles of international law with regard to the environment[32] and establishes a system of mutual responsibility and co-operation.[33] Where the Community does not act itself, the Member States are the trustees for the benefit of the Community.[34] On the other hand, the Community has the duty to use its

---

[27] On the concept of co-operative Community law see J. Wuermeling, *Kooperatives Gemeinschaftsrecht* (N. P. Engel, Kehl am Rhein, 1988), 2 ff. Specifically in the field of the environment see Scheuing, n. 26 above, 167 and 171; A. Epiney and T. M. J. Möllers, *Freier Warenverkehr und nationaler Umweltschutz* (Heymann, Köln, 1992), 16; G. Bothe, 'Umweltschutz in der Europäischen Gemeinschaft' in P. Behrens and H.-J. Koch (eds.), *Umweltschutz in der Europäischen Gemeinschaft* (Nomos, Baden-Baden, 1991), 180 at 182.

[28] On the significance of Art. 5 see e.g. E. Grabitz, Art. 5 in E. Grabitz and M. Hilf (eds.), *Kommentar zur EU* (2nd edn., C. H. Beck, München, 1990 ff.); M. Zuleeg, Artikel 5, para. 5 in H. v. d. Groeben, J. Thiesing, and C.-D. Ehlermann (eds.), *Kommentar zum EWG-Vertrag* (Nomos, Baden-Baden, 1983 ff.).

[29] See in detail Kahl, n. 23 above, 120 and 121, who calls this the environmental co-operation rule.

[30] See the Court's language in Case 61/77 *Commission* v. *Ireland (Sea Fisheries I)* [1978] *ECR* 447 at 449, Case 141/78 *France* v. *United Kingdom (Sea Fisheries II)* [1979] *ECR* 2923 at 2942, and Case 32/79 *Commission* v. *United Kingdom (Sea Fisheries Conservation Measures)* [1980] *ECR* 2403 at 2432. For more references see Kahl, n. 23 above, 120. See also P. J. G. Kapteyn and P. VerLoren van Themaat, *Introduction to the Law of the European Communities* (2nd edn., Kluwer Deventer, 1989), 85 ff.

[31] See Joined cases 6 and 11/69 *Commission* v. *France (Rediscount Rate for Export Claims)* [1969] *ECR* 523 at 540. Case 77/77 *Benzine en Petroleum Handelsmaatschappij BV* v. *Commission* [1978] *ECR* 1513 at 1525; see also e.g. D. Lasok and J. W. Bridge, *The Law and Institutions of the European Communities* (5th edn., Butterworths, London, 1993), 39, or Kapteyn and VerLoren van Themaat, n. 30 above, 89.

[32] See e.g. Kapteyn and VerLoren van Themaat, n. 30 above, 89.

[33] See e.g. V. Constantinesco, 'L'article 5 CEE, de la bonne foi à la loyauté communautaire' in F. Capotorti *et al.* (eds.), *Du droit international au droit de l'intégration—Liber Amicorum Pescatore* (Nomos, Baden-Baden, 1987), 97 at 114: 'il apparaît que l'article 5 du traité CEE et l'utilisation qui en est faite par la Cour permettent de voir dans cette disposition l'énoncé d'un véritable principe fondamental du droit communautaire: le principe de co-opération' (it seems that Art. 5 EC and the way it is used by the Court in its case law point in the direction that this provision is a true founding principle of Community law in general: the principle of co-operation), with reference to Joined cases 205 to 215/82 *Deutsche Milchkontor* v. *Germany* [1983] *ECR* 2665. See also Kahl, n. 23 above, 120 to 143.

[34] See Case 804/79 *Commission* v. *United Kingdom (Sea Fisheries Conservation Measures)* [1981] *ECR* 1045 at 1075; See also M. Pechstein, *Die Mitgliedstaaten der EG als 'Sachwalter des gemeinsamen Interesses' und Gesetzgebungsnotstand im Gemeinschaftsrecht* (Duncker & Humblot, Berlin, 1987).

competence in a way which takes into account the needs and preferences of the different regions and Member States.[35] Thus, Community environmental acts should include whenever possible derogations for higher national standards[36] or even include regionally adequate protection levels.[37]

Implementation and Enforcement of Community Environmental Law

In the field of the protection of the environment, one of the most important aspects of the principle of loyalty under Article 5 is the Member States' obligation *to implement Community directives and to enforce the existing Community environmental law*. Only the strict application of the measures adopted ensures the efficient and effective protection of the environment. The Community relies predominantly on Member States for the realization of the Community legal order and it is the Member States' obligation to co-operate and guarantee the proper implementation of Community law. This is particularly important in the field of the environment, especially where specific habitats or species have been declared of European interest or where specific measures have been adopted for the establishment of the common market. In spite of the basic principle, the non-fulfilment of obligations arising from the Community's environmental law and the insufficient or incomplete implementation of Community environmental directives is one of today's most urgent problems concerning the environmental order of the Community.[38]

Mutual Recognition of Standards and Protection Measures

If one considers the duty to implement and enforce Community environmental acts as properly being one of the positive consequences of Article 5, the duty to abstain from any action which jeopardizes the objectives of the Community can be described as its negative consequence.[39] Both the protection of the environment and the achievement of the general objectives of the Treaty through the establishment of the common market are aims which have to be favoured and facilitated by the Member States. In the initial phase, Member States were completely precluded from adopting additional rules in areas where the Community had adopted exhaustive measures.[40] The pre-emptive effect of Community law was, and is, an instrument to allow the Community to implement a common

[35] Art. 130r(3) and (2).

[36] Art. 130r(2), second para., or Art. 130s(5) concerning financial aids or temporary derogations for less advanced regions or Member States.

[37] See e.g. the different protection levels according to different needs in Council Dir. 88/609/EEC on the limitation of emissions of certain pollutants into the air from large combustion plants [1988] *OJ* L336/1; see also Kahl, n. 23 above, 122.

[38] See e.g. also the detailed descriptions by U. Everling, 'Durchführung und Umsetzung des Europäischen Gemeinschaftsrechts im Bereich des Umweltschutzes unter Berücksichtigung der Rechtsprechung des EuGH' [1993] *NVwZ* 209 at 212 or M. Zuleeg, 'Umweltschutz in der Rechtsprechung des Europäischen Gerichtshofs' [1993] *NJW* 31 at 34 to 37.

[39] See for this distinction Constantinesco, n. 33 above, 99.

[40] See Chs. 5 and 8.

legal order and to rely on national administrative bodies and judges to ensure its realization.[41]

Nevertheless, with the coming into force of the Single European Act the Community has changed or rather amended its regulatory system in view of the urgent need for a high level of protection for the environment,[42] health,[43] worker safety[44] etc. Obviously, the general guiding principles of Community law such as its pre-emptive effect or the primacy of Community law remain the most important pillars of the Community's legal order. However, through the introduction of new provisions the system has been modified in order to strike a balance between different Community objectives. The introduction of explicit safeguard provisions, such as those incorporated in Article 100a(4) or 130t and in a somewhat modified way in Articles 100a(5) and 130r(2), allows for the introduction or maintenance of higher standards in fields of Community harmonization. The development which had started much earlier, by the introduction of explicit derogations in secondary Community acts, has been extended and is now used to ensure the protection of the environment at a high level. These new provisions give the Member States further responsibilities which have to be carried out within the limits prescribed by the Treaty provisions and the general spirit of the Treaty. The co-operative system can be conceptualized more easily by reference to systems of corporate federalism such as those known in the United States or other federal systems.[45]

While the Member States retain the power to adopt more stringent environmental legislation within their own territory according to national or regional preferences and within the framework provided for by the Treaty, the spirit of the Treaty demands on the other hand the mutual recognition of environmental choices and standards by other Community partners. The principle of solidarity and co-operation between Member States requires them to abstain from any measures which affect another Member State's right and responsibility to ensure the desired level of protection within its own territory.[46] Once a Community environmental measure has been implemented correctly by a Member State, it has fulfilled its basic tasks and duties under the Treaty. Where divergent environmental standards are unsatisfactory because of the alleged competitive effects or possible transboundary effects, Member States have to rely on the Community mechanisms for the adoption of common standards.

[41] See on the role of domestic judges and administrative bodies in the creation of a Community legal order e.g. F. Snyder, 'The Effectiveness of European Community Law' (1993) 56 *MLR* 19 to 54.
[42] Arts. 100a(4) and 130t.   [43] Art. 100a(4).
[44] Art. 100a(4) or Art. 118a; see also C.-O. Lenz, 'Immanente Grenzen des Gemeinschaftsrechts' [1993] *EuGRZ* 57 at 63.
[45] See the most interesting comparison by A. Sbragia, 'The European Community: A Balancing Act' [1993] *Publius—The Journal of Federalism* 23 at 37 or Kahl, n. 23 above, 121, with reference to German legal writing.
[46] See e.g. U. Everling, 'Die Wiederaufbereitung abgebrannter Brennelemente in anderen Mitgliedstaaten der Europäischen Gemeinschaft' [1993] *RIW*, suppl. 2, or H.-W. Rengeling, 'Schadlose Verwertung radioaktiver Reststoffe durch Wiederaufbereitung in anderen EG-Mitgliedstaaten' [1991] *DVBl.* 916 with reference to the territoriality principle.

Each Member State has to take into account the other Member States' needs and claims with regard to the protection of the environment.[47] This is particularly important in cases where the protection of the environment has transboundary effects and benefits or needs co-operation for a beneficial outcome.[48] If other Member States wish to attain a higher level of protection within the Community as a whole they have to use the Community procedures and are prevented from relying on any unfriendly acts or trade measures to influence another Member State's policy.[49] As such, where a territorial separation of environmental policies would be inefficient in cases where environmental problems have a transnational character or where environmental issues of a European or global concern are at stake, the Community provides an important forum for the adoption of high level environmental legislation at a common European level.[50] In areas, however, where no such issues are concerned, Member States have to abstain from influencing another Member State's environmental policy through the use of unilateral trade actions or similar measures. The use of import and export restrictions linked to extraterritorial environmental issues should be regulated through common European legislation and not by applying unilateral pressure.[51] As the Community is based predominantly on a system of law, the Member States are obliged to use the Community procedures and existing instruments to co-operate for the protection of the Common European and global environment.

As with the protection of the common European heritage or the life quality of the Member States' citizens, the Community has the ability to adopt measures which are aimed at the establishment of the common market through the harmonization of production and processing standards.[52] In these areas the alleged effect on competition of divergent national measures may lead to the adoption of common rules at a European level. In most cases the existing Community system ensures the maintenance of a minimum level of environmental protection and leaves Member States the power to adopt higher stan-

---

[47] See e.g. L. Krämer, Art. 130r, para. 92 in Groeben, Thiesing, and Ehlermann (eds.), n. 28 above, or Zuleeg, n. 38 above, 38.

[48] See e.g. the Court's considerations in Case C–9/89 *Spain* v. *Commission* (*Common Fisheries Policy Catch Limitations*) [1990] *ECR* I–1383 at 1410 concerning fish catch quotas.

[49] See Ch. 5 on the geographical scope of Art. 36 EC and e.g. Everling, n. 46 above; Rengeling, n. 46 above, 916, with reference to the territoriality principle.

[50] See e.g. the Community acts on trade in waste such as Commission Dir. 85/339/EEC on the supervision and control within the European Community of the transfrontier shipment of hazardous waste [1985] *OJ* L272/1 or for the reduction of air emissions such as Council Dir. 89/369/EEC on the prevention of air pollution from new municipal waste incineration plants [1989] *OJ* L163/32.

[51] See Ch. 5 on the geographical scope of Art. 36 EC; this does not rule out action by the Member States for the extraterritorial protection of the environment in cases where certain species or habitats have been declared 'the common heritage' as e.g. in Dir. 79/409/EEC on the conservation of wild birds [1979] *OJ* L103/1. See also Krämer, n. 11 above, 118.

[52] See Chs. 7 and 8 or the Court's considerations in Case 91/79 *Commission* v. *Italy* (*Detergents*) [1980] *ECR* 1099 at 1106, or more recently in Case C–300/89 *Commission* v. *Council* (*Titanium Dioxide*) [1991] *ECR* I–2867.

dards. Such domestic measures may have important competitive effects but they also represent different national choices and needs.[53]

When a Member State adopts higher standards within its territory, the national or regional choice will be accepted by the Community but does not automatically lead to the possibility of compensation for higher environmental costs.[54] As with the case of unilateral trade measures for the protection of the extraterritorial environment, Member States have to abstain from unilateral measures used to compensate the alleged loss of competitiveness through higher national environmental standards. While the 'polluter pays' principle and the responsibility for national environmental choices would prohibit all kind of state aids or investment aids for the avoidance of pollution or other environmentally harmful emissions, the Commission's practice under Articles 92(3) searches for a pragmatic balance to provide incentives for the introduction of (legally binding or voluntary) higher environmental standards combined with financial aids without allowing Member States to compensate for such regulatory differences wholly through the use of competition distorting state aids.[55]

An important consequence of the solidarity principle is the mutual recognition of equivalent product standards and environmental and health control measures.[56] The need for a high level of protection of the environment should never be abused for discriminatory or protectionist objectives.[57] While a Member State retains important discretion as far as the protection of its own territory or the common European heritage is concerned,[58] the Community order requires the Member States to accept standards and control measures which exist in other Member States and are equivalent to domestic standards. In these cases the protection of the environment does not justify the imposition of national standards which are not necessary for a higher level of protection within the importing country.[59] On the other hand, the establishment of the common market is based on the mutual recognition of standards, in particular when no harmonized European standards exist. This principle has been applied by the Court in its *Cassis de Dijon* case law[60] and has also found its way into the Single European Act (Article 100b).[61]

---

[53] See Ch. 2 on the possible 'disadvantages' arising from higher environmental standards for national undertakings.

[54] See also Ch. 6 on the role of state aids and Case 173/73 *Italy* v. *Commission (Family Allowances)* [1974] *ECR* 709 at 720.

[55] See Ch. 6 and EC Commission, *Guidelines on State Aids for Environmental Protection* [1994] *OJ* C72/3 to 9.

[56] See Ch. 5 on this principle and the abundant case law of the Court quoted there.

[57] See Ch. 5 on Art. 36. or the case law developed by the Court: see e.g. C-195/90 *Commission* v. *Germany (Charge on Heavy Goods Vehicles)* [1992] *ECR* I-3141; see also Ch. 9.4.

[58] See on the Court's case law concerning the level of protection in health and environmental issues Ch. 5.

[59] See e.g. Case 302/86 *Danish Bottles*, n. 6 above, or Case 178/84 *Commission* v. *Germany (German Purity Law)* [1987] *ECR* 1227.

[60] See Ch. 4.   [61] See also Pernice, n. 11 above, 48 and 49.

Co-operative Development of Environmental Law

Since the late 1960s the Community has adopted environmental measures which have become fairly extensive. We can probably differentiate schematically between three kinds of environmental measures although their objectives are often closely linked: (a) product standards, (b) production standards for the establishment of the common market, and (c) strictly environmental measures.

In its initial phase the Community adopted mainly environmental measures related to the consumption and production of goods. Production and processing standards were introduced to avoid the alleged competitive disadvantage which more advanced Member States feared from the autonomous introduction of higher environmental standards for the undertakings within their territories. At the same time the Community introduced product standards to allow the free movement of goods. In both areas the harmonization of environmental standards was intended to facilitate the establishment of the common market.[62] Thus, Member States were usually allowed to introduce higher environmental production and processing measures within their territory provided they did not extend their national standards through trade measures. Such standards raise the question whether this leads to discrimination against nationals (reverse discrimination[63]) but they do not affect the trade order of the Community.

The Community has also introduced common standards for end-products in order to allow these goods to move freely within the common market. The need for the acceptance of foreign products without abolishing all kinds of security and safety standards has led the Community to introduce its own safety measures, also in the field of the environment. On the other hand, Member States have always been allowed to apply environmental product standards if they were not completely harmonized at Community level, necessary for a legitimate objective, used in a non-discriminatory manner, and proportionate.[64]

The development of a genuine environmental policy on the basis of Article 130r is the extension of the incidental environmental measures which were taken in relation to establishment of the common market.[65] All the environmental measures which were adopted under Articles 100 and 235 or 43, 75, 84(2) etc. had important environmental effects. This remains true after the introduction of Articles 100a and 130r; in particular the case law concerning the appropriate legal basis for a Community act which has effects on both the common or internal market and the environment shows the close relationship between the environmental and economic effects of Community environmental law.[66] In any case the Community today has the power to adopt environmental measures in all areas.

---

[62] See Chs. 7 and 8.   [63] See Ch. 2.   [64] See Ch. 5.
[65] See Ch. 7 on the development of the environmental policy and Ch. 9 on Art. 130r.
[66] See Chs. 8 and 9; in particular see the case law in Case C–300/89 *Titanium Dioxide*, n. 52 above, or Case C–155/91 *Commission* v. *Council (Waste Directive)* [1993] *ECR* I–939.

Notification Procedures and Mutual Information

An important condition for the functioning of the Community's system for the co-ordination of national environmental measures and its own objectives of a high level of environmental protection and the establishment of the common market is mutual information between Commission and Member States.[67] It is a direct consequence flowing from the existence of a shared competence and the general principles of loyalty and solidarity.[68] The established information and notification procedures are a key element of co-ordination under the Treaty. These procedures usually provide for a standstill period and an examination of the measures in question by the Commission.

While for many years the Member States had no duty to inform the Commission about planned environmental measures which might concern the common market there is now an elaborate set of procedures. The gentlemen's agreement of 1973 on the notification of national draft environmental legislation has been largely replaced by more stringent provisions. Directive 83/189/EEC requires the notification of all national draft legislation providing product specification.[69] The broad interpretation by the Commission covers most national environmental legislation. In relation to national trade-related environmental measures against non-member countries, Directive 288/ 82/EEC provides for a similar procedure.[70]

The specific safeguard clauses of the relevant harmonizing Community measures usually require the execution of a specific notification and examination procedure to be applicable.[71] This notification requirement has been institutionalized under Articles 100a(5)[72] and 130r(2).[73] Article 100a(5) explicitly mentions the application of a 'control procedure', while Article 130r(2) refers to an 'inspection procedure'. The systematic application of diverging measures under Articles 100a(4)[74] and 130t[75] requires notification to the Commission.

The Commission as the guardian of the Treaty is required to control the application of all diverging national measures and examine their compatibility with the provisions invoked and the system of the Treaty in general. If it doubts the lawfulness of national measures it may take action against the Member State concerned in the European Court of Justice.[76] At the same time the Commission has to give a detailed statement of the reasons behind its decisions concerning national measures. Other Member States have the capacity to intervene before

---

[67] See also for details Kahl, n. 23 above, 136 to 138, or Middeke, n. 10 above, 213 to 218.

[68] See e.g. Kapteyn and VerLoren van Themaat, n. 30 above, 114, referring to the first limb of Art. 5 or Kahl, n. 23 above, 136 to 138.

[69] See Ch. 8, on notification and examination procedures, and Krämer, n. 26 above, 173.

[70] See Ch. 11 on Art. 113 EC and the implementing legislation.

[71] See Chs. 8, 9 and 10 on safeguard clauses.

[72] See Ch. 8 on Art. 100a(5).   [73] See Ch. 9 on Art 130r(2) EC.

[74] See Ch. 8 on Art. 100a(4) EC.   [75] See Ch. 9 on Art. 30t EC.

[76] See the procedural aspects in Chs. 6, 8, and 9, and also the descriptions by Middeke, n. 10 above, 213 to 218, or Kahl, n. 23 above, 136 to 138.

the Court and the latter has underlined the importance of such procedural aspects and information requirements.[77] Similarly, the exceptional admissibility of voluntary agreements under Article 85 and state subsidies under Article 92 is subject to very strict information and control procedures.[78]

COMMON MARKET AND ENVIRONMENT: FINDING THE BALANCE

The Protection of the Environment and Social Regulation

To install a proper environmental policy, the Member States of the European Community use a diversified set of instruments depending on the problems concerned.[79] They are all aimed at reducing environmental damage or pollution and preserving our natural habitats and quality of life. While economic instruments such as pollution charges or environmental taxes, as well as tradeable pollution permits, aim at the internalization of external costs of production and consumption processes,[80] prohibitions and standards for products or their components, and for certain production methods or processes, aim at the precautionary elimination of certain environmental dangers and risks.[81] While the first category becomes increasingly important in view of the efficient allocation of costs and resources through the price or market mechanism, the latter retains its importance in areas where the evaluation of costs is difficult or the potential risk too high or not clearly recognizable.[82]

A third category of instruments is voluntary agreements between the authorities and certain undertakings. Even in cases where such agreements are concluded only between private undertakings, the authorities may favour, allow, or facilitate them and thus use these agreements as an element of their own environmental policy. Particularly in view of the existing implementation and enforcement problems of legally binding rules, voluntary agreements are becoming increasingly important elements of domestic administrative and environmental law.[83]

Finally, Member States may want to use financial incentives such as general state aids or investments aids as well as tax reductions or exemptions to facili-

---

[77] See Case C–41/93 *France* v. *Commission (PCP Decision)* [1994] *ECR* I–1829.

[78] See e.g. Ch. 6 on state aids and the Commission's practice as established in Communication of the Commission [1983] *OJ* C318/3.

[79] See on the optimal intervention for specific market failures e.g. H. G. Johnson, 'Optimal Trade Intervention in the Presence of Domestic Distortions', in P. Baldwin *et al.* (eds.), *Trade, Growth and the Balance of Payments* (Rand McNally, Chicago, 1965) or the general observations by E.-U. Petersmann in *Constitutional Functions and Constitutional Problems of International Economic Law* (Fribourg University Press, Fribourg, 1991), 57 ff.

[80] See, more specifically, Chs. 1, 3, and 10 on these economic arguments; see also on the 'polluter pays' principle Ch. 6.3.7.   [81] See Ch 4.

[82] See e.g. H. Siebert, *Economics of the Environment* (3rd. edn., Springer, Berlin, 1992).

[83] See Ch. 6 on voluntary agreements.

tate certain environmental behaviour.[84] While these measures are, in principle, contrary to the 'polluter pays' principle and do not really internalize external cost, they may still have positive environmental effects and be legitimate in cases where political or legal implications preclude the application of other instruments.[85]

Economic Freedoms against Interventionist Abuse

All these interventionist state measures aim at correcting market failures arising from the public or common good character of the environment. At the same time every state intervention concerning the economic process in general, as well as the competition of undertakings, may be abused by the authorities a phenomenon we call government failure.[86] As is the case for all economic measures described, national environmental measures, such as product standards, production requirements, prohibition of certain substances, specific environmental taxes, and state aids, can hinder trade and/or have an important impact on the competitive situation in the common market.[87]

As the establishment of the common market relies on the principles of undistorted trade and competition, such domestic action in principle jeopardizes the achievement of the Community's objectives.[88] Thus, the Treaty establishing the European Community includes an important number of rules and principles which should avoid the abuse of domestic policy instruments by Member States or regions within the European Community. Apart from the general rules derived from Article 5,[89] the Treaty's economic constitution[90] is predominantly based on the prohibitions of certain domestic actions which hinder trade or distort competition.[91]

As we have seen, domestic environmental measures may easily infringe the Treaty's provisions concerning the free movement of goods (Articles 30 and 34),[92] the prohibition of tax discrimination (Article 95),[93] the Member States' duties under Article 85 (in conjunction with Article 5),[94] and the prohibition of

---

[84] See Ch. 6 on the specific problems arising from tax cuts and state aids.

[85] See also the ambivalent but pragmatic approach by the Commission in its guidelines on state aids for environmental protection, n. 55 above.

[86] See e.g. Petersmann, n. 79 above, 96 ff.

[87] See Chs. 7 and 8 on these competition arguments leading to the harmonization of environmental laws at an early stage.

[88] See for details Ch. 2.   [89] See above on Art. 5 EC.

[90] See also the important principles concerning other human rights established mainly through the practice by the Court in its abundant case law, see e.g. H.-W. Rengeling, *Grundrechtschutz in der Europäischen Gemeinschaft* (C. H. Beck, München, 1993) or e.g. Case 29/69 *Criminal Proceedings against Stauder* [1969] *ECR* 419 at 430; Case 4/73 *Criminal Proceedings against Nold* [1974] *ECR* 491 at 516; Case 44/79 *Criminal Proceedings against Hauer* [1979] *ECR* 3727; Case C-260/89 *Criminal Proceedings against ETA* [1991] *ECR* I-2927 at 2963.

[91] On the similarities of the established trade rules with the global trade system and economic theory see Ch. 2 and W. Molle, *The Economics of European Integration* (Brookfield, Aldershot, 1990), 83 to 115.

[92] See Ch. 3.   [93] See Ch. 3 on Art. 95 EC.

[94] See Ch. 6 on state aids on agreements between undertakings.

state aids (Article 92).[95] In general, these Treaty provisions are directed at trade
and competition distortive and discriminatory state measures, but in some cases
their scope is far-reaching and goes well beyond the classical non-discrimination
principle.[96] This has been recognized very early on, following the Court's case
law in *Dassonville*,[97] where it seems that the Court's original interpretation went
much further than the Treaty drafters had planned and where the Court itself
had to reinterpret and concretize its own 'integrating case law'.[98]

Apart from pure discrimination cases,[99] the Community had and has to face
the problem of environmentally positive or useful domestic measures which
employ instruments principally prohibited by the Treaty or its interpretation by
the Court.[100] From the objective of the prohibitions referred to it, however,
becomes evident that domestic measures which do not distort trade or competition are not within their scope. In particular, in cases where the protection of
the environment is achieved by non-discriminatory measures, the Court's interpretation of Articles 34, 95, 92, and even 85 leaves space for domestic environmental measures. The issue is somewhat more difficult in cases where measures
fall under the Court's broad conception of Article 30. Nevertheless, under the
rule of reason the Court has found a way to moderate its integrative interpretation of this provision in a way which incorporates care for the environment
into the concept of Article 30.[101]

Even in cases where environmental measures have a limited distorting
effect,[102] all the Treaty guarantees referred to include specific exceptions which
can be used in the interest of certain public policy goals. Despite the lack of an
environmental consciousness of the Treaty drafters, the existing exceptions have
all been used for environmental measures. Article 36 is the most famous and discussed exception clause, which is partly due to the fact that prohibitions and
standards which easily fit into the Court's interpretation of 'measures having
equivalent effect' as trade restrictions were and are the most common instruments of traditional environmental policy.[103] On the other hand, we have noted

---

[95] See Ch. 6 on state aids.
[96] See on the integrative function of these provisions and the issue of 'negative integration' Ch. 2.
On Arts. 30 and 85 see also Kapteyn and VerLoren van Themaat, n. 30 above, 92 ff. and 355 ff.
[97] Case 8/74 *Procureur du Roi* v. *Dassonville* (*Dassonville*) [1974] *ECR* 837; see for details Ch. 3.
[98] See Ch. 3 on the *Dassonville* formula and with regard to Joined cases C–267 and 268/91
Criminal Proceedings against Bernard Keck and Daniel Mithouard, 24 Nov. 1993 and the *Cassis de Dijon* case
law.
[99] See on the importance of the non-discrimination principle Ch. 2 and the relevant considerations under Arts. 36 (Ch. 5), 76 (Ch. 9), and 95 (Ch. 3).
[100] See Chs. 1, 2, and 7 referring to the general development of the Community's environmental
policy.
[101] See Chs. 4 and 5.
[102] See on the limits of distortion in form of the proportionality principle under Art. 36 and the
rule of reason Ch. 5; for Art. 85 see the Commission's considerations on the 'unduly distortive effect
of such measures' Ch. 6 and EC Commission, *XXII Report on Competition Policy*, n. 7 above, 106, or
on the 'quasi-proportionality test' concerning environmental state aids see EC Commission, 55
above.   [103] See Ch. 4 and 5.

how Articles 92(3) and 85(3) are used to enable the Member States to use 'green' voluntary agreements between undertakings and state and investment aids in their domestic environmental policy.[104]

Nevertheless, all these exceptions are constructed to allow environmentally justified and necessary measures. Any abuse has to be avoided and the Court has developed a detailed set of conditions to be fulfilled before a distorting domestic measure is given the benefit of the Treaty's exception clauses, in particular under Article 36.[105] The Commission is considered to be the 'watchdog' of Community law and therefore one of the main actors for the detection of domestic abuses of environmental measures. The procedure under Article 169 is its main instrument for challenging the lawfulness of national laws,[106] rules, and administrative practices under Article 36. In the notification and control procedures under Articles 85(3) or 92(3) the Commission has a strong influence on the Member States' use of voluntary agreements and state aids for environmental aims.[107] Similarly, the quasi-constitutional character of Articles 30 and 34 leads to strict control of domestic measures through private claims before national courts and the possibility of preliminary rulings before the European Court of Justice.[108]

Specific Environmental Aspects

Through the interpretation of the scope of specific prohibitions and the possible exceptions, the Community has integrated the safeguarding of certain recognized public interests into the Treaty. The possible exceptions[109] to and the scope[110] of the Treaty's provisions concerning the prohibition of certain domestic measures generate the same considerations for all kinds of domestic actions of public interest, irrespective of their particular objective. Nevertheless, the principles developed by the Court leave abundant room for environmental considerations in fields where the justification of a measure is at stake. Even before the coming into force of Article 130r, the case law of the Court shows that the Court generally takes ecological considerations into account when applying and interpreting the Treaty provisions.[111] Similarly, one may say that the Commission refers regularly to environmental principles and considerations when deciding on domestic measures under Article 85 or 92. This seems particularly appropriate in view of the existence of Article 130r(2), the so-called integration clause,[112] which underlines the importance of the European

---

[104] See the relevant sects. in Ch. 6.   [105] See Ch. 5.   [106] See Ch. 8 on Art. 36 EC.
[107] See Ch. 6 on notification and control procedures in competition matters.
[108] See on the constitutional character of international rules Petersmann, n. 79 above, 299 ff., or 341 ff. and the importance of private actors in their enforcement e.g. Snyder, n. 41 above, 303 ff.
[109] See Arts. 36, 85(3), 92(3), and the relevant Chs. 3 and 6.
[110] See, in particular, Arts. 9, 30, 34, 85, 92, and 95 and the relevant Chs. 3 to 5 and 6.
[111] e.g. Case C–2/90 *Walloon Waste Case*, n. 6 above.
[112] See Ch. 9 and e.g. Kahl, n. 23 above, 27 or Pernice, n. 11 above, 50.

Community's commitment to a high level and efficient environmental policy for all areas of Community action.[113]

With the entry into force of the Single European Act (SEA), Article 130r(2) incorporated the protection of the environment as a general point of concern into all Community policies.[114] Community environmental policy had already been integrated into the Community order before the coming into force of the SEA through the case law of the Court of Justice on the appropriateness of specific Treaty provisions to adopt environmentally relevant harmonization measures, such as under Articles 43[115] or 100.[116] Similarly, the Court integrated domestic environmental concerns into the policy for the establishment of the common market at an early stage and introduced the concept of the 'protection of the environment' as a 'mandatory requirement of the Treaty' which has to be taken into account under Article 30.[117] Likewise, the Court and the Commission have included concern for the environment in the interpretation of the Treaty's exception clauses.[118]

The principles according to which the Community should pursue its environmental policy are enumerated in Article 130r(2) and are the recognized general principles of environmental law and policy, such as the precautionary principle, the principle of correction at source, and the 'polluter pays' principle.[119] Apart from Community secondary law, these principles have also found their way into the Court's and the Commission's application and interpretation of the Treaty. Nevertheless, their concrete application is still incidental and an important group of scholars has thus argued for an extension of the environmental provisions in the Treaty and the introduction of explicit procedures and organs.[120]

---

[113] See e.g. M. Schweitzer and W. Hummer, *Europarecht* (4th edn., Metzner, Neuwied, 1993), 388.

[114] Art. 130r(2) is the so-called integration clause: see Ch. 9.

[115] e.g. Case 68/86 *United Kingdom* v. *Council (Substances having a Hormonal Action)* [1988] *ECR* 855, see Ch. 9.3.2.

[116] E. g. Case 91/79, n. 52 above, 1106; see also Ch. 8 on Art. 100 EC.

[117] See Chs. 3 and 4, in particular Joined cases 3, 4, and 6/76 *Kramer*, n. 6 above, 1313, or Case 240/83 *ADBHU*, n. 6 above, 549. The leading case remains, however, Case 302/86 *Danish Bottles*, n. 6 above.

[118] See Ch. 4 on the relationship between Art. 36 EC and rule of reason. On Art. 85(3) see Ch. 6 and, in general, the Commission's *Report on Competition Policy*. For an environmental case see, e.g., the proceedings concerning 'Vereniging Van Onafhankelijke Tankopstang Bedrijven' (VOTOB) in EC Commission, *XXII Report on Competition Policy*, n. 7 above, 106 to 108, also discussed in Ch. 6. On the Commission's view of Art. 92(3) see EC Commission, *Guidelines on State Aids for Environmental Protection*, n. 55 above, and Joined cases 62 and 72/87 *Exécutif Régional Wallon* v. *Commission* [1988] *ECR* 1573 (paras. 22 to 25), discussed in Ch. 6.

[119] For a detailed description of all the principles involved see L. Krämer, *EEC Treaty and Environmental Protection* (Sweet & Maxwell, London, 1990), 51 ff.

[120] See the proposals by the 'European Environmental Union' Committee (including among others Hans-Christoph Binswanger, Peter Häberle, Michael Kloepfer, Jörg Paul Müller, Eckhard Rehbinder, Peter Saladin) on 'Aims and Principles of the Environmental Policy of the European Union (Umweltpolitische Ziele und Grundsätze für die Europäische Union—Vorschläge des Arbeitskreises 'Europäische Umweltunion'), issued on 20 Jan. 1994; reprinted in past in *Neue Zürcher Zeitung* (21 Jan. 1994, no. 17), 28.

At an early stage the Court incorporated the precautionary principle into its case law on domestic safeguard measures in fields such as health protection or protection of the environment.[121] Although not always explicitly referring to the precautionary principle, the Court's case law with regard to the level of proof of the existence of an environmental danger or the appropriate national level of protection relies on the application of this principle. The acceptance of a high level of domestic protection despite the disrupting effects on the common or internal market is particularly important under the precautionary principle. The Court leaves the Member States with significant discretion regarding the measures to be chosen,[122] the evaluation of environmental risks,[123] and the level of protection desired.[124] Most cases where domestic environmental measures have been considered to be unlawful under the Treaty have concerned discriminatory measures or situations where the Member States were not able to justify the measures applied.[125] To find the balance between the precautionary principle and the interest in market integration is a particularly difficult task.[126]

The 'polluter pays' principle is also playing an increasingly important role within the Community environmental order.[127] The use of charges and the internalization of external costs,[128] in general, are postulates of Community environmental policy.[129] In particular, in the procedures for the exceptional acceptance of domestic environmental state aids, the Commission regularly refers to the 'polluter pays' principle and makes it an important element for the evaluation of domestic measures.[130] In the application of Article 85(3) the Commission has shown a certain interest in the use of the 'polluter pays' principle, too.[131] Nevertheless, the Commission does not enforce the principle in all

[121] See for an example of the application of the precautionary principle by judges in American law with regard to wildlife protection e.g the decision by a New York State District Court in *Palladio v. Diamond*, 321 F Supp. 630 at 633 (SDNY, 1970) as referred to by Geradin, n. 1 above, 150: '[t]he state's list of endangered species may be broader than the federal simply because the State Legislature did not see fit to wait until only a handful of species remained before it passed a law affording protection. We cannot overrule the legislature for being cautious. Extinct animals, like lost time, can never be brought back. They are gone forever.'

[122] See the views of Epiney and Möllers, n. 27 above, 85, or K. Hailbronner, 'Der "nationale Alleingang" im Gemeinschaftsrecht am Beispiel der Abgasstandards füe PKW' [1989] *EuGRZ* 101 at 119.

[123] See e.g. Case 40/82 *Commission v. United Kingdom (Newcastle Disease)* [1984] *ECR* 283 at 299 or C-375/90 *Commission v. Greece (Scientific Uncertainty)* [1993] *ECR* I-2055; see Ch. 5.

[124] See e.g. Case 302/86 *Danish Bottles*, n. 6 above, and Ch. 5.

[125] See Ch. 5 for details.

[126] See below Ch. 12 for an analysis of the balancing process in the Community.

[127] See e.g. the *Vth Action Programme*, n. 7 above, and the comments in Ch. 7.

[128] See Ch. 3 on Art. 95 EC and, in particular, Ch. 10.

[129] See also on tolls and environmental charges the Court's reasoning in Case C-195/90 *Charge on Heavy Good Vehicles*, n. 57 above, the Community secondary law on tolls and charges for the use of motorways, Dir. 93/89/EEC [1993] *OJ* L279/32 and Case C-21/94 *Parliament v. Council* [1995] *Proceedings of the Court* (no. 20) 1.

[130] See Ch. 6 on state aids and EC Commission, *Guidelines on State Aids for Environmental Protection*, n. 55 above.

[131] See Ch. 6 on anti-competitive behaviour and in particular the procedure against VOTOB, n. 118 above.

areas and the abundance of regional and national state aids for environmentally beneficial behaviour is only explicable in view of the existing reluctance of Member States to implement a severe internalization of environmental costs.[132]

The principle of correction at source[133] and the related principles of proximity and self-sufficiency[134] have recently been given a central role in the general waste policy of the Community. In an unexpected development, the Court has integrated these principles into the general framework of trade in waste and thereby modified the general principle of free movement of goods.[135] While the particular decision in the relevant case may have been influenced by the difficult and emotional dispute about trans-frontier movements of waste in general at the time,[136] the principles have now definitely found their way into Community secondary law[137] and international conventions such as the Basel Convention[138] which are an integrative part of the Community order.

The Court's findings in the *Walloon Waste Case*,[139] in particular, show how new environmental principles can reshape a basic element of the Community order such as the free movement of goods.[140] While the development is warmly welcomed by certain authors, in principle, for ecological reasons, it is criticized by others who underline the fact that the treatment and disposal of waste are not always optimally guaranteed within the region of origin.[141]

Apart from the explicit environmental principles enumerated in the Treaty, the general development of the Court's case law and the Commission's practice shows how environmental concepts and considerations have reshaped certain general economic premises of the Treaty. In particular, under the non-discrimination principle, the differentiation according to ecological characteristics has important environmental effects and allows adequate treatment of environmental needs and objectives.[142] Examples from the case law of the Court show that ecological considerations can justify specific distinctions and a particular treatment of environmentally important situations. In the leading case, Case 302/86 *Commission* v. *Denmark* (*Danish Bottles*) the ecological effect of recyclable

---

[132] See Ch. 6 on state aids or Ch. 10 on the problems with the introduction of an energy-tax, Proposal for a Council Directive introducing a tax on carbon dioxide emissions and energy [1992] *OJ* C196/1.

[133] Art. 130r(2); on the development see Krämer, n. 119 above, 62.

[134] Elements of the Convention on the Control of Transboundary Movements of Hazardous Wastes and their Disposal, signed in Basel on 22 Mar. 1989, reprinted e.g. in (1989) 28 *ILM* 657.

[135] See Case C–2/90 *Walloon Waste Case*, n. 6 above. See e.g. D. Geradin, 'The Belgian Waste Case' (1993) 18 *ELRev.* 144 to 153.

[136] See e.g. the references in Everling, n. 38 above, 210.

[137] Dir. 91/156/EEC [1991] *OJ* L78/32.

[138] Convention on the Control of Transboundary Movements of Hazardous Wastes and Their Disposal, n. 134 above.

[139] Case C–2/90 *Walloon Waste Case*, n. 6 above.

[140] See for details and criticism Ch. 5.

[141] See for details the case analysis in Ch. 5.

[142] See in general on differentiation and discrimination Chs. 2 and, on Art. 36 EC and the rule of reason, 5.

bottles as opposed to non-recyclable drink containers was considered to be a valid characteristic for distinguishing the two kinds of containers,[143] while the fact that a species of bird is endangered obviously justifies specific treatment in comparison to non-endangered species.[144]

On the other hand, the mere fact that waste originates in another region has been considered by the Court to be sufficient to allow different treatment in comparison to local waste.[145] The latter case shows how the principle of correction at source also reshapes the non-discrimination principle in a way which is completely foreign to traditional trade theory.[146] In general, the origin of a product is not an objective reason which would allow for any differentiation between goods and any differential treatment is considered to be mere protectionism or unjustified discrimination.[147] In the case law of the Court and in Community secondary law,[148] however, the place of origin becomes, in the case of waste, the decisive characteristic of a product. Despite the possible criticism deriving from the optimal allocation of costs and resources, as well as the conceptual difficulties the case raises,[149] this is a meaningful example for the importance of environmental considerations and principles in the case law of the Court and in today's Community legal order. It will be interesting to see how far the principles of sustainability or bio-diversity, as they are listed in the *V Environmental Action Programme* in accordance with the decisions at the 1992 Rio Earth Summit, will influence the development of the Community order.[150]

In Search of a Balance

We have seen that the Community order requires the pursuit of different objectives and the use of distinct instruments for their achievement.[151] In a situation like this it is unavoidable that different objectives do not necessarily converge under certain conditions but require different measures. The alleged opposition

[143] Case 302/86 *Danish Bottles*, n. 6 above. See also Ch. 5 analysing the case.
[144] See Case C–169/89 *Criminal Proceedings against Gourmetterie Van den Burg BV (Scottish Red Grouse)* [1990] *ECR* I–2143 and Art. 14 of the relevant Community Dir. 79/409/EEC on the protection of wild birds, n. 51 above. See Ch. 5 for the analysis of the case.
[145] See Case C–2/90 *Walloon Waste Case*, n. 6 above. See e.g. Geradin, n. 135 above.
[146] See Ch. 5 on the Member States' remaining responsibilities. On the fundamental importance of the non-discrimination principle for the Community order see Ch. 2.
[147] This is e.g. the reasoning the US Supreme Court has applied in similar cases such as *Philadelphia* v. *New Jersey*, 437 US 617 (1978) where the Supreme Court held that differential treatment of non-local waste constituted discrimination against 'articles from outside the state unless there is some reason, apart from their origin, to treat tem differently'. See also Geradin, n. 10 above, 157.
[148] See Chs. 3 and 5.
[149] See e.g. E.-U. Petersmann, 'Freier Warenverkehr und nationaler Umweltschutz in EWG und EWR' [1993] *Aussenwirtschaft* 95 at 121.
[150] See EC Commission, n. 7 above, and Ch. 2. See also Ch. 5 on the Member States' remaining responsibilities.
[151] See the Preamble to the Treaty and Art. 2.

between trade and environment[152] is mainly based on cases where economic integration and local protection of the environment would require different solutions. In these cases the Court or the relevant Community institutions has to evaluate the interests at stake and to balance them in view of the objectives pursued. Economic integration is a means for the achievement of a set of Community objectives. It should, however, only be pursued in a way which guarantees a high level of environmental protection and allows for the sustainable use of natural habitats and resources.[153] Thus the co-ordination of environmental protection and economic integration asks for a continuous balancing.[154]

In many cases environmental interests may coincide with specific regional or national interests as opposed to the Community interest in economic integration through market freedoms and harmonization of standards. To find the balance between such territorial claims and interests of the Community as a whole is another task of the Community. Alberta Sbragia defines this situation by comparison with the United States as follows: '[t]he European Community is distinctive precisely because it deals with the claims of territory in a variety of ways. It is constantly searching for balance. . . . As the Community continues to undergo construction, it is inevitable that this constant searching for balance will continue'.[155]

While Articles 9, 12, 34, and 95 aim mainly at national measures applied in a discriminatory way, Article 30 covers also domestic measures which are applied equally to imported and domestic goods but affect inter-state trade in an excessive way. In particular in the field of the free movement of goods and in the case law concerning 'measures having equivalent effect' to restrictions on trade the Court has established a highly integrative approach[156] and consequently has had to establish a very sensitive set of conditions for the balancing of justified environmental measures and their disintegrative effect on the common market. For specific interests, Article 36 and similarly the case law of the European Court of Justice on the rule of reason allow for justified exceptions to the general prohibition of Article 30.[157] The protection of the environment is such an exception which allows national measures if they are justified, applied in a non-discriminatory way, and proportionate.

---

[152] See on the vivid criticism of economic growth and integration e.g. J. Bhagwati, 'Environmentalists against GATT' in *The Wall Street Journal* (European edn., 25 Mar. 1993), or E. Brown Weiss, 'Environment and Trade as Partners in Sustainable Development: A Commentary' [1992] *AJIL* 728 ff.

[153] See Art. 2 EC.

[154] See on the ranking between the different objectives of the Treaty e.g. Kahl, n. 23 above, 161 to 203. Most authors support the equal ranking of economic and ecological objectives, see e.g. E. Grabitz, Art. 130r in Grabitz and Hilf (eds.), n. 28 above; K. Heinz and A. Körte, 'Die Ziele Umweltschutz und Binnenmarkt zwischen gemeinschaftlicher Kompetenz und nationaler Verantwortung—Zu den neuen Umweltvorschriften im EWG-Vertrag' [1991] *JA* 41 at 46, T. Oppermann, *Europarecht* (C. H. Beck, München, 1991), para. 2010, or U. Beyerlin, 'Die "neue" Umweltpolitik der Europäischen Gemeinschaft' [1989] *UPR* 361 at 362.

[155] Sbragia, n. 45 above, 37.   [156] See Ch. 2.   [157] See Ch. 4.

While the Court has proved again and again its intention of avoiding any abuse of Article 36 or the rule of reason for protectionist and discriminatory domestic measures, it has also shown in many cases that it recognizes the importance of environmental protection in general and the need for domestic local and regional measures in particular.[158] Domestic environmental measures which do not fall within a field which is completely harmonized at Community level and are neither discriminatory nor a means of disguised protectionism are lawful under the system of Articles 30 and 36 if they are proportionate. As in other fields of social regulation, the proportionality test, as developed by the Court, is the Community's main instrument for the balancing of integration interests and environmental protection.[159]

Domestic measures have to be reasonable means for the achievement of a justified environmental objective. Apart from the set level of protection, Member States have to use the least trade restrictive measure available. The keystone of the system applied, however, is the question whether the trade restrictive character of a measure is excessive in relation to the environmental benefit achieved. The question of the excessive character of a measure, i.e. the request that a measure has to be proportionate to the aim pursued, is a crucial test which should balance the different interests concerned. In particular the judgment in Case 302/86 *Danish Bottles* has shown the importance of this element in the general Community system.[160] The Court has to weigh the interests concerned, a task which calls for a weighing of the different objectives at stake.[161]

While the Court has given the proportionality principle an important place in its general jurisdiction and in particular under Article 36 and the rule of reason, the Commission has adopted a related approach in its evaluation of environmental instruments which infringe the Community rules on undistorted competition. The Commission refers explicitly to the principle of proportionality when evaluating the lawfulness of voluntary agreements or the state aids.[162] In these cases the Commission is often confronted with instruments which may have positive environmental effects despite their competition distorting effect.[163] Like the Court, the Commission tries in these cases to balance the interests at stake. While the Commission, in principle, has to safeguard the Community order with regard to the free movement of goods and undistorted competition, it also has to consider the local and regional needs with regard to environmental policy.

---

[158] See Case 240/83 *ADBHU*, n. 6 above, 548; Case 302/86 *Danish Bottles*, n. 6 above; see Ch. 7 on the role of the Court.

[159] See Ch. 5.

[160] See e.g. K. Hailbronner, 'EG-Verkehrspolitik und Umweltschutz' in H.-W. Rengeling (ed.), *Umweltschutz und andere Politiken der Europäischen Gemeinschaft* (Heymann, Köln, 1993), 149 at 159.

[161] See for a detailed analysis of the Court's proportionality test under Arts. 30 and 36, Ch. 5, Middeke, n. 10 above, 198 ff. or Kahl, n. 23 above, 204 to 211.

[162] See e.g. EC Commission, *XXIII Report on Competition 1993* (EC, Brussels, 1994), and COM(94)161 final, 85; or the *Guidelines on State Aids for Environmental Protection*, n. 55 above.

[163] See e.g. also L. Krämer, 'Die Integrierung umweltpolitischer Erfordernisse in die gemeinschaftliche Wettbewerbspolitik' in H.-W. Rengeling (ed.), n. 160 above, 47 at 60.

Apart from the 'polluter pays' principle and the non-discrimination principle, the proportionality principle plays an important role in the Commission's considerations under both Article 85(3) and 93(3).[164] The Commission approves certain measures, which are in principle prohibited, provided they have positive environmental effects and do not 'unduly' restrict competition.[165]

The Commission and the Court are thus constantly in search of a balance between the different objectives of the Treaty. As in other legal systems,[166] this leaves judges, in particular, with an important discretion in situations where two objectives of a legal system have to be combined and eventually be ranked in the case at issue.[167] While the judges of the European Court should find certain guidance in the precautionary principle and the subsidiarity principle, the outcome of the balancing analysis may be somewhat unpredictable.[168] For reasons of legal certainty and predictability, harmonization at Community level and the negotiated balancing of interests by the Member States may lead to a more satisfactory and less controversial result. Undoubtedly, the Court has played a very important role in the development of environmental protection issues within the Community,[169] but in the long term important decisions on the place of environmental protection issues within the economic integration process have to be regulated in the Treaty and secondary Community law.[170] This does not require an exhaustive harmonization of standards at Community level and thus does not preclude Member States from adopting more stringent measures.[171]

The Court's decisions on the mandatory nature of environmental protection[172] within the Treaty system even before the entry into force of the Single European Act and the judgment in Case C-2/90 *Walloon Waste Case* are good examples of the important guiding role of the Court.[173] At the same time the introduction of the detailed environmental provisions under the Single European

---

[164] See Ch. 6.

[165] See e.g. the Commission's decision in the proceedings against VOTOB, n. 118 above; see also Ch. 6 analysing these proceedings.

[166] See e.g. the balancing test applied by the US Supreme Court, the Swiss Federal Court, or the German Constitutional Court, as refered to in Ch. 5; for the case of the United States see also Geradin, n. 10 above, 194.

[167] See for details Kahl, n. 23 above, 161, and in particular Case 302/86 *Danish Bottles*, n. 6 above.

[168] See e.g. the very similar situation concerning the trade in waste within the Community and the United States and the divergent case law by the Supreme Court and the Court of Justice Ch. 5 or Geradin, n. 10 above, 141 ff. See also the divergent opinions by Slynn AG in Case 302/86 *Danish Bottles*, n. 6 above, 4626, or the different reasoning by Jacobs AG in Case C-2/90 *Walloon Waste Case*, n. 6 above, 4456 ff.

[169] See Chs. 4 and 7.

[170] See e.g. also the openly admitted incapacity of the US Supreme Court to balance two different interests at stake in *American Can Co.* v. *Oregon Liquor Control Comm'n*, 517 P. 2d 691 (1972) at 697, as quoted by Geradin, n. 10 above, 159, who called for such harmonization.

[171] See the next section on harmonization in the EC.

[172] See Ch. 4 and, in particular, Case 240/83 *ADBHU*, n. 6 above, and Case 302/86 *Danish Bottles*, n. 6 above.

[173] See also the call for harmonization after the *Walloon Waste* decision, Geradin, n. 10 above, 196 to 197.

Act in 1987[174] and the introduction of Community secondary law concerning the transport and disposal of waste[175] show the importance of transparent and predictable rules for the Community actors.

THE HARMONIZATION OF EUROPEAN ENVIRONMENTAL LAW

Integration through Law

The general principle of non-discrimination and specific safeguard clauses for public interest reasons are integrated into most trade agreements.[176] The European Community, however, has further reaching objectives. As long as the members of a trade area are allowed to maintain very different rules for environmental reasons, the elimination of trade obstacles is limited. The harmonization of national laws and rules which hinder trade is one of the most specific elements of the Community in relation to ordinary international economic institutions. The harmonization of product-related national measures allows the elimination of different standards hindering trade and, at the same time, guarantees the maintenance of certain safety standards in the public interest.[177] In the field of environmental product measures the Community may also harmonize national standards and thereby eliminate obstacles to trade which otherwise would be covered by the exception clause of Article 36[178] or lawful as applied in a non-discriminatory way. In the field of environmental production measures[179] and indirect taxation[180] the harmonization of laws is rather in the interest of the elimination of differences in the competitive situations in Member States.[181]

The general harmonization of differing national rules hindering the establishment of the common market is based on Articles 100 and 100a. They are also appropriate for the harmonization of certain environmental measures.[182] Other provisions exist in the Treaty for the harmonization of rules in specific fields. Particularly important for the harmonization of environmental measures are: Article 43 (agriculture),[183] Articles 75 and 84(2) (transport),[184] Article 130s (environment)[185] etc. Specific environmental taxes used as economic instruments

---

[174] See Ch. 7.

[175] See, in particular, the literature referred to in Ch. 3 on waste.

[176] e.g. GATT Arts. I, III, and XX.

[177] See Ch. 8 and, in particular, Case 91/79 *Detergents*, n. 52 above.

[178] See e.g. Case 272/80 *Criminal Procedure against FNMBP (Plant Protection Products)* [1981] *ECR* 3277 at 3290.

[179] See also Ch. 8 and e.g. Case C–300/89 *Titanium Dioxide*, n. 52 above.

[180] See Ch. 10.

[181] See Cases 91/79 *Detergents*, n. 52 above, and 92/79 *Commission* v. *Italy (Maximum Sulphur Content of Liquid Fuels)* [1980] *ECR* 1099 and 1115; see Ch. 8, on Art. 100 EC.   [182] See Ch. 8.

[183] See Ch. 9 on the CAP.   [184] See Ch. 9 on transport.

for the protection of the environment can also fall under Article 99 (indirect taxation).[186] Article 130r(4) also empowers the Community to adopt measures which concern environmental co-operation with non-member countries.[187]

With regard to the external relations the Community has exclusive power under Article 113 to adopt measures concerning the common commercial policy.[188] Since more and more trade measures are used for the protection of the environment, Article 113 is applied to relations with non-member countries in a similar way to Article 100a within the internal market to harmonize trade-related environmental measures (TREMs).[189] As new trade-hindering obstacles may derive from different national environmental measures with regard to imports from non-member countries, the Community has the power to adopt a common position for the whole territory of the common market.[190]

The European Environment and European Law

Under the rubric of environmental protection, the harmonization of national laws is acceptable as long as the level attained in the Community guarantees efficient protection. Several provisions in the Treaty imply that the Community level of protection is intended to be high.[191] Nevertheless, the harmonization of environmental rules is not intended to eliminate justified environmental concerns in the Member States in the interest of the free movement of goods. As under Article 36, again here both objectives, the establishment of the common market and the protection of the environment, have to be respected equally.

Apart from product- and production-related harmonization measures linked to the establishment of the common market and the external commercial policy, the Community has also developed an important set of genuinely environmental measures. While the choice of the correct legal basis has become more difficult, the introduction of a genuine environmental competence under Article 130s EC indicates the development from a purely economic Community to a comprehensive legal system which has established an important ecological order.[192] A particularly interesting development is the recognition of a common European natural heritage which demands measures and financial support at a European level.[193]

---

[185] See Ch. 9 on Arts. 130r–130t EC.   [186] See Ch. 10.   [187] See Ch. 11.
[188] See Ch. 11.   [189] See Ch. 11 on Art. 113.
[190] See Case C–62/88 *Greece* v. *Council* (*Chernobyl I*) [1990] *ECR* I–1545; see Ch. 11 analysing the case.
[191] See Ch. 7 on this development.   [192] See also Ch. 7.
[193] See e.g. Dir. 79/409 on the conservation of wild birds, n. 51 above, or the intentions to protect habitats in the Mediterranean area, see e.g. Krämer, n. 119 above, 13 to 15. See also Ch. 5 on Art. 36 EC and the rule of reason and in particular Case C–169/89 *Van den Burg*, n. 144 above, or Case 252/85 *Commission* v. *France* (*Conservation of Wild Birds*) [1988] *ECR* 2243 and Krämer, n. 11 above, 118.

Harmonization *v.* Diversity

As has been indicated above, the Community is in continuous search for a balance between territorial claims and non-territorial claims, i.e. Community claims. While the common market requires for its functioning and establishment a certain harmonization and co-ordination of domestic standards, regional, local, and national environmental preferences and needs may diverge. At the same time the development of Community environmental law has shown that in many cases the existence of harmonized European environmental standards and their enforcement by the Commission and the Court are favourable for the state of the environment.[194]

The common or internal market is basically built on the principles governing a free trade area and a customs union. In many respects it follows the principles of global trade liberalization as laid down in the GATT system. To support the unity of the market and to ease the flow of goods, the harmonization of domestic rules and the establishment of certain common policies constitute important integrative elements of the Community legal order. The harmonization measures under Articles 100 and 100a, as well as common policies, are important instruments to reduce technical obstacles to trade and competition distortions within the Community. Apart from the general non-discrimination principle, the Court has given the Treaty provisions on the free movement of goods, in particular Article 30, a strongly integrative character, which is often referred to as negative harmonization.

The principles developed by the Court under Article 30, and in particular the notion of 'measures having equivalent effect', as well as the pre-emptive effect of Community secondary law, should prevent Member States from erecting new barriers to the free flow of goods within the Community. The establishment of the common market should not be jeopardized through new technical or administrative rules. The 'balkanization' of the Community is contrary to the spirit of economic integration underlying the Treaty.[195]

---

[194] See on the implementation problems and the many Treaty violations as a consequence of the non-fulfilment of Community environmental law L. Krämer, *Focus on European Environmental Law* (Sweet & Maxwell, London, 1993), 194 ff.; see also Ch. 8.

[195] See the terminology used by the US Supreme Court where market integrity is concerned, e.g. D. Kommers and M. Waelbroeck, 'Legal Integration and the Free Movement of Goods: The American and European Experience' in M. Cappelletti, M. Seccombe, and J. H. H. Weiler (eds.), *Integration through Law* (W. de Gruyter, New York, 1985), 165 at 221.

[194] See on the implementation problems and the many Treaty violations as a consequence of the non-fulfilment of Community environmental law L. Krämer, *Focus on European Environmental Law* (Sweet & Maxwell, London, 1993), 194 ff.; see also Ch. 8.2.6.

[195] See the terminology used by the US Supreme Court where market integrity is concerned, e.g. D. Kommers and M. Waelbroeck, 'Legal Integration and the Free Movement of Goods: The American and European Experience' in M. Cappelletti, M. Seccombe, and J. H. H. Weiler (eds.), *Integration through Law* (W. de Gruyter, New York, 1985), 165 at 221.

On the other hand, the Member States and the Community have to take into consideration the different needs of local conditions in the various regions of the Community. The ability to uphold autonomous domestic environmental measures or introduce divergent national measures within Community environmental law is an important means of satisfying different needs and preferences within the Community. The diversity of situations and conditions in the various regions of the Community has to be integrated within the concept of market unity. The search for a balance between market unity and diverging environmental conditions calls for legal mechanisms which allow for a limited application of more stringent environmental measures according to local-needs without giving way to the balkanization of the common market. To combine market integration and optimal protection of the environment the Community has to establish its own environmental policy at an already high level of protection and at the same time allow Member States to adopt more stringent measures where they seem reasonably justified.

The Single European Act has confirmed the developments introduced by the Court and has established a broad set of legal instruments which allow for a high-level Community environmental policy within the establishment of the common market and simultaneously has given the Member States the power to introduce and apply generally more stringent environmental measures.

In particular, in harmonized areas, this has changed the general Treaty structure.[196] The opportunity for Member States to apply more stringent environmental measures is one element within the Community environmental order which should ensure the ecologically sound character of the Community system. At the same time the Community will have to adopt harmonized measures to facilitate the establishment of the common market and safeguard the protection of the Community environment. The principles of subsidiarity and competition between legal or regulatory systems as well as the achievement of the optimal protection of the environment should be guidelines for the implementation of the shared responsibility and competence for the protection of the environment through Community action and domestic measures.

---

[196] See the criticism by Pescatore, n. 25 above (*CMLRev.*), 9, 18 and others; see for a review of the criticism Kahl, n. 23 above, 264.

Summary

COMMUNITY ENVIRONMENTAL MEASURES AND DOMESTIC MEASURES

The *protection of the environment* is a *shared responsibility* of the Community and its Member States. In the promotion of its objectives the Community has to respect the environment and to achieve a high level of environmental protection. The existence of environmental measures at Community and Member State level will help to ensure the best possible protection for the environment. As a divided power-system the Community legal order has developed instruments to co-ordinate Community, national, and local measures without jeopardizing the Common Market. *Domestic and Community measures complement each other where appropriate for the protection of the environment at a high level.*

Whenever the existing Community acts provide for the adoption of more stringent domestic environmental rules or in the absence of relevant Community law, national, regional, and local entities are entitled to take necessary action provided they do not jeopardize the Community legal order and, in particular, the establishment of the Common Market. *The abuse of environmental measures by national authorities for the hindrance of trade or the distortion of competition* has to be avoided through the strict application of the Community principles. Nevertheless, the *compatibility* of domestic environmental measures with the basic freedoms and rules governing the common market and Community law in general must be interpreted in the light of the established principles of Community environmental policy and in view of the achievement of a high level of environmental protection.

BASIC PRINCIPLES OF THE COMMON MARKET
AND DOMESTIC MEASURES (PART I)

2.1 Arbitrary Discrimination and Protectionism (Chapters 2 and 3)

Environmental measures shall not be abused for *discriminatory or protectionist goals* (see Articles 6, 30, 34, 36, 76, 95). The distinction between arbitrary discrimination and *justified differentiation* has to take into account ecological considerations and the existing principles such as the principle of correction at source or the 'polluter pays' principle (Article 130r(2)).

2.2 Distortive Action and Trade Barriers (Chapters 3 and 6)

Domestic environmental measures shall not rely on *instruments which are per se incompatible with the Common Market* (see Articles 9, 12, 30, 34, 37, 85, 92). The existing *exceptions* (Articles 36, 85(3), 92(2) and (3)) will, however, be interpreted and applied with a view to the possible environmental gains and in application of the principles of the Community's environmental policy. *Voluntary restrictions* of ecologically harmful activities and investments in clean technology should be favoured where this is possible without distorting competition and respecting the 'polluter pays' principle (Articles 42, 77, 85, 92).

2.3 Justified Limitations on the Free Movement of Goods (Chapter 4)

In consideration of the *importance of the principles of the free movement of goods and the integrative effect of the Court's case law* (*Dassonville* formula), environmental measures have to fulfil the requirements established by the Court in its interpretation and application of Article 30. Nevertheless, the protection of the health of humans, animals and plants as well as the more general protection of the environment are *important recognized aspects of the Community's objectives which allow for restrictions on trade*. Domestic environmental measures have, however, to satisfy the *reasonableness, necessity, and proportionality tests* of the Court. (Article 36, rule of reason)

2.4 Domestic Environmental Objectives and Evaluations (Chapter 5)

When assessing *national environmental objectives* the Court has to take into account the existing principles of Community environmental policy. Under the precautionary principle and in view of the principle of subsidiarity the Member States should be granted a sufficient discretion for the establishment of their desired level of protection and their assessment of the existing dangers and needs.

2.5 Reasonableness, Necessity, and Equivalent Measures (Chapter 5)

These principles should also be taken into account when the *reasonableness and the necessity* of a chosen measure are at stake. The choice of a concrete locally suitable measure and the evaluation of alternatives should allow sufficient discretion to the local authorities without opening loopholes for unjustified restrictions to trade. The *equivalence* of measures for the protection of the environment applied by other Member States should be mutually recognized if the maintenance of additional measures leads to no justified improvement in environmental quality or protection of health (Article 101b, rule of reason).

2.6 Proportionality: The Establishment of the Balance (Chapter 5)

The establishment of the Common Market is not a means in itself. It is, however, one of the main instruments for the promotion of the Community's objectives including, *inter alia*, sustainable growth and the raising of quality of life. The objectives of the Community rely on the preservation of our natural habitats and the common heritage of the Community. These aspects of the Community's tasks and aims have to be respected when *establishing the balance between gains from trade and domestic environmental measures under the proportionality test* as applied by the Court.

REMAINING DIFFERENCES AND COMMUNITY HARMONIZATION (PART II)

Very early in its existence the Community started to adopt its own environmentally relevant measures. During an initial phase they were predominantly adopted to avoid maintaining differences in product and production-related domestic environmental measures which would hinder the establishment of the common market. With the growing awareness of today's environmental problems, however, the protection of the European environment has become an equally important issue of European primary and secondary law. The harmonization of environmental standards, however, raises many questions with regard to the desirable extent of Community regulation and the level at which measures should be taken. The principle of subsidiarity and economic ideas in favour of competition among regulatory systems may be helpful in deciding on the optimal use of regulatory measures and economic instruments for the protection of the environment at a local, national, regional, and European level. The Treaty itself provides for several instruments which allow for the implementation of a locally adequate, high-level environmental policy without jeopardizing the Community's other objectives.

3.1 Community Measures and the Environment (Chapters 7 to 11)

Under Article 130s the Community shall adopt its *own environmental policy*. It will also *integrate the protection of the environment* when harmonizing national rules for the establishment of the Common Market (Articles 99, 100, 100a, and, in the establishment of its common policies (see Articles 43, 75, 84(2), 113). In all these activities the Community measures must integrate high-level environmental-protection requirements (see Articles 130r(2), 100a(3)).

3.2 Exclusiveness and Pre-emption of Community Law (Chapters 7 and 11)

Under certain provisions (e.g. Articles 43, 75, 84(2), 99, 100, 113, 235, 238) the Community can adopt exhaustive measures which, in principle, preclude the Member States from the adoption of additional environmental measures regulating the same field. The *exclusiveness* of Community measures and the *pre-emptive character* of Community law in a certain area, however, must be interpreted in respect of the principle of subsidiarity (Article 3b) and the achievement of an optimal protection of the environment and health (e.g. Articles 130s(2) and 30). If the Community measures do not achieve the level of protection necessary with respect to the diversity of situations in the various regions of the Community, national and local measures may and should complement them. *Mixed agreements* allow for the participation of both Community and Member States in the negotiation and ratification of conventions for international environmental co-operation (Article 130r(4)).

3.3 Specific Safeguard Clauses and Minimum Standards (Chapters 8 to 11)

In order to achieve the optimal protection of the environment according to different local needs and preferences the Community must provide for the application of more stringent local measures, whenever this is possible without jeopardizing the existing Community system. *Specific safe-guard clauses and minimum standards in the relevant Community acts* which allow for the application of more stringent national or local environmental measures are appropriate means for this objective. Articles 100a(5) and 130r(2), second subparagraph, establish a principle which is common practice under the existing secondary law in most areas (e.g. Articles 43, 75, 84(2), 99, 100, 235, 238). The *implementation of directives* is another means of allowing certain local choices. Nevertheless, the Community has to safeguard the objectives and effectiveness of the adopted measures.

3.4 The General Opting-out Provisions (Chapters 8 and 9)

Under specific Treaty provisions the Member States are *generally entrusted to apply more stringent environmental measures, even after an exhaustive harmonization of national rules* has taken place. Under Articles 100a(4) and 130t the Member States will complement the adopted Community secondary law with their own local and national measures if they ensure the protection of the environment at a higher level and are compatible with the other obligations under the Treaty. The principle of pre-emption has been modified in the interest of the protection of the environment and other recognized interests.

3.5 Co-ordination, Notification, and Community Inspection (Chapters 8 to 11)

For the co-ordination of domestic and Community measures in all these cases there are *notification and inspection procedures* under the Treaty and secondary law which facilitate the co-operation and co-ordination within the Community legal order (e.g. Articles 100a(4) and (5), 130r(2), and 130t or Directive 88/189/EEC).

Annex I: Principal Environmental Provisions in the Treaty

1. TREATY OBJECTIVES AND MEANS

Article 2

The Community shall have as its task, by establishing a common market and an economic and monetary union and by implementing the common policies or activities referred to in Articles 3 and 3a, to promote throughout the Community a harmonious and balanced development of economic activities, sustainable and non-inflationary growth respecting the environment, a high degree of convergence of economic performance, a high level of employment and of social protection, the raising of the standard of living and quality of life, and economic and social cohesion and solidarity among Member States.

Article 3

For the purposes set out in Article 2, the activities of the Community shall include, as provided in this Treaty and in accordance with the timetable set out therein:

. . .

(k) a policy in the sphere of the environment;

. . .

2. FREE TRADE PROVISIONS AND NON-DISCRIMINATORY TAXATION

Article 30

Quantitative restrictions on imports and all measures having equivalent effect shall, without prejudice to the following provisions, be prohibited between Member States.

Article 34

1. Quantitative restrictions on export, and all measures having equivalent effect, shall be prohibited between Member States.

2. Member States shall, by the end of the first stage at the latest, abolish all quantitative restrictions on exports and any measures having equivalent effect which are in existence when this Treaty enters into force.

Article 36

The provisions of Articles 30 to 34 shall not preclude prohibitions or restrictions on imports, exports or goods in transit justified on grounds of public morality, public policy or public security; the protection of health and life of humans, animals or plants; the protection of national treasures possessing artistic, historic or archæological value; or the protection of industrial and commercial property. Such prohibitions or restrictions shall not, however, constitute a means of arbitrary discrimination or a disguised restriction on trade between Member States.

Article 95

No Member State shall impose, directly or indirectly, on the products of other Member States any internal taxation of any kind in excess of that imposed directly or indirectly on similar domestic products.

Furthermore, no Member State shall impose on the products of other Member States any internal taxation of such a nature as to afford indirect protection to other products.

. . .

3. COMPETITION RULES OF THE COMMUNITY

Article 85

1. The following shall be prohibited as incompatible with the common market: all agreements between undertakings, decisions by associations of undertakings and concerted practices which may affect trade between Member States and which have as their object or effect the prevention, restriction or distortion of competition within the Common Market, and in particular those which:

(a)   directly or indirectly fix purchase or selling prices or any other trading conditions;

(b)   limit or control production, markets, technical development, or investment;

(c)   share markets or sources of supply;

(d)   apply dissimilar conditions to equivalent transactions with other trading parties, thereby placing them at a competitive disadvantage;

(e)   make conclusion of contracts subject to acceptance by the other parties as supplementary obligations which, by their nature according to commercial usage, have no connection with the subject of such contracts.

2. Any agreement or decision prohibited pursuant to this Article shall be automatically void.

3. The provisions of paragraph 1 may, however, be declared inapplicable in the case of:

—any agreement or category of agreements between undertakings;
—any decision or category of decisions by associations of undertakings;
—any concerted practice or category of concerted practices;

which contribute to improving the production or distribution of goods or to promoting technical or economic progress, while allowing consumers a fair share of the resulting benefit, and which does not:

(a) impose on the undertakings concerned restrictions which are not indispensable to the attainment of these objectives;
(b) afford such undertakings the possibility of eliminating competition in respect of a substantial part of the products in question.

Article 86

Any abuse by one or more undertakings of a dominant position within the common market or in a substantial part of it shall be prohibited as incompatible with the common market in so far as it may affect trade between Member States.

Such abuse may, in particular, consist in:

(a) directly or indirectly imposing unfair purchase or selling prices or other unfair trading conditions;
(b) limiting production, markets or technical development to the prejudice of consumers;
(c) applying dissimilar conditions to equivalent transactions with other trading parties, and thereby placing them at a competitive disadvantage;
(d) making the conclusion of contracts subject to acceptance by the other parties of supplementary obligations which, by their nature or according to commercial usage, have no connection with the subject of such contracts.

Article 92

1. Save as otherwise provided in this Treaty, any aid granted by a Member State or through State resources in any form whatsoever which distorts or threatens to distort competition by favouring certain undertakings or the production of certain goods shall, in so far as it affect trade between Member States, be incompatible with the Common Market.

2. The following shall be compatible with the Common Market.

(a) aid having a social character, granted to individual consumers, provided that such aid is granted without discrimination related to the origin of the products concerned;
(b) aid to make good the damage caused by natural disasters or exceptional occurrences;

. . .

3. the following may be considered to be compatible with the Common Market:

(a)   aid to promote the economic development of areas where the standard of living is abnormally low or where there is serious underemployment;

(b)   aid to promote the execution of an important project of common European interest or to remedy a serious disturbance on the economy of a Member State;

Article 93

1. The Commission shall, in co-operation with the Member States, keep under constant review all systems of aid existing in those States. It shall propose to the latter any appropriate measures required by the progressive development or by the functioning of the common market.

2. If, after giving notice to the parties concerned to submit their comments, the Commission finds that aid granted by a State or through State resources is not compatible with the Common Market having regard to Article 92, or that such aid is being misused, it shall decide that the State concerned shall abolish or alter such aid within a period of time to be determined by the Commission.

If the State concerned does not comply with this decision within the prescribed time, the Commission or any interested State may, in derogation from the provisions of Articles 169 and 170, refer the matter to the Court of Justice direct.

On application by a Member State, the Council, may, acting unanimously, decide that aid which that State is granting or intends to grant shall be considered to be compatible with the Common Market, in the derogation from the provisions of Article 92 or from the regulations provided for in Article 94, if such a decision is justified by exceptional circumstances. If, as regards the aid in question, the Commission has already initiated the procedure provided for in the first sub-paragraph of this paragraph, the fact that the State concerned has made its application to the Council shall have the effect of suspending that procedure until the Council has made its attitude known.

. . .

4. APPROXIMATION OF LAWS

Article 100

The Council shall, acting unanimously on a proposal from the Commission and after consulting the European Parliament and the Economic and Social Committee, issue directives for the approximation of such laws, regulations or administrative provisions of the Member States as directly affect the establishment or functioning of the Common Market.

Article 100a

1. By way of derogation from Article 100 and save where otherwise provided in this Treaty, the following provisions shall apply for the achievement of the objectives set out in Article 7a. The Council shall, acting in accordance with the procedure referred to in Article 189b and after consulting the Economic and Social Committee, adopt the measures for the approximation of the provisions laid down by law, regulation and administrative action in Member States which have as their object the establishment and functioning of the internal market.

2. Paragraph 1 shall not apply to fiscal provisions, to those relating to the free movement of persons nor to those relating the rights and Interests of Employed persons.

3. The Commission, in its proposals envisaged in paragraph 1 concerning health, safety, environmental protection and consumer protection, will take as a base a high level of protection.

4. If, after the adoption of a harmonization measure by the Council acting by a qualified majority, a Member State deems it necessary to apply national provisions on grounds of major needs referred to in Article 36, or relating to protection of the environment or the working environment, it shall notify the Commission of these provisions.

The Commission shall confirm the provisions involved after having verified that they are not a means of arbitrary discrimination or a disguised restriction on trade between Member States.

By way of derogation from the procedure laid down in Articles 169 and 170, the Commission or any Member State may bring the matter directly before the Court of Justice if it considers that another Member State is making improper use of the powers provided for in this Article.

5. The harmonization measures referred to above shall, in appropriate cases, include a safeguard clause authorizing the Member States to take, for one or more of the non-economic reasons referred to in Article 36, provisional measures subject to a Community control procedure.

Article 235

If action by the Community should prove necessary to attain, in the course of the operation of the Common Market, one of the objectives of the Community and this Treaty has not provided the necessary powers, the Council shall, acting unanimously on a proposal from the Commission and after consulting the European Parliament, take the appropriate measures.

4. ENVIRONMENTAL POLICY OF THE EC

Article 130r

1. Community policy on the environment shall contribute to pursuit of the following objectives:

—preserving, protecting and improving the quality of the environment;
—protecting human health;
—prudent and rational utilization of natural resources;
—promoting measures at international level to deal with regional or world-wide environmental problems.

2. Community policy on the environment shall aim at a high level of protection taking into account the diversity of situations in the various regions of the Community. It shall be based on the precautionary principle and on the principles that preventive action should be taken, that environmental damage should as a priority be rectified at source and that the polluter should pay. Environmental protection requirements must be integrated into the definition and implementation of other Community policies.

In this context, harmonization measures answering these requirements shall include, where appropriate, a safeguard clause allowing Member States to take provisional measures, for non-economic environmental reasons, subject to a Community inspection procedure.

3. In preparing its policy on the environment, the Community shall take account of:

—available scientific and technical data;
—environmental conditions in the various regions of the Community;
—the potential benefits and costs of action or of lack of action;
—the economic and social development of the Community as a whole and the balanced development of its regions.

4. Within their respective spheres of competence, the Community and the Member States shall co-operate with third countries and with the competent international organizations. The arrangements for Community co-operation may be the subject of agreements between the Community and the third parties concerned, which shall be negotiated and concluded in accordance with Article 228.

The previous subparagraph shall be without prejudice to Member States' competence to negotiate in international bodies and to conclude international agreements.

Article 130s

1. The Council, acting in accordance with the procedure referred to in Article 189c and after consulting the Economic and Social Committee, shall decide what action is to be taken by the Community in order to achieve the objectives referred to in Article 130r.

2. By way of derogation from the decision-making procedure provided for in paragraph 1 and without prejudice to Article 100a, the Council, acting unanimously on a proposal from the Commission and after consulting the European Parliament and the Economic and Social Committee, shall adopt:

—provisions primarily of a fiscal nature;

—measures concerning town and country planning, land use with the exception of waste management and measures of a general nature, and management of water resources;

—measures significantly affecting a Member State's choice between different energy sources and the general structure of its energy supply.

The Council may, under the conditions laid down in the preceding subparagraph, define those matters referred to in this paragraph on which decisions are to be taken by a qualified majority.

3. In other areas, general action programmes setting out priority objectives to be attained shall be adopted by the Council, acting in accordance with the procedure referred to in Article 189b and after consulting the Economic and Social Committee.

The Council, acting under the terms of paragraph 1 or paragraph 2 according to the case, shall adopt the measures necessary for the implementation of these programmes.

4. Without prejudice to certain measures of a Community nature, the Member States shall finance and implement the environment policy.

5. Without prejudice to the principle that the polluter should pay, if a measure based on the provisions of paragraph 1 involves costs deemed disproportionate for the public authorities of a Member State, the Council shall, in the act adopting that measure, lay down appropriate provisions in the form of:

—temporary derogations, and/or

—financial support from the Cohesion Fund to be set up no later than 31 December 1993 pursuant to Article 130d.

Article 130t

The protective measures adopted pursuant to Article 130s shall not prevent any Member State from maintaining or introducing more stringent protective measures. Such measures must be compatible with this Treaty. They shall be notified to the Commission.

5. SPECIFIC ASPECTS OF THE EXTERNAL RELATIONS OF THE EC

Article 113*

1. The common commercial policy shall be based on uniform principles, particularly in regard to changes in tariff rates, the conclusion of tariff and trade agreements, the achievement of uniformity¹ in measures of liberalization, export policy and measures to protect trade such as those to be taken in the event pf dumping or subsidies.

2. The Commission shall submit proposals to the Council for implementing the common commercial policy.

3. Where agreements with one or more States or international organizations need to be negotiated, the Commission shall make recommendations to the Council, which shall authorize the Commission to open the necessary negotiations.

The Commission shall conduct these negotiations in consultation with a special committee appointed by the Council to assist the Commission in this task and within the framework of such directives as the Council may issue to it.

The relevant provisions of Article 228 shall apply.

4. In exercising the powers conferred upon it by this Article, the Council shall act by a qualified majority.

Article 228

1. Where this Treaty provides for the conclusion of agreements between the Community and one or more States or international organizations, the Commission shall make recommendations to the Council, which shall authorize the Commission to open the necessary negotiations. The Commission shall conduct these negotiations in consultation with special committees appointed by the Council to assist it in this task and within the framework of such directives as the Council may issue to it.

In exercising the powers conferred upon it by this paragraph, the Council shall act by a qualified majority, except in the cases provided for in the second sentence of paragraph 2, for which it shall act unanimously.

2. Subject to the powers vested in the Commission in this field, the agreements shall be concluded by the Council, acting by a qualified majority on a proposal from the Commission. The Council shall act unanimously when the agreement covers a field for which unanimity is required for the adoption of internal rules, and for the agreements referred to in Article 238.

3. The Council shall conclude agreements after consulting the European Parliament, except for the agreements referred to in Article 113(3), including cases where the agreement covers a field for which the procedure referred to in Article 189b or that referred to in Article 189c is required for the adoption of

---

* As amended by Article G(28) TEU.

internal rules. The European Parliament shall deliver its opinion within a time-limit which the Council may lay down according to the urgency of the matter. In the absence of an opinion within that time-limit, the Council may act.

By way of derogation from the previous subparagraph, agreements referred to in Article 238, other agreements establishing a specific institutional framework by organizing cooperation procedures, agreements having important budgetary implications for the Community and agreements entailing amendment of an act adopted under the procedure referred to in Article 189b shall be concluded after the assent of the European Parliament has been obtained.

The Council and the European Parliament may, in an urgent situation, agree upon a time-limit for the assent.

4. When concluding an agreement, the Council may, by way of derogation from paragraph 2, authorize the Commission to approve modifications on behalf of the Community where the agreement provides for them to be adopted by a simplified procedure or by a body set up by the agreement; it may attach specific conditions to such authorization.

5. When the Council envisages concluding an agreement which calls for amendments to this Treaty, the amendments must first be adopted in accordance with the procedure laid down in Article N of the Treaty on European Union.

6. The Council, the Commission or a Member State may obtain the opinion of the Court of Justice as to whether an agreement envisaged is compatible with the provisions of this Treaty. Where the opinion of the Court of Justice is adverse, the agreement may enter into force only in accordance with Article N of the Treaty on European Union.

7. Agreements concluded under the conditions set out in this Article shall be binding on the institutions of the Community and on Member States.

Article 234

The rights and obligations arising from agreements concluded before the entry into force of this Treaty between one or more Member States on the one hand, and one or more third countries on the other, shall not be affected by the provisions of this Treaty.

To the extent that such agreements are not compatible with this Treaty, the Member States or State concerned shall take all appropriate steps to eliminate the incompatibilities established. Member States shall, where necessary, assist each other to this end and shall, where appropriate, adopt a common attitude.

In applying the agreements referred to in the first paragraph, Member States shall take into account the fact that the advantages accorded under this Treaty by each Member State form an integral part of the establishment of the Community and are thereby inseparably linked with the creation of common Institutions, the conferring of powers upon them and the granting of the same advantages by all other Member States.

Annex II: Guidelines on State Aid for Environmental Protection, [1994] OJ C72/3–9

1. INTRODUCTION

1.1. In the 1970s and early 1980s, the Community's environmental policy was mainly concerned with setting and implementing standards for the main parameters of the environment. The Commission's memorandum of 6 November 1974 on State aid in environmental matters[1] reflects this approach. The framework, which was extended with certain amendments in 1980[2] and again in 1986,[3] provided that aid could be authorized mainly to help firms carry out investment necessary to achieve certain mandatory minimum standards. The use of state aid was considered to be a transitional stage, paving the way for gradual introduction of the 'polluter pays' principle, under which economic agents would bear the full cost of the pollution caused by their activities.[4]

1.2. In the Single European Act a new section on the environment was added to the EC Treaty which gives the Community express powers in the environmental field.[5] The new provisions confirm the 'polluter pays' principle but go further, calling for the requirements of environmental protection to be included in defining and implementing the Community's other policies and stressing the need for prevention. The theme of integrating the environment into other policies is taken up, along with the concept of 'sustainable development', in the Community's fifth programme on the environment.[6] This acknowledges that the traditional approach, based almost exclusively on regulation and particularly standards, has not been wholly satisfactory. It therefore argues for a broadening of the range of policy instruments. Different instruments (regulation, voluntary action, and economic measures) or various combinations of these may be the best way of achieving desired environmental objectives in a given situation, depending on the legal, technical, economic, and social context. Both positive financial incentives, i.e. subsidies, and disincentives, namely taxes and levies, have their place. The need to integrate environmental with other policies also means taking into account the objectives of economic and social cohesion in the

[1] Letter to Member States SEC(74)4264 of 6 Nov. 1974; *IV Report on Competition Policy*, paras. 175 to 182.

[2] Letter to Member States SG(80)D/8287 of 7 July 1980; *X Report on Competition Policy*, paras. 222 to 226.

[3] Letter to Member States SG(87)D/3795 of 23 Mar. 1987; *XVI Report on Competition Policy*, para. 259. The 1986 version of the framework, which was due to expire at the end of 1992, was extended for a further year: see letters to Member States of 18 Jan. and 19 July 1993.

[4] See Council recommendation of 3 Mar. 1975, [1975] OJ L194.

[5] Arts. 130r, 130s, and 130t EC.

[6] COM(92)23 final, Vol. ii, 27 Mar. 1992 and Council resolution of 1 Feb. 1993.

Community, the requirements of maintaining the integrity of the single market, and international commitments in the environmental field.

1.3. The application of the EC Treaty rules on state aid must reflect the role economic instruments can play in environmental policy. This means taking account of a broader range of financial measures in this area. Aid control and environmental policy must also support one another in ensuring stricter application of the 'polluter pays' principle.

1.4. Subsidies may be a second-best solution in situations where the 'polluter pays' principle—which requires all environmental costs to be 'internalized', i.e. absorbed in firms' production costs—is not yet fully applied. However, such aid, particularly in the most polluting sectors of agriculture and industry, may distort competition, create trade barriers, and jeopardize the Single Market. The fact is that firms in all Member States have to invest to make their plant, equipment, and manufacturing processes meet environmental requirements, so gradually internalizing external environmental costs. State aid is liable to give certain firms an advantage over their competitors in other Member States not receiving such aid, even though subject to the same environmental constraints.

1.5. A description is given below of the main types of state support for environmental protection that have been notified in recent years. The various types of aid are divided into the three broad categories: investment aid, horizontal support measures, and operating aid.

1.5.1. Investment Incentives, Possibly Associated with Regulation or Voluntary Agreements

In many areas of environmental policy, firms are required to meet certain standards by law. Such mandatory standards may transpose international agreements or Community legislation into national law, or they may be set solely on the basis of national, regional, or local objectives. The common feature in such situations is that there is a legal requirement.

However, to achieve or restore a satisfactory quality of the environment in heavily industrialized areas in particular, it is necessary gradually to raise levels of protection and to encourage firms to go beyond legal requirements.

The ultimate objective of investment incentives in this sphere is to facilitate a gradual raising of the quality of the environment. Support for investment typically falls into one of the following categories:

- aid under programmes designed to help existing firms adapt their plant to new standards or encourage them to reach such standards more rapidly (aid available for a limited period to speed up the process of implementing new standards),
- aid to encourage efforts to improve significantly on mandatory standards through investment that reduces emissions to levels well below those required by current or new standards,

- aid granted in the absence of mandatory standards on the basis of agreements whereby firms take major steps to combat pollution without being legally required to do so or before they are legally required to do so,
- aid for investment in fields in which environmental action is a matter of priority, but benefits the community at large more than the individual investor and is therefore undertaken collectively. This may be the case, for example, with waste disposal and recycling,
- aid to repair past environmental damage which the firms are not under any legal obligation to remedy.

1.5.2. Aid for Horizontal Support Measures

Horizontal support measures are designed to help find solutions to environmental problems and to disseminate knowledge about such solutions so that they are applied more widely. The wide range of activities in this field includes:

- research and development of technologies that cause less pollution,
- provision of technical information, consultancy services and training about new environmental technologies and practices,
- environmental audits in firms,
- spreading information and increasing awareness of environmental problems among the general public, general promotion of ecological quality labels and of the advantages of environmentally friendly products, etc.

1.5.3. Operating Aid in the Form of Grants, Relief from Environmental Taxes or Charges, and Aid for the Purchase of Environmentally Friendly products

Despite the progress achieved in reducing pollution and in introducing cleaner technologies, there are many activities which damage the environment but whose environmental costs are not passed on in production costs and product prices. Conversely, the environmental benefits of products and equipment that cause less pollution are normally not fully reflected in lower prices to consumers. A clear trend is nevertheless apparent in Member States towards measures to internalize some of these external costs and benefits through taxes or through charges for environmental services, on the one hand, and through subsidies, on the other.

The introduction of environmental taxes and charges can involve state aid because some firms may not be able to stand the extra financial burden immediately and require temporary relief. Such relief is operating aid. It may take the form of:

- relief from environmental taxes introduced in some Member States, where it is necessary to prevent their firms being placed at a disadvantage compared with their competitors in countries that do not have such measures,

- grants to cover all or part of the operating cost of waste disposal or recycling facilities, water treatment plant, or similar installations, which may be run by semi-public bodies with users being charged for the service.
- Cost-related charges for environmental services are in line with the 'polluter pays' principle. However, it may be necessary to delay the introduction of full charging or to cross-subsidize some users at the expense of others, especially during the transition from traditional waste disposal practices to new recycling or treatment techniques. The State may also cover part of the investment costs of such facilities.

Among the subsidies designed to reflect the positive environmental benefits of certain technologies are:

- grants or cross-subsidies to cover the extra production costs of renewable energies, and
- aid that encourages consumers and firms to purchase environmentally friendly products[7] rather than cheaper conventional ones.

1.6. These guidelines aim to strike a balance between the requirements of competition and environment policy, given the widespread use of state aid in the latter policy. Such aid is normally only justified when adverse effects on competition are outweighed by the benefits for the environment. The guidelines are intended to ensure transparency and consistency in the manner in which the Treaty provisions on state aid are applied by the Commission to the wide range of instruments described above (regulation, taxes and subsidies, training and information measures) that are used by Member States for environmental protection purposes. The following section therefore states the criteria the Commission will apply in assessing whether state aid of various types for environmental protection purposes is compatible with Article 92 EC. The intention is not to encourage Member States to grant aid, but, when Member States wish to do so, to guide them as to what types and levels of aid may be acceptable.

2. SCOPE OF THE GUIDELINES

2.1. These guidelines apply to aid in all the sectors governed by the EC Treaty, including those subject to specific Community rules on state aid (steel processing, shipbuilding, motor vehicles, synthetic fibres, transport, agriculture, and fisheries), in so far as such rules do not provide otherwise. In the agricultural sector[8] the guidelines do not apply to the field covered by Council Regulation 2078/92/EEC.[9]

---

[7] General criteria for environmentally friendly products are listed in Council Reg 880/92 EEC of 23 Mar. 1992 on a Community eco-label award scheme [1992] OJ L99/1.

[8] Aid relating directly or indirectly to the production and/or marketing of products, excluding fisheries products, listed in Annex II EC.

[9] Council Reg. 2078/92/EEC of 30 June 1992 on agricultural production methods compatible with the requirements of the protection of the environment and the maintenance of the countryside [1992] OJ L215/85.

2.2. The guidelines set out the approach followed by the Commission in the assessment pursuant to Article 92 of state aid for the following purposes in the environmental field:

- investment,
- information activities, training, and advisory services,
- temporary subsidies towards operating costs in certain cases, and
- purchase or use of environmentally friendly products.

They apply to aid in all forms.[10]

2.3. Aid for energy conservation will be treated like aid for environmental purposes under the guidelines in so far as it aims at and achieves significant benefits for the environment and the aid is necessary, having regard to the cost savings obtained by the investor. Aid for renewable energy, the development of which is an especially high priority in the Community,[11] is also subject to these guidelines, in so far as aid for investment is concerned. However, higher levels of aid than provided for in paragraph 3.2 may be authorized in appropriate cases. Operating aid for production of renewable energies will be judged on its merits.

2.4. State aid for research and development in the environmental field is subject to the rules set out in the Community framework for state aid for research and development.[12]

3. APPLICABILITY OF THE STATE AID RULES

3.1. Assessment of Aid for Environmental Protection pursuant to Article 92 EC

Article 92(1) EC prohibits, subject to possible exceptions, government financial assistance to specific enterprises or industries that distorts or threatens to distort competition and may affect trade between Member States. State aid for environmental protection often fulfils the criteria laid down in Article 92(1). It confers an advantage on particular enterprises, unlike general measures which benefit firms throughout the economy, and it can affect intra-Community trade.

However, where aid meets the conditions set out below, the Commission may consider that it is eligible for one of the exemptions provided for in Article 92 EC. Naturally, exemption is conditional on compliance with other provisions of Community law as well, in particular those governing the Single Market.

---

[10] The principal forms are grants, subsidized loans, guarantees, tax relief, reductions in charges, and benefits in kind.
[11] See Council Decision 93/500/EEC of 13 Sept. 1993 concerning the promotion of renewable energies in the Community (Altener programme) [1993] OJ L235/41.
[12] [1986] OJ C83/2.

3.2. Aid for Investment

3.2.1. Aid for investment in land (when strictly necessary to meet environmental objectives), buildings, plant, and equipment intended to reduce or eliminate pollution and nuisance or to adapt production methods in order to protect the environment may be authorized within the limits laid down in these guidelines. The eligible costs must be strictly confined to the extra investment costs necessary to meet environmental objectives. General investment costs not attributable to environmental protection must be excluded. Thus, in the case of new or replacement plant, the cost of the basic investment involved merely to create or replace production capacity without improving environmental performance is not eligible. Similarly, when investment in existing plant increases its capacity as well as improving its environmental performance, the eligible costs must be proportionate to the plant's initial capacity.[13] In any case aid ostensibly intended for environmental protection measures but which is in fact for general investment is not covered by these guidelines. This is true, for example, of aid for relocating plant to new sites in the same area. Such aid is not covered by the guidelines because recent cases have shown that it may conflict with competition and cohesion policy. It will therefore continue to be considered on a case-by-case basis until sufficient experience has been built up for more general rules to be issued.

3.2.2. The rules for investment aid in general also apply to aid for investment to repair past damage to the environment, for example by making polluted industrial sites again fit for use. In cases where the person responsible for the pollution cannot be identified or called to account, aid for rehabilitating such areas may not fall under Article 92(1) EC in that it does not confer a gratuitous financial benefit on particular firms or industries. Such cases will be examined on their merits.

3.2.3. As a general rule, aid for environmental investment can be authorized up to the levels set out below.[14] These provisions apply both to investment by individual firms and investment in collective facilities.

---

[13] For aid concerning the disposal of animal manure, the Commission also applies by analogy the criteria set out in Annex III to Council Dir. 91/676/EEC of 12 Dec. 1991 concerning the protection of waters against pollution caused by nitrates from agricultural sources [1991] OJ L375/1.

[14] The rules for investment aid laid down in these guidelines are without prejudice to those provided by other Community legislation existing or yet to be enacted, in particular in the environmental field. For investments covered by Art. 12(1) and (5) of Council Reg. 2328/91/EEC of 15 July 1991 on improving the efficiency of agricultural structures ([1991] OJ L218/1) the maximum aid level is 35%, or 45% in areas referred to in Council Dir. 75/268/EEC of 28 Apr. 1975 on mountain and hill farming and farming in certain less-favoured areas ([1995] OJ L128/1). These maximum aid levels apply irrespective of the size of the enterprise. Consequently, the maxima may not be increased for SMEs as provided for below in this section. For investments in Objectives 1 and 5b regions, the Commission reserves the right, on a case-by-case basis, to accept higher aid levels than the above, where the Member State demonstrates to the satisfaction of the Commission that this is justified.

A. Aid to Help Firms Adapt to new Mandatory Standards

Aid for investment to comply with new mandatory standards or other new legal obligations and involving adaptation of plant and equipment to meet the new requirements can be authorized up to the level of 15 per cent gross[15] of the eligible costs. Aid may be granted only for a limited period and only in respect of plant which has been in operation for at least two years when the new standards or obligations enter into force.

For small and medium-sized enterprises[16] carrying out such investment an extra 10 per cent gross of aid may be allowed. If the investment is carried out in assisted areas[17] aid can be granted up to the prevailing rate of regional aid authorized by the Commission for the area, plus, for SMEs, 10 per cent gross in Article 92(3)(c) areas and 15 per cent gross in Article 92(3)(a) areas.[18]

In keeping with the 'polluter pays' principle, no aid should normally be given towards the cost of complying with mandatory standards in new plant. However, firms that instead of simply adapting existing plant more than two years old opt to replace it by new plant meeting the new standards may receive aid in respect of that part of the investment cost that does not exceed the cost of adapting the old plant.

If both Community and national mandatory standards exist for one and the same type of nuisance or pollution, the relevant standard for the purposes of this provision shall be the stricter one.

B. Aid to Encourage Firms to Improve on Mandatory Environmental Standards

Aid for investment that allows significantly higher levels of environmental protection to be attained than those required by mandatory standards may be authorized up to a maximum of 30 per cent gross of the eligible costs. The level of aid actually granted for exceeding standards must be in proportion to the improvement of the environment that is achieved and to the investment necessary for achieving the improvement.

If the investment is carried out by SMES, an extra 10 per cent gross of aid may be allowed. In assisted areas, aid can be granted up to the prevailing rate of regional aid authorized by the Commission for the area, plus, where appropriate, the supplements for SMEs referred to above.[19]

---

[15] That is the nominal before-tax value of grants and the discounted before-tax value of interest subsidies as a proportion of the investment cost. Net figures are after tax.

[16] As defined in the Community guidelines on state aid for SMEs [1992] OJ C213/2.

[17] That is, areas covered by national regional development schemes independent of the Structural Funds. In areas designated as eligible for aid from the Structural Funds pursuant to Objectives 2 or 5b but not nationally assisted areas, the level of aid will be decided in relation to each scheme.

[18] See the guidelines on state aid for SMES. If the aid available for environmental investment in a non-assisted area under these guidelines exceeds the prevailing rate of regional aid authorized for an Art. 92(3)(c) assisted area in the same country, then the rate of aid in the assisted area can be raised to that available in the non-assisted area.

[20] As in the case of aid for adapting to standards, if the aid available for environmental investment in a non-assisted area exceeds the prevailing rate of regional aid authorized for an Art. 92(3)(c) assisted area in the same country, then the rate of aid in the assisted area can be raised to that available in the non-assisted area. See also n. 17.

If both Community and national mandatory standards exist for one and the same type of nuisance or pollution, the relevant standard for the purposes of applying this provision shall be the stricter one.

Where a project partly involves adaptation to standards and partly improvement on standards, the eligible costs belonging to each category are to be separated and the relevant limit applied.

C. Aid in the Absence of Mandatory Standards

In fields in which there are no mandatory standards or other legal obligations on firms to protect the environment, firms undertaking investment that will significantly improve on their environmental performance or match that of firms in other Member States in which mandatory standards apply may be granted aid at the same levels and subject to the same condition of proportionality as for going beyond existing standards (see above).

Where a project partly involves adaptation to standards and partly measures for which there are no standards, the eligible costs belonging to each category are to be separated and the relevant limit applied.

3.3. Aid for Information Activities, Training, and Advisory Services

Aid for publicity campaigns to increase general environmental awareness and provide specific information about, for example, selective waste collection, conservation of natural resources, or environmentally friendly products may not fall within Article 92(1) EC at all where they are so general in scope and distant from the marketplace as not to confer an identifiable financial benefit on specific firms. Even when aid for such activities does fall within Article 92(1), it will normally be exemptable.

Aid may also be authorized for the provision of training and consultancy help to firms on environmental matters. As provided under the SME aid guidelines, for SMEs such aid may be granted at rates of up to 50 per cent of the eligible costs.[20] In assisted areas aid of at least the authorized rate of investment aid may be authorized for training and consultancy services for both SMEs and larger firms.

3.4. Operating Aid

In accordance with longstanding policy the Commission does not normally approve operating aid which relieves firms of costs resulting from the pollution or nuisance they cause. However, the Commission may make an exception to this principle in certain well-defined circumstances. It has done so so far in the fields of waste management and relief from environmental taxes. The

[20] See n. 16.

Commission will continue to assess such cases on their merits and in the light of the strict criteria it has developed in the two fields just mentioned. These are that the aid must only compensate for extra production costs by comparison with traditional costs, and should be temporary and in principle degressive, so as to provide an incentive for reducing pollution or introducing more efficient uses of resources more quickly. Further more, the aid must not conflict with other provisions of the EC Treaty, and in particular those relating to the free movement of goods and services.

In the field of waste management, the pubic financing of the additional costs of selective collection, recovery, and treatment of municipal waste for the benefit of businesses as well as consumers may involve state aid but can in that case be authorized provided that businesses are charged in proportion to their use of the system or to the amount of waste they produce in their enterprise. Aid for the collection, recovery, and treatment of industrial and agricultural waste will be considered on a case-by-case basis.

Temporary relief from new environmental taxes may be authorized where it is necessary to offset losses in competitiveness, particularly at international level. A further factor to be taken into account is what the firms concerned have to do in return to reduce their pollution. This provision also applies to reliefs from taxes introduced pursuant to EC legislation in which the Member States have discretion as to the relief or its amount.

3.5. Aid for the Purchase of Environmentally Friendly Products

Measures to encourage final consumers (firms and individuals) to purchase environmentally friendly products may not fall within Article 92(1) EC because they do not confer a tangible financial benefit on particular firms. Where such measures do fall within Article 92(1), they will be assessed on their merits and may be authorized provided that they are applied without discrimination as to the origin of the products, do not exceed 100 per cent of the extra environmental costs,[21] and do not conflict with other provisions of the Treaty or legislation made under it[22] with particular reference to the free movement of goods.

3.6. Basis of the Exemption

Within the limits and on the conditions set out in paragraphs 3.2 to 3.5, aid for the above purposes will be authorized by the Commission under the exemption

---

[21] Unless Community legislation does not allow as much as 100% (see, e.g., Council Dir. 91/441/EEC of 26 June 1991 amending Dir. 70/220/EEC on the approximation of the laws of the Member States relating to measures to be taken against air pollution by emissions from motor vehicles [1991] OJ L242/1.

[22] e.g. the car emissions Dir. (which also contains notification requirements) and Council Dir. 83/189/EEC of 28 Mar. 1983 laying down a procedure for the provision of information in the field of technical standards and regulations[1983] OJ L109/8.

provided for in Article 92(3)(c) EC for 'aid to facilitate the development of certain activities . . ., where such aid does not adversely affect trading conditions to an extent contrary to the common interest'. However, aid for environmental purposes in assisted areas pursuant to Article 92(3)(a) EC may be authorized under that provision.

3.7. Important Projects of Common European Interest

Aid to promote the execution of important projects of common European interest which are an environmental priority and will often have beneficial effects beyond the frontiers of the Member State or States concerned can be authorized under the exemption provided for in Article 92(3)(b) EC. However, the aid must be necessary for the project to proceed and the project must be specific and well-defined, qualitatively important, and must make an exemplary and clearly identifiable contribution to the common European interest. When this exemption is applied, the Commission may authorize aid at higher rates that the limits laid down for aid authorized pursuant to Article 92(3)(c).

3.8. Cumulation of Aid from Different Sources

The limits set above on the level of aid that may be granted for various environmental purposes apply to aid from all sources, including Community aid when this is combined with national aid.

4. NOTIFICATION, EXISTING AUTHORIZATIONS, DURATION, AND REVIEW OF GUIDELINES AND REPORTING REQUIREMENTS

4.1. Except in so far as aid classed as *de minimis* is concerned[23] these guidelines do not affect the obligation of Member States pursuant to Article 93(3) EC to notify all aid schemes, all alterations of such schemes, and all individual awards of aid made to firms outside authorized schemes. In the notification, Member States must supply the Commission with all relevant information showing, *inter alia*, the environmental purpose of the aid and the calculation of eligible costs. The rules for the accelerated clearance procedure for SME aid schemes and amendments of existing schemes[24] and on the notification of cumulations of aid remain applicable.[25] When it authorizes aid schemes, the Commission may require individual notification of aid awards above a certain threshold or in certain sectors, apart from those referred to in paragraph 2.1 or in other appropriate cases.

---

[23] See SME aid guidelines [1992] OJ C213/2.
[24] *Ibid.* 10.   [25] [1985] OJ C3.

4.2. The guidelines are without prejudice to schemes that have already been authorized when the guidelines are published. However, the Commission will review such existing schemes pursuant to Article 93(1) EC by 30 June 1995. Furthermore, the Commission will monitor the effects of approved aid schemes and will propose appropriate measures pursuant to Article 93(1) if it finds the aid in question to be creating distortions of competition contrary to the common interest.

4.3. The Commission will follow these guidelines in its assessment of aid for environmental purposes until the end of 1999. Before the end of 1996 it will review the operation of the guidelines. The Commission may amend the guidelines at any time should it prove appropriate to make changes for reasons connected with competition policy, environmental policy, and regional policy or to take account of other Community policies and of international commitments.

4.4. The Commission will require Member States to supply it with reports on the operation of aid schemes for environmental protection in accordance with its notice of 24 March 1993 on standardized notifications and reports.

Bibliography

ALT, WILFRIED, and SACK, JÖRN, 'Nationale Werbebeschränkungen und freier Warenverkehr' [1990] EuZW 311.

ALONSO GARCIA, ENRIQUE, El derecho ambiental de la Comunidad Europea (2 volumes, Civitas, Madrid, 1993).

AMERICAN CHAMBER OF COMMERCE IN BELGIUM, The EC Environment Guide 1994 (Catermill Publishing, London, 1995).

ANDERSON, TERRY L. (ed.), NAFTA and the Environment (Pacific Research Institute for Public Policy, San Francisco, 1993).

BALDI, MARINO, 'Direct Applicability of the Free Trade Agreement between the EEC and the EFTA Countries from a Swiss Perspective' [1985] Swiss Review of International Competition Law 31.

BALL, SIMON, and BELL, STEWART, Environmental Law (Blacksotone Press, London, 1991).

BAIL, CHRISTOPH, 'The Promotion of Policy Coherence on Trade and Environment: A Role for the European Community' in Cameron, James, Demaret, Paul, and Geradin, Damien (eds.), Trade and the Environment: The Search for Balance (Cameron May, London, 1994) 333.

BARENTS, RENÉ, 'The Community and the Unity of the Common Market' (1990) 33 GYIL 9 .

—— 'The Prohibition of Fiscal Discrimination in Article 95 of the EEC Treaty' (1981) 18 CMLRev. 521.

—— 'Milieu en interne markt'[1993] SEW 5.

—— 'Artikel 95 en de gemeenschappelijke markt' [1983] SEW 438.

BARRINGTON, DONALD, 'The Emergence of a Constitutional Court' in O'Reilly, James (ed.), Human Rights and Constitutional Law (Round Hall Press, Dublin, 1992), 251.

BARTLING, HARTWIG, 'National unterschiedliche Produktstandards und Produkthaftung unter aussenwirtschaftlichem Aspekt' (1988) 39 Jahrbuch für Sozialwissenschaften 145.

BASEDOW, JÜRGEN, 'Besprechung zu EuGH Urteil C–195/90' [1992] JZ 868.

BAUDENBACHER, CARL, 'Kartellrechtliche und verfassungsrechtliche Aspekte gesetzesvertretender Vereinbarungen zwischen Staat und Wirtschaft' [1988] JZ 689.

BAUMOL, WILLIAM J., and OATES, WALLACE E., The Theory of Environmental Policy (2nd. edn., Cambridge University Press, Cambridge, 1988).

BECKER, ULRICH, Der Gestaltungsspielraum der EG-Mitgliedstaaten im Spannungsfeld zwischen Umweltschutz und freiem Warenverkehr (Nomos, Baden-Baden, 1991).

BEHRENS, FRITZ, Rechtsgrundlagen der Umweltpolitik der Europäischen Gemeinschaften (Beiträge zur Umweltgestaltung, Heft A 55, Berlin, 1976).

—— 'Die Umweltpolitik der Europäischen Gemeinschaften und Art. 235 EWGV' [1978] DVBl. 462 to 469.

BEHRENS, PETER, 'Die Konvergenz der wirtschaftlichen Freiheiten im europäischen Gemeinschaftsrecht' [1992] EuR 145.

BEHRENS, PETER, and KOCH, HANS-JOACHIM (eds.), Umweltschutz in der europäischen Gemeinschaft (Nomos, Baden-Baden, 1991).

BERGMANN, JAN MICHAEL, 'Principle of preemption' versus Nationaler Alleingang—Eine Erörterung *am Beispiel der Umweltpolitik* (Vorträge, Reden und Berichte aus dem Europa-Institut, no. 251, Saarbrücken, 1993).

BEUTLER, BENGT, BIEBER, ROLAND, PIPKORN, JÖRN, and STREIL, JOCHEN, *Die Europäische Gemeinschaft—Rechtsordnung und Politik* (3rd edn., Nomos, Baden-Baden, 1987, and 4th edn., Nomos, Baden-Baden, 1993).

BEYER, THOMAS C. W., 'Europa 1992: Gemeinschaftsrecht und Umweltschutz nach der Einheitlichen Europäischen Akte' [1990] *JuS* 962.

BEYERLIN, ULRICH, 'Die "neue" Umweltpolitik der Europäischen Gemeinschaft' [1989] *UPR* 361.

BIEBER, ROLAND, 'Mutual Completion of Overlapping Systems' (1988) 13 *ELRev.* 147.

BINDER, CHRISTINE, 'Wege der Rechtsangleichung am Beispiel des Umweltrechts' in Korinek, Karl, and Rill, Heinz-Peter (eds.), *Österreichisches Wirtschaftsrecht und das Recht der EG* (Orac, Wien, 1990), 163.

BLECKMANN, ALBERT, 'Die umgekehrte Diskriminierung' [1985] *RIW* 917.

—— *Europarecht* (5th edn., Heymann, Köln, 1990).

BOCK, MATTHIAS, 'Umweltrechtliche Prinzipien in der Wettbewerbsordnung der Europäischen Gemeinschaft' [1994] *EuZW* 47.

BONGAERTS, JAN, 'The German Packaging Ordinance' [1992] *Environmental Business Law Review* July, 53.

BORER, JÜRG, *Massnahmen gleicher Wirkung wie mengenmässige Beschränkungen im Freihandelsabkommen Schweiz–EWG* (Stämpfli, Bern, 1988).

BORRIES, REIMER VON, 'Das Subsidiaritätsprinzip im Recht der Europäischen Union' [1994] *EUR* 263.

BÖRNER, BODO, 'Subventionen—Unrichtiges Europarecht?' in Böner, Bodo, *et al.* (eds.), *Einigkeit und Recht und Freiheit, Festschrift für Carl Carsten* (Heymann, Köln, 1984), 63.

BOVET, CHRISTIAN, 'Concurrence et environnement' [1995] *SZW/RSDA—Swiss Review of Business Law* 169.

BRAUNS, HANS JOACHIM, and RIEDEL, NORBERT, 'EG-Verträglichkeit von "Autobahn-Gebühren" ' [1991] *RIW* 224.

BREIER, SIEGFRIED, 'Das Schicksal der Titaniumdioxid-Richtlinie' [1993] *EuZW* 315.

—— 'Verbesserung der Kraftstoffqualität im Wege des nationalen Alleingangs?' [1994] *EuZW* 624 .

—— 'Ausgewählte Probleme des gemeinschaftlichen Umweltrechts' [1994] *RIW* 584.

BREUER, RÜDIGER, 'Die internationale Orientierung von Umwelt- und Technikstandards im deutschen und europäischen Recht' [1989] *Jahrbuch des Umwelt- und Technikrechts* 43.

—— 'Umweltrechtliche und wirtschaftslenkende Abgaben im europäischen Binnenmarkt' [1992] *DVBl.* 485.

BRIDGE, JOHN, 'Case 68/86 UK versus Council, Judgment of 23 February 1988' (1988) 22 *CMLRev* 733.

BRINKHORST, LAURENS JAN, 'Subsidiarity and European Environmental Policy' in *Subsidiarity: The Challenge of Change, Working Document Proceedings of the Jacques Delors Colloquium* (European Institute for Public Administration, Maastricht, 1991).

—— 'Subsidiaity and European Community Environment Policy—A Pandora's Box?' [1993] *European Environmental Law Review*, January, 16.

BROUWER, ONNO *et al.* , *Environment and Europe: European Union Environment Law and Policy and its Impact on Industry* (Stibbe, Simont, Monahan and Duhot, Deventer, 1994).

BRUNETTI, OLIVER, *EG-Rechtsverträglichkeit als Kriterium der nationalen Umweltpolitik* (Schulthess and Stämpfli, Zürich and Bern, 1993).

BUNGARTEN, HARALD, *Umweltpolitik in Westeuropa* (Europa Union, Bonn, 1978).

BURROWS, F., *Free Movement in European Community Law* (Oxford Unversity Press, Oxford, 1987).

CAMERON, JAMES, and MAKUCH, ZEN, 'Implementation of the United Nations Framework Conventions on Climate Change: Trade Law Implication' in Cameron, James, Demaret, Paul, and Geradin, Damien (eds.), *Trade and the Environment: The Search for Balance* (Cameron May, London, 1994), 116.

—— and WARD, HALINA, *The Uruguay Round's Technical Barriers to Trade Agreement* (WWF International Research Report, Gland, January 1993).

CAPPELLETTI, MAURO, 'Is the European Court of Justice "running wild"?' (1987) 12 *ELRev.* 3.

—— SECCOMBE, MONICA, and WEILER, JOSEPH, 'Introduction' in Cappelletti, Mauro, Seccombe, Monica, and Weiler, Joseph (eds.), *Integration through Law* (W. de Gruyter, Berlin and New York, 1986) i, book 1, 3.

CASS, D. Z., 'The Word that Saves Maastricht? The Principle of Subsidiarity and the Division of Powers within the European Community' (1992) 29 *CMLRev.* 1107.

CAVES, RICHARD E., FRANKEL, JEFFREY A., and JONES, RONALD W., *World Trade and Payments* (6th edn., Harper Collins College Publishers, New York, 1993).

CHEYNE, ILONA, 'International Agreements and the European Community Legal System' (1994) 19 *ELRev.* 581.

CHARNOVITZ, STEVE, 'Exploring the Environmental Exceptions in the GATT Article XX' [1991] *JWT* 37.

COASE, RONALD H., 'The Problem of Social Cost' (1960) 3 *Journal of Law and Economics* 1.

COENEN, REINHARD, and JÖRISSEN, JULIANE, *Umweltverträglichkeitsprüfung in der Europäischen Gemeinschaft* (Schmidt, Berlin, 1989).

COLIN, JEAN-PIERRE, *Le gouvernement des juges dans les Communautés Européennes* (Librairie générale de droit et de jurisprudence, Paris, 1966).

CONGRESS OF THE UNITED STATES, *Trade and Environment* (Congress of the United States of America, Background Paper, Washington, DC, 1992).

CONSTANTINESCO, VLAD, 'L'article 5 CEE, de la bonne foi à la loyauté communautaire' in Capotorti, Franceso, *et al.* (eds.), *Du droit international au droit de l'intégration—Liber Amicorum Pierre Pescatore* (Nomos, Baden-Baden, 1987), 97.

CORDEN, MAX W., 'The Normative Theory of International Trade' in Jones, Ronald W., and Kenen, Peter B., *Handbook of International Economics* (North-Holland, Amsterdam, 1984) 63.

COVA, COLETTE, 'Lomé IV: Une convention pour 10 ans' [1990] *RMC* 1.

CROSS, EUGENE DANIEL, 'Preemption of Member State Law in the European Economic Community: A Framework for Analysis' (1992) 29 *CMLRev.* 447.

DANNECKER, GERHARD, and APPEL, IVO, 'Auswirkungen der Vollendung des Europäischen Binnenmarktes auf den Schutz der Gesundheit und der Umwelt' (1990) 89 *Z Vgl. R Wiss.* 127.

DANUSSO, M., and DENTON, R., 'Des the EC Court of Justice Look for a Protectionist Motive Under Article 95?' [1990] *LIEI* 67.

DAUSES, MANFRED A., 'Dogmatik des freien Warenverkehrs in der Europäischen Gemeinschaft' [1984] *RIW* 197.

DAUSES, MANFRED A., 'Die rechtliche Dimension des Binnenmarktes' [1991] *EuZW* 8 .
—— 'L'interdiction des mesures d'effet équivalent à des restrictions quantitatives à la lumière de la jurisprudence de la CJCE' [1992] *RTDE* 607.
—— 'Die Rechtsprechung des EuGH zum Verbraucherschutz und zur Werbefreiheit im Binnenmarkt' [1995] *EuZW* 425.
DE SADELEER, N., 'La directive 92/43/ECEE concernant la conservation des habitats naturels ainsi que de la faune et de la flore sauvages: vers la reconnaissance d'un patrimoine naturel de Communautée Européenne' [1993] *RMC* 25.
DEMARET, PAUL, 'Environmental Policy and Commercial Policy: The Emergence of Trade-Related Environmental Measures (TREMs) in the External Relations of the European Community' in: Maresceau, M. (ed.), *The European Community's Commercial Policy after 1992: The Legal Dimension* (Martinus Nijhoff, Dordrecht, 1993), 315.
—— 'Trade-Related Environmental Measures (TREMs) in the External Relations of the European Community' in: Cameron, James, Demaret, Paul, and Geradin, Damien (eds.), *Trade and the Environment: The Search for Balance* (Cameron May, London, 1994) 277.
—— and STEWARDSON, RAOUL, 'Border Tax Adjustments under GATT and EC Law and General Implications for Environmental Taxes' [1994] *JWT* 5.
DEMIRAY, DAVID A., 'The Movement of Goods in a Green Market' [1994] *LIEI* 73.
DEMMKE, CHRISTOPH, *Die Implementation von EG-Umweltpolitik in den Migliedstaaten— Umsetzung der Trinkwasserrichtlinie* (Nomos, Baden-Baden, 1994).
DE RUYT, JEAN, *L'acte unique européen—Commentaire* (2nd edn., Editions de l'Université de Bruxelles, Bruxelles, 1989).
DIECKMANN, MARTIN, *Das Abfallrecht der Europäischen Gemeinschaft* (Nomos, Baden-Baden, 1994).
DIEDERICHSEN, LARS, 'Ein neues Umweltzeichen für Europa' [1993] *RIW* 224.
DOUMA, WYBE TH., 'Wallon Waste Import Ban' [1993] *European Business Law Review*, February, 32.
DÖRR, OLIVER, 'Die Warenverkehrsfreiheit nach Art. 30 EWG-Vertrag—doch bloss ein Diskriminierungsverbot?' [1990] *RabelsZ* 677.
DUBACH, ALEXANDER, 'Der freie Warenverkehr in der neuesten Rechtsprechung des Europäischen Gerichtshofs' [1994] *SZW/RSDA* 219.
DÜERKOP, MARCO, 'Trade and Environment: International Trade Aspects of the Proposed EC Directive Introducing a Tax on Carbon Dioxide Emissions and Energy' (1994) 31 *CMLRev.* 807.
DURIC, HANS PETER, *Die Freihandelsabkommen EG–EFTA: Die rechtliche Problematik* (Nomos, Baden-Baden, 1991).
DUSCHANEK, ALFRED, 'Umweltschutzsubventionen in der EG und in Österreich' in Griller, Stephan, and Rill, Heinz-Peter (eds.), *Europäischer Binnenmarkt und österreichisches Wirtschaftsverwaltungsrecht* (Orac, Wien, 1991), 355.
EBENROTH, CARSTEN THOMAS, *et al.*, 'Vereinbarkeit des Strassenbenutzungsgebührengesetzes mit dem EWG-Vertrag' [1990] *BB* 2125.
EHLE, DIETRICH, and MEIER, GERD, *EWG-Warenverkehr* (O. Schmidt, Köln, 1971).
EHLERMANN, CLAUS-DIETER, 'The Internal Market Following the Single European Act' (1987) 24 *CMLRev.* 360.
EICKHOF, NORBERT, and FRANKE, MARTIN, 'Die Autobahngebühr für Lastkraftwagen' [1994] *Wirtschaftsdienst* 244.

EMILIOU, NICHOLAS, 'Opening Pandora's Box: The Legal Basis of Community Measures before the Court of Justice' (1994) 19 *ELRev.* 488.

EMMERT, FRANK, *Lange Stange im Nebel oder neue Strategie?*, Basler Schriften zur europäischen Integration, Nr. 7 (Europa Institut der Universität Basel, Basel, 1994).

EPINEY, ASTRID, 'Gemeinschaftsrechtlicher Umweltschutz und Verwirklichung des Binnenmarktes—"Harmonisierung" auch der Rechtsgrundlagen?' [1992] *JZ* 564.

—— 'Einbeziehung gemeinschaftlicher Umweltschutzprinzipien in die Bestimmung mit- gliedstaatlichen Handlungsspielraums' [1993] *DVBl.* 93.

—— 'Subsidiarität als verfassungsrechtlicher Grundsatz' in *Swiss Reports Presented at the XIVth International Congress of Comparative Law* (Schulthess, Zürich, 1994), 9 .

—— *Umgekehrte Diskriminierungen* (Heymann, Köln, 1995).

—— and FURRER, ANDREAS, 'Umweltschutz nach Maastricht' [1992] *EuR* 369.

—— and MÖLLERS, THOMAS M.J., *Freier Warenverkehr und nationaler Umweltschutz* (Heymann, Köln, 1992).

ESTY, DANIEL C., *Greening the GATT—Trade, Environment, and the Future* (Institute for International Economics, Washington, DC, 1994).

EUROPAINSTITUT DER UNIVERSITÄT BASEL (ed.), *Subsidiarität—Schlagwort oder Kurskorrektur?* Tagungsband, Basler Schriften zur europäischen Integration Nr. 1 (Europainstitut der Universität Basel, Basel, 1994).

EVERLING, ULRICH, 'Zur neueren EuGH-Rechtsprechung zum Wettbewerbsrecht' [1982] *EuR* 301.

—— 'Zur föderalen Struktur der Europäischen Gemeinschaft' in Hailbronner, Kay, Ress, Georg, and Stein, Torsten (eds.), *Staat und Völkerrechtsordnung—Festschrift für K. Doehring* (Duncker & Humblot, Berlin, 1989), 179.

—— 'Probleme der Rechtsangleichung zur Verwirklichung des Europäischen Binnen- marktes' in Baur, Jürgen F., Hopt, Klaus J., and Mailänder, Peter K. (eds.), *Festschrift für Ernst Steindorff zum 70. Geburtstag am 13. März 1990* (Duncker & Humblot, Berlin and New York, 1990), 1155.

—— 'Abgrenzung der Rechtsangleichung zur Verwirklichung des Binnenmarktes nach Art. 100a EWGV durch den Gerichtshof' [1991] *EuR* 179.

—— 'Durchführung und Umsetzung des Europäischen Gemeinschaftsrechts im Bereich des Umweltschutzes unter Berücksichtigung der Rechtsprechung des EuGH' [1993] *NVwZ* 209.

—— 'Die Wiederaufbereitung abgebrannter Brennelemente in anderen Mitgliedstaaten der Europäischen Gemeinschaft' [1993] *RIW* (supplement 2 to issue 3).

—— SCHWARTZ, IVO, and TOMUSCHAT, CHRISTIAN, 'Die Rechtsetzungsbefugnisse der EWG in Generalermächtigungen, insbesondere Art. 235 EWGV' [1976] *EuR* (special issue) 1.

FALKENSTEIN, ALFRED, *Freier Warenverkehr in der EG* (Nomos, Baden-Baden, 1989, looseleaf).

FALOMO, LUCA M., 'L'incidenza del Trattato die Maastricht sul Diritto Comunitario Ambientale' [1992] *Rivista di Diritto Europeo* 587.

FIDLER, DAVID P., 'Competition Law and International Relations' [1992] *ICLQ* 563.

FLYNN, JAMES, 'How Will Article 100a(4) work? A Comparison with Article 93' (1987) 24 *CMLRev.* 689.

FORWOOD, NICHOLAS, and CLOUGH, MARC, 'The Single European Act and Free Movement' (1989) 14 *ELRev.* 383.

FRIAUF, KARL HEINRICH, 'Abfallrechtliche Rücknahmenpflichten' in Baur, J. F., Müller-

GRAFF, P.-C., and ZULEEG, M. (eds.), *Europarecht, Energierecht, Wirtschaftsrecht, Festschrift für B. Börner* (Heymann, Köln, 1992), 701.

FÜLGRAFF, GEORGES, 'Forschung für die Umwelt' in Gündling, Lothar, and Weber, Beate (eds.), *Dicke Luft in Europa* (Müller Juristischer Verlag, Heidelberg, 1988), 95.

—— *Die Sperrwirkung des sekundärrechtlichen Gemeinschaftsrechts auf die nationalen Rechtsordnungen* (Nomos, Baden-Baden, 1994).

FURRER, ANDREAS, 'Nationale Umweltschutzkompetenzen in der EG und im EWR' [1992] *AJP* 1517.

GALLIGAN, D. J., *Discretionary Powers* (Clarendon Press, Oxford, 1990).

GARRONE, PIERRE, 'La discrimination indirecte en droit communautaire: vers une théorie générale' [1994] *RTDE* 425.

GATT SECRETARIAT, *Trade and Environment* (GATT, Geneva, 1992).

—— (ed.), *The Final Results of the Uruguay Round—The Legal Texts* (GATT, Geneva, 1994).

GERADIN, DAMIEN, 'The Belgian Waste Case' (1993) 18 *ELRev.* 144.

—— 'Free Trade and Environmental Protection in an Integrated Market: A Survey of the Case Law of the United States Supreme Court and the European Court of Justice' (1993) 2 *Journal of Transnational Law and Policy* 141.

—— 'Trade and Environmental Protection: Community Harmonization and National Environmental Standards' [1993] *YEL* 151.

—— 'Balancing Free Trade and Environmental Protection—The Interplay between the ECJ and the Community Legislator' in Cameron, James, Demaret, Paul, and Geradin, Damien (eds.), *Trade and the Environment: The Search for Balance* (Cameron May, London, 1994) 204.

GILSDORF, PETER, 'Die Grenzen der Gemeinsamen Handelspolitik' in Ress, Georg (ed.), *Rechtsprobleme der Rechtsangleichung*, Vorträge, Reden, und Berichte aus dem Europa-Institut, no. 137 (Europainstitut der Universität des Saarlandes, Saarbrücken, 1988), 35.

GIRSCH, HERBERT, 'Subsidiarität statt Vereinheitlichung' in *Neue Zürcher Zeitung* (28–29 March 1992, no. 74), 85.

GLAESNER, HANS-JOACHIM, 'Die Einheitliche Europäische Akte' [1986] *EuR* 119.

GLATZ, HANS R., 'Die Verträglichkeit nationaler umweltpolitischer Initiativen mit dem EWG-Vertrag: Das Beispiel der PKW-Schadstoffbegrenzung' in Schwarze, J. and Bieber, R. (eds.), *Das europäische Wirtschaftsrecht vor der Herausforderung der Zukunft* (Nomos, Baden-Baden, 1985), 161.

GOETZ, VOLKMAR, 'Anmerkungen zu den Gerichtsurteilen des Europäischen Gerichtshofs Rs 68/86 und 131/86 vom 23.2.1988' [1988] *EuR* 298.

GORMLEY, LAURENCE, ' "Actually or Potentially, Directly or Indirectly"? Obstacles to the Free Movement of Goods' [1989] *German Yearbook of European Law* 197.

—— 'Recent Case Law on the Free Movement of Goods: Some Hot Potatoes' (1990) 27 *CMLRev.* 825.

—— *Prohibiting Restrictions on Trade within the E.E.C.* (North Holland, Amsterdam, New York, and Oxford, 1985).

GORNIG, GILBERT, and SILAGI, MICHAEL, 'Vom Ökodumping zum Ökoprotektionismus— Umweltzeichen im Lichte von EWG-Vertrag und GATT' [1992] *EuZW* 753.

GRABITZ, EBERHARD, *Stillhalteverpflichtungen vor dem Binnenmarkt—Unvereinbarkeit der Erdgassteuer mit Gemeinschaftsrecht* (Engel, Kehl a. Rhein, 1988).

—— 'Handlungsspielräume   der   EG-Mitgliedstaaten   zur   Verbesserung   des

Umweltschutzes—Das Beispiel der Umweltabgaben und -subventionen' [1989] *RIW* 623.

—— and HILF, MEINHARD (eds.), *Kommentar zur Europäischen Union* (looseleaf, 2nd edn., C. H. Beck, München, 1990, looseleaf).

—— and SASSE, CHRISTOPH, *Umweltkompetenz der Europäischen Gemeinschaften*, Beiträge zur Umweltgestaltung, Heft 59 A (E. Schmidt, Berlin, 1977).

—— and ZACKER, CHRISTIAN, 'Scope for Action by EC Member States for the Improvement of Environmental Protection under EEC Law: The Example of Environmental Taxes and Subsidies' (1989) 26 *CMLRev.* 423.

—— and ZACKER, CHRISTIAN, 'Die neuen Umweltkompetenzen der EWG' [1989] *NVwZ* 297.

GRILLER, STEFAN, *Europäische Normung und Rechtsangleichung—Der Abbau technischer Handelshemmnisse in Europa unter besonderer Berücksichtigung Österreichs* (Signum-Verlag, Wien, 1990).

GROEBEN, HANS VON DER, THIESING, JOCHEN, and EHLERMANN, CLAUS-DIETER (eds.), *Kommentar zum EWG-Vertrag* (3rd. edn., Nomos, Baden-Baden, 1983, looseleaf).

GRÖNER, HELMUT, 'Umweltschutzbedingte Produktnormen als nichttarifäres Handelshemmnis', in Gutzler, Helmut (ed.), *Umweltpolitik und Wettbewerb* (Nomos, Baden-Baden, 1981), 142.

GROSSMANN, HARALD, 'Einseitige Maßnahmen der EG gegenüber unfairen Handelspraktiken' (1993) IX *Wirtschaftsdienst* 487.

GROUX, JEAN and MANIN, PHILIPPE, *The European Communities in the International Order* (Commission of the European Communities, Brussels, 1985).

GUHLMANN, CLAUS, 'The Single European Act—Some Remarks from a Danish Perspective' (1987) 24 *CMLRev.* 31.

GYSELEN, LUC, 'The Emerging Interface between Competition Policy and Environmental Policy in the EC' in Cameron, James, Demaret, Paul, and Geradin, Damien (eds.), *Trade and the Environment: The Search for Balance* (Cameron May, London, 1994), 242.

HÄFELIN, ULRICH, and MÜLLER, GEORG, *Grundriss des Allgemeinen Verwaltungsrechts* (Schulthess, Zürich, 1990).

HAIGH, NIGEL, *EEC Environmental Law and Policy and Britain* (2nd edn., Longman, Harlow (Essex), 1989).

—— 'The European Community and International Environmental Policy' in Hurrel, Andrew, and Kingsbury, Benedict (eds.), *The International Politics of the Environment* (Clarendon Press, Oxford, 1994).

HAILBRONNER, KAY, *Der nationale Alleingang im EG-Binnenmarkt—Vortrag gehalten vor der Juristischen Gesellschaft zu Berlin, 17.Mai 1989* (Schriftenreihe der Juristischen Gesellschaft zu Berlin, Heft 116, Berlin, 1989).

—— 'Der "nationale Alleingang" im Gemeinschaftsrecht am Beispiel der Abgasstandards für PKW' [1989] *EuGRZ* 101.

—— 'EG-Verkehrspolitik und Umweltschutz' in Rengeling, H.-W. (ed.), *Umweltschutz und andere Politiken der Europäischen Gemeinschaft* (Heymann, Köln, 1993), 149 .

—— KLEIN, ECKART, MAGIERA, SIEGFRIED, and MÜLLER-GRAFF, PETER-CHRISTIAN, *Handkommentar zum EWG-Vertrag* (Heymann, Köln, 1991).

HANSMEYER, K.-H., 'Marktwirtschaftliche Elemente in der Umweltpolitik—Eine Zusammenfassung der Argumente' [1988] *ZfU* 231.

HAUSER, HEINZ, 'Harmonisierung oder Wettbewerb nationaler Regulierungssysteme in einem integrierten Wirtschaftsraum' [1993] *Aussenwirtschaft* 459.

HAUSER, HEINZ, and HÖSLI, MADELEINE, 'Harmonization or Regulatory Competition in the EC (and the EEA)?' [1991] *Aussenwirtschaft* 497.

—— and VALLENDER, KLAUS, *Zur Bindung des Wirtschaftsgesetzgebers durch Grundrechte* (Stämpfli, Bern, 1989).

HEINZ, KERSTEN, 'Nochmals: Die Fahrverbotsregelungen der Smogverordnungen auf dem Prüfstand des EG-Rechts' [1989] *NVwZ* 1035.

—— and KÖRTE, ALTMUT, 'Die Ziele Umweltschutz und Binnenmarkt zwischen gemeinschaftlicher Kompetenz und nationaler Verantwortung—Zu den neuen Umweltvorschriften im EWG-Vertrag' [1991] *JA* 41.

HEISTER, JOHANNES, MICHAELIS, PETER, and MOHR, ERNST, 'The Use of Tradable Emission Permits for Limiting CO_2-Emissions' [1992] *European Economy* (The Economics of Limiting CO_2-Emissions, special edn.), 27.

HENKE, JÖRG, *EuGH und Umweltschutz* (VVF, München, 1992).

HERZOG, PETER E., and SMIT, HANS, *The Law of the European Economic Communities—Commentary* (Bender, New York, 1976, looseleaf).

HESELHAUS, SEBASTIAN, 'Gemeinschaftsrechtliche Vorgaben für Stassenbenützungsgebühren für den Schwerverkehr' [1993] *EuZW* 311.

HILDEBRAND, PHILIPP M., 'The European Community's Environmental Policy, 1957 to 1992: From Incidental Measures to an International Regime' [1992] *Environmental Politics* 13.

—— 'EG-Aussenkompetenzen in Grenzen' [1995] *EuZW* 7.

HILF, MEINHARD, 'Umweltabgaben als Gegenstand von Gemeinschaftsrecht und -politik' [1992] *NVwZ* 107.

HOCHLEITNER, FERDINAND, *Die Kompetenzen der Europäischen Wirtschaftsgemeinschaft auf dem Gebiet des Umweltschutzes* (VWGO, Wien, 1990).

HOFFERT, URSULA, *Europarecht und nationale Umweltpolitik: nationale Abweichungsmöglichkeiten von der gemeinschaftlichen Rechtsangleichung und Ausnahmen vom Grundsatz des freien Warenverkehrs am Beispiel des Umweltschutzrechts* (Springer, Wien, 1993).

HOFFMANN, MICHAEL, *Grundfragen der grenzüberschreitenden Verbringung von Abfall nach nationalem Recht und nach EG-Recht* (Duncker & Humblot, Berlin, 1994).

HOFFMANN-RIEM, WOLFGANG, 'Gemeinschaftspolitik zwischen Marktfreiheit und Umweltschutz' in Behrens, Peter, and Koch, Hans-Joachim (eds.), *Umweltschutz in der Europäischen Gemeinschaft* (Nomos, Baden-Baden, 1991), 9 .

HOLLINS, STEVE, and MACRORY, RICHARD, *A Source Book of European Community Environmental Law* (Oxford University Press, Oxford, 1995).

HOLZINGER, KATHARINA, 'Does Legal Harmonization Really "Harmonize" the National Environmental Policies in the European Community?' in Pal, Leslie A., and Schultze, Rainer-Olaf (eds.), *The Nation-State versus Continental Integration* (Universitätsverlag Dr. N. Brockmeyer, Bochum, 1991), 297.

—— *Politik des kleinsten gemeinsamen Nenners? Umweltpolitische Entscheidungsprozesse in der EG am Beispiel der Einführung des Katalysatorautos* (Duncker & Humblot, Berlin, 1994).

HOWARTH, WILLIAM, 'The Single European Market and the Problem of Fish Movements' (1990) 15 *ELRev.* 34.

HUGLO, JEAN-GUY, 'L'application par les Etats membres des normes communautaires en matière d'environnement' [1994] *RTDE* 451.

IPSEN, HANS-PETER, *Europäisches Gemeinschaftsrecht* (Mohr, Tübingen, 1972).

IUCN, UNEP, and WWF, *Caring for the Earth, A Strategy for Sustainable Living* (WWF, Gland, 1991).

JACHMANN, MONIKA, 'Die Einführung einer Nahverkehrsabgabe durch Landesgesetz' [1992] *NVwZ* 932.

JACHTENFUCHS, MARKUS, 'The European Community and the Protection of the Ozone Layer' [1990] *JCMS* 261.

JACKSON, JOHN H., *The World Trading System* (MIT Press, Cambridge, Mass., 1989).

—— 'World Trade Rules and Environmental Policies: Congruence or Conflict?' (1992) 49 *Washington & Lee Law Review* 1227.

—— and DAVEY, WILLIAM J., *Legal Problems of International Economic Relations* (2nd. edn., West Publishing Co., St. Paul, Minn., 1986).

JACOT-GUILLARMOD, OLIVIER, *Le juge national face au droit communautaire: perspective suisse et communautaire* (Bruylant, Bruxelles, 1993).

JACQUÉ, JEAN-PAUL, 'L'Acte Unique Européen' [1986] *RTDE* 575.

JADOT, B., 'Mesures nationales de police de l'environnement, libre circulation des marchandises et proportionnalité' [1990] *CDE* 408.

JANS, JAN H., 'Article 7 EEC and a Non-Discriminatory Transfrontier Environmental Policy [1988] *LIEI* 21.

—— 'European Environmental Law' [1989] *Journal of the Law Society of Scotland* 211.

JAHNS-BÖHM, JUTTA, 'Die umweltrechtliche Querschnittklausel des Art. 130 r II 2 EWGV' [1992] *EuZW* 49.

—— *Umweltschutz durch europäisches Gemeinschaftsrecht am Beispiel der Luftreinhaltung* (Duncker & Humblot, Berlin, 1994).

JARASS, HANS D., 'Binnenmarktrichtlinien und Umweltschutzrichtlinien' [1991] *EuZW* 530.

JENKINS, CHARLES, 'The Maastricht Treaty' [1992] *European Trends*, March, 1.

JOERGES, CHRISTIAN, 'European Law, the Nation State and the Maastricht Treaty' in Dehousse, Renaud (ed.), *The European Union Treaty* (C. H. Beck, München, 1993), 1.

—— FALKE, JOSEF, MICKLITZ, HANS-WOLFGANG, and BRÜGGEMEIER, GERT, *Die Sicherheit von Konsumgütern und die Entwicklung der Europäischen Gemeinschaft* (Nomos, Baden-Baden, 1988).

JOHNSON, ESTHER, and O'KEEFFE, DAVID, 'From Discrimination to Obstacles to Free Movement: Recent Developments Concerning the Free Movement of Workers 1989–1994' (1994) 31 *CMLRev.* 1313.

JOHNSON, H. G., 'Optimal Trade Intervention in the Presence of Domestic Distortions' in Baldwin, Robert E., *et al.* (eds.), *Trade, Growth and the Balance of Payments* (Rand McNally, Chicago, 1965).

JOHNSON, STANLEY P., and CORCELLE, GUY, *The Environmental Policy of the European Community* (Graham & Trotman, London, 1989, and 2nd edn., 1995).

KAHL, WOLFGANG, *Umweltprinzip und Gemeinschaftsrecht* (Müller Juristischer Verlag, Heidelberg, 1993).

KAMMINGA, M., 'Who Can Clean Up the Rhine: the European Community or the International Rhine Commission?' [1978] *NILR* 63.

KAPTEYN, PIETER J. G. and VERLOREN VAN THEMAAT, PIETER, *Introduction to the Law of the European Communities* (2nd edn., Kluwer, Deventer, 1989).

KARL, H., 'Europäische Umweltpolitik im Spannungsfeld zwischen Zentralität und Dezentralität' in Zimmermann, Klaus W., *et al.* (eds.), *Umwelt und Umweltpolitik in Europa* (Europa-Union-Verlag, Bonn, 1995), 139.

KELLER, HELEN, and TOBLER, CHRISTA, 'PCP-Verbot im Gemeinschaftsrecht' [1994] *AJP/PJA* 1562.

KEMPIS, KARL VON, 'Überlegungen zur derVereinbarkeit des Grundsatzes de Abfallbeseitigung im Inland mit dem EWG-Vertrag' [1985] *UPR* 354.

KEWENIG, W., *Der Grundsatz der Nichtdiskriminierung im Völkerrecht der internationalen Handels beziehungen, Band 1: Der Begriff der Diskriminierung* (Athenäum, Frankfurt a. M., 1972).

KIRCHGÄSSNER, GEBHARD, 'Ansatzmöglichkeiten zur Lösung europäischer Umwel probleme' [1992] *Aussenwirtschaft* 55.

KISS, ALEXANDRE, and SHELTON, DINAH, *Manual of European Environmental Law* (Grotius Cambridge, 1993).

KLEIER, ULRICH F., 'Freier Warenverkehr (Art. 30 EWG-Vertrag) und di Diskriminierung inländischer Erzeugnisse' [1988] *RIW* 623.

KLOEPFER, MICHAEL, 'Umweltschutz als Kartellprivileg' [1980] *JZ* 781.

—— 'Kartellrecht und Umweltrecht' in Gutzler, Helmut (ed.), *Umweltpolitik un Wettbewerb* (Nomos, Baden-Baden, 1981), 57.

—— and THULL, RÜDIGER, 'Rechtsprobleme einer CO$_2$-Abgabe' [1992] *DVBl.* 195.

KOERS, ALBERT T., 'The External Authority of the EEC in Regard to Marine Fisheries (1977) 14 *CMLRev.* 269.

KOHLEPP, KAY H., 'Beschränkung des freien Warenverkehrs in der EG durch national Umweltschutzbestimmungen' [1989] *DB* 1455.

KOMMERS, DONALD, and WAELBROECK, MICHEL, 'Legal Integration and the Fre Movement of Goods: The American and European Experience' in Cappelletti, Mauro Seccombe, Monica, and Weiler, Joseph (eds.), *Integration through Law* (W. de Gruyter Berlin/New York, 1985) i, book 3, 165.

KOPPEN, IDA, *The European Community's Environmental Policy*, EUI Working Paper no 88/238 (European University Institute, San Domenico di Fiesole, 1988).

—— *The Role of the European Court of Justice in the Development of the European Community Environmental Policy*, EUI Working Paper, no. 92/18 (European University Institute, Sa Domenico di Fiesole, 1993).

KRÄMER, LUDWIG, 'The Single European Act and Environmental Protection' (1987) 2 *CMLRev.* 659.

—— 'Grundrecht auf Umwelt und Gemeinschaftsrecht' [1988] *EuGRZ* 285.

—— 'Einheitliche Europäische Akte und Umweltschutz: Überlegungen zu einigen neuer Bestimmungen im Gemeinschaftsrecht' in Rengeling, Hans-Werner (ed.), *Europäische Umweltrecht und europäische Umweltpolitik* (Heymann, Köln, 1988), 137.

—— 'Das Verursacherprinzip im Gemeinschaftsrecht' [1989] *EuGRZ* 353.

—— *EEC Treaty and Environmental Protection* (Sweet & Maxwell, London, 1990).

—— 'EWG-Umweltrecht und nationale Alleingänge' [1990] *UTR* 437.

—— 'The Implementation of Environmental Laws by the European Economic Communities' [1991] *GYIL* 9.

—— 'Community Environmental Law—Towards a Systematic Approach' [1992] *YEI* 151.

—— *Focus on Environmental Law* (Sweet & Maxwell, London, 1993).

—— *European Environmental Law—Casebook* (Sweet & Maxwell, London, 1993).

—— 'L'environnement et le marché unique européen'[1993] *RMC* 45.

—— 'Environmental Protection and Article 30 EEC Treaty' (1993) 30 *CMLRev.* 111.

—— 'Die Integrierung umweltpolitischer Erfordernisse in die gemeinschaftliche Wettbewerbspolitik' in Rengeling, Hans-Werner (ed.), *Umweltschutz und andere Politiken der Europäischen Gemeinschaft* (Heymann, Köln, 1993), 47.

—— 'Die Rechtsprechung des Gerichtshofs der Europäischen Gemeinschaften zum Umweltrecht 1992—1994' [1995] *EuGRZ* 45.

—— *EC Treaty and Environmental Law* (2nd edn., Sweet & Maxwell, London, 1995, revised edition of Krämer, Ludwig, *EEC Treaty and Environmental Protection*, above).

KRAVIS, IRVING BERNARD, *Domestic Interests and International Obligations: Safeguards in International Trade Organizations* (University of Pennsylvania Press, Philadelphia, 1963).

KREUTZBERGER, ROBERT, 'Der Umweltschutz als Aufgabe der Europäischen Gemeinschaften' [1986] *ZfU* 169.

KROMAREK, PASCALE, 'Environmental Protection and Free Movement of Goods: The Danish Bottle Case' [1990] *J Env. L* 87.

KUPFER, DIETRICH, 'Rechtschöpfung oder Rechtsharmonisierung? Tendenzen des Europäischen Umweltrechts' [1989] *AgrarR* 57.

KUSCHEL, HANS-DIETER, 'Das neue Lomé-Abkommen zwischen der EG und den AKP-Ländern' [1980] *EA* 330.

LASOK, D., and BRIDGE, J. W., *The Law and Institutions of the European Communities* (5th edn., Butterworths, London, 1991).

LANGEHEINE, BERND, 'Rechtsangleichung unter Art. 100 a EWGV' [1988] *EuR* 235.

LAURENCE, DUNCAN, and WYNNE, BRIAN, 'Transporting Waste in the European Community: A Free Market?' [1989] *Environment*, July/August, 12 and 34.

LEE, NORMAN, 'Environmental Policy' in Artis, Mike, and Lee, Norman (eds.), *The Economics of the European Union: Policy and Analysis* (Oxford University Press, Oxford, 1994), 238.

LENSEN, ANTON, *Environment and Subsidiarity*, Working Paper (European Parliament, Directorate General for Research, Luxembourg, 1993).

LENZ, CARL-OTTO, 'Immanente Grenzen des Gemeinschaftsrechts' [1993] *EuGRZ* 57.

LEYTON-BROWN, DAVID, 'Continental Harmonization and the Canada–U.S. Free Trade Agreement' in Pal, Leslie A., and Schultze, Rainer-Olaf (eds.), *The Nation-State versus Continental Integration* (Universitätsverlag Dr. N. Brockmeyer, Bochum, 1991), 149.

LIEFFERINK, J. D. *et al.* (eds.), *European Integration and Environmental Policy* (Belhaven Press, London, 1993).

LIER, A. (ed.), *Tax and Legal Aspects of EC Harmonisation* (Martinus Nijhoff, Deventer, 1993).

LIETZMANN, KURT, 'Einheitliche Europäische Akte und Umweltschutz: Die neuen Umweltbestimmungen im EWG-Vertrag', in Rengeling, Hans-Werner (ed.), *Europäisches Umweltrecht und europäische Umweltpolitik* (Heymann, Köln, 1988), 163.

LÖW, NORBERT, *Der Rechtsschutz des Konkurrenten gegenüber Subventionen aus gemeinschaftsrechtlicher Sicht* (Nomos, Baden-Baden, 1992).

LOW, PATRICK (ed.), *International Trade and the Environment*, World Bank Discussion Paper (World Bank, Washington, DC, 1992).

LÜDER, TILMAN, 'Mars: Zwischen Keck und Cassis' [1995] *EuZW* 609.

LÜTKES, STEFAN, *Zulässigkeit von Geschwindigkeitsbeschränkungen auf Autobahnen nach dem EWG-Vertrag—insbesondere unter Berücksichtigung der gemeinschaftsrechtlichen Verkehrs- und Umweltpolitik sowie des freien Warenverkehrs in der EG* (Kommentator-Verlag, Neuwied/Frankfurt a.M., 1990).

—— 'Kompetenz der EG für Geschwindigkeitsbeschränkungen für PKW auf Autobahnen' [1991] *EuZW* 277.

MACRORY, RICHARD, The Enforcement of Community Environmental Laws: Some Critical Issues' (1992) 29 *CMLRev.* 347.

MARTEN, KAI-UWE, and SCHMID, SONJA, 'Die EU-Öko-Audit-Verordnung und der Britis Standard (BS 7750)' [1995] *RIW* 754.

MARTI, HANS, *Die Wirtschaftsfreiheit der schweizerischen Bundesverfassung* (Helbing & Lichtenhahn, Basel/Stuttgart, 1976).

MASCLET, JEAN-CLAUDE, 'Les articles 30, 36 et 100 à la lumière de l'arrêt "cassis d Dijon"' [1980] *RTDE* 611.

—— 'La libre circulation des marchandises dans les communautés européennes' [1986 *RTDE* 243.

MASTELLONE, CARLO, 'The External Relations of the E.E.C. in the Field o Environmental Protection' [1981] *ICLQ* 104 .

MATTERA, A., 'L'arrêt "Cassis de Dijon": Une nouvelle approche pour la réalisation et l bon fonctionnement du marché intérieur' [1990] *RMC* 505.

MATUSCHAK, HOLGER, 'Die Bedeutung des neuen Art. 130s Abs. 2 EGV im Rahmen de EG-vertraglichen Umweltrechts [1995] *DVBl.* 81.

MCKEAN, W. A., 'The Meaning of Discrimination in International and Municipal Law [1970] *BYIL* 177.

MEIER, GERT, 'Einheitliche Europäische Akte und freier EG-Warenverkehr' [1987] *NJW* 537.

—— *Die Cassis-Rechtsprechung des Gerichtshofes der Europäischen Gemeinschaften: eine Entschei dungssammlung mit Einführung von Gert Meier* (Behr, Hamburg, 1988, looseleaf).

MERTENS DE WILMARS, J., 'Het Hof van Justitite van de Europese Gemeenschappen n. de Europese Akte' [1986] *SEW* 601.

MIDDEKE, ANDREAS, *Nationaler Umweltschutz im Binnenmarkt* (Heymann, Köln, 1993).

MOENCH, CHRISTOPH, 'Die Fahrverbotsregelungen der Smog-Verordnungen auf den Prüfstand des EG-Rechts' [1989] *NVwZ* 325.

MOLLE, WILLEM, *The Economics of European Integration* (Brookfield, Aldershot, 1990).

MØLLER, ØSTROM J., 'Binnenmarkt und Umweltschutz, Artikel 100a der Einheitlichen Europäischen Akte' [1987] *EA* 497.

MONTAG, FRANK, 'Umweltschutz, Freier Warenverkehr und Einheitliche Europäische Akte' [1987] *RIW* 935.

MÖSCHEL, WERNHARD, 'Altautoverwertung und europäisches Gemeinschaftsrecht' in Baur, J. F., Müller-Graff, P.-C., and Zuleeg, M. (eds.), *Europarecht, Energierecht, Wirtschaftsrecht, Festschrift für B. Börner* (Heymann, Köln, 1992), 289.

MORTELSMANN, KAMIEL, 'Article 30 of the Treaty and Legislation Relating to Market Circumstances: Time to Consider a New Definition?' (1991) 28 *CMLRev.* 115.

MÜCKENHAUSEN, PETER, 'Die Harmonisierung der Abgaben auf den Strassengüterverkehr in der Europäischen Gemeinschaft' [1994] *EuZW* 519.

MÜLLER, JÖRG-PAUL, *Die Grundrechte der schweizerischen Bundesverfassung* (Schulthess, Zürich, 1991).

MÜLLER-GRAFF, PETER-CHRISTIAN, 'Die Rechtsangleichung zur Verwirklichung des Binnenmarketes' [1989] *EuR* 107.

MURSWIEK, DIETRICH, 'Freiheit und Freiwilligkeit im Umweltrecht' [1988] *JZ* 985.

NICOLAIDES, PHEDON, 'Competition Among Rules' [1992] *JWT* 113.

NICOLAYSEN, GERT, 'Inländerdiskriminierung im Warenverkehr' [1991] *EuR* 95.

NIEMEYER, HANS-JÖRG, 'Recent Developments in EC State Aid Law' [1993] *EuZW* 273.

—— 'Die Anwendbarkeit der Art. 85 und 86 EG-Vertrag auf staatliche Massnahmen' [1994] *WuW* 721.

NOELLKAEMPER, ANDRÉ, 'The European Community and International Environmental Co-operation: Legal Aspects of External Community Powers' [1987] *LIEI* 55.

OATES, WALLACE E., 'Market Incentives for Environmental Protection: A Survey of Some Recent Developments' in Peston, M. H., and Quandt, R. E. (eds.), *Prices, Competition and Equilibrium* (P. Allan, Oxford, 1986), 251.

OECD (Council at ministerial level), *Trade and Environment* (OECD, Paris, 1991).

—— *Environmental Labelling in OECD Countries* (OECD, Paris, 1991).

OEHMICHEN, ALEXANDER, *Die unmittelbare Anwendbarkeit der völkerrechtlichen Verträge der EG— Die Freihandels- und Assoziierungsabkommen* (Diss., Saarbrücken, 1992).

OFFERMANN-CLAS, CHRISTEL, 'Die Kompetenzen der Europäischen Gemeinschaften im Umweltschutz' [1983] *ZfU* 47.

D'OLIVEIRA, HANS ULRICH JESSURUN, 'Das Rheinchloridabkommen und die EWG' [1983] *RIW* 322.

OLIVER, PETER, *Free Movement of Goods in the E.E.C.* (2nd edn., European Law Centre, London, 1988).

O'KEEFFE, DAVID, and SCHERMERS, HENRY G. (eds.), *Mixed Agreements* (Kluwer, Deventer, 1983).

OPPERMANN, THOMAS, *Europarecht* (C. H. Beck, München, 1991).

PALME, CHRISTOPH E., *Nationale Umweltpolitik in der EG—Zur Rolle des Art. 100aIV im Rahmen der Europäischen Umweltgemeinschaft* (Duncker & Humblot, Berlin, 1992).

PAPPAS, SPYROS A., 'The Legal Basis for Action to Be Taken by the European Community in the Field of the Environment' in *Subsidiarity: The Challenge of Change, Working Document Proceedings of the Jacques Delors Colloquium* (European Institute of Public Administration, Maastricht, 1991).

PECHSTEIN, MATTHIAS, *Die Mitgliedstaaten der EG als 'Sachwalter des gemeinsamen Interesses' und Gesetzgebungsnotstand im Gemeinschaftsrecht* (Duncker & Humblot, Berlin, 1987).

PERNICE, INGOLF, 'Kompetenzordnung und Handlungsbefugnisse der Europäischen Gemeinschaft auf dem Gebiet des Umwelt- und Technikrechts' [1989] *DV* 1.

—— 'Auswirkungen des europäischen Binnenmarktes auf das Umweltrecht— Gemeinschafts(verfassungs-)rechtliche Grundlagen' [1990] *NVwZ* 201.

—— 'Gestaltung und Vollzug des Umweltrechts im europäischen Binnenmarkt— Europäische Impulse und Zwänge für das deutsche Umweltrecht' [1990] *NVwZ* 414.

—— 'Rechtlicher Rahmen der europäischen Unternehmenskooperation im Umwelt- bereich unter besonderer Berücksichtigung von Art. 85 EWGV' [1992] *EuZW* 139.

—— 'Kritierien der normativen Umsetzung von Umweltrichtlinien der EG im Lichte der Rechtsprechung des EuGH' [1994] *EuR* 325.

PERSAUD, INGRID, 'The Packaging and Packaging Waste Directive' [1995] *ELR* 318.

PESCATORE. PIERRE, 'La carrence du législateur et le devoir du juge' in Lüke, G. *et al.* (eds.), *Rechtsvergleichung, Europarecht und Staatsintegration, Gedächtnisschrift für Leontin-Jean Constantinesco* (Heymann, Köln, 1983), 559.

—— 'Die "Einheitliche Europäische Akte"—Eine ernste Gefahr für den gemeinsamen Markt' [1986] *EuR* 153.

—— 'Some Critical Remarks on the "Single European Act" ' (1987) 24 *CMLRev.* 9.

PETERSMANN, ERNST-ULRICH, *Constitutional Functions and Constitutional Problems of International Economic Law* (Fribourg University Press, Fribourg i.Ue., 1991).

—— 'Trade Policy, Environmental Policy and the GATT: Why Trade Rules and Environmental Rules Should Be Mutually Consistent' [1991] *Aussenwirtschaft* 197.

PETERSMANN, ERNST-ULRICH, 'Constitutionalism, Constitutional Law and European Integration' [1991] *Aussenwirtschaft* 247.
—— 'Umweltschutz und Welthandelsordnung im GATT-, OECD- und EWG-Rahmen' [1992] *EA* 257.
—— 'Freier Warenverkehr und nationaler Umweltschutz in EWG und EWR' [1993] *Aussenwirtschaft* 95.
—— 'International Competition Rules for the GATT—MTO World Trade and Legal System' [1993] *JWT* 35.
—— 'Constitutional Principles Governing the EEC's Commercial Policy' in Maresceau, M. (ed.), *The European Community's Commercial Policy after 1992* (Kluwer, Deventer, 1993), 21.
—— 'International Trade Law and International Environment Law—Prevention and Settlement of International Disputes in GATT' [1994] *JWT* 43.
—— 'Trade and Environmental Protection: Practice of GATT and the EC Compared' in Cameron, James, Demaret, Paul, and Geradin, Damien (eds.), *Trade and the Environment: The Search for Balance* (Cameron May, London, 1994), 147.
—— 'Settlement of International Environmental Disputes in GATT and the EC— Comparative Legal Aspects' in Blokker, Niels, and Muller, Sam (eds.), *Towards More Effective Supervision by International Organizations, Essays in Honour of Henry G. Schermers* (Martinus Nijhoff, Dordrecht, 1994), 165.
—— *International and European Trade and Environmental Law after the Uruguay Round* (Kluwer, London, 1995).
—— 'International and European Trade and Environmental Law after the Uruguay Round' in Academy of European Law (ed.), *Collected Courses of the Academy of European Law* (Martinus Nijhoff, Dordrecht, 1995).
PETSCHKE, MATTHIAS, 'Die Warenverkehrsfreiheit in der neuesten Rechtsprechung des EuGH' [1994] *EuZW* 107.
PIEPER, STEFAN ULRICH, *Subsidiarität* (Heymann, Köln, 1994).
PIPKORN, JÖRN, 'Das Verbot von Maßnahmen gleicher Wirkung wie mengenmässige Beschränkungen' in Fuss, Ernst-Werner (ed.), *Der Beitrag des Gerichtshofes der europäischen Gemeinschaften zur Verwirklichung des Gemeinsamen Marktes* (Nomos, Baden-Baden, 1981), 9.
POPHAM HAIK LAW FIRM, 'Subsidiarity and the Environment—US Lessons' [1993] *European Environmental Law Review* 15.
PORTWOOD, TIMOTHY, *Competition Law and the Environment* (Cameron May, London, 1994).
PUTTLER, ADELHEID, 'Non-Tariff Trade Barriers to the Free Movement of Goods' in Pal, Leslie A., and Schultze, Rainer-Olaf (eds.), *The Nation-State versus Continental Integration* (Universitätsverlag Dr. N. Brockmeyer, Bochum, 1991) 261.
QUICK, REINHARD, 'Der Gemeinschaftsrahmen für Umweltschutzbeihilfen' [1994] *EuZW* 620.
RABE, HANS-JÜRGEN, 'Vorbehaltene Kompetenzen der Mitgliedstaaten der EG auf dem Gebiete des Umweltschutzes' [1987] *EuR* 177.
RASMUSSEN, HJALTE, *On Law and Policy in the European Court of Justice* (Martinus Nijhoff, Dordrecht, 1986).
REHBINDER, ECKARD, and STEWART, RICHARD, *Environmental Protection Policy—Integration Through Law* (W. de Gruyter, Berlin/New York, 1985), ii.
REICH, NORBERT, 'Competition Between Legal Orders: A New Paradigm of EC Law' (1992) 29 *CMLRev.* 861.

RENGELING, HANS-WERNER, 'Das Beihilferecht der europäischen Gemeinschaften' in Börner, Bodo and Neudörfer, Konrad (eds.), *Recht und Praxis der Beihilfen im Gemeinsamen Markt—KSE vol 32*. (Heymann, Köln, 1984), 23.

—— 'Schadlose Verwertung radioaktiver Reststoffe durch Wiederaufarbeitung in anderen EG-Mitgliedstaaten' [1991] *DVBl.* 914.

—— 'Gemeinschaftsrechtliche Apekte der Abfallentsorgung' in Baur, J. F., Müller-Graff, P.-C., and Zuleeg, M. (eds.), *Europarecht, Energierecht, Wirtschaftsrecht, Festschrift für B. Börner* (Heymann, Köln, 1992), 359.

—— *Grundrechtsschutz in der Europäischen Gemeinschaft* (C. H. Beck, München, 1993).

—— and HEINZ, KERSTEN, 'Die dänische Pfandflaschenregelung' [1990] *JuS* 613.

RESS, GEORG, 'Luftreinhaltung als Problem des Verhältnisses zwischen europäischem Gemeinschaftsrecht und nationalem Recht' in *150 Jahre Landgericht Saarbrücken* (Heymann, Köln, 1985), 355.

RIDEAU, JOEL, 'Les accords internationaux dans la jurisprudence de la Cour de justice des Communautés Européennes' [1990] *Revue Générale de Droit International Public* 289.

ROBINSON, JONATHAN, 'The Legal Basis of EC Environmental Law' [1992] *J Env. L* 109.

RODI, MICHAEL, *Umweltsteuern: das Steuerrecht als Instrument der Umweltpolitik* (Nomos, Baden-Baden, 1993).

ROLLER, GERHARD, 'Der "Blaue Engel" und die "Europäische Blume" ' [1992] *EuZW* 499.

ROMI, RAPAHEL, *L'Europe et la protection juridique de l'environnement* (Victoires Editions Litec, Paris, 1993).

RÖTTINGER, MORITZ, 'Bedeutung der Rechtsgrundlage einer EG-Richtlinie und Folgen einer Nichtigkeit' [1993] *EuZW* 117.

SANDALOW, TERRANCE and STEIN, ERIC, 'On the Two Systems' in Sandalow, Terrance, and Stein, Eric (eds.), *Courts and Free Markets* (Oxford University Press, Oxford, 1982) i, 1.

SANDS, PHILIPPE, 'European Community Environmental Law: Legislation, the European Court of Justice and Common-Interest Groups' (1990) 53 *MLR* 685.

—— 'European Community Environmental Law: The Evolution of a Regional Regime of International Environmental Protection' (1991) 100 *Yale Law Journal* 2510.

—— and TARASOFSKY, RICHARD G., *Documents in European Community Environmental Law—Principles of International Environmental Law* (Manchester University Press, Manchester, 1995), iii.

SBRAGIA, ALBERTA, 'The European Community: A Balancing Act' [1993] *Publius: The Journal of Federalism* 23.

SCHAEFER, DETLEF, *Die unmittelbare Wirkung des Verbots nichttarifärer Handelshemmnisse (Art. 30 EWGV) in den Rechtsbeziehungen zwischen Privaten: Probleme der horizontalen Wirkung des Gemeinschaftsrechts gezeigt am Beispiel des Art. 30 EWGV* (Peter Lang, Frankfurt a. M., 1987).

SCHAEFER, GUENTHER F., 'The Subsidiarity Principle and European Environmental Policy' in *Subsidiarity: The Challenge of Change, Working Document, Proceedings of the Jacques Delors Colloquium* (European Institute of Public Administration, Maastricht, 1991).

SCHERER, JOACHIM, 'Umweltrecht: Handelshemmnis im EG-Binnenmarkt?' [1992] *URP/DEP* 76.

—— 'Regional Perspectives of Trade and the Environment: The European Union' in Lang, Winfried (ed.), *Sustainable Development and International Law* (Graham and Trotman, London, 1994) 253.

SCHEUING, DIETER H., 'Umweltschutz auf Grundlage der Einheitlichen Europäischen Akte' [1989] *EuR* 152.

SCHEUING, DIETER H., *Grenzüberschreitende atomare Wiederaufarbeitung im Lichte des europäischen Gemeinschaftsrechts* (Nomos, Baden-Baden, 1991).

SCHILLER, THEO, 'Social Policy and European Integration' in Pal, Leslie A., and Schultze, Rainer-Olaf (eds.), *The Nation-State versus Continental Integration* (Universitätsverlag Dr. N. Brockmeyer, Bochum, 1991), 131.

SCHMIDHAUSER, BARBARA, *Kartellrecht und Umweltschutz—Schweiz, Deutschland, Europäische Gemeinschaft* (Diss., Universität Basel, Basel, 1993).

SCHMIDT, ALKE, 'Transboundary Movements of Waste Under EC Law: The Emerging Regulatory Framework' [1992] *J Env. L* 57.

——— 'Trade in Waste Under Community Law' in Cameron, James, Demaret, Paul, and Geradin, Damien (eds.), *Trade and the Environment: The Search for Balance* (Cameron May, London, 1994), 184.

SCHMIDT-RÄNTSCH, ANNETTE, 'Besitz und Vermarktung von geschützten Tieren und Pflanzen nach der Vollendung des EG-Binnenmarktes' [1982] *NuR* 49.

SCHMITT, VEIT, 'Die Harmonisierung der Wettbewerbsbedingungen in der EG-Binnenverkehrspolitik' [1993] *EuZW* 305.

SCHNEIDER, G., 'Die Erhaltung und Bewirtschaftung der Fischereiressourcen im Rahmen der Gemeinsamen Fischereipolitik der EG' [1989] *RIW* 873.

SCHOENBAUM, THOMAS, 'Free International Trade and Protection of the Environment' [1992] *AJIL* 700.

SCHRÖER, THOMAS, *Die Kompetenzverteilung zwischen der Europäischen Wirtschaftsgemeinschaft und ihren Mitgliedstaaten auf dem Gebiet des Umweltschutzes* (Duncker & Humblot, Berlin, 1992).

——— 'Abgrenzung der Gemeinschaftskompetenzen zum Schutze der Gesundheit vor radioaktiver Strahlung, Anmerkungen zum Urteil des EuGH vom 4.10.1991 in Rs C–70/88' [1992] *EuZW* 207.

SCHRÖMBGES, ULRICH, 'EG-Binnenmarkt und Steuerharmonisierung' [1989] *DB* 2558.

SCHWARZE, JÜRGEN, *European Adminstrative Law* (Sweet & Maxwell, London, 1992), also in German: Schwarze, Jürgen, *Europäisches Verwaltungsrecht* (Nomos, Baden-Baden, 1988).

——— 'Le principe de subsidiarité dans la perspective du droit constitutionnel allemand' [1993] *RMCUE* 615.

SCHWARZER, STEPHAN, 'Nationale und internationale Verpackungsreglementierung als Unternehmensdatum' [1993] *ÖZW* 16.

SCHWEITZER, MICHAEL, und HUMMER, WALDEMAR, *Europarecht* (4th edn., Metzner, Neuwied, 1993).

SCHWEIZER, RAINER J., 'Betrachtungen zum Vorentwurf eines Bundesgesetzes über den Binnenmarkt' [1994] *AJP* 739.

SCHUTT, WOLFGANG, and STEFFENS, JOACHIM, 'EuGH-Entscheidung zu Verpackungs-vorschriften in Dänemark' [1989] *RIW* 447.

SEIDEL, MARTIN, 'Umweltrecht in der Europäischen Gemeinschaft—Träger oder Hemmnis des Fortschritts' [1989] *DVBl.* 441.

SEDEMUND, JOCHIM, and MONTAG, FRANK, 'Die Entwicklung des Europäischen Gemeinschaftsrechts' [1994] *NJW* 625.

SEMRAU, FRANK W., 'Conflict and Co-operation in Continental Policy-Making: The Case of Canada and the U.S.' in Pal, Leslie A., and Schultze, Rainer-Olaf (eds.), *The Nation-State versus Continental Integration* (Universitätsverlag Dr. N. Brockmeyer, Bochum, 1991), 315.

SEVENSTER, H. G., 'Van schone auto's EEG-dingen' [1989] *NJB* 556.

SEXTON, TONY, 'Enacting National Environmental Laws More Stringent than Other States' Laws Under the European Community' (1991) 24 *Cornell International Law Journal* (1991) 563.

SIEBERT, HORST, *Umweltpolitik in der europäischen Gemeinschaft—Zentralisierung oder Dezentralisierung?* Kieler Reprints (Insitut für Weltwirtschaft an der Universität Kiel, Kiel, 1991).

—— *Economics of the Environment: Theory and Policy* (3rd edn., Springer, Berlin, 1992).

SINN, STEPHAN, *The Taming of Leviathan: Competition among Governments: Constitutional Political Economy* (Institut für Weltwirtschaft an der Universität Kiel, Kiel, 1992), 177.

SKORDAS, ACHILLES, *Umweltschutz und freier Warenverkehr in EGW-Vertrag und GATT* (Apelt, Steinbach, 1986).

—— 'Das Griechische Bierreinheitsgebot und die erforderliche Reform des Lebensmittelsrechts' [1992] *RIW* 977.

SMITH, T., and SARNOFF, V., 'Free Commerce and Sound Waste Management: Some International Comparative Perspectives' [1992] *International Environmental Reporter* 207.

SNYDER, FRANCIS, *Law of the Common Agricultural Policy* (Sweet & Maxwell, London, 1985).

—— 'The Common Agricultural Policy in the Single European Market' in Academy of European Law (ed.), *Collected Courses of the Academy of European Law* (Martinus Nijhoff, Dordrecht, 1992), ii, book 1, 303.

—— 'The Effectiveness of European Community Law' (1993) 56 *MLR* 19.

SOELL, HERMANN, 'Finanz- und steuerrechtliche Fragen' in Salzwedel, Jürgen (ed.), *Grundzüge des Umweltrechts* (E. Schmidt, Berlin, 1982), 635.

—— 'Überlegungen zum europäischen Umweltrecht—Zur umweltrechtlichen Situation nach Inkrafttreten der EEA' [1990] *NuR* 155.

SOMSEN, HAN, 'Comments on Case C–300/89' (1992) 29 *CMLRev.* 140.

STÄHLER, FRANK, 'Eine Analyse möglicher Instrumente zur Reduktion von CO_2-Emissionene in der Bundesrepublik Deutschland' [1990] *Zeitschrift für Energiewirtschaft* 178.

STAKER, CHRISTOPHER, 'Free Movement of Goods in the EEC and Australia: A Comparative Study' [1990] *YEL* 209.

STEIN, ERIC, 'Towards a European Foreign Policy?' in Cappelletti, Mauro, Seccombe, Monica, and Weiler, Joseph (eds.), *Integration through Law* (W. de Gruyter, Berlin/New York, 1986), i, book 3, 3.

STEINDORFF, ERNST, 'Probleme des Art. 30' [1984] *ZHR* 338.

—— 'Umweltschutz in Gemeinschaftshand?' [1984] *RIW* 767.

STEINER, JOSEPHINE, 'Drawing the line: Uses and Absuses of Article 30 EEC' (1992) 29 *CMLRev.* 749.

STENGER, JÜRGEN, *Das Steuerrecht als Instrument des Umweltschutzes—Möglichkeiten und Grenzen eines Einsatzes des Steuerrechts zur Erfüllung umweltpolitischer Ziele* (Peter Lang, Frankfurt a.M./Bern, 1995).

STEWART, RICHARD, 'Pyramids of Sacrifice? Problems of Federalism in Mandating State Implementation of National Environmental Policy' (1977) 86 *Yale Law Journal* 1196.

STRAUCH, VOLKMAR, 'Nationale Umweltschutzsubventionen als wettberwerbspolitisches Störpotential' in Gutzler, H. (ed.), *Umweltpolitik und Wettbewerb* (Nomos, Baden-Baden, 1981), 125.

STREINZ, RUDOLF, 'Das Problem umgekehrter Diskriminierungen im Bereich de' Lebensmittelrechts' [1990] *Zeitschrift für das gesamte Lebensmittelrecht* 487.

STREIT, M. E., *Systemwettbewerb und Harmonisierung im europäischen Integrationsprozess, Diskussions beitrag 09/95* (Max Planck Institut zur Erforschung von Wirtschaftssystemen, Jena, 1995)

TEMPLE LANG, JOHN, 'The European Community Directive on Bird Conservation' [1982 *Biological Conservation* 11.

——— 'ERTA Judgment and Court's Case Law' [1986] *YEL* 183.

THIEFFRY, PATRICK, 'Les nouveaux instruments juridiques de la politique communautair de l'environnement' [1992] *RTDE* 669.

THIEL, JÜRGEN MICHAEL, *Umweltrechtliche Kompetenzen in der Europäischen Union* (Brockmeyer Bochum, 1995).

THOMÉ-KOZMIENSKY, SOPHIE, *Die Verpackungsverordnung—Rechtmässigkeit, 'Duales System' Europarecht* (Duncker & Humblot, Berlin, 1994).

TIMMERMANS, C. W. A., 'Verboden discriminatie of (geboden) differentiatie' [1982] *SEW* 426.

TOBEY, JAMES A., 'The Effects of Domestic Environmental Policies on Patterns of World Trade: An Empirical Test' [1990] *Kyklos* 191.

TOSTMANN, STEFAN, 'EuGH-Verbot des Ablagerns von Abfall aus einem anderen Mitgliedstaat' [1992] *EuZW* 577.

TOTH, A. G., 'The Principle of Subsidiarity in the Maastricht Treaty' (1992) 29 *CMLRev* (1992) 1079.

TRIBE, LAURENCE H., *American Constitutional Law* (2nd edn., Foundation Press, Mineola, NY, 1988).

UMWELTBUNDESAMT (ed.), *Rechtsakte der EG auf dem Gebiet des Umweltschutzes*, Stand 1.3.1991 (Umweltbundesamt, Berlin, 1991).

UNEP, *Selected Multilateral Treaties in the Field of the Environment* (Grotius, Cambridge, 1991).

USHER, JOHN A., 'Protection of the Environement through Trade Restrictions and the Community Internal Relations: The Respective Competence of the Community and its Member States' in Cameron, James, Demaret, Paul, and Geradin, Damien (eds.), *Trade and the Environment: The Search for Balance* (Cameron May, London, 1994), 261.

VALLENDER, KLAUS, *Wirtschaftsfreiheit und begrenzte Staatsverantwortung* (2nd edn., Stämpfli, Bern, 1991).

VAN DER WOUDE, MARC, 'The Limits of Free Circulation: The Torfaen Borough Case' [1990] *Leiden Journal of International Law* 57.

VAN RIJN, THOMAS, 'A Review of the Case Law of the Court of Justice on Articles 30–36 in 1986 and 1987' (1988) 25 *CMLRev.* 593.

VANDERKERCKHOVE, KAREN, 'The Polluter Pays Principle in the European Community' [1993] *YEL* 200.

VANDERMEERSCH, DIRK, 'The Single European Act and the Environmental Policy of the EC' (1987) 12 *ELRev.* 407.

——— 'Twintig jaar EG-Milieurecht in retrospectief: van casuïstik naar modern beleid?' [1992] *SEW* 532.

VARIAN, HAL R., *Intermediate Microeconomics* (3rd edn., W. W. Norton, New York, 1993).

VERLOREN VAN THEMAAT, PIETER, *Rechtsgroundlagen van een nieuwe internationale economische orde, Studies in internationaal economisch recht* (Asser Institute, s'Gravenhage, 1979), ii.

——— 'La libre circulation des marchandises après l'arrêt "Cassis de Dijon" ' [1982] *CDE* 123.

VERMULST, ERWIN A., 'A European Practitioner's View of the GATT-System: Should Competition Law Violations Distorting International Trade Be Subject to GATT Panels?' [1993] *JWT* 55.

VIGNES, DANIEL, 'Le rapprochement des législations méritetil encore son nom?' in *Mélanges pour J. Boulouis, L'Europe et le droit* (Dalloz, Paris, 1991), 533.

VOGELAAR, FLORIS, O. W., 'Towards an Improved Integration of EC Environmental Policy and EC Competition Policy: An Interim Report', Paper presented at the Fordham Corporate Law Institute, 21st Annual Conference on International Antitrust Law & Policy, New York 27–28 October, 1994 (on file with author).

VÖLKER, EDMOND L. M., *Leading Cases and Materials on the External Relations Law of the European Community (with Emphasis on the Common Commercial Policy)* (Kluwer, Deventer, 1985).

VORWERK, AXEL, *Die umweltpolitischen Kompetenzen der Europäischen Gemeinschaft und ihrer Mitgliedstaaten nach Inkrafttreten der EEA* (VVF, München, 1990).

VOSS, ULRIKE and WENNER, GREGOR, 'Der EuGH und die gemeinschaftsrechtliche Kompetenzordnung—Kontinuität oder Neuorientierung?' [994] *NVwZ* 332.

WAELBROECK, MICHAEL, 'Le rôle de la Cour de Justice dans la mise en œuvre de l'acte unique européen' [1989] *CDE* 41.

WÄGENBAUER, ROLF, 'Ein Programm für die Umwelt' [1993] *EuZW* 241.

WALDHÄUSL, MARTIN, 'EuGH zum freien Warenverkehr: Das Keck-Urteil' [1994] *Ecolex* 367.

WALKER, SANDRA, *Environmental Protection versus Trade Liberalization: Finding the Balance* (Publications des Facultés Universitaires Saint-Louis, Bruxelles, 1993).

WEALE, ALBERT, and WILLIAMS, ANDREA, 'Between Economy and Ecology? The Single Market and the Integration of Environmental Policy' in Judge, David (ed.), *A Green Dimension for the European Community—Political Issues and Processes* (F. Cass, London, 1993).

WEILER, JOSEPH H. H., 'The Community System: The Dual Character of Supranationalism' [1981] *YEL* 267.

—— *Il sistema comunitario europeo* (Molino, Bologna, 1985).

—— 'The Transformation of Europe' (1991) 100 *Yale Law Journal* 2403.

—— 'Journey to an Unknown Destination: A Restrospective and Prospective of the European Court of Justice in the Arena of Political Integration [1993] *JCMS* 417.

WEINSTOCK, ULRICH, 'Nur eine europäische Umwelt? Europäische Umweltpolitik im Spannungsfeld von ökologischer Vielfalt und ökonomischer Einheit' [1983] *ZfU* 1.

WERDER, AXEL VON and NESTLER, ANKE, 'Grundsätze ordnungsgemässiger Umweltschutzorganisation als Maßstab des europäischen Umweltaudit' [1995] *RIW* 296.

WHEELER, MARINA, 'The Legality of Restrictions on the Movement of Wastes under Community Law' [1993] *Journal of Environmental Law* 133.

WHITE, ERIC L., 'In Search of the Limits to Article 30 of the EEC Treaty' (1989) 26 *CMLRev.* 235.

WIEBE, ANDREAS, 'EG-rechtliche Grenzen des deutschen Werberechts am Beispiel der Umweltwerbung' [1994] *EuZW* 41.

WILKINSON, DAVID, 'Maastricht and the Environment: The Implications for the EC's Environment Policy of the Treaty on European Union' [1992] *J Env. L* 221.

WILMOWSKY, PETER VON, *Abfallwirtschaft im Binnenmarkt* (Werner Verlag, Düsseldorf, 1990).

—— 'Abfall und freier Warenverkehr: Bestandesaufnahme nach dem EuGH-Urteil zum wallonischen Einfuhrverbot' [1992] *EuR* 414 .

WILMOWSKY, PETER VON, 'Waste Disposal in the Internal Market: The State of Play after the ECJ's Ruling on the Walloon Import Ban' (1993) 30 *CMLRev.* 541.

WILS, WOUTER P. J., 'La protection d'habitats naturels en droit communautaire' [1994 *CDE* 398.

WINKLER, TOBIAS D., *Wo kein Kläger, da kein Richter—Die Verwirklichung der gegenseitige. Anerkennung von Produktregulierungen in der Europäischen Union, Diskussionsbeitrag 07/95* (Max Planck-Institut zur Erforschung von Wirtschaftssystemen, Jena, 1995).

WOOLCOCK, STEPHEN, 'The European "acquis" and Multilateral Trade Rules: Are the Compatible?' [1993] *JCMS* 539.

—— *The Single European Market: Centralization or Competition among National Rules* (The Roya Institute of International Affairs, London, 1994).

WUERMELING, JOACHIM, *Kooperatives Gemeinschaftsrecht* (N. P. Engel, Kehl am Rhein, 1988)

WYATT, DERRICK, 'European Court of July 14, 1976, cases 3, 4, and 6/76' (1977) *ELRev.* 41 and 47.

—— and Dashwood, Alan, *European Community Law* (3rd edn., Sweet & Maxwell, London 1993).

ZÄCH, ROGER, *Wettbewerbsrecht der Europäischen Union* (C. H. Beck, München, 1994).

ZAELKE, DURWOOD, ORBUCH, PAUL, and HOUSMAN, ROBERT F. (eds.), *Trade and th Environment—Law, Economics, and Policy* (Island Press, Washington, DC, 1993).

ZAGARIS, BRUCE, 'The Transformation of Environmental Enforcement Cooperatio between Mexico and the United States in the Wake of NAFTA' (1993) 18 *North Carolin Journal of International Law and Commercial Regulation* 59.

ZOHLNHÖFER, WERNER, 'Umweltschutz und Wettbewerb—Grundlegende Analyse' ir Gutzler, H. (ed.), *Umweltpolitik und Wettbewerb* (Nomos, Baden-Baden, 1981), 15.

ZULEEG, MANFRED, 'Vorbehaltene Kompetenzen der Mitgliedstaaten der Europäischer Gemeinschaft auf dem Gebiet des Umweltschutzes' [1987] *NVwZ* 280.

—— 'Umweltschutz in der Rechtsprechung des Europäischen Gerichtshofs' [1993] *NJW* 31.

Index